LET'S
PUT ON
A MUSICAL!

LET'S PUT ON A MUSICAL!

PETER FILICHIA

AVON BOOKS ◆ NEW YORK

LET'S PUT ON A MUSICAL! is an original publication of Avon Books. This work has never before appeared in book form.

AVON BOOKS
A division of
The Hearst Corporation
1350 Avenue of the Americas
New York, New York 10019

Library of Congress Cataloging in Publication Data:
Filichia, Peter.
  Let's put on a musical! : how to choose the right show for your
school, community or professional theater / by Peter Filichia.
      p. cm.
    1. Musicals—Production and direction.   2. Musicals—Stage guides.
I. Title.
MT955.F54   1993   93–3128
792.6—dc20   CIP
                                          MN

First Avon Books Trade Printing: August 1993

The author dedicates this book to
Frank Roberts
for suggesting the project

Thanks, too, to Steve Allen, Peter Atlas, Paulette Attie, Mark Auerbach, Steve Aznavourian, Alan Bailey, David Barbour, Lisa A. Barnett, Roger Bean, Christopher Berg, Bob Bezubka, Judy Blazer, Ken Bloom, Christopher Catt, Theodore S. Chapin, Jay S. Clark, David Cleaver, Douglas J. Cohen, Bruce Colville, Keith Crowningshield, Debbie Dustin, Sherry Eaker, Marilyn Egol, Joshua Ellis, Lehman Engel, Marty Erskine, Gareth Esersky, Bert Fink, Steve Flaherty, Charles Fontana, David Gersten, Steve Hanan, Sheldon Harnick, John Harris, John Harrison, Holly Hill, Tom Howard, Suzanne Ishee, Michael Kerker, Michael Kerley, Bruce Kimmel, John Kinsman, Skip Koenig, Linda Konner, Alix Korey, John Kroll, Valerie and Kevin LaCount, Melanie Larch, Ruth Lepie, Judy Malloy, Ken Mandelbaum, Daniel Marcus, David N. Matthews, Kevin McAnarney, Philip Wm. McKinley, Gerry Morris, Sam Norkin, Paul C. Norton, Richard Norton, Joseph Patton, Gene Paul, John Pike, Jody Rein, Michael Riedel, Paul Roberts, Howard Rogut, Bill Rosenfield, Gloria Rosenthal, Dick Rousseau, Mike Salinas, Bob Sandla, Paul Seltzer, Mark Shenton, Robert Sher, Thomas Z. Shepard, Bert Silverberg, John Sloman, Michael Sommers, Mary Stout, Jeff Sweet, Jordan Tinsley, Danny Troob, Frank Verlizzo, Sean Wengroff, Frank Wildhorn, Walter Willison, David Wolf, and Maury Yeston.

CONTENTS

7
"MEN!"
Musicals with Predominantly Male Casts
107

8
"WHERE ARE THE MEN?"
Musicals with Predominantly Female Casts
124

9
"KIDS!"
Musicals for Grade School and Junior High School Students
141

10
"YOU ARE 16 GOING ON 17"
Musicals for High Schoolers
153

11
"HOW DO YOU DO, MIDDLE AGE?"
Musicals with Parts for Middle-Aged Performers
175

12
"THANK GOD I'M OLD!"
Shows That Don't Depend on Young Casts
186

13
"COMEDY TONIGHT!"
Musicals Out for Laughs
194

14
"PUT ON YOUR SUNDAY CLOTHES!"
Musicals That Rely Heavily on Costumes
208

15
"SEVEN AND A HALF CENTS DOESN'T BUY A HELLUVA LOT"
Musicals That Can Be Done on a Small Budget
227

16
"MISTER, YOU CAN BE A HERO"
Cult Shows That Haven't Yet Found Their Audience
237

17
"STRIKE UP THE BAND!"
Musicals for Musicians Who Also Want to Act
252

18
"DON'T TELL MAMA!"
Musicals for Sophisticated Communities
266

24
"THAT'S ENTERTAINMENT!"
Musicals Simply Out for Fun
340

APPENDIX
355

INDEX
357

LET'S PUT ON A MUSICAL!

INTRODUCTION

One of the worst productions I ever saw was Gilbert and Sullivan's *H.M.S. Pinafore* at an Alabama community theater. Many of the actors and actresses just couldn't keep up with Gilbert's trippingly difficult patter, and more than a dozen times during the first act, the performers just stopped mid-song and stood there embarrassed. Measures of music went without lyrics, either because the actors had forgotten the challenging words, or because they were simply unable to sing them in rhythm. To make matters worse, the lass who played the Lass That Loved a Sailor was much too young for the More-Than-Middle-Aged Man playing opposite her.

As soon as the first act ended, I was on my way to my car—wondering all the way, *Why did this company choose this show?* Did the board of directors include a few big G-and-S fans who thought their group should give tribute to these nineteenth-century giants? If that was their intention, it backfired: A couple who'd already beaten me to the door were agreeing that they'd "always hated Gilbert and Sullivan anyway," unaware that they might have felt differently had they seen a different production.

If only the theater group had better matched its talents to its production! Chances are they could have put on a terrific show. The sailor, for example, would have been fine as one of the chorus of businessmen in *Promises, Promises*, but putting him in this lead was a problem; the sophisticated and carefree woman playing the lass would have made an excellent Sally Bowles in *Cabaret*.

Now, Gilbert and Sullivan will survive such productions, but will your local

1

community theater, church group, or high school drama club? Before casting, before rehearsing, it's crucial to pick the right show. So here's a handbook of what's available, do-able, and enjoyable for your audience.

HOW TO USE THIS BOOK

The discussion of each musical includes the following information.

CREATORS: Who wrote the book, music, and lyrics? When anyone is famous for other shows, movies, or songs that information is usually also cited; for example, in a listing for *Little Me*, the composer is mentioned as Cy (*The Will Rogers Follies*) Coleman.

BACKGROUND: When was the original production produced, how many performances did it last, and how many Tony nominations and/or awards did it receive? (Remember that off-Broadway musicals aren't eligible for Tonys.) If a show failed, but for a specific reason that shouldn't affect your production (i.e., miscasting, producers who ran out of money), that's also mentioned.

STORY: What are the plot and theme? Who's it about? What happens? When and where does it take place?

ASSETS: What could make you choose this show above all others?—such as ease of production, or absence of expensive sets, costumes, or props. The score and book are also assessed, with commentary on what makes us care about the characters, or what (if anything) the show is trying to say. Most shows are admittedly no more complicated than "Morals tomorrow; comedy tonight!" but others have more on their minds.

LIABILITIES: What problems might you encounter when doing this show that you're better off knowing now rather than in your third week of rehearsal? Some are problems that plagued the professionals during the original production; others are issues that especially tend to harass nonprofessionals.

RECOGNIZABLE SONGS: One aspect of a musical that audiences most enjoy is discovering that a certain song comes from a show—the I-didn't-know-that-came-from-there experience. Songs that have managed to become familiar, be it through a hit record or a TV commercial, are listed.

WHO YOU'LL NEED: Here you'll find listed the most important characters in the piece (basically in order of importance); in many cases you can decide if the roles should be played by a man or a woman. We're living in an age where, if we may borrow from *A Chorus Line*, there's more emphasis on "How many people does he need?" than on "How many boys? How many girls?" Still, we've included the names of some stars greatly associated with certain roles—or stars who'd be good for the shows—in case you have a Tommy Tune type or a Patti LuPone clone. If the show uses (or can use) a chorus, that's also noted.

DESIGNATED DANCES: How much or how little choreography is needed? For which dancers (or would-be dancers)?

SUGGESTED SETS: Directors who contributed to this book almost unanimously agreed on one point: Don't use flats, for they take too long to lug on and off, and they never look that good anyway. Instead, play against a dark cyclorama (if you're in a small black-box theater, this is already taken care of), roll on some pieces of furniture, and that's your set. As a result, the suggested sets listed here are the sets you might emulate—but you'll save yourself much grief and expense if you play it simple and let the audience fill in the rest.

COSTUMES: We offer an overview of the types of clothes you'll need—from which century, and in what style. Specific costumes—such as the tarred-and-feathered outfit in *Big River*—are also listed, if they pose a particular problem.

IMPORTANT PROPS: This section gives you an idea of just what type of scavenger hunt you'll have to undertake—especially for such arcane items as a bicycle with no pedals for *Ben Franklin in Paris*, enormous beach balls on which your *No, No, Nanette* dancers can perch, or a horse for *Happy Hunting*.

SPECIAL EFFECTS: If a musical needs voice-overs, important sound cues, thunder and lightning, fog, or all of these, you'll find that noted here.

PROVIDED INSTRUMENTATION: Here are listed which orchestral parts are printed and available for musicians. Of course, as the 1992 revival of *The Most Happy Fella* proved, all you may really need are a couple of pianos, but the sound of an orchestra can be fun—if your musicians are competent.

ADVERTISING AND MARKETING: Some directors can't think of that catchy phrase that can provide a good lead for a press release; here you'll find some ideas that will give you a start on writing those releases to send to newspapers. Also included are some suggestions for bumper stickers, ad campaigns, and marketing opportunities that could help get you a broader base of support.

SUGGESTIONS: Many directors feel that staging a show exactly the way it was presented on opening night on Broadway is the best service they can give their audiences. If, they reason, this is the way the pros did it, then this is the way it should be done, and they'll replicate it right down to the very last bit of blocking. Other directors like to do things their own way, even to the point where they disassemble and reassemble the musical, then present it with a few extra scenes or eliminate scenes or songs. Here are some unconventional ideas that have been known to work (or may just deserve a chance)—though you'd best clear these and your own through the organization that is licensing your show.

RESOURCES: Was an original cast album made? Is it available on compact disc, tape—or even an old-fashioned vinyl record? Was there a movie version? A taped TV special? Here's a list of what's been made—*not* necessarily what's available in print, but what it is at least theoretically possible to find. The more you work in the theater, the more people you'll encounter who have some of the more arcane items listed here. And, of course, new titles are being released and rereleased on CDs or cassettes each month, so check if a cast album isn't listed here.

In addition, some shows now have CDs on which a rehearsal pianist plays—called "Rehearscores"—as well as study guides or videocassettes with author interviews. These are also listed.

RIGHTS: Most musicals are available through five licensing organizations: Dramatists Play Service, Music Theatre International, Rodgers and Hammerstein, Samuel French, and Tams-Witmark. The addresses and telephone and fax numbers are listed in the appendix.

BEFORE YOU START REHEARSALS

Decide whether you want your cast to watch the movie version of the show. Because of videotape, nonprofessional actors now often have the option to rent or buy the movie version of the show they'll soon be in. This can be dangerous: Many professional actors who have been cast in a revival make a point not to watch someone else's interpretation; they fear that it might influence their performances too much.

On the other hand, nonprofessionals (or not-*yet*-professionals) sometimes benefit from seeing a (presumably) good performer deliver a professional performance. Your choice! And of course *you'll* have to decide if you want to see a tape.

Some directors don't stop at banning the cast from watching the movie. Take the Cedar Rapids, Iowa, director who decided to stage *110 in the Shade*, the musical version of *The Rainmaker*. Now there's no movie of *110*, but this director made his actors vow that they wouldn't even listen to the original cast album, because he wanted to see what they would come up with just from reading the music, without a "definitive interpretation" to influence them. "And it was fascinating," recalls a member of the company, "when after the run we finally did hear the record and hear the differences. We came up with a musical that had more of the triumphant gumption of *The Rainmaker* instead of that lyric soprano quality that wouldn't have played too well in Cedar Rapids."

Lastly, *don't get discouraged*. If you're just starting your own little company on a shoestring budget, may you live to be a hundred. Don't forget that there was a time when theater people had no idea where East Haddam, Connecticut, was—but in the past twenty-five years, they've sure learned how to find it. Were it not for that town's Goodspeed Opera House, Broadway might have never seen *Annie* or *Man of La Mancha*. Now almost all musical theater aficionados have made a pilgrimage to Goodspeed to see vintage musicals. Many, in fact, attend a matinee, so that in the evening they can head off to nearby Chester, where Goodspeed's *second* theater functions as a showcase for newer, sometimes experimental musicals.

You may be a long way off from establishing your first theater, let alone your second, but, as Dorothy Fields wrote in *Seesaw*, "It's not where you start, it's where you finish." And to be sure that you do triumphantly reach the finish line, make certain that you pick musicals you love—and that you do them justice.

"WHY, IT'S GOOD OLD RELIABLE..."

The Classic Musicals

"My customers," says Robert Eagle, Artistic Director of the Reagle Players in Waltham, Massachusetts, "want shows whose names they recognize. We've occasionally tried to give them less familiar shows, but they don't come out for them. Even those who *have* come seem a little disappointed that we didn't offer them a show they knew and loved."

As Coca-Cola discovered some years ago, people *like* classics. So if you too are in a community that buys tickets only for the most famous titles in the Broadway canon, here are your bread-and-butter musicals.

ANNIE GET YOUR GUN

CREATORS: Book by Herbert and Dorothy Fields (who later wrote the book for *Redhead*) music and lyrics by Irving ("White Christmas") Berlin.

BACKGROUND: The 1946 production was supposed to be composed by Jerome Kern, but he died before he began to work on it. Producers Richard Rodgers and Oscar Hammerstein II could have written it themselves, but they opted to ask Irving Berlin, whose score propelled the musical to run 1,147 performances—then the third-longest run in musical theater history.

STORY: 1885, the Midwest. Annie Oakley may be a sharpshooter, but she isn't sharp where men are concerned. When she meets handsome Frank Butler, she wants him—though he clearly states he wants a more feminine type. She signs to appear in Buffalo Bill's Wild West Show in which Frank stars, and is soon outshooting him, which further alienates him. Annie eventually decides to let Frank win a match so that he will marry her.

ASSETS: *Dramatics* magazine reports this is one of the most performed titles of stock, college, and amateur groups throughout the country. It's also one of the most hit-laden scores in musical theater history, has a very funny book, and offers many well-defined characters that nonprofessionals can happily manage.

LIABILITIES: The ending—in which a woman supresses her abilities so a man will stay in love with her—demeans both leads. (How much nicer it would have been if Frank as well as Annie kept missing the targets as the curtain descended.) "But," says Jeffrey Dunn, who has directed the production in European tours, "you can have your Frank play it as if he knows she's thrown the match."

There's also a problem with the characterization of the "Indians"; a half-century has passed since most Native American roles were written into the play solely to be mocked (one joke's punch line states, "50 squaws are worth two dollars.") Yes, the authors do a bit better by making Sitting Bull most savvy, but there's still some condescension here. The song "I'm an Indian, Too" is a problem for more than ethical reasons: It's also a dance diversion that stalls a steadily building book; the song comes just before Annie has inadvertently one-upped Frank, who walks out on her; a slow curtain would work just fine here, instead of the song followed by a letter from Frank saying he's leaving.

RECOGNIZABLE SONGS: "Doin' What Comes Natur'lly," "The Girl That I Marry," "You Can't Get a Man with a Gun," "There's No Business Like Show Business," "They Say It's Wonderful," "I Got the Sun in the Morning," "Anything You Can Do (I Can Do Better)."

WHO YOU'LL NEED: *Lead Singing Roles*: An endearing sharpshooting woman (who's been played by everyone from Ethel Merman to Mary Martin to Suzi Quatro); the handsome and rugged love of her life. *Supporting Singing Roles*: Annie's young brother and three sisters; three show business promoters (two male, one female). *Other Roles*: Buffalo Bill; Sitting Bull; Pawnee Bill, a show business entrepreneur; a chorus to play Native Americans, conductors, porters, waiters, major domos, and various society types. *Maximum*, 56; *minimum*, 27.

DESIGNATED DANCES: Five production numbers involving most of the company; some steps for Annie and her siblings; a ballyhoo; two Native American ceremonial dances.

SUGGESTED SETS: Inside and outside a hotel; a Pullman parlor; fairgrounds; a tent arena; the deck of a boat; a ballroom; a ferry; outside a fort. Your least costly option, though, may be a rough-hewn wood unit set replete with wagon wheels and cowhead skeletons.

COSTUMES: Wild West attire: cowboy hats and boots, derbies and pin-check suits; porter uniforms; a white wig, handlebar mustache, and goatee for Buffalo Bill; boas, crinolines, feathered hats, bonnets, and high-buttoned shoes. Annie's costumes start out as glorified rags but become progressively more feminine.

IMPORTANT PROPS: An ear trumpet; steamer trunks; musical instruments for a parade; various flags, including an American one with forty-five stars; placards to announce both Buffalo Bill and Pawnee Bill's shows; posters that announce Annie and Frank as star attractions; guns, holsters, and rifles that shoot blanks and are quickly reloadable; an optional motorcycle.

SPECIAL EFFECTS: Annie shoots birds that drop from above.

PROVIDED INSTRUMENTATION: Flute, oboe, clarinet, bassoon, horn, two trumpets, three trombones, two percussion, four violins, viola, cello, bass, harp, guitar, piano-conductor.

ADVERTISING AND MARKETING: List the song titles in a display ad—followed by "You'll hear them all if you come to *Annie Get Your Gun* beginning on . . ."

SUGGESTIONS: Merman was famous for her "goon look" (the script read "Annie looks at Frank, and, in a second, falls in love with him forever"), but styles have changed, and today's musical subtleties suggest that your Annie not be as goony.

A 1992 production at the Westchester (New York) Broadway Theater made some fascinating choices: Upon her entrance, Annie "shot" the orchestra leader when first trying to prove that she's a crack shot; Pawnee Bill was played by a woman and became Pawnee Jill; and though Annie traditionally travels with her young brother and three sisters, this production gave her only one brother in whom she confided, and this one-on-one relationship added depth and poignancy.

RESOURCES: The 1991 studio cast album conducted by John McGlinn (the most complete) on CD and cassette, though there are two albums featuring Merman, one with Martin, and even one with Judy Garland singing the main songs; the faithful 1950 movie on videotape; the very faithful 1957 Mary Martin TV version.

RIGHTS: Rodgers and Hammerstein.

CAROUSEL

CREATORS: Book and lyrics by Oscar Hammerstein II, music by Richard Rodgers (who had recently collaborated on *Oklahoma!*).

BACKGROUND: Hammerstein took the Ferenc Molnar play *Liliom*, moved its locale from Hungary to New England, and, most importantly, changed the ending from one of despair to one of hope. Throughout rehearsals, Hammerstein feared what Molnar would think, but when the playwright attended, he told Hammerstein that it was what he liked best about the show. Critics agreed, and the 1945 production ran 890 performances.

STORY: Late 1870s, New England. Billy Bigelow, a carousel barker, quickly falls in love with and marries Julie Jordan. Both lose their jobs, and being out of work so frustrates Billy that he becomes involved in a bungled robbery. When he's caught, he kills himself. Julie gives birth to their daughter, and is left to raise her; Billy, from heaven, sees them, wishes to seek redemption—and asks the Starkeeper for one day on earth, which is granted—15 years after the fact. At first he does a bad job of confronting his teenage daughter, but he does eventually bring her some happiness.

ASSETS: Great book and score, a most moving story, with characters that are more complex than those in the average musical and therefore command our attention.

LIABILITIES: Some schools don't much like the idea that Billy commits suicide. And, as is the case with *Oklahoma!*, Hammerstein wrote very regional dialogue that is tough reading ("fust" for "first," "keering" for "caring," and "perlice" for "police"), and will mean an awkward first few readings by your cast.

RECOGNIZABLE SONGS: "If I Loved You," "June Is Bustin' Out All Over," "You'll Never Walk Alone."

WHO YOU'LL NEED: *Leading Singing Roles* (all with legit voices): A virile carousel barker (John Raitt); the young but strong girl who loves and marries him. *Supporting Singing Roles:* Julie's levelheaded best friend; her even more levelheaded husband; her spa owner cousin; a sinister sailor (who can fling a girl over his shoulder). *Other Roles:* Billy's female boss; Julie's sobersided sideburned boss; their daughter at fifteen; her would-be suitor; a captain; a policeman; a school principal; a man in a bear suit; a ballerina; a clown; nine children of varying ages; two angels, a Starkeeper (read: God) who is written to double as a doctor; townspeople who can be in the ballet. *Maximum*, 57; *minimum*, 18.

DESIGNATED DANCES: Musical staging for the opening carousel waltz; a rousing dance for the spa owner and the sailors; a hornpipe for the sailors; a ballet for Billy and Julie's grown daughter, a would-be suitor, and townspeople.

SUGGESTED SETS: An amusement park; a tree-lined path; an ocean-front house; a more modest dwelling; outside a schoolhouse; an island and its wharf; a beach; a place that suggests heaven (a ladder and a clothesline on which stars are hung is all you'll need).

COSTUMES: Late-nineteenth-century New England sea-town work wear: striped shirts and tams; a shawl; a woman's large hat; graduation robes (or suits);

fine clothes for nine children; policemen uniforms of the era; a bear suit; a clown suit; a ballerina outfit. And make certain that your very best costumes are saved for the clambake; this is, after all, their once-a-year day.

IMPORTANT PROPS: A bench; an ice-cream wagon; fishnets; picnic baskets; pies, cakes, trays of doughnuts, and coffee cups; rolling pins; jugs; suitcases; a gun; a translucent star; and, of course, a carousel.

SPECIAL EFFECTS: Fog; a knife trick in which the sinister sailor demonstrates his expert knife-throwing ability (a knife must emerge from where he's "thrown" it).

PROVIDED INSTRUMENTATION: Flute, oboe, clarinet, bassoon, two horns, trumpet, two trombones, tuba, percussion, two violins, viola, cello, bass, harp, piano-conductor.

ADVERTISING AND MARKETING: Is there an amusement park carousel in your area? If you've scheduled your production during a time when it's in operation, arrange to have your actors stop by (on the carousel's busiest night, of course) a few weeks prior to performance and sing selections from your upcoming production. This gives your cast a chance to perform before an audience, which will give them some good experience for opening night. Of course, have posters everywhere advertising your production, and have advance ticket sales available.

SUGGESTIONS: Some productions are done *without* a carousel—miming that effect—and others use representational ones. Your choice.

RESOURCES: The 1966 revival cast album on CD, cassette, and LP is the most complete; the very faithful 1956 movie on videotape and laserdisc; Ferenc Molnar's play *Liliom*, on which the musical is fairly faithfully based.

RIGHTS: Rodgers and Hammerstein.

FIDDLER ON THE ROOF

CREATORS: Book by Joseph (*Take Me Along*) Stein, music by Jerry Bock, lyrics by Sheldon Harnick (who had collaborated on *Fiorello!*).

BACKGROUND: The 1964 Broadway production opened in Detroit during a newspaper strike, so the only review was *Variety's*—and it was negative. Director-choreographer Jerome Robbins didn't panic, however, but said that he'd "fix one thing every day"—and apparently did, for the show went on to receive ten Tony nominations, won nine awards—including Best Musical—and went on to a then-record 3,242-performance run.

STORY: Jewish (and all) tradition—and its breakdown in Anatevka, a town in 1905 Czarist Russia. Tevye the milkman and his wife, Golde, enlist a matchmaker, as is the tradition, to find husbands for their five daughters, but each of the eldest three finds a husband on her own—one a tailor, one a revolutionary, and one a Gentile. While Tevye can accept the first two, he cannot sanction the third. Tevye struggles as his world comes to an end—literally as well as figuratively—for he and all the other Jews in town are ejected from their homeland and must emigrate to America as the play ends.

ASSETS: *Dramatics* magazine reports this is one of the most performed titles of stock, college, and amateur groups throughout the country. Great score, fine book, engaging characters, dramatic situations that, though Jewish-oriented, are so engrossing they are universal. In fact, the Japanese production of the show caused one Asian theatergoer to wonder how the show could be about Jews and written by Americans—"because it is *so* Japanese."

LIABILITIES: Many think the 1990 Broadway revival, which won the Tony as Best Revival but still closed at a financial loss, proved that *Fiddler* has been seen one time too many—so check to see when the last production occurred in your area.

RECOGNIZABLE SONGS: "Tradition," "Matchmaker," "If I Were a Rich Man," "Sunrise, Sunset," "Now I Have Everything."

WHO YOU'LL NEED: *Lead Singing Roles:* A humble but wise milkman (Zero Mostel). *Supporting Singing Roles:* His no-nonsense wife; their three eldest daughters; a meddlesome matchmaker (Beatrice Arthur); a shy tailor who becomes a mensch; a young and handsome teacher with revolution on his mind (and a legit voice); a wealthy and hefty butcher; a rabbi and his son; a bookseller; ghosts of a grandmother and the butcher's wife (the former ideally on stilts). *Other Roles:* Peasant villagers; onstage musicians; two teenage boys; a tall blond Gentile; the tailor's mother; a beggar, a priest, a constable, and an innkeeper; and, of course, a fiddler on the roof. *Maximum, 46; minimum, 22.*

DESIGNATED DANCES: Two circle dances; a rousing peasant folk dance for the men; a short dance between Tevye and the fiddler; a polka for the young lovers; a ballet for Golde, the daughters, and their lovers. Most challenging will be the bottle dance, in which four men dance while balancing bottles on their hats. (In addition, the daughters must make the brooms "dance" a bit in the "Matchmaker" song.)

SUGGESTED SETS: A shtetl village community: inside and outside Tevye's house; the local inn; a tailor's shop; a barn; a railroad station; and various streets of Anatevka.

COSTUMES: Early twentieth-century Russian Jewish peasant wear: boots; vests; caps; yarmulkes (skull caps); prayer shawls; bandanas; black silk wedding hats; nightshirts, nightcaps, and nightgowns; costumes representing ghosts.

IMPORTANT PROPS: A milkman's cart; a sewing machine; brooms; pots and pans; a bed with quilts and pillows; Bibles; bundles of books; menorahs (candelabra); candles and candlesticks; a wedding canopy; bottles; goblets; a glass that can be covered with cloth and smashed for each performance; dishes that can be broken; stilts; straw trunks; a violin for the fiddler.

SPECIAL EFFECTS: One character flies in a dream sequence, which could be enhanced by fog.

PROVIDED INSTRUMENTATION: Five reeds, three trumpets, trombone, horn, accordion, guitar, percussion, three violins, viola, cello, bass, piano.

ADVERTISING AND MARKETING: "You say that if you were a rich man, you'd come see our show? You don't have to be that rich—because for only [price], you can see *Fiddler on the Roof*..."

SUGGESTIONS: Stresses David Wolf, the assistant stage manager for some of the original Broadway run, "Do not overemphasize the 'Jewishness' of the piece by adopting Lower East Side accents. *Fiddler* is a universal story, and should be played that way." Adds Melanie Larch of the Charleston (West Virginia) Light Opera Guild, "Consult with your local Orthodox synagogue and invite the rabbi to come speak to the cast. We did that, and the observations he gave us enriched our show."

RESOURCES: The original cast album on CD, cassette, and LP; the 1970 faithful movie version on videotape and laserdisc; Sholom Aleichem's *Tevye's Daughters*, on which the musical is loosely based; a "Rehearscore" disc for Macintosh and IBM systems that eliminates the need for a rehearsal pianist; study guides.

RIGHTS: Music Theatre International.

GUYS AND DOLLS

CREATORS: Book by Jo Swerling and Abe (*How to Succeed in Business*) Burrows, music and lyrics by Frank (*Where's Charley?*) Loesser.

BACKGROUND: Did Jo Swerling write the book as his son insists, or was it Abe Burrows, as most others assert? Whoever wrote what resulted on stage in the 1950 production certainly complemented Frank Loesser's fabulous score. Critics gave the production unanimous raves, and the show won five Tony awards—including Best Musical—en route to a 1,200-performance run. It was the 1992 Tony winner for Best Revival.

STORY: 1950's, New York City. Nathan Detroit is always looking for a place to run a crap game, to the consternation of his longtime fiancée, Adelaide. He needs a thousand dollars, and bets Sky Masterson that Sky can't get Sarah Brown of the faltering Save-a-Soul Mission to fly with him to Havana—but Sky does it. The two fall in love—until Sarah discovers that the gamblers used the mission while she and Sky were away. Sarah then refuses to have anything to do with him, leading Sky to try to "win" sinners in a dice game so that they will attend a prayer meeting and keep the mission going. Sky wins his sinners, and he and Sarah then marry—as do Adelaide and a most unhappy Nathan.

ASSETS: *Dramatics* magazine reports this is one of the most performed titles of stock, college, and amateur groups throughout the country. In addition to a great score and a funny book, the show gives an opportunity for four of your best performers to shine, for *Guys and Dolls* is one of the few musicals that could be said to offer four leading roles: Sky Masterson and Sarah Brown have approximately the same stage time as Nathan Detroit and Miss Adelaide.

LIABILITIES: Just one word: "Obadiah." In the first act, Sky Masterson confides to Sarah that that's his real name, and stresses that he doesn't tell it to anyone—but in the show's last scene, the moment after he and Sarah are married, Obadiah is precisely what she calls him in front of all his confederates. Not nice, or a good omen for the marriage.

RECOGNIZABLE SONGS: "A Bushel and a Peck," "Guys and Dolls," "If I Were a Bell," "I've Never Been in Love Before," "Luck Be a Lady," "Sit Down, You're Rockin' the Boat."

WHO YOU'LL NEED: *Lead Singing Roles:* A (sure-singing) gambler for whom the sky's the limit (a Scott Bakula type); the pure missionary lass (with legit voice) who inadvertently falls in love with him; a comic crap-game promoter; the stripper who's been in love with him for fourteen years. *Supporting Singing Roles:* Three good-natured hoods. *Other Roles:* Salvation Army types (Sarah's father, their boss, and onstage musicians); a beefy and imposing visiting high-roller; a suspicious police lieutenant; a waiter; a drunk; a chorus of gamblers and nightclub cuties. *Maximum, 39; minimum, 29.*

DESIGNATED DANCES: Four numbers involving much musical staging; two schlocky nightclub numbers; heavy dance and modern dance ballet in "Luck Be a Lady."

SUGGESTED SETS: Various locations on and around Broadway; outside and inside a mission; a cheap nightclub; the streets of Havana and one of its night spots; a sewer.

COSTUMES: Garish pin-stripe suits and loud ties; 1950s-styles suits and dresses for the women; Salvation Army–type uniforms; exotic Cuban costumes for both entertainers and night-spot patrons; silly and outlandish nightclub girl costumes; policemen's uniforms; detective suits; wedding dresses and tuxes.

IMPORTANT PROPS: A phone booth; newspapers and racing tip sheets; a blind man's cane; Bibles; samplers with biblical quotations; restaurant tables and chairs; coconut shell glasses; a vaporizer; onstage musicians' bass drum, trumpets, and trombones; a ladder by which gamblers climb into and out of the sewer; many pairs of dice.

PROVIDED INSTRUMENTATION: Five reeds, three trumpets, trombones, French horn, four violins, cello, bass, percussion.

ADVERTISING AND MARKETING: If there's a bingo hall in your community, arrange for your cast to visit, sing a few songs, sell a few tickets, and even give away a pair to the big bingo winner that night.

SUGGESTIONS: The opening section, "Runyonland," in which we meet all the colorful characters who inhabit Times Square, was originally conceived as a long choreographed sequence, but as the wildly successful 1992 revival proved, it doesn't have to be all that lengthy.

RESOURCES: The original cast album on CD, cassette, and LP; the 1992 revival cast album on CD and cassette; the rather faithful 1955 movie version on videotape and laserdisc; Damon Runyon's story, "The Idyll of Miss Sarah Brown," on which the musical is loosely based; a "Rehearscore" disc for Macintosh and IBM systems that eliminates the need for a rehearsal pianist.

RIGHTS: Music Theatre International.

HELLO, DOLLY!

CREATORS: Book by Michael *(Bye Bye Birdie)* Stewart, music and lyrics by Jerry *(Mame)* Herman (though other writers have often been rumored to have written some of the score).

BACKGROUND: The 1964 production opened in Detroit to mediocre reviews, but with the addition of "Before the Parade Passes By," it opened on Broadway to great reviews, received eleven Tony nominations, won ten awards—including Best Musical—and became the town's hottest ticket. After two and a half years, though, it declined precipitously, prompting producer David Merrick to bring in an all-black cast headed by Pearl Bailey. It was the shot in the arm that regained much of the momentum to carry the show to a then-record 2,844-performance run.

STORY: Turn-of-the-century Yonkers—and New York City. "Mrs. Levi is a wheeler-dealer of a matchmaker," says original Dolly Carol Channing, "who admits up front that she's tired and out to marry for money." Horace Vandergelder, Yonkers's most successful merchant, is the object of her affection, but she doesn't let him know it until he's come to New York and humiliated himself chasing a younger woman. Meanwhile, Vandergelder's two clerks, Cornelius and Barnaby, also come to New York, meet and fall in love with milliner Irene and her assistant Minnie, and lead the women to believe they have money. When they discover the men don't, the women don't care, and everyone ends up happily in love.

ASSETS: *Dramatics* magazine reports this is one of the most performed titles of stock, college and amateur groups throughout the country. In addition to a funny book, there's a marvelous opening number, a terrific first-act curtain, an even better eleven o'clock number, and, in between, the greatest second-act showstopper in a generation's worth of shows.

LIABILITIES: "All of Dolly's songs come in Carol Channing's original keys," says John Pike, Assistant to the Executive Director at the Goodspeed Opera House in East Haddam, Connecticut, "so unless your leading lady has an *extraordinarily* atypical voice, you'll have to transpose them."

RECOGNIZABLE SONGS: "Hello, Dolly!" "Before the Parade Passes By."

WHO YOU'LL NEED: *Lead Singing Role:* A middle-aged matchmaker (Channing) who's the type who remembers the waiters' names in the restaurant she hadn't frequented in years. *Supporting Singing Roles:* A tight-fisted half-a-millionaire; his timid clerk and even more timid assistant; a legit-voiced milliner and her assistant. *Other Roles:* A struggling artist suitor and his silly girlfriend; a heavyset young woman; an old woman; two actors to play a horse; a judge; a court clerk; a maitre d' who's a major domo; a chorus of men who are the speediest waiters in New York. *Maximum, 39; minimum, 19.*

DESIGNATED DANCES: When a show has a song called "Dancing," you know there'll be a good deal of it—and *Hello, Dolly!* does have plenty: There's much musical staging in the opening, and an abundance of stylized in-tempo dancing, marching, and walking throughout. In addition to a polka and three production numbers—including that big second-act title song showstopper—the waiters have a "gallop" in which they demonstrate their speed and dexterity.

SUGGESTED SETS: The streets of New York and Yonkers in the 1890s. Also, a feed store (ideally with a trap door and a second level); a train station; inside and outside a hat shop (with a closet); a courtroom; a most marvelous restaurant with private dining rooms. If you can somehow manage to mimic the original production's runway around the orchestra pit, do it.

COSTUMES: Late 1890s finery for everyone—including Sunday clothes and hats; waiters' tuxedos; a most elaborate red dress for Dolly. You'll also need a horse costume for two cast members.

IMPORTANT PROPS: A horsecar; parade instruments (especially a bass drum); luggage on a big cart; a pushcart; tables with tablecloths that reach the floor; hats; mannequins; trays with attached food; skewers; ice buckets; champagne bottle (with poppable cork); a loving cup; a box of chocolates; artificial cherries.

SPECIAL EFFECTS: Sounds of an explosion, smoke.

PROVIDED INSTRUMENTATION: Four reeds, three trumpets, two trombones, three violins, cello, bass, two percussion, guitar-banjo; piano-celeste, piano-conductor.

ADVERTISING AND MARKETING: "Hear the music that kept the Beatles from number one on the Top 40 for much of 1964."

SUGGESTIONS: You'll have to come up with the train that takes Dolly and everyone else from Yonkers to New York for the big "Put on Your Sunday Clothes" number, but you have an option to use a big cardboard cutout of the train, and have your cast walk through it. Yes, it's considerably less glamorous to reduce what was a big number on Broadway to a mere in-one (a scene played in front of the curtain), but it does also serve to give your techies extra time to get the next scene's dress shop set in place.

RESOURCES: The original cast album on CD, cassette, and LP; the 1969 faithful movie on videotape and laserdisc; Thornton Wilder's play *The Matchmaker* on which the musical is fairly faithfully based.

RIGHTS: Tams-Witmark.

THE KING AND I

CREATORS: Book and lyrics by Oscar Hammerstein II, music by Richard Rodgers (who had recently collaborated on *South Pacific*).

BACKGROUND: The 1951 production was much acclaimed for its new discovery, Yul Brynner, as well as for its legendary leading lady, Gertrude Lawrence. Although Lawrence died during its run, the production, winner of five Tony Awards—including Best Musical—was so strong that it ran 1,246 performances.

STORY: 1860s, Siam. East meets West as widowed Anna and her son come to Siam to teach English to the King's children. She finds the King a difficult man, but also sees that he has an inherent goodness, and that pride of being king keeps him from admitting that she has her good points. Anna does influence his favorite son and head wife, and even begins to get somewhere with him. The King discovers that one of his wives loves a young boy and wants to flog the girl—but cannot, because he knows Anna disapproves. The inner conflict this creates deals the King a fatal blow, and he soon dies. His son, the new king, plans to make some humane changes, and, with Anna's help, we know that he will be a better king than his father as the curtain falls.

ASSETS: In addition to a moving score and intelligent book, the show, more than forty years after its conception, still functions as a platform for women's rights; the King's wives are convinced they're lower than men, and Anna works very hard to point out how worthy they are.

LIABILITIES: The show doesn't have many fun moments for which Broadway musicals are famous; its charms are quieter, and an audience smiles much more than it will laugh out loud. There's also a politically incorrect implication that the best way for the Asians to impress the English is to dress and act exactly like them.

RECOGNIZABLE SONGS: "I Whistle a Happy Tune," "Getting to Know You," "Hello, Young Lovers," "Shall We Dance?"

WHO YOU'LL NEED: *Lead Singing Roles*: A strong, no-nonsense early middle-aged legit-voiced woman (nice if she can also whistle!). *Supporting Singing Roles*: A despotic but intelligent king; his head wife; his newest young (soprano) wife and the young man (a tenor) who loves her; Anna's pre-teen son (he should whistle, too); the King's favorite prepubescent son. *Other Roles*: A prime minister; a secretary; a boat captain; an interpreter; a British ambassador; royal dancers; royal wives; Amazons; priests; slaves; enough "Siamese" children to parade in a march. *Maximum, 49; minimum, 21.*

DESIGNATED DANCES: Your biggest challenge will be "The Small House of Uncle Thomas," a Siamese version of *Uncle Tom's Cabin*—a fifteen-minute sequence in which there is much stylized movement, and demands a lead dancer who can sustain hopping on one foot for a long time. Also, a spirited "Shall We Dance?" for Anna and the King.

SUGGESTED SETS: A boat at a dock; the palace corridor and grounds; the King's study; a schoolroom; a bedroom; a theater.

COSTUMES: Mid-nineteenth-century finery for Anna (hoop skirts) and her son; Siamese garb for men, women, and slaves (penangs, pantaloons, etcetera, etcetera, etcetera); an angel's outfit; priest's robes. Broadway costumer Irene Sharaff always maintained that the success of the "Shall We Dance?" number was largely due to the great bare-shouldered hoop dress that she designed for Anna. Get one for her, and ones just like it for the many Siamese women who'll wear them in a second-act scene.

IMPORTANT PROPS: A bed; a bullwhip; a large Bible; parade gear of oversized banners and elongated dragons; two maps (one of the world, and one fictitious map that shows a very large Siam and a very small Burma). For "The Small House of Uncle Thomas," you'll need a drum and gong; two doghouse-sized cabins; masks; a huge sword; a very long strip of light blue fabric to represent a river; a golden horn; giant snowflakes suspended from poles.

SPECIAL EFFECTS: Fireworks at end of act one.

PROVIDED INSTRUMENTATION: Two flutes, oboe, two clarinets, bassoon, two horns, two trumpets, two trombones, tuba, two percussion, three violins, viola, cello, bass, harp, piano-conductor.

ADVERTISING AND MARKETING: "Before there was Elvis, there was another King. Come see *The King and I* on . . ."

SUGGESTIONS: If you've found that your audience enjoys laughing above all else, choose another show.

RESOURCES: The 1977 revival cast album on CD, cassette, and LP offers the most material; the faithful 1956 movie on videotape and laserdisc; Margaret Landon's novel *Anna and the King of Siam* and its 1946 movie adaptation on which the musical is rather loosely based.

RIGHTS: Rodgers and Hammerstein.

MAN OF LA MANCHA

CREATORS: Book by Dale Wasserman (who wrote the play *One Flew over the Cuckoo's Nest*), music by Mitch (*Chu Chem*) Leigh, lyrics by Joe (*Shinbone Alley*) Darion.

BACKGROUND: The 1965 Broadway production did not play the midtown theater district, but instead opened in a prefabricated building on the New York University campus. It's often been said that during previews many patrons walked out after act one, but those who stayed were thrilled by the "Impossible Dream" ending, so management cut the intermission to keep people in their seats to get more cheers at the end. Once the show opened, it received seven Tony nominations, won five awards—including Best Musical—and settled in for a 2,328-performance run, and the intermission was restored.

STORY: While in a Spanish prison during the Inquisition, Miguel de Cervantes tells inmates his story of Don Quixote, the knight born three hundred years too late, a man who feels that "Facts are the enemy of truth," and sees the world as it ought to be rather than as it is. Quixote meets and is smitten by Aldonza, a bar wench who believes that "the world is a dungheap and we are all maggots in it." Still, Don Quixote believes that she is special, and convinces her and many others of that by the time of his death. Is Cervantes too optimistic a writer? No, for by show's end, he is released from prison.

ASSETS: A stirring score, and a book that offers the audience hope.

LIABILITIES: Is Quixote merely old and crazy? He turns the other cheek one time too many, and when he says that he "never had the courage to believe in nothing," is he profound or guilty of doubletalk? (Still, some of these problems can be alleviated if your Quixote is a loving messiah, and less arch in tone.) And how will your audiences feel about the rape of Aldonza?

RECOGNIZABLE SONGS: "The Impossible Dream."

WHO YOU'LL NEED: *Lead Singing Roles:* A vigorous nobleman-poet who, with makeup, becomes an old and eccentric knight-errant (Raul Julia); a rough-and-tumble bar wench with legit voice (who is tossed around by the male chorus) who finds her inner beauty. *Supporting Singing Roles:* A comic man-servant; a (soprano) niece who pretends to be concerned about her uncle; a tenor-voiced padre; a housekeeper; a doctor; a muleteer; a barber; an innkeeper. *Other Roles:* The innkeeper's wife; a duke; a governor; a captain; a guitarist;

many prisoners who double as muleteers and horses. (Considering that the show takes place in a prison in which all sorts of prisoners are incarcerated, there's really no reason why females can't play many of the male roles.) *Maximum, 29; minimum, 19.*

DESIGNATED DANCES: Much stylized movement for the muleteers; some steps for your horses.

SUGGESTED SETS: One unit set with a few iron gates, but you really should have a long gangplank staircase situated centerstage for easy (yet dramatic) entrances and exits into the bowels of the prison. Trap doors (representing wells) could enhance a production, but aren't necessary; in fact, the set could easily be adapted for a black-box theater—but keep that gangplank, to give the sense that we're really immersed in a prison.

COSTUMES: Late-sixteenth-century noble and peasant wear: a battered knight's suit for Quixote, but impressive period military uniforms and vest armor; gentlemen's clothes for his tormentors; glorified burlap rags for Aldonza and the inmates; Alhambran finery for women; Spanish metal helmets with adorning features (one with a face shield); robes for academics, monks, and a padre (the monks and padre will also need skullcaps, cinctures, and beads); horse heads; mantillas; serapes; robes; nightgown and nightcaps; a steel barber's hat that can double as a bowl; an exaggerated goatee, eyebrows, and mustache.

IMPORTANT PROPS: Sawhorses; large mirror shields; lances, scabbards, and swords (one that can easily become bent after an offstage struggle); cooking pot; mugs and steins; large serving trays; wooden bowls and spoons; wine casks and goatskins; buckets with rope handles; bullwhips; hunting horns; money bags; a theatrical trunk; a makeup case; a barber's razor and clipping shears; a parchment letter; a makeshift bed; a portable writing desk with quill pen; long ladder; a book representing *Don Quixote.*

SPECIAL EFFECTS: Shadows of windmill blades.

PROVIDED INSTRUMENTATION: Five reeds, two horns, two trumpets, two trombones, bass, two guitars, two percussion.

ADVERTISING AND MARKETING: Late in the original Broadway run, the management enjoyed running an ad that said, "What?! You've seen *Man of La Mancha* only once?!" Because the show is still so beloved, you might again try this strategy.

SUGGESTIONS: In the 1987 Paris revival, the *Don Quixote* book was made of greatly oversized, ragged pages held together by a makeshift cover and rope. When Cervantes was released from prison, he almost forgot the book—but halfway up the ramp remembered it, turned to call for it, and caught it when it was thrown to him. It was very exciting to watch not only Cervantes the man, but also *Don Quixote* the masterpiece get out of prison.

RESOURCES: The original cast album on CD, cassette, and LP; the 1972 fairly faithful (though bad) movie; Miguel de Cervantes's novel *Don Quixote*.

RIGHTS: Tams-Witmark.

MY FAIR LADY

CREATORS: Book and lyrics by Alan Jay Lerner, music by Frederick Loewe (who later collaborated on *Camelot*).

BACKGROUND: Lerner and Loewe first started musicalizing George Bernard Shaw's play *Pygmalion* in the early 1950s, but couldn't get anywhere with it; a few years later Lerner realized that if he showed the offstage action that Shaw only described, he could make a richer show. Raves greeted his and Loewe's 1956 musical, which received ten Tony nominations and won six awards—including Best Musical—and audiences attended for a then-record musical run of 2,717 performances.

STORY: 1912, London. Henry Higgins bets Colonel Pickering that he is a skilled enough teacher to turn Eliza, a flower girl, into someone who could fool upper-class people into thinking she was to the manor born. Eliza, wanting to better herself, goes along, and though she finds learning difficult at first, she eventually emerges triumphant. Higgins, however, views the triumph as his own, which infuriates Eliza, and nearly sends her into the arms of Freddy, a highborn lad who has fallen in love with her. By curtain's end Higgins realizes what he's lost, and Eliza returns to him.

ASSETS: A witty and engaging book with a score to match; indeed, at one time, the show's original cast album was the best-selling record of all time (*not* merely the best-selling show record).

LIABILITIES: Your production may not cost a million, but it must look it in both sets and costumes. What's more, Higgins, Mrs. Higgins (his mother), Colonel Pickering, and Freddy all must articulate the King's English without error; have you the actors who can pull this off?

RECOGNIZABLE SONGS: "Wouldn't It Be Loverly," "With a Little Bit of Luck," "The Rain in Spain," "I Could Have Danced All Night," "On the Street Where You Live," "Get Me to the Church on Time," "I've Grown Accustomed to Her Face."

WHO YOU'LL NEED: *Lead Singing Roles:* A megalomaniacal English professor (a Richard Chamberlain type); a (legit-voiced) flower girl capable of being transformed into much more (Julie Andrews). *Supporting Singing Roles:* A young (legit-voiced) society swell who falls madly in love; a vigorous dustman;

an amiable colonel; a no-nonsense housekeeper. *Other Roles:* Two high-class mothers; a hirsute Hungarian; the Queen of Transylvania and her consort; a common-law wife; servants; a chauffeur; three costermongers; two cronies; an angry bartender; a policeman; a butler; a footman; another flower girl; a chorus of Londoners, both plain and fancy. *Maximum, 45; minimum, 22.*

DESIGNATED DANCES: Two music hall turns for Eliza's father and his cronies, the second one also involving much of the company; an impromptu tango for Higgins, Eliza, and Pickering; some musical staging for a gavotte for most of the company; a waltz for most of the company.

SUGGESTED SETS: Outside the Royal Opera House; near some tenements; Higgins's study; in and around the Ascot Race Track; on the street where Higgins lives; a promenade and ballroom; the Covent Garden flower market; Mrs. Higgins's conservatory.

COSTUMES: Early twentieth-century London finery for the upper class (opera and ball gowns, tuxedos with top hats and tails, capes), and glorified rags for the lower class (shoddy shawl, coarse apron, hat with ostrich feathers); a policeman's uniform. The famous black-and-white costume design for everyone who attends the Ascot races isn't *de rigueur.*

IMPORTANT PROPS: A smudge-pot fire; flower baskets with violets; a nosegay; a wing chair; two pouffes; a telephone; a bird cage; a bust of Plato; a small xylophohone; a gramophone with speaker horn; a metronome; a burner with active flame; marbles; a tray of chocolates; tea and strawberry tarts; a decanter; a Chinese fan; jewels; a suitcase; an ice bag for Higgins's head; Higgins's slippers.

SPECIAL EFFECTS: Voice-overs of various British accents reciting phonics—some played at unlikely high speeds—as well as Eliza's voice.

PROVIDED INSTRUMENTATION: Two violins, viola, cello, bass, flute/piccolo, oboe/English horn, two clarinets, bassoon, two horns, three trumpets, two trombones, tuba, percussion, harp, piano-conductor.

ADVERTISING AND MARKETING: "In 1956, it was called the musical of the century. Nearly 40 years later, that's still accurate."

SUGGESTIONS: The movie misses a joke used in the original production: in Act One, Scene Three, Higgins gives Eliza, who'd just wiped her nose on her sleeve, a handkerchief "to wipe any part of your face that feels moist. Remember, that's your handkerchief, and that's your sleeve." But Eliza then again wipes her nose on her sleeve, and *then* wipes it off with the handkerchief.

RESOURCES: The original cast album on CD, cassette, and LP; the faithful 1964 movie version on videotape and laserdisc; George Bernard Shaw's play *Pygmalion*, on which the musical is fairly faithfully based and its movie version.

RIGHTS: Tams-Witmark.

OKLAHOMA!

CREATORS: Book and lyrics by Oscar Hammerstein II, music by Richard Rodgers (who then went on to collaborate on *Carousel*).

BACKGROUND: When the very different 1943 production debuted in New Haven under the title *Away We Go!* the New Yorkers who came to see it decided that it had "No legs, no jokes, no chance." But this new-styled show that didn't open with a bevy of chorus girls, and relied on characterization for humor instead of one-liners, garnered the attention of Broadway critics and audiences, who responded to the retitled *Oklahoma!* and kept it running for a then-record 2,212 performances.

STORY: 1907, in the "Indian territory" above Texas. Though Aunt Eller encourages a relationship between her niece Laurey and Curly, the two can't admit their affection for each other. (It's not a problem for secondary lovers Will and Ado Annie—though Annie does have difficulty in settling for one man.) But when hired hand Jud—an unsavory type with a passion for pornography—expresses interest in Laurey, Curly stakes his claim and weds her. Jud then tries to kill Curly, but is accidentally slain with his own knife. At a very quick trial, Curly is acquitted by reason of self-defense, and he and Laurey begin their honeymoon.

ASSETS: *Dramatics* magazine reports that this is one of the most performed titles of stock, college and amateur groups throughout the country. Great score, fine book, funny and engagingly well-written characters throughout.

LIABILITIES: If the show were written today, Hammerstein might have had more pity for Jud, and might not have had Curly, in an early scene, encouraging him to commit suicide; to today's audiences, Curly seems very insensitive to a mentally disturbed person. Also, as is the case with *Carousel*, Hammerstein wrote very regional dialogue that is tough reading ("yer" for "your," "whur" for "where," and "shore" for "sure"), and will mean an awkward first few readings by your cast.

RECOGNIZABLE SONGS: "Oh, What a Beautiful Mornin'," "The Surrey with the Fringe on Top," "People Will Say We're in Love," "Oklahoma."

WHO YOU'LL NEED: *Lead Singing Roles* (each with legit voices): A handsome cowboy who can spin a rope; the pretty, independent girl he wants to court. *Supporting Singing Roles:* A flirtatious girl and her skeptical would-be suitor (who can dance); her father; a savvy peddler; a good-natured aunt; an unhappy and unbalanced base (*and* bass) hired hand. *Other Roles:* A flibbertigibbet girl; a girl who enjoys telling fortunes; a chorus of farmers and cowmen, their wives and girlfriends; ballet counterparts for Laurey, Curly, and Jud; dance hall girls. *Maximum, 53; minimum, 23.*

DESIGNATED DANCES: A two-step for Will and Aunt Eller; a ragtime dance for Will and four cowboys; a waltz for Curly and the flibbertigibbet; a spritely dance for Laurey and her girlfriends; an up tempo dance for Ado Annie and Will; some musical staging for the title song; two square dances; an extensive ballet for Laurey, Curly, and Jud's counterparts.

SUGGESTED SETS: The front and back of Laurey's farmhouse (with a slammable door and fence); the exterior and interiors of a smokehouse (a particularly difficult set change); a grove; a ranch; a kitchen porch.

COSTUMES: Early twentieth-century Western wear; a wedding dress and bridal veil; nightgown; corset; apron; garter; red flannel drawers.

IMPORTANT PROPS: A butter churn; a pot-bellied stove; a clothesline; a quilt; lunch hampers; tin pans and spoons; a saddle, horse collars; hoes, rakes, and axes; a spittoon; lanterns; firewood; a bulging suitcase; a bottle of elixir; a kaleidoscope; a shotgun and pistols; a knife.

PROVIDED INSTRUMENTATION: Flute, oboe, two clarinets, bassoon, horns, trumpet, trombone, percussion, four violins, viola, cello, bass, guitar, harp, piano-conductor.

ADVERTISING AND MARKETING: "See why *Oklahoma!* has been a hit in every state."

SUGGESTIONS: "The concerns that Curly and Laurey have in trying not to admit their love is the type that very young people have," says Jeffrey Dunn, who directed a 1991 European tour, "so cast them with kids who are virtual teenagers."

RESOURCES: The 1979 revival cast album on CD, cassette, and LP offers the most material; the faithful 1955 movie version on videotape and laserdisc; Lynn Riggs's play *Green Grow the Lilacs*, on which the musical is fairly faithfully based.

RIGHTS: Rodgers and Hammerstein.

SHOW BOAT

CREATORS: Book and lyrics by Oscar (*Oklahoma!*) Hammerstein II, music by Jerome (*Leave It to Jane*) Kern.

BACKGROUND: Critic Alexander Woolcott read Edna Ferber's novel, *Show Boat*, called Jerome Kern, and urged the composer to musicalize it. Ferber didn't see a musical in her book about love gone wrong and miscegenation, but agreed in hopes that esteemed producer Florenz Ziegfeld would produce. Even though the show contained only one number that showed off his trademark girls, and he was wary of the show's success, Ziegfeld offered the 1927 production, which ran for a then-impressive 572 performances.

STORY: 1880's–1920's on the Mississippi. Cap'n Andy claims that his show boat is "one big happy family"—and that includes his wife, daughter Magnolia, as well as stars Julie and husband Steve, and black help Queenie and Joe. But it won't be for long; because a river rat's love for Julie goes unrequited, and he informs the sheriff that she's a "half-breed" with Negro blood. Steve knowing this was coming, pricks her finger and sucks her blood so that he too will have black blood in him. Julie and Steve must leave the show boat, which greatly upsets Magnolia, who adores Julie; she is mollified, however, when Steve is replaced on the boat by Gaylord, with whom she immediately falls in love. Magnolia and Gaylord wed; it's a bad match, however, for Gaylord is not the marrying kind, and in time winds up abandoning his wife and their daughter after they too have left the boat. Magnolia needs a job, and fate brings her back to Julie, who pretends to be drunk when auditioning for a show once she sees that Magnolia needs it even more than she does. But the sadder-but-wiser Magnolia is found by her father, and they are reunited at curtain's fall.

ASSETS: Not only a great score, but a book that's still an astonishing achievement sixty years later. No musical up to that time had ever had an ingredient as subtle and clever as having an audience suspect that Julie has black blood in her because she knows a "black" song; nor had there ever been anything as dramatic as the scene in which her husband "infects" himself with her blood. Even today, these scenes, among many others, hold an audience spellbound.

LIABILITIES: You'll have to build an elaborate show boat. Some—especially young audiences—will find the music much too operetta-like in quality. (Do your principals have the voices to carry this demanding score?) And the second act has many too many reprises of its first-act songs. Some of the language describing blacks is now offensive. And on a very minor level, some of the least sophisticated members of your audience may inappropriately laugh at the many times Gaylord is referred to by his nickname, *Gay*.

RECOGNIZABLE SONGS: "Make Believe," "Ol' Man River," "Can't Help Lovin' Dat Man," "Life upon the Wicked Stage," "Why Do I Love You?" "Bill," "After the Ball."

WHO YOU'LL NEED: *Lead Singing Roles:* A naive young girl who grows to a sadder-but-wiser woman; her suave but phony gambler husband (each has a strong legit voice); an accomplished actress, her far less accomplished but decent husband. *Supporting Singing Roles:* A lovably crusty captain; his shrewish wife; their granddaughter (both as a child and a young adult), a male-female vaudeville team; a black earthmother and her unambitious husband (who must have an amazing bass voice). *Other Roles:* A river rat; a pilot; a sheriff; a woman on the levee; three barkers; an Egyptian dancer; nuns; wealthy theatergoers; waiters; many black dock workers and their wives; a large chorus of men, women, and children. *Maximum, 59; minimum 32.*

DESIGNATED DANCES: Heavy. The vaudevillians appear in three soft-shoe production numbers, but there's also a high-stepping kick-line for Julie, Magnolia, Queenie and the ladies; a skirt-swishing ballyhoo for Queenie and the chorus; a wedding dance; a cakewalk for most of the company; a pseudo can-can for the female chorus.

SUGGESTED SETS: An elaborate show boat; its kitchen; its auditorium; outside a gambling saloon; at the 1893 Chicago World's Fair; inside a boardinghouse; a convent; outside a newspaper office.

COSTUMES: Much finery of all periods is used; top hats and canes; waistcoats for the men; bustle dresses; feathered hats; parasols for the women; an Egyptian dancer's scanty costume; nuns' habits; masks on sticks; a captain's uniform with admiral's hat; a preacher's black suit; waiters' uniforms. A difficult show, because it spans forty years in which styles greatly changed.

IMPORTANT PROPS: Bushels, baskets, and bales of cotton; placard promoting the show boat's stars; makeshift theater curtain; megaphones; many tables and chairs for various locales; kitchen equipment; pots and pans; flower seller's tray; champagne flutes; mistletoe.

PROVIDED INSTRUMENTATION: Flute, oboe, clarinet, bassoon, horn, two trumpets, three trombones, two percussion, four violins, viola, cello, bass, harp, guitar, piano-conductor.

ADVERTISING AND MARKETING: Do some numbers at a local marina, and sell tickets there.

SUGGESTIONS: While Gaylord is often nicknamed "Gay" in the script, you may be better off using his full name, so that the less enlightened in your audience won't spoil the show with snickers.

RESOURCES: The best (and most complete) album is the 1990 studio cast album on EMI-Angel on CD, cassette, and LP. The 1936 fairly faithful film version, which is far superior to the 1951 rendition; the Edna Ferber novel on which the musical is somewhat faithfully based; the book *Show Boat*, a history of the show, by Miles Kreuger.

RIGHTS: Rodgers and Hammerstein.

SOUTH PACIFIC

CREATORS: Book and lyrics by Oscar Hammerstein II, music by Richard Rodgers (who next wrote *The King and I*).

BACKGROUND: The 1949 production proved that Rodgers and Hammerstein's serious effort, the unsuccessful *Allegro*, did not mean that the team was defeated; indeed, *South Pacific* received unanimous raves, won eight Tony Awards, and ran 1,925 performances.

STORY: Prejudice. It's World War II in the South Pacific. Nellie Forbush, a young woman from Little Rock, has become an ensign in the armed forces. She believes she is less prejudiced about other races than her parents were, but when she's faced with the reality that Emile de Becque, the Frenchman with whom she's fallen in love, has fathered children by a Polynesian woman, she is repulsed. By show's end, she loses her prejudice, partly because she's seen and sanctioned the love of a young lieutenant and a Polynesian girl.

ASSETS: *Dramatics* magazine reports this is one of the most performed titles of stock, college, and amateur groups throughout the country. A score as great and deserving as its reputation, two star roles, and a musical that does have "redeeming features" in trying to say something about prejudice—and succeeding.

LIABILITIES: By today's standards, Emile is not a nice man; he asks Nellie to marry him in their very first scene, but conveniently avoids telling her that he's had two children with a Polynesian woman. (And why doesn't he teach English to his French-speaking kids?) What's more, the interracial romance between the lieutenant and the Polynesian girl, based on love at first sight and physical attraction, today seems shallow.

RECOGNIZABLE SONGS: "Some Enchanted Evening," "There Is Nothin' Like a Dame," "Bali Ha'i," "I'm Gonna Wash That Man Right Outa My Hair," "(I'm in Love with) A Wonderful Guy," "Younger Than Springtime," "Happy Talk," "Honey Bun," "This Nearly Was Mine."

WHO YOU'LL NEED: *Lead Singing Roles:* A tomboyish ensign (Mary Martin); her older and more sophisticated would-be lover; each has a legit voice. *Supporting Singing Roles:* An enterprising Polynesian woman; her innocent daughter; the tenor-voiced lieutenant who loves her. *Other Roles:* A captain; an enterprising enlisted man; a commander; a yeoman; two sergeants; two seamen; two Seabees; a radio operator; a Marine; a male lieutenant and a female lieutenant; eight female ensigns; two half-Polynesian children; a chorus of islanders, sailors, and officers. *Maximum, 51; minimum, 22.*

DESIGNATED DANCES: Some musical staging for the sailors' two numbers; a soft-shoe for the Seabees; some strutting for Nellie and the ensigns after she washes her hair and in her onstage number; and a quick jitterbug.

SUGGESTED SETS: A terrace of a plantation home; a bamboo and canvas shop; the edge of a palm grove near the beach; a native hut; at a fountain; inside the commander's office; a beach; a makeshift stage and its backstage area; a communications office.

COSTUMES: Uniforms for nurses, officers, Seabees, and sailors (including oversized regulation whites for Nellie); bathing suits for men and women; tattered shirts; grass skirts; one "South Seas siren" outfit (for a man—a straw fright wig and a brassiere made of coconuts); native-style garb for both sexes; nuns' habits.

IMPORTANT PROPS: Bamboo and native tapa-cloth curtains; a shrunken head; a boar-tooth bracelet; a package of clean laundry; large shells; native hats; canoes; bales of equipment; tin tubs; microphone; roll of cable; flower bouquet; gold watch; earphones; a bottle of Scotch; a rustic wooden—but operable—shower which can be as crude as a bucket with holes in it; plenty of shampoo.

PROVIDED INSTRUMENTATION: Flute, oboe, clarinet, bassoon, horn, two trumpets, two trombones, tuba, percussion, four violins, viola, cello, bass, harp.

ADVERTISING AND MARKETING: "Anyone bringing a bottle of shampoo with which Nellie can wash that man right out of her hair gets a ticket for half-price." You can then donate the shampoo to a homeless shelter.

SUGGESTIONS: Says Donovan Marley, Artistic Director of the Denver Theatre Center, "I've cast blacks in the roles of the Polynesians, and have found that works well."

RESOURCES: The original cast album on CD, cassette, and LP; the faithful 1958 movie on videotape and laserdisc; two stories, "Fo' Dolla" and "Our Heroine" from James Michener's book *Tales of the South Pacific* on which the musical is rather faithfully based.

RIGHTS: Rodgers and Hammerstein.

Also See: *Anything Goes; Babes in Arms; Bells Are Ringing; Brigadoon; Camelot; Damn Yankees; Gigi; Good News!; Kiss Me, Kate; Mame; The Music Man; No, No, Nanette; Oliver!; The Pajama Game; Peter Pan; Singin' in the Rain; The Sound of Music; Sugar Babies; West Side Story; The Wizard of Oz.*

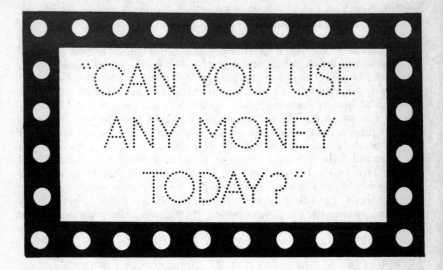

"CAN YOU USE ANY MONEY TODAY?"

The More Recent Moneymakers

"Can you use any money today?" Ethel Merman asked in *Call Me Madam*—and which of us could not? "Then," says Tina Williams, of Tallahassee Young Actors' Theatre, "you'd better do a newer classic, one presented after *Oklahoma!* or *Hello, Dolly!* but still old enough to be famous."

If you—and your audiences—feel the same way, here are some of the more recent classics.

ANNIE

CREATORS: Book by Thomas (*I Remember Mama*) Meehan, music by Charles (*Bye Bye Birdie*) Strouse, lyrics by Martin (*Two by Two*) Charnin.

BACKGROUND: The Goodspeed Opera House in Connecticut produced the musical in 1976, where it opened in shambles; the original Annie was fired early in the run, and by the end, it was clear that the actress playing Miss Hannigan would also have to go. Mike Nichols came on as producer, Dorothy Loudon as Miss Hannigan took the reins of the orphanage, some rewriting occurred, and the result was a bevy of great reviews, ten Tony nominations, seven wins—including Best Musical—and a 2,377-performance run.

STORY: New York City during the Depression. Annie, an orphan determined to find her parents, escapes from an orphanage, but is found and returned just as Grace Farrell, secretary to wealthy Oliver Warbucks, is there on her annual visit to choose a boy whom Warbucks can host for the Christmas holidays. Miss Hannigan, the scurrilous orphanage head, is furious when Annie charms Grace into choosing her, and more angry still when Warbucks takes to the young girl. (Grace comes to tell a furious Miss Hannigan that Annie will be staying a bit longer, bumping into Hannigan's brother Rooster and his doxy Lily on her way out.) The entrepreneur eventually becomes so taken with Annie that he wants to adopt her—but to his surprise, she doesn't accept, for she still wants to find her real parents. Warbucks loves her enough to offer a fifty-thousand-dollar reward to anyone who can prove they're Annie's real parents. That's when Rooster and Lily, fortified with information about Annie that only Hannigan knows, decide to impersonate Annie's parents. The ruse seems to work—until Rooster again bumps into Grace and jogs her into remembering where she's seen him before. It's discovered that Annie's parents died some time ago, so she and Warbucks become father and daughter by curtain's fall.

ASSETS: Who can resist the sight of little girls singing and dancing—especially to such a good score? The book is amazingly touching, especially considering that its source is a comic strip, and has genuine emotional pull.

LIABILITIES: There's a touching scene in which Annie finds a dog and wants to save him from the pound by claiming he's hers—and must prove it by having the dog immediately come to her; can you find a manageable dog who'll cooperate? Adds Paul C. Norton, Associate Professor of Theatre Arts at Bay Path College in Longmeadow, Massachusetts, "Do not, under any circumstances, allow any parents into auditions or, if possible, allow them to have anything to do with the show."

RECOGNIZABLE SONGS: "(The Sun'll Come Out) Tomorrow."

WHO YOU'LL NEED: *Lead Singing Roles:* A spunky yet warm young girl (with a legit voice). *Supporting Singing Roles:* A feisty and disappointed spinster; her nefarious brother; his empty-headed squeeze; a wealthy and sincere industrialist (with a strong baritone); his lovely well-bred secretary; a butler; three maids; an aspiring actress; a radio entertainer; his two-girl backup; Franklin Delano Roosevelt and five Cabinet members; six adorable little orphan girls. *Other Roles:* A sound-effects man; a chief justice; an NBC page; a chorus of homeless people, servants, and New Yorkers, a shaggy dog. *Maximum,* 55; *minimum,* 24.

DESIGNATED DANCES: The orphans have an opening number which involves choreographing their mop-and-pail movements and a kick-line that opens the second act; Hannigan, Rooster, and Lily have a couple of struts;

some musical staging by Warbucks's servants on two numbers; a soft-shoe duet for Annie and Warbucks.

SUGGESTED SETS: An orphanage with a barracks of beds; a New York City street; a homeless community; a mansion's main hall and its study; along Sixth Avenue and Broadway; an NBC radio studio; inside the White House.

COSTUMES: 1930s wear, both plain (orphans' dresses, housecoats, homeless peoples' clothes, and cheap-flamboyant outfits) and fancy (sharp suits, immaculate servant costumes, nice dresses for Annie—as well as for the six orphans who emerge at the curtain in different colors); policemen's uniforms; soft-shoe outfit for radio entertainer.

IMPORTANT PROPS: A limousine; mops and pails; a large laundry basket on wheels; barrels; two silver lockets; a radio sound effects table; applause signs; a trick hat Rooster can control with a string.

PROVIDED INSTRUMENTATION: Five reeds, two trumpets, two trombones, tuba, violin, cello, bass, guitar/banjo, two percussion, piano-conductor.

ADVERTISING AND MARKETING: "Christmas, adorable children, a dog— Yup, we're doing *Annie!*"

SUGGESTIONS: There's a temptation to fill the stage with a chorus of little girls for the opening number—but let the caster beware; how will you keep them busy and quiet when they're not onstage?

RESOURCES: The original cast album on CD, cassette, and LP; the fairly faithful 1982 movie version on videotape and laserdisc; a "Rehearscore" CD for Macintosh and IBM systems that eliminates the need for a rehearsal pianist; the Harold Gray comic strips on which the musical is loosely based.

RIGHTS: Music Theatre International.

GODSPELL

CREATORS: Book conceived by John-Michael Tebelak, music and additional lyrics (to buttress some traditional hymn lyrics) by Stephen (*Pippin*) Schwartz.

BACKGROUND: What began as a college show at Carnegie-Mellon University moved to off-off-Broadway's Cafe La Mama, then to a small off-Broadway theater, then a larger off-Broadway theater—playing 2,124 performances—and still wasn't through, moving to Broadway for 527 more performances, where it received a Tony nomination for Best Score.

STORY: A folk-rock look at the last days and nights of Jesus of Nazareth: his betrayal by Judas, his denial by Peter, his trial at the hands of Pontius Pilate, his crucifixion and death—but done in a charming, tuneful, and imaginative way.

ASSETS: *Dramatics* magazine reports this is one of the most performed titles by stock, college, and amateur groups throughout the country. "I'm about as far removed from religion as you can get," says Steve Allen, a St. Louis director, "but even I get a little born-again when doing this show. The 'Last Supper' sequence always pulls a cast together tighter than any show I've ever been in."

LIABILITIES: A production can often suffer from "the cutes" when the cast gives the audience too much peace, brotherhood, and smiling.

RECOGNIZABLE SONGS: "Day by Day."

WHO YOU'LL NEED: *Ensemble Roles:* Six men and four women—each with a simple (*not* simplistic) quality—not to mention lankiness, clowning ability, and good rock voices. But casting *Godspell* offers a wild card of possibilities; don't hesitate to do it with grade-school children. A little child's sense of innocence and wonder beautifully lends itself to the material. *Maximum,* 30; *minimum,* 10.

DESIGNATED DANCES: Three production numbers for the entire cast; a soft-shoe for Jesus and John the Baptist.

SUGGESTED SETS: Though the original production set the action in front of a floor-to-ceiling chain-link fence, you can use an empty stage with a few steamer trunks full of clothes and props.

COSTUMES: You have a freer hand here than you do with most musicals, for *Godspell* has a (pardon the oxymoron) devil-may-care, choose-what-you-have-backstage feeling—though Jesus is traditionally costumed in a T-shirt with a parody of Superman's great big red "S."

IMPORTANT PROPS: Gallons of wine and little plastic cups to serve it during intermission, as has always been the *Godspell* custom. If you're doing it with kids, grape juice will suffice.

PROVIDED INSTRUMENTATION: Piano, guitar, percussion.

ADVERTISING AND MARKETING: Before you start rehearsals, advertise that "In only [number] days, we'll be presenting *Godspell.* To do a good job, we're going to need a number of costumes. Lucky for us, to costume *Godspell,* all we really need are old clothes. Our truck will be coming around on [date] to pick up any old clothes that you think will be good for *Godspell*; in exchange, we'll give you a buy-one-ticket-get-one-free voucher."

Once you're closer to performance, take an ad that's headlined, "Come to *Godspell*—the drinks are on us." Then explain that during intermission, you'll serve wine. See if you can get a local wine merchant to donate the wares. (It's up to you—and your wine donor—if you'll acknowledge the donation in the program, but one of the themes of the show is that when you do something nice for somebody, you really shouldn't look to get credit for it.) And check to see if in your community you can serve even this modicum of liquor.

The week before performances, let the local churches know that you're doing the show (many announce upcoming events from the pulpit), for some will be especially willing to promote a play with a religious theme.

SUGGESTIONS: "Have a dynamic Jesus," says Schwartz, "but remember that this is an ensemble show. Too many productions I've seen have an actor come out, really sell his number, then not try too hard for the rest of the show. Meanwhile, other actors are trying to top the previous actor's big moment, and the can-you-top-this competition ruins the show."

"And be prepared," laments Deborah Voss, who directed the show for Cheyenne (Wyoming) Little Theater Players, "to have many debates on religious philosophy with cast members who have different views from yours and the script's."

RESOURCES: The original cast album on CD, cassette, and LP; the faithful 1973 movie on videotape and laserdisc, and, of course, the Gospel According to St. Matthew, on which the musical is fancifully based.

RIGHTS: Theater Maximus, 1650 Broadway, New York, NY 10019; 212–765–5913.

GREASE

CREATORS: Book, music, and lyrics by Jim Jacobs and Warren Casey.

BACKGROUND: Despite the 1972 production's shaky start—not-so-good reviews, and a very small advance sale—there was enough interest in the 1950s to create a demand for tickets. Seven Tony nominations (albeit no awards) helped, and a then-record 3,338-performance run resulted.

STORY: The 1950s in Anytown. Greaser Danny Zuko met Sandy Dumbrowski, a young innocent, during the summer, and it was love at first sight; Danny showed his sensitive side, for he didn't expect to see her at Rydell High the first day of school. But his friends are watching him, so he reverts to his greaser personality. All this does is make Sandy join the female version of the greaser life—the Pink Ladies—though the worldly-wise Rizzo distrusts her. The two become closer when Rizzo has a pregnancy scare, but it's just that— and all ends happily—even for the reunited Danny and Sandy.

ASSETS: *Dramatics* magazine reports this is among the most performed titles by stock, college, and amateur groups throughout the country. A fun score.

LIABILITIES: The show can look a little ragged if you don't have convincing-looking cars.

RECOGNIZABLE SONGS: "Summer Nights," "Greased Lightning."

WHO YOU'LL NEED: *Lead Singing Roles:* An ultra-cool guy who's nicer than he cares to admit; the innocent young girl who loves him. *Supporting Singing Roles:* Four Pink Ladies (a tough one (with a legit voice); a good-natured dreamer, a beauty, a compulsive eater); four Burger Palace Boys (a tough one, an innocent guitarist, a clown, a wheeler-dealer); a cheerleader; a slovenly blind date; a valedictorian; a deejay, a wannabe rock-'n'-roll star; a falsetto singer; an elderly schoolteacher. *Maximum, 17; minimum, 16.*

DESIGNATED DANCES: 1950s stomping; jitterbug; stepping in tempo; Elvis hip action for virtually all the company.

SUGGESTED SETS: School cafeteria; schoolyard; outside steps; gym; a teen girl's bedroom; a street corner; a park; a burger palace; a drive-in movie.

COSTUMES: Pink Lady jackets; leather jackets; poodle skirts; beauty smocks and curlers; panties; garter belts; bras.

IMPORTANT PROPS: 1950s jalopies; tire iron; auto antenna; picnic table; bar with stools; cafeteria trays; brown lunch bags; beer bottles; Coke cans; "church key" can openers; box of Saran Wrap; water pistol; batons; police siren air horn; hubcaps; pennants; oversized red foam dice; stuffed animals; a View-Master; 45-rpm records; guitar; live mike; radios (home and transistor); telephones.

PROVIDED INSTRUMENTATION: Two saxophones, two guitars, bass, drums, electric piano, piano-conductor.

ADVERTISING AND MARKETING: "We tried selling greasy foods during intermission," said one director who *insisted* on remaining anonymous. "I urge you not to make that mistake."

SUGGESTIONS: A great show for high-schoolers, who tend to enjoy "acting out" by playing these benignly asocial characters.

RESOURCES: The original cast album on CD, cassette, and LP; the somewhat faithful 1978 movie on videotape and laserdisc (which does contain some hit songs that the musical doesn't have).

RIGHTS: Samuel French.

JESUS CHRIST SUPERSTAR

CREATORS: Book and lyrics by Tim Rice, music by Andrew Lloyd Webber (who later collaborated on *Evita*).

BACKGROUND: The authors revolutionized the way musicals were produced—first doing an album, but having a produced stage musical in mind all along. The record became so popular that the public virtually demanded a 1971 Broadway production—and 720 performances resulted.

STORY: The last days and nights of Jesus of Nazareth: his betrayal by Judas, his denial by Peter, his trial at the hands of Pontius Pilate, his crucifixion and death—not in *Godspell's* innocent way, but in a grand rock-opera style with meatier characters.

ASSETS: A terrific score; not a difficult show to produce and one that kids love to be in; a show that can have many elaborate sets and a design as grand as your designer's imagination, but one that can also be produced on a shoestring budget.

LIABILITIES: In addition to the score being vocally demanding, there may still be an influental person or two in your community who doesn't enjoy seeing one of the most significant events in the history of the world treated as a rock musical.

RECOGNIZABLE SONGS: "Everything's Alright," "I Don't Know How to Love Him," "Superstar."

WHO YOU'LL NEED: *Lead Singing Roles:* Jesus; Peter; Judas; Mary Magdalene (all with legit voices) *Supporting Singing Roles:* Ten other apostles; five high priests; Pontius Pilate; a very flamboyant Herod. *Other Roles:* A chorus to play lepers, merchants, tormentors, and reporters. *Maximum, 45; minimum, 20.*

DESIGNATED DANCES: Any time there's more than one performer on stage, you'll need some musical staging, but the only real "number" is the mock-vaudeville turn done by Herod and his followers.

SUGGESTED SETS: A spot in the Bethany desert; a street in Jerusalem; Pilate's house; the Last Supper table, the Garden of Gethsemane; the top of Calvary.

COSTUMES: You can simply have togas of various designs (one production in Omaha had Jesus and eleven of the apostles in white, while Judas was in *off*-white), though fanciful turbans and grandiose accoutrements for the high priests are a must.

IMPORTANT PROPS: Palms; a bag containing thirty pieces of silver; a cup of wine; swords; a large cross.

SPECIAL EFFECTS: In the rock tradition, hand mikes are often used.

PROVIDED INSTRUMENTATION: Three options: A rock combo (electric/acoustic guitar, electric bass guitar, piano/organ, drums/percussion); for bandstration, add two trumpets, trombone, French horn, flute/piccolo, flute/clarinet, oboe, bassoon; for orchestration, add two violins, viola, cello, piano-conductor.

ADVERTISING AND MARKETING: "Are you ready for the show that put Andrew Lloyd Webber on the map? *Jesus Christ Superstar* will be returning to this area on . . ."

SUGGESTIONS: A 1991 production by the Walnut Street Theater Company in Philadelphia once again proved that this show can be done without elaborate scenery—that just a unit set of "stone" bricks and tablets suffices.

RESOURCES: The original cast album on CD, cassette, and LP; the original two-disc studio recording that led to the stage production; the faithful 1973 movie version on videotape and laserdisc; and, of course, Matthew, Mark, Luke, and John's gospels in the Bible.

RIGHTS: Music Theatre International.

LITTLE SHOP OF HORRORS

CREATORS: Book and lyrics by Howard Ashman, music by Alan Menken (the authors of *The Little Mermaid* movie).

BACKGROUND: The 1982 production opened strong at the off-off Broadway WPA Theater, causing over thirty producers to bid for the rights for an extended commercial off-Broadway run. Record producer David Geffen, producer Cameron Mackintosh (*Cats, Les Miserables, Phantom of the Opera, Miss Saigon*), and the Shuberts were the winners; the show received seven Drama Desk nominations, won three awards, and 2,209 performances resulted.

STORY: 1950s on Skid Row. Seymour, a nerdy clerk in a plant store, loves Audrey, whose taste runs to tougher men (given that she has a bad self-image)—though she is flattered when Seymour names his new plant Audrey II in her honor. But the plant only thrives when it is fed blood, and when Audrey's newest boyfriend abuses her one time too many, Seymour feeds him to Audrey II. The voracious plant wants more and more, and eventually consumes everyone in sight.

ASSETS: A fine score buttressing a very funny book—especially remarkable, considering the original movie may strike you as unwatchable.

LIABILITIES: The ending is a downer. And try telling an auditioning actor that he's landed the part—of manipulating the plant's big mouth. (Actually, you need a puppeteer, not an actor.) And speaking of that plant, you're going to have to create not one, but three—to show Audrey II's various stages of growth. But there is available (at extra charge) a blueprint and pattern sheet from the licensers.

WHO YOU'LL NEED: *Lead Singing Roles:* A good-natured nerd; the masochistic, legit-voiced woman he loves. *Supporting Singing Roles:* Three Motown-style singers; a sadistic dentist; the at-first nasty, then obsequious store owner; the deep, rich voice of Audrey II. *Other Roles*: A derelict; an actor to manipulate the plant's mouth. *Maximum, 14; minimum, 9.*

DESIGNATED DANCES: No choreography as such—just some musical staging in two numbers.

SUGGESTED SETS: Inside and outside a plant store.

COSTUMES: Low-rent mid-1950s fashions; for the dentist, regulation whites, "Supremes"–like costumes, and a leather outfit.

IMPORTANT PROPS: A dentist's chair and tools; a clear-plastic bubble headdress; flowers for the shops—and, of course, those three plants of varying sizes. "You'd be surprised," says Melanie Larch of the Charleston (West Virginia) Light Opera Guild, "how many groups still have the plants from their productions, and would be happy to rent or sell you theirs."

SPECIAL EFFECTS: That plant, of course, and a myriad of vines that fall from the ceiling at play's end.

PROVIDED INSTRUMENTATION: Guitars, bass, drums, three keyboards, piano-conductor.

ADVERTISING AND MARKETING: Make sure that you recruit your local florists to take ads in your program.

SUGGESTIONS: You may think about playing the show without an intermission—the authors did originally—but the actor inside the plant needs to get out for a few minutes—as the authors soon found with the original production.

RESOURCES: The original cast album on cassette and LP; the fairly faithful 1986 movie version on videotape and laserdisc; the original 1960 low-budget movie on which the musical is somewhat faithfully based.

RIGHTS: Samuel French.

PIPPIN

CREATORS: Book by Roger O. (*Walking Happy*) Hirson, music and lyrics by Stephen (*Godspell*) Schwartz.

BACKGROUND: The 1972 Broadway production opened to good reviews, received eleven Tony nominations, won five awards and ran 1,944 performances.

STORY: The Holy Roman Empire, 780 A.D. A Leading Player (read: master of ceremonies) tells us the story of Pippin, who not only finds it difficult being the son of a great man—Charlemagne—but also has a tough time finding his purpose in life. Pippin tries going to war, but doesn't take to it; he tries sleeping around, and while it is pleasurable, he ultimately doesn't feel fulfilled. He tries painting, then religion; he tries protesting, and even has a fantasy in which he kills his father and takes over as emperor—only to find it a difficult job, and one he's not up to. That sends him to the countryside, where he happens upon a widow and her young son, with whom he stays on their farm. And though he gets some satisfaction out of being a father to the boy who needs him, he still isn't fulfilled patching the roof and pitching the hay, so, after six months, he leaves them. That's when the Leading Player confronts him with the prospect of suicide, but Pippin certainly doesn't want that. He realizes that he'll take his happiness where he can find it, and contentedly settles for being "trapped—but happy" with his new wife and stepson.

ASSETS: Yes, the score is terrific, but the book is much underrated: it's a work of startling maturity, and it teaches a good lesson on what's really important in life.

LIABILITIES: "Its logical structure," complains Thomas R. Stretton, who's directed the show at Philadelphia high schools. "The show seems to end in the present, when the Leading Player tells the orchestra to stop playing. But up to now, the show's been set in the Middle Ages." But Stretton has a solution: "We began the show as if it were a rehearsal, and during the big magic effect in 'Magic to Do,' the company changed onstage into medieval costumes. Then the end of the show seemed to make more sense when Pippin, his wife, and stepson are stripped to rehearsal clothes."

RECOGNIZABLE SONGS: "Corner of the Sky."

WHO YOU'LL NEED: *Lead Singing Roles:* An innocent young (baritone) man who grows to become a mensch; an emcee (originally played by a man, but can be played by a woman). *Supporting Singing Roles:* A Holy Roman Emperor who's too preoccupied to be a father; his scheming second wife; a feisty grandmother; an average ordinary kind of woman who loves Pippin. *Other Roles:* A brave but stupid stepbrother; an eight-year-old boy; a chorus of vaudevillians and dancers. *Maximum 24; minimum,* 8.

DESIGNATED DANCES: Heavy for the chorus: Some athletic maneuverings for the opening number; a production number that includes slow-motion fighting; a march. Also a male and female dancer come out together twice to do a dance representing an unsuccessful and then a successful sexual experience.

SUGGESTED SETS: The scenes are demarcated through themes—"War," "The Flesh," "Revolution," etc. suggesting that anything from a black box to scaffolding to a unit set with drapes—anything but realism—will do.

COSTUMES: The musical is purposely structured to take place in a netherworld; the setting is no more medieval than is the score, so it's the type of show, not unlike Schwartz's *Godspell,* where any type of fanciful or ragtag costuming feels at home (though you should have something to suggest armor for the war sequences). Use leotards, stretch pants, halter tops, motorcycle jackets, fishnet stockings, and you'll have yourself a show.

IMPORTANT PROPS: A duck and a pig (stuffed animals will do); a theater worklight; an oversized board done in a Gregorian chant design that has the music staffs, notes, and lyrics to "No Time at All" fancifully printed so that your audience can sing along.

SPECIAL EFFECTS: Stresses Stretton, "The opening song, 'Magic to Do,' *does* demand magic"—so at least spend the money to have the flashpots create flames.

PROVIDED INSTRUMENTATION: Two reeds, French horn, trumpet, trombones, guitar, harp, violin, viola, cello, bass (electric bass), piano/harpsichord, piano/organ, percussion, drums, piano-conductor.

ADVERTISING AND MARKETING: Near the apple bins in grocery stores and supermarkets, place posters that say, "We're offering another kind of *Pippin* that's just as juicy. Come see our *Pippin* at . . ."

SUGGESTIONS: Do borrow director-choreographer Bob Fosse's marvelous device in "With You," where Pippin learns about mindless sex: One chorus member holds his legs, another his arms, and, as girls roll across the stage in assembly line fashion, the two "holders" press him onto the girl then take him off as the next girl rolls on, and press him down again.

RESOURCES: The original cast album on CD, cassette, and LP; the 1977 videotape of a touring production; a "Rehearscore" disc for Macintosh and IBM systems that eliminates the need for a rehearsal pianist.

RIGHTS: Music Theatre International.

TO BE LICENSED AT A FUTURE DATE:

CATS

Andrew *(The Phantom of the Opera)* Lloyd Webber set his music to T. S. Eliot's poems on the lives and times of alley cats; both the 1981 London production and the 1982 Broadway production may make good on their promises to run for "now and forever." The musical does have a terrific score—including the hit "Memory"—and some genuine excitement, but the real appeal of the show may be our love of cats; their actor counterparts are just as much fun to watch.

When you are able to do the musical, you'd best have some limber bodies available—for, as Bonnie Simmons, a member of the original cast who played nearly 4,000 performances, says, "This is a very tough show on the human body, which was not meant to move around like a cat."

LES MISERABLES

The Claude-Michel Schonberg–Alain Boubil adaptation of the Victor Hugo novel opened to not-so-hot reviews in 1985, but you'd never know it from the worldwide sensation it's created. In case you haven't seen it, or have forgotten the novel, it's about Jean Valjean, who was once desperate enough to steal a loaf of bread and was incarcerated for it, but escaped to a new town where he now lives a model life and serves as mayor. Inspector Javert, however, believes the law is the law, and mercilessly pursues him. The mesmerizing score (including "I Dreamed a Dream") will be challenging to most groups, not only because of the intense vocal demands, but also because there are no fewer than thirty-five songs. You'll also have to find early eighteenth-century French costumes and military uniforms, and build something resembling the big second-act barricade. Don't forget that the original production greatly relied on an almost constantly moving turntable.

MISS SAIGON

The Claude-Michel Schonberg—Alain Boubil adaptation of *Madama Butterfly* may be a better show than its reviews have indicated. The story of the young soldier who falls in love with a young Vietnamese girl, but leaves her behind and forever wonders about her, was not written in a linear fashion; halfway through the first act, there seems to be a missing scene—which does come in act two, when the now-famous helicopter arrives during the fall of Saigon to separate the lovers; *then* events become clear. Perhaps the juxtaposition occurred because the authors didn't want to blow their big helicopter effect in the first act—but given that nonprofessional groups probably won't be able to create a helicopter, maybe the writers will rethink the show and put the musical events in a logical order for amateur productions. One further irony: This musical is really a very small show, and will be more engrossing when done in a small space.

THE PHANTOM OF THE OPERA

Andrew (*Cats*) Lloyd Webber and Charles Hart's musical will perhaps represent the biggest challenge your costume and scenic designers ever face; the first scene alone involves a production of *Hannibal* at the Paris Opera House that should be sumptuous. After that, you'll have to replicate the Phantom's candelabra-lit lair—and what will you do for the famous falling chandelier? If your answer is, "Mime it in slow motion," fine—but you will also have to teach your cast a very demanding score.

"I'M THE GREATEST STAR!"

Musicals That Showcase Your Finest Performer

Sometimes an organization finds it can boast one performer who is so good that he or she is worth showcasing in a musical. "They're often the people who are the most serious," says producer Debbi Dustin of the Arlington (Massachusetts) Friends of the Drama, "and they should be the stars if they've got that much dedication and talent."

So if you have a star, here are some musicals with powerhouse parts originated by stars who either won Tonys or just narrowly missed winning them.

APPLAUSE

CREATORS: Book by Betty Comden and Adolph Green (who collaborated on the *Singin' in the Rain* movie), music by Charles Strouse, and lyrics by Lee Adams (who collaborated on *Bye Bye Birdie*).

BACKGROUND: The 1970 production opened in Baltimore in wonderful shape, causing strong word-of-mouth in a season that had been mediocre; it received seven Tony nominations, won four awards—including Best Musical—and ran 896 performances.

STORY: 1970, New York City. Margo Channing is a major Broadway star whose generosity of heart compels her to bring big fan Eve Harrington into her inner circle—only to have Eve try to take her next starring role and Bill, her man. Eve succeeds in acquiring the former, but doesn't get the latter, as Margo and Bill live (presumably) happily ever after.

ASSETS: "A show about show business always seems to turn on a cast more than others," reports St. Louis director Steve Allen, "and this one has a plot with some real bite in it." Indeed, those who don't know the story beforehand might assume during act one that Margo is paranoid and Eve is guiltless.

LIABILITIES: Here's one of those musicals that, though entertaining, suffers in comparison with the original movie. *All About Eve* is a classic, and while *Applause* is fun, it isn't as good as that—especially considering that poisonous critic Addison De Witt from the movie is not a character in the musical. The music is also considered difficult for nonprofessionals.

WHO YOU'LL NEED: *Lead Singing Role:* A legendary star (a Lauren Bacall or Kathleen Turner type). *Supporting Singing Roles:* Her confident (tenor) director-lover; an ambitious woman who wants to be a star but can convincingly hide it; a male hairdresser; a worrisome playwright (who plays or fakes banjo); his well-bred wife; a charming out-of-work actress with aspirations (Bonnie Franklin)—though you could use a man here—especially considering that the lyric refers to "You're losing your hair" and "You're the king of it all." *Other Roles:* A forceful producer; a stage manager; an agent; a pianist; a columnist; waiters; first nighters; gay bar patrons; coffee-commercial staff; male and female chorus dancers; three onstage musicians (one should play the bass fiddle). *Maximum, 41; minimum, 20.*

DESIGNATED DANCES: Margo is involved in the production number in the gay bar; a jitterbug; a short tarantella; a waltz; some small impromptu steps. The chorus has two production numbers, including the title song that includes a *homage* to other hit musicals, but you needn't keep it—or even the montage of tap-dancing, ballet steps, baton-twirling, juggling, and roller-skating that ends it.

SUGGESTED SETS: Margo's dressing room, split-level living room, and bedroom; two night spots: one in Greenwich Village with walls of photographs, one representing midtown's Joe Allen's (or any theater restaurant); a Connecticut home; backstage; a podium and oversized medallion to represent the Tony Awards ceremony.

COSTUMES: Opening night duds; wigs; formal party wear; a pailetted evening gown that can fit both Margo and Eve; smart and sexy dresses; upscale winter coats; feather boa; fur stole; more casual street clothes; "Village boys" flashy clothes; rehearsal togs; waiter uniforms; dressing gown, pajamas, robes, and slippers; costume party wear (including an East Indian outfit and Babylonian female slave outfit).

IMPORTANT PROPS: Dressing table; mirror; screen; floral bouquets; a brass bed and furniture befitting a star's bedroom; jukebox; "Welcome Home" banner; small signs on strings for a party game; swivel chair; coffee tables; jars and tins of instant coffee, enough cups to break one each performance; a TV; saxophone; banjo; couches with pillows; armchairs; bar units; party carts; restaurant tables; chairs; red-checkered tablecloths; a high-domed serving dish; a Tony Award.

SPECIAL EFFECTS: Snow; tape-recorded voice-overs for Margo, the playwright, and a telephone operator. If you have camcorder and monitor capabilities, use them for the Tony ceremonies. The "gypsy" who sings the title song should be able to do that famous trick of pulling a tablecloth from a table without disturbing what's on top. ·

PROVIDED INSTRUMENTATION: Five reeds, three trumpets, three trombones, two violins, viola, cello, bass and electric bass, two percussion, harp, electric organ, guitar, banjo, mandolin, piano-celeste, piano-conductor.

ADVERTISING AND MARKETING: "We present *Applause* to you, in hopes that you'll present us with applause."

SUGGESTIONS: During your curtain call, when your Margo Channing is centerstage, singing the reprise of "Applause" with her cast surrounding her, at the last possible moment, have your Eve Harrington (who'll be next to her, of course) suddenly step in front of the star and take a deep bow.

RESOURCES: The original cast album on cassette and LP. Keep an eye out for a rebroadcast of the faithful 1973 TV production.

RIGHTS: Tams-Witmark.

BELLS ARE RINGING

CREATORS: Book and lyrics by Betty Comden and Adolph Green (who later collaborated on *Applause*); music by Jule (*Gentlemen Prefer Blondes*) Styne.

BACKGROUND: Though Comden, Green, and star Judy Holliday had worked together and had been friends for a long time, the struggles in writing this original musical caused them strain out of town; Holliday was especially peeved that even by then they hadn't yet written a closing number for her. "Jule Styne," said original conductor Milton Rosenstock, "always says, 'Look to your book for good song ideas'—and when he noticed that Judy's line of dialogue about 'The Bonjour Tristesse Brassiere Company' got a laugh each night, he decided that that should be the subject of the song." Holliday was certainly pleased by "I'm Goin' Back," arguably the Broadway musical's best eleven o'clock number, and the result helped to garner four Tony nominations, two awards, and a 924-performance run.

STORY: 1950's, New York City. Ella Peterson is a switchboard operator for Susanswerphone, an answering service. Her boss (and cousin) Sue always chides her for becoming too involved in the lives of her clients—a dentist and an actor, but most especially playwright Jeff Moss, who's suffering from writer's block. Ella even shows up at his apartment in hopes of motivating him to work, but pretends to be "Melisande Scott," assuming he'd have no interest in the real her. Moss does fall in love with Melisande, and that bothers Ella even more. She suddenly disappears, sending Jeff on a hunt all over town. Eventually, Moss meets the dentist and actor, the truth is unraveled, and Jeff is happy to love Ella instead of Melisande.

ASSETS: In addition to a fine score and a most lovable heroine, its charming book represents one of the most clever original musicals ever written. The subplot is especially strong: Ella's boss falls in love with a "record executive" who's really using her office as a bookie joint. His clients call up and code-order Beethoven's (meaning Belmont Park) Tenth Symphony (horse number ten), Opus 3 (third race), on LP (to win)—but when a delivery boy points out that Beethoven only wrote *nine* symphonies, Ella changes the order to the Ninth Symphony—which is horse number nine . . .

LIABILITIES: The show has dated, not only because we're in an age of answering machines that virtually eliminate the need for a telephone answering service, but also because the lyrics in the "Drop That Name" song all refer to then-famous people, most of whom are now dead or forgotten. And when has an apartment front door ever been left unlocked in New York? Jeff's is—because the plot needs it.

RECOGNIZABLE SONGS: "Just in Time," "The Party's Over."

WHO YOU'LL NEED: *Lead Singing Roles:* A lovable telephone switchboard operator (Judy Holliday); the once-successful (baritone) playwright she loves. *Supporting Singing Roles:* Her no-nonsense cousin and boss (Jean Stapleton); the pseudo-elegant con man she loves. *Other Roles:* A plump co-worker; a harried producer; a frustrated dentist who yearns to be a songwriter; a friendly delivery boy; two dim-witted detectives; two henchmen; a flashy brunette; a calculating actress; an emcee; four dancing boys and girls; Marlon Brando and Elvis Presley impersonators; a telephone installer; neighborhood friends; party guests; bookies; subway commuters. *Maximum, 42; minimum, 13.*

DESIGNATED DANCES: Three big production numbers, a cha-cha, some soft-shoe.

SUGGESTED SETS: A basement apartment dominated by a telephone switch-board; a bachelor-apartment living room; a penthouse living room; a gypsy cafe; a nightclub in Egyptian decor; a dentist's office; a drugstore; various New York streets; a park; a subway car.

COSTUMES: 1950s everyday wear; pajamas and robe; leather motorcycle jackets; jeans; white mittens; Hawaiian shirt and straw hat; men's and women's formal wear; a Brooks Brothers suit; nightclub girls' costumes; gold jackets; a mop-head "wig"; a red dress worthy of *La Traviata*.

IMPORTANT PROPS: *Many* dial telephones; a bird cage; a typewriter; small floral bouquets; coffee and Danish; a phone booth; a dentist's chair and air hose; copies of *Variety*; a bevy of identical musical score books.

SPECIAL EFFECTS: Voice-overs for men, women, and children.

PROVIDED INSTRUMENTATION: Five reeds, two horns, three trumpets, two trombones, four violins, viola, cello, bass, percussion, harp, piano-celeste, piano-conductor.

ADVERTISING AND MARKETING: "Come with bells on to see *Bells Are Ringing*, and we'll let you in for half-price."

SUGGESTIONS: Do the show as a period piece, a loving valentine to a simpler era. As the audience enters before the show, prepare them for the era by playing pre-Elvis 1950s hits ("Love Is a Many Splendored Thing," "Three Coins in the Fountain" etc.).

RESOURCES: The original cast album on CD, cassette, and LP; the somewhat faithful 1960 movie version on videotape and laserdisc.

RIGHTS: Tams-Witmark.

FIORELLO!

CREATORS: Book by Jerome (*I Can Get It for You Wholesale*) Weidman and George (*Where's Charley?*) Abbott, music by Jerry Bock and lyrics by Sheldon Harnick (who later collaborated on *Fiddler on the Roof*).

BACKGROUND: The 1959 production wanted Mickey Rooney to star as the "Little Flower," but he didn't—leaving the part to then-unknown Tom Bosley, who excelled—as did the script, which became the third musical to win the Pulitzer Prize. Add to that seven Tony nominations, four awards—including Best Musical—and a 796-performance run.

STORY: It's before World War I in New York City, and Fiorello H. LaGuardia, a lawyer who helps the oppressed, defends women who are on strike against an oppressive shirtwaist factory, and meets Thea, with whom he falls in love—to the dismay of his longtime and very loyal secretary, Marie. Fiorello fully admits part of the reason he's helping Thea is to have an issue that will gain him attention and votes to win an election as a Republican Congressman in a heavily Democratic district, which ward boss Ben thinks is impossible. But he wins one election, then goes to Washington, where he supports the draft—

and enlists himself. He doesn't tell Marie he plans to marry Thea once he comes home; Marie is disappointed when he steps off the returning boat and proposes to Thea.

Ten years later, a happily married Fiorello (though his wife is ill) is battling to become mayor of New York City, pitted against James J. Walker. Ben suggests that Fiorello may have lost some of his humanity by always being right and incorruptible, and he bristles and fires Ben from the campaign. Marie tells Fiorello that she's heard from a friend that a threat may be made on his life, so he dispatches his two office assistants to thwart the plan. When at the site they hear that Thea has died, they leave, and Fiorello is almost killed in the process. He's furious with them until he learns why they left. He loses the election to Walker, and goes into a three-year funk. Marie, aware of the corruption of the Walker administration, at first tries to reconcile Fiorello with Ben, but realizes she must forget him and "marry the very next man" who asks her. As it turns out, it's a grateful LaGuardia who is ready to battle Walker as the show ends.

ASSETS: A strong book, a good character, a fine score. And the authors were very smart to start the show with the one incident for which people most remember Fiorello: his reading the comics to the kids on the news when the newspapers were on strike.

LIABILITIES: A pejorative term for Italian will offend some, but the bigger problem is the nonjudgmental attitude expressed toward the three references to men beating women. It may have been common then, but we needn't be reminded of it. Dropping two of the incidents won't be so difficult, but the third will be a problem, because it's a lyric in the last song.

WHO YOU'LL NEED: *Lead Singing Role:* A charismatic and decent politician. *Supporting Singing Roles:* A charming wife; a devoted secretary (each is a soprano); two loyal assistants; a ward boss and his seven hacks; a militant female striker. *Other Roles:* A cop who advances through the ranks; a conservative senator; a judge; a commissioner; a mobster and his bodyguards; a butler; a switchboard operator; a chorus of women strikers, minority clients, and chorines. *Maximum, 52; minimum, 30.*

DESIGNATED DANCES: A tarantella, a hora, and a waltz for the cast; a Charleston production number for the chorines.

SUGGESTED SETS: Fiorello's New York law office and reception room; his Washington office; his Manhattan residence; a political meeting house with a prominent card table; a drab tenement roof; an Art Deco penthouse; a radio station; outside a factory. When Fiorello gave speeches on the streets of Little Italy and the Lower East Side in the original production, the same set was used, but rotating street signs in Italian and Hebrew suggested that they were different neighborhoods.

COSTUMES: Pre–World War I fashions and Roaring Twenties garb; party frocks; doughboy uniforms; a flier's uniform; kimonos and mules; Fiorello's famous large black hat.

IMPORTANT PROPS: A fire alarm box; an "On the Air" sign and radio mike; a Sunday newspaper comic section; tea set and cups; hatboxes; picket signs; a stepladder; telephones; decks of cards; a crumpled black suit; a set of false teeth; a raw pork chop; a tearable shirt for each performance.

SPECIAL EFFECTS: Sound effects of fire sirens; a Pathé newsreel to show the World War I efforts.

PROVIDED INSTRUMENTATION: Five reeds, three trumpets, three trombones, horn, two violins, cello, bass, two percussion, guitar-banjo, piano-celeste, piano-conductor.

ADVERTISING AND MARKETING: "Statistics show that LaGuardia is the fourth most difficult airport in the country. You'll be much more pleased when coming to *our* LaGuardia. We're doing *Fiorello!* at . . ."

SUGGESTIONS: If the Pathé newsreel is a problem, you can drop the sequence or use a radio reporter to convey the information.

RESOURCES: The original cast album on CD, cassette, and LP.

RIGHTS: Tams-Witmark.

FUNNY GIRL

CREATORS: Book by Isobel (*Love Me or Leave Me*) Lennart, music by Jule Styne, lyrics by Bob Merrill (who collaborated on *Sugar*).

BACKGROUND: The 1964 production went through more rewriting and adding of new songs than most musicals, and even called on Jerome Robbins to help. With a lesser star, it might not have gotten by, but as Walter Kerr began his review, "Everyone knew that Barbra Streisand would be a star and now she is." The show itself had become a household name by the time Streisand left in late 1965, and remained on Broadway for 1,348 performances.

STORY: Before and after World War I in New York City. Ugly duckling Fanny Brice's rise from a vaudeville comedienne to genuine Ziegfeld star is fast, but her romance with a "gorgeous" gambler Nick Arnstein happens faster. When his luck runs out, Fanny sees no problem in her supporting them, but he won't have it, becoming so desperate that he becomes involved in embezzlement and goes to jail. Once he's paroled, Fanny wants a reconciliation, but when she sees Nick doesn't, she pretends she doesn't, either, for his sake, and they part amicably.

ASSETS: A chance for the funny and not too attractive woman in your company to clown, play serious scenes, and sing some of the most dynamic solos in Broadway history. Nice, too, that the book doesn't try for a happy ending.

LIABILITIES: Nick Arnstein's resenting being "Mr. Brice" is a pretty predictable story. Today a musical biography wouldn't dare just tell the tale of a famed performer's life, and not only because it would run out of gas and "stop the show" in the worst sense, but because it would have to have a point of view; *Funny Girl* has none. Add to this that it is a very expensive show to mount, thanks to period costumes and a multitude of sets.

RECOGNIZABLE SONGS: "People;" "Don't Rain on My Parade."

WHO YOU'LL NEED: *Lead Singing Role:* An ugly duckling with great singing and comedic talent who loves not wisely but too well (a Barbra Streisand or Patti LuPone type). *Supporting Singing Roles:* A sharp-looking but ultimately unsuccessful gambler; the quintessential Jewish mother and her three card-playing friends; a song-and-dance man who's Fanny's best friend; a Ziegfeld Follies tenor. *Other Roles:* Florenz Ziegfeld Jr.; a stage manager; a director; an agent; a music hall owner; a maid; a five-piece back-up band; a chorus to play showgirls, waiters, and a household staff of servants. *Maximum 55; minimum, 30.*

DESIGNATED DANCES: Stylized walking down the stairs in the Ziegfeld tradition; a tap-dance production number; a waltz for most of the company; some uncomplicated musical staging.

SUGGESTED SETS: A theater dressing room with table and fourth-wall "mirror"; inside, outside, and backstage at a music hall and later at a Broadway theater (in which you have two onstage Ziegfeld Follies numbers on staircases); in and around a saloon; a kitchen; a Lower East Side block party; a private dining room; a railroad station; a Long Island mansion and its study.

COSTUMES: Street clothes of the late teens and early 1920s; showgirl outfits with headdresses; a bridal gown; military uniforms; a formal tux (with cape) and ruffled shirt; a fancy blue dress.

IMPORTANT PROPS: A piano; a lunch box; a sewing machine, ashcans; "Congratulations!" banner; candalabra; chaise longue; champagne magnums; roses; a blue marble egg; fancy luggage; stuffed animals; balloons; a card table.

PROVIDED INSTRUMENTATION: Five reeds, three trumpets, three trombones, horn, two violins, cello, bass, two percussion, guitar-banjo, piano-celeste, piano-conductor.

ADVERTISING AND MARKETING: "Mirror, mirror, on the wall; who's the funniest girl in town? We have a very *Funny Girl* at the . . ."

SUGGESTIONS: If you prefer "My Man" to "The Music That Makes Me Dance," see if the licensers will let you use it.

RESOURCES: The original cast album on CD, cassette, and LP; the 1968 (reasonably faithful) movie on videotape and laserdisc.

RIGHTS: Tams-Witmark.

GYPSY

CREATORS: Book by Arthur (*West Side Story*) Laurents, music by Jule (*Funny Girl*) Styne, lyrics by Stephen (*Follies*) Sondheim.

BACKGROUND: Sondheim had hoped to write the music for this 1959 musical, but star Ethel Merman had just had a disappointment with *Happy Hunting* by a new composer and decided that Sondheim, who had not yet been represented on Broadway as a composer, would only write the lyrics. As great a composer as Sondheim is, would he have written a better score than Jule Styne's? The show received seven Tony nominations, won (believe it or not) *none*, but racked up 702 performances in that run, 120 in a limited-run 1974 revival with Angela Lansbury (who won a Tony), and 502 in the 1989 Tony-winning revival with Tyne Daly, (who won a Tony).

STORY: 1920, Seattle. Rose is determined that her daughters June and Louise will have the vaudeville career denied her. While June is talented, Louise is not, but Rose won't say die, even after June runs away, and Rose's agent-suitor Herbie begs her to give up. Without June, the act must play burlesque, which disgusts Herbie and causes him to leave, but turns out to be a blessing in disguise for Louise, who becomes famous stripper Gypsy Rose Lee—to first the contempt and then the admiration of her mother.

ASSETS: A great score and one of the most compelling books in musical theater history, replete with fascinating characters. (Many feel that the show should have been called *Rose*, because it's really more about her than about Gypsy Rose Lee.)

LIABILITIES: Rose is a tough lady with whom to spend an evening, and this has always turned off some audiences; indeed, for a show of this quality, it has never run as long as its reviews and achievement merits. "Audiences," laments original producer David Merrick, "just aren't interested in the problems of show people."

RECOGNIZABLE SONGS: "Small World," "Everything's Coming Up Roses," "Together Wherever We Go," "Let Me Entertain You."

WHO YOU'LL NEED: *Lead Singing Role*: A don't-try-to-stop-me legit-voiced stage mother. (Although such veteran performers as Ethel Merman and Angela Lansbury have played the part of Rose, there is no need to cast the character as an older woman; after all, when the show begins, June and Louise are very little girls, so their mother could conceivably be younger than thirty.) *Supporting Singing Roles*: A very, *very* talented girl and her slightly older counterpart; a less talented girl and her teenage counterpart who can later portray a dynamic and successful stripper; a candy salesman turned agent who can be pushed around for only so long; a young male dancer with big plans; three broken-down strippers. *Other Roles*: A kiddie show host and kiddie show performers; a landlord; backstage workers; Rose's irascible father; a bunch of young boys and their teenage counterparts; a not-so-attractive group of young adult women; two kids to play a cow; a snippy theatrical secretary; a waitress, a live small dog and little lamb. *Maximum, 55; minimum, 35.*

DESIGNATED DANCES: Heavy: An audition piece that involves a few steps for the young girls; two complete vaudeville numbers and one in rehearsal; a march; a tiny fox-trot for Rose and Herbie; a stunning tap dance by one boy in which Louise joins; an arm-in-arm dance for Rose, Louise, and Herbie; a romp for three strippers; some stylized stripteases for the older Louise.

SUGGESTED SETS: A Seattle theater stage; a kitchen; on the road; on stage and backstage of vaudeville houses; two adjoining hotel rooms; a Chinese restaurant; a theatrical office; a theater alley; a railroad terminal; the Texas desert; onstage, backstage, and the dressing rooms of a burlesque house; the Garden of Eden; a posh dressing room.

COSTUMES: Street clothes of the 1920s and 1930s; vaudeville costumes for three different acts (hats and canes); children's wear (knickers, a muff); pajamas for Rose, Louise, June, and the boys; an Uncle Sam outfit; a Boy Scout uniform; a young girl's dress embellished with balloons; a cow costume; many blond wigs; G-strings and other stripper wear; Louise's breakaway dress, gloves, and effluvia for her strip.

In one scene, Rose mentions that some drapes would make nice coats; in a subsequent scene, we see from the coats they're wearing that she's made good on her suggestion—so you'll need matching, eye-catching material for those drapes and coats to get that laugh.

IMPORTANT PROPS: A car; a caboose; a gold plaque; a cow head; a trumpet; an American eagle with flags surrounding it; a bathtub; Chinese food; a birthday cake; tables and chairs, a trumpet; cutlery at home and in restaurants; electric lights that spell out "ROSE."

SPECIAL EFFECTS: Voice-overs; black light that allows a scene in which the young kids can go offstage while their older replacements come on, making the effect look effortless. One of your stripper outfits must be wired for lights with a switch that your actress can control.

PROVIDED INSTRUMENTATION: Five reeds, three trumpets, three trombones, horn, two violins, cello, bass, two percussion, guitar-banjo, piano-celeste, piano-conductor.

ADVERTISING AND MARKETING: Have a promotion with a local florist, offering a free ad in your program in exchange for a bunch of roses to be given at the end of the show to one lucky ticketholder.

SUGGESTIONS: Scene one takes place in a Seattle vaudeville theater where Rose is successful in getting her kids into a local kiddie show. But in scene two, which takes place in Rose's father's home, she is upset that they'll only be getting ten dollars, so she asks her father for eighty-eight dollars to spruce up the act and get them to Los Angeles—so they won't wind up working their whole lives (as he did) with nothing but a gold plaque as recognition. When he turns her down, Rose exits with the plaque, which she'll pawn. It's a wonderful scene, but it does involve building a separate interior set that is never again used. So you might consider having Rose's father show up at the theater (he had a hunch she'd be here, auditioning the kids, and followed her), play their confrontation there, have her talk about the plaque, and, after he walks out in disgust, have her open her purse and show us that she's already taken it.

RESOURCES: The original and 1974 and 1989 revival cast albums on CD, cassette, and LP; the 1962 very faithful movie on videotape and laserdisc; Gypsy Rose Lee's memoir *Gypsy*, on which the musical is very faithfully based.

RIGHTS: Tams-Witmark.

HOW TO SUCCEED IN BUSINESS WITHOUT REALLY TRYING

CREATORS: Book by Jack Weinstock and Willie Gilbert (though Abe [*Guys and Dolls*] Burrows is reputed to have done much of the work), music and lyrics by Frank (*The Most Happy Fella*) Loesser.

BACKGROUND: The 1961 production received unanimous raves, eight Tony nominations, seven Tonys—including Best Musical—and then went on to win the Pulitzer Prize (amazing, given that this was in an era when Pulitzers went to more serious fare). The result was a 1,417-performance run.

STORY: 1960s, New York City. J. Pierpont Finch will do anything to rise to the top of World Wide Wickets, and, thanks to a trusty manual, he goes from the mail room to vice president of advertising in no time at all. His jealous rival, Bud Frump—nephew of J. B. Biggley, president of the company—works hard to see that he fails, but Finch always winds up smelling like a rose, and along the way finds an understanding woman in secretary Rosemary.

ASSETS: A good score supports a very funny book replete with memorable characters—especially Finch, who can be played by the young man in your company who hitherto has played supporting juvenile roles and deserves more of a chance.

LIABILITIES: This show has an antiquated and benign take on what we'd now consider sexual harassment.

RECOGNIZABLE SONGS: "I Believe in You."

WHO YOU'LL NEED: *Lead Singing Role:* An aggressive but likable young man. *Supporting Singing Roles:* His charming female admirer; the blustery company president; the president's foppish nephew; a sexy, incompetent female secretary; a young unglamorous female secretary; an older more unglamorous female secretary; a middle-management boss; a mailroom clerk. *Other roles:* Business executives; their secretaries; an unctuous voice-over. (But men *could* play secretaries, and women bosses, of course.) *Maximum,* 40; *minimum* 16.

DESIGNATED DANCES: A big eleven o'clock number for all the men and the older unglamorous secretary; a production number featuring mock-pirate girls; one frenetic number and one involving some musical staging for all the minor office workers.

SUGGESTED SETS: Outside and inside the World Wide Wicket Company (its corridors, in the mailroom, at the elevator, in the men's executive wash-room, and the outer and inner offices of Finch and Biggley); a television studio.

COSTUMES: 1960s office wear; gray flannel three-button suits; trenchcoats; "nice" dresses; World Wide Wicket blazers; window-washer outfit; golfing outfit with tam o'shanter; policeman's suit. The joke behind one number ("Paris Original") is that every woman shows up at a party in the same dress—so you'll have to have that dress exactly replicated for a minimum of five women.

IMPORTANT PROPS: Big overstuffed CEO's chair; office desks and chairs on rollers; in-out bins; steno pads; umbrellas; attache cases; scrub mops and pails; golf clubs in a bag; two sets of knitting and needles; big coffee urn; small coffeepot; Styrofoam cups; an easel; mock-ups of *Time, Newsweek,* and *Sports Illustrated* with your CEO's picture on each; electric shavers; an enormous Bible; a book with a "How to Succeed" logo on its cover. Typewriters can be mimed fourth-wall.

PROVIDED INSTRUMENTATION: Five reeds, three trumpets, horn, three trombones, four violins, cello, bass, harp, guitar, two drums.

ADVERTISING AND MARKETING: "Now who wouldn't want to know *How to Succeed in Business Without Really Trying?* We'll tell you, beginning on . . ."

SUGGESTIONS: Keep the show in its time period, so that the audiences will excuse the "unraised consciousness" of the piece.

RESOURCES: The original cast album on CD, cassette, and LP; the faithful 1967 movie on videotape and laserdisc, the Shepherd Mead mock-manual on which the musical was very loosely based.

RIGHTS: Music Theatre International.

ME AND MY GIRL

CREATORS: Book by L. Arthur Rose, Douglas Furber, Stephen Fry, and Mike Ockrent, music by Noel Gay, lyrics by Rose and Furber.

BACKGROUND: The 1986 production opened to raves for its leading man, Robert Lindsay, but the show itself was so good—twelve Tony nominations and three awards—that it kept running through Lindsay's two replacements, totaling 1,420 performances.

STORY: 1930s, London. Bill Snibson may be the newly found heir to a great nobleman's fortune, but he's been raised in lowlife Lambeth, where he fell in love with Sally Smith. While not terribly resistant to gentrification, Bill does draw the line at abandoning his girl, despite protests from his well-bred relatives, the duchess and Sir John. But the latter on the sly comes up with a solution that neatly solves the problem: He sends Sally to Henry Higgins, who teaches her to become a lady, thus making her "worthy" of the new Bill.

ASSETS: As good as the score is—and it is—it's the book that really shines here. In too many musicals, a man and woman fall in love at first sight, and we're expected to root for this couple who don't really know each other. But Bill and Sally have been in love for some time, so when he comes into a fortune and refuses to abandon her for someone else, he's a true hero for whom we can cheer. And when she's willing to give him up so that he can live his new posh life, we see that she loves him, too—and we love her for it.

LIABILITIES: The songs and book have a distinctly British feel (and we don't mean Andrew Lloyd Webber) that may be off-putting to some of your audience. More than that, though, you must have a singer-actor-dancer-comedian-charmer (have we made our point?) of extraordinary proportions, for this is one of the most demanding roles in musical theater.

WHO YOU'LL NEED: *Lead Singing Roles:* An uneducated Cockney with a heart as big as all outdoors—and a talent to match as a song-and-dance man; his sunny but realistic girlfriend. *Supporting Singing Roles:* A fortune-hunting beauty; her idiotic but harmless swain; a duchess and her distinguished long-ago suitor; the foppish family solicitor; the head manservant. *Other Roles:* A lord and a lady; a stockbroker; a cook; a landlady; a chorus of highbrow guests, servants, footmen, and Lambeth locals. *Maximum, 55; minimum, 25.*

DESIGNATED DANCES: Two dances for Bill and Sally; one for Bill and Sir John; a solo dance for the family solicitor; a big production number with some tap dancing; a second-act ballet for Bill, Sally, and the Lambeth locals, a most vigorous "Lambeth Walk" for the entire company.

SUGGESTED SETS: A Mayfair road; a mansion's exterior, main hall with fireplace, drawing room, terrace, garden, and library; a Lambeth street and pub.

COSTUMES: 1930s finery (formal dresses, riding clothes, cricket and tennis clothes, hunting hats and coats, three wedding tuxedos and gowns, and suspenders); staff uniforms for male and female servants; working-class clothes (some of it especially garish when the Cockneys attend a party at the mansion). In addition, British judicial wigs; a Richard III outfit (complete with hump); an oversized flowing ermine-trimmed red cape and gold coronet, a set of knight's armor which is immobile during the first scene—and then walks off when scene two merges into scene three.

IMPORTANT PROPS: A touring car; an onstage piano; classical busts; a tiger-skin rug; ancestral portraits (which come to life via cast members); a huge ancient volume; croquet mallets and balls; a bicycle; a very large feathered fan; an ear trumpet; suitcases both pristine and tattered; *many* identical gold watches on chains to perform many tricks.

PROVIDED INSTRUMENTATION: Five reeds, three trumpets, horn, three trombones, four violins, cello, bass, harp, guitar, two drums.

ADVERTISING AND MARKETING: "Take you and your girl to *Me and My Girl*."

SUGGESTIONS: Don't overdo Bill's first entrance. There is the temptation to have him come in and whoop it up the way a true low-class lout would; that, however, only makes us want to see him taken down a peg. The brilliant Robert Lindsay immediately got us on Bill's side by entering and looking shy, overwhelmed, and intimidated by the assembled nobles. Every one of us can empathize with the feeling.

RESOURCES: The original cast album on CD, cassette, and LP.

RIGHTS: Samuel French.

THE MUSIC MAN

CREATORS: Book, music, and lyrics by Meredith Willson (who later wrote *The Unsinkable Molly Brown*).

BACKGROUND: The 1957 production wasn't given much of a chance when it started rehearsals; leading man Robert Preston was a Hollywood has-been, and the author was a fifty-five-year-old Broadway rookie. But the show received unanimous raves, eight Tony nominations, and five awards—including Best Musical (even beating out *West Side Story*)—and ran 1,375 performances.

STORY: Early 1900s in Iowa. Harold Hill, a traveling con man, comes to River City, allegedly to start a children's band, even though we soon learn he can't read a lick of music. Almost everyone in town is fooled by him, except Marian, the local librarian, who's incensed that he's taking over the town. But when she sees her chronically shy young brother Winthrop (he stutters) come alive when handed his cornet, she immediately falls in love with Hill, and conspires to keep the truth from the town. Eventually the day of reckoning comes, and the kids must perform for their elders; they're terrible, but the parents don't care, because they are so proud to see their sons and daughters in a band. Looks like Harold is going to stay in River City for a while—with Marian.

ASSETS: A terrific score and a very moving book. That first-act curtain where Marian finally sees Winthrop enthusiastic about something is one of the most moving in the history of musical theater. The show's also a nice valentine to a simpler and gentler America that's long gone, but is worth remembering.

LIABILITIES: Oh, there are a great many words set to music in this show. Not only must Harold Hill be nimble with words—remember "Trouble" and the verse to "Seventy-six Trombones"?—but the opening number has *nine* men speaking and pulsating in rhythm to a highly percussive number; if they don't do it well, it gets your show off to a very nervous start.

RECOGNIZABLE SONGS: "Seventy-six Trombones," "Till There Was You."

WHO YOU'LL NEED: *Lead Singing Roles:* A dazzling and charming con man; the aloof (soprano) librarian who comes to love him. *Supporting Singing Roles:* A mature mother with a thick Irish brogue; her stuttering young son; an endearing second-rate con man; a haughty mayor's wife and her four equally judgmental best friends; her teenage daughter and the misunderstood young man she loves and who loves her; four men who can become a convincing barbershop quartet. *Other Roles:* Eight traveling salemen and a train conductor who *speak* the opening number; an irate mayor; a constable; a young girl taking piano lessons; a chorus of townspeople, boys, and girls. *Maximum, 55; minimum, 39.*

DESIGNATED DANCES: The big "Seventy-six Trombones" march; a production number with Harold, Marian, and library patrons; a rousing act one closer for the entire company; a cakewalk for the secondary con man and the company.

SUGGESTED SETS: A railway coach; River City's town square, town park, school gymnasium, and assembly hall; outside and inside the town's library; outside and inside a modest Iowa house; outside a hotel.

COSTUMES: Turn-of-the-century wear; unsuitably loud suits for the traveling salesmen and more sedate ones for the Iowa men; everyday housedresses and special-occasion tiered dresses for the local women; knickers for the boys; bloomers for the girls; Greco-Roman togas for the townswomen's pageant; a constable outfit. But the biggest order to fill will be the uniforms for your marching band, not to mention a jacket for Hill that, when turned inside out, immediately becomes a band uniform coat, and an "ordinary" hat that converts to his bandleader's hat.

IMPORTANT PROPS: Suitcases; many books to be carried in the library scene; a bandleader's baton; a band instrument for every boy and girl.

PROVIDED INSTRUMENTATION: Three violins, cello, bass, flute, five reeds, three trumpets, three trombones, percussion, and piano-conductor.

ADVERTISING AND MARKETING: Here's a chance to give an award to your town's premier "music man." Be he a conductor or a very good musician, make him the honorary chairperson of opening night, or even have him conduct the overture.

SUGGESTIONS: A good show to do in cooperation with your school or local band; after all, they already have the uniforms for the finale.

RESOURCES: The original cast album on CD, cassette, and LP; the very faithful 1962 movie on videotape and laserdisc; a "Rehearscore" disc for Macintosh and IBM systems that eliminates the need for a rehearsal pianist.

RIGHTS: Music Theatre International.

THE UNSINKABLE MOLLY BROWN

CREATORS: Book by Richard Morris, music and lyrics by Meredith (*The Music Man*) Willson.

BACKGROUND: The 1960 production didn't quite live up to *The Music Man*, but its bringing a new star to Broadway—Tammy Grimes, who won the show's only Tony—kept the show alive for 532 performances.

STORY: Early 1900s in rural Colorado. Molly Brown may only be a girl from a rural Colorado town, but she wants to be famous and marry a millionaire, and sets out to do just that. She starts out by playing piano in a Leadville saloon, where she meets Johnny Brown, a miner who soon proposes. She likes him but feels she'd better resist. However, when he builds her a house and furnishes it with a brass bed, she succumbs. Afterward, he goes off to mine—and returns with three hundred thousand dollars he got from striking silver. Molly hides it in the stove for safekeeping, and when Johnny starts cooking, it burns, so he sets out to make more money, which he promptly does. They move to Denver and build a big house, but find that the "beautiful people of Denver" don't like the house, their taste, or them. A monsignor gently suggests that they become "more polished," and though Johnny is reluctant, Molly convinces him to head to Europe. There Molly is considered the darling of the international set simply because of her American rough-and-tumble nature. She brings many of her European friends back to Denver with her, so she can show them off to the Denver society at a party. But Johnny's friends from Leadville come, too, and a brawl erupts. Molly decides to return to Europe, but Johnny flatly refuses to go. They separate, and a Prince soon asks Molly to marry him. She almost does but decides she must rejoin Johnny, and takes the next boat home—the *Titanic*. When it sinks, she is the heroine who keeps everyone's body and spirit buoyed, and returns to Denver acclaimed by one and all—including Johnny.

ASSETS: The song that opens the show—"I Ain't Down Yet"—and the one that follows—"Belly Up to the Bar, Boys"—are as good as anyone could hope. The book is stronger than often alleged. And the title role provides a character with a large range—from illiterate to nouveau riche to genuine heroine.

LIABILITIES: Johnny Brown's songs are a bit maudlin; the scene involving the *Titanic* is a letdown because it is not at all spectacular and is rather perfunctory. And would anyone really put money in a stove for safekeeping?

WHO YOU'LL NEED: *Lead Singing Roles:* A rags-to-riches heroine who tries to be high-class but better enjoys being herself; the suddenly wealthy (baritone) prospector who's content to live simply. *Supporting Singing Roles:* Molly's three rough-and-tumble brothers; a prince and princess; three (optional) policemen. *Other Roles:* Molly's raucous father; a saloon owner; a parish priest; a monsignor; a sheriff; a butler; a professor; a baron; a count and countess; a duke and duchess; a grand duchess; a chorus to play miners, prostitutes, and the beautiful people of Denver. *Maximum, 57; minimum, 26.*

DESIGNATED DANCES: Three large production numbers for the entire company, a cakewalk for Molly and her brothers; some soft-shoe for the policemen; a tango for the Europeans.

SUGGESTED SETS: Outside a Colorado shack; inside and outside a garish saloon; inside and outside a log cabin; a tasteful Denver mansion; a far-less-tasteful decorated-in-red mansion; a Paris salon; a Monte Carlo club; on a lifeboat in the middle of the Atlantic; at the base of the Rocky Mountains.

COSTUMES: Early twentieth-century wear; glorified rags for the rustic Coloradoans (including jeans, patched overalls, and cowboy hats and boots; garish prostitute clothes); finery for the beautiful people of Denver (formal clothes and long dresses); elegant clothes for the Europeans (handsome suits, long dresses, and large hats); policemen, butler, and priest outfits; tuxedos and ruffled vests.

IMPORTANT PROPS: Pot-bellied wood-burning stove; upright onstage piano; picks and shovels; a brass bed; champagne magnum in cart; a lifeboat (ideally one that can rock in the "waves").

PROVIDED INSTRUMENTATION: Two violins, cello, bass, three reeds, three trumpets, two trombones, three horns, percussion, piano-conductor.

ADVERTISING AND MARKETING: "A musical about a real survivor."

SUGGESTIONS: If you don't feel like casting three policemen and teaching them a song and a dance, and don't need time to change from the tasteful Denver mansion to Molly's ebullient one, see if you can convince the licensers to allow you to cut "The Denver Police" song and scene, which was originally an in-one scene used to kill time while the new set was being assembled behind the scrim.

RESOURCES: The original cast album on CD, cassette, and LP; the rather faithful 1964 movie on videotape and laserdisc.

RIGHTS: Music Theatre International.

WOMAN OF THE YEAR

CREATORS: Book by Peter (1776) Stone, music by John Kander, lyrics by Fred Ebb (who had recently collaborated on The Act).

BACKGROUND: The 1981 production received six Tony nominations and won four awards—but it was star power that kept the production afloat, first from Lauren Bacall, and later from Raquel Welch, whom many said was better. Debbie Reynolds even came on to play for a few weeks before the show ended its 770-performance run.

STORY: Just before talk show host Tess Harding is to be named "Woman of the Year," she reminisces about her difficult marriage to cartoonist Sam Craig. They met after Tess had given an on-air editorial about the worthlessness of "the funnies," and soon became husband and wife. Problem is, Sam wants more of a wife than Tess is equipped to be; she's especially busy chasing a Russian ballet dancer who's defected. Eventually, though, the dancer tells her he intends to return to Russia because his wife is there—and his private life is more important than his career. Tess sees the light, and the couple decide to work it out as the curtain falls.

ASSETS: A good score, and a chance for audiences to see their own lifestyles validated by the struggles of two-income-household spouses.

LIABILITIES: You'll find many names-in-the-news (Andropov, Haldeman, Erlichman) that no longer appear in the headlines, but more problematic is the dated aspect of the Russian dancer who's defected. There's also a mean-spiritedness about the secondary characters, who gleefully sing such songs as "I Told You So" and "It Isn't Working" when the marriage isn't. And it's demeaning to realize that Tess believes she is right about the inanity of cartoons—but immediately apologizes as soon as she sees that the cartoonist is a hunk.

WHO YOU'LL NEED: Lead Singing Role: A dynamic, take-charge, talk show hostess (a Kathleen Turner type). Supporting Singing Roles: Her equally intense and rugged cartoonist husband; her fey male secretary; her Germanic maid; her vain co-host; her former husband and his unglamorous comic hausfrau; a Russian ballet dancer; four cartoonists; two FBI agents; a saloon keeper; a doorman; a chairwoman; committee women; TV technicians; bar patrons. Maximum, 30; minimum, 16.

DESIGNATED DANCES: One big production number for Tess and the cartoonists; a ballet rehearsal for the Russian and his dancers.

SUGGESTED SETS: A hotel ballroom; a TV studio with a kitchen set; a cartoonist's studio; a tavern; a posh apartment; a ballet rehearsal room; a Colorado house.

COSTUMES: Contemporary formal wear and street clothes; an inexpensive housecoat.

IMPORTANT PROPS: A large blow-up of your star; a very large stuffed animal; large floral bouquet; cups of pens; bottles of ink; rolls of paper; champagne; flutes; a vodka bottle; tea set and trays; cassette recorder and microphone; load of wood; a beeper; hairspray; an apron, galoshes. Your biggest challenge: Tess prepares and bakes an onstage cake.

PROVIDED INSTRUMENTATION: Five reeds, three trumpets, two horns, three trombones, percussion, drums, two violins, two cellos, bass, harp, keyboard-conductor.

ADVERTISING AND MARKETING: Who could be judged the "Woman of the Year" in your community? Choose one, tell the local papers and photographers, and make her the honored guest on your opening night.

SUGGESTIONS: There was a scene in the original production in which Sam discussed with Katz—his cartoon character—the pros and cons of his romance with Tess. Katz was an actual animated character who was projected on a scrim. The movie is available from the licenser, but if you don't have the wherewithal to show it, have an actor play Katz and let him interact with Sam.

RESOURCES: The original 1942 *Woman of the Year* movie of the same name with Spencer Tracy and Katherine Hepburn on which the musical is loosely based and the original cast album on CD, cassette and LP.

RIGHTS: Samuel French.

ALSO WORTH A LOOK

The Act

With book by George (*Company*) Furth, music by John Kander, and lyrics by Fred Ebb—the *Cabaret* team—is a good bet if you'd like to stage a show in a nightclub setting. After all, the show takes place at the Hotel Miramar in Las Vegas, where Michelle Craig, a former movie star who has fallen on hard times, is back on the nightclub circuit singing and discussing the secrets of her past. If you've got four men in your group who are good actors but poor singers, you can use them in this show, which has meaty dramatic parts for them all. There is a four-man, two-woman chorus, and they're used in seven loud, garish, Vegas-style numbers—six of which involve your star in the role that won a Tony for Liza Minnelli. Rights: Samuel French.

Barnum

Has fine music by Cy Coleman, lyrics by Michael Stewart, and book by Mark Bramble, but it also has a dynamic leading man who promises, "Tonight you are going to see—bar none—every sight, wonder, and miracle." That will be the biggest barrier to your success. Creating an entire under-the-bigtop setting will be difficult, and finding a cast who can do the many stunts—clowns, jugglers, stilt-performers—will be harder, not to mention that your leading man must finish act one by doing a highwire act. Then you'll have to costume your characters in both nineteenth-century street clothes and bigtop costumes. It might all be worth it if Michael Stewart's book didn't merely deal with a man with great dreams who's always discouraged by his earthbound wife who wants him to run a clock factory. And we're supposed to root for them to stay together? Rights: Tams-Witmark.

George M!

Gives your older audience a chance to hear "Give My Regards to Broadway," "Yankee Doodle Dandy," "Harrigan," "Over There," "You're a Grand Old Flag," and other George M. Cohan standards. Your cast may have a head start on the score from their days in school or choral groups. "But," stresses Joan Dillon of the Venice (Florida) Little Theatre, "the chorus is always onstage, except when they all file offstage to change costumes, of which there are many. You've got to have dressers who are *great* at their jobs." Still, if you have a feisty performer who's right for the part—and will be able to carry a book that isn't terribly interesting and a show that's been described as "a string of finales," the show might be worthwhile. Rights: Tams-Witmark.

Musicals with Great Vocal Demands

Once upon a time, there was a woman named Florence Foster Jenkins who wanted to sing more than anything else. She rented Carnegie Hall, made her debut, and unfortunately received notices saying that "her singing at its finest suggests the untrammeled swoop of some great bird," that "in high notes, she sounds as if she were afflicted by a low, nagging backache," and that she had "a subtle ghastliness that defies description."

Luckily for the musical theater, Mrs. Jenkins's forays were in the world of opera—but if she had decided on a Broadway career, we would have certainly advised her to stay clear of the following musicals that have very heavy vocal demands.

CANDIDE

CREATORS: Revised book by Hugh (A *Little Night Music*) Wheeler from Lillian Hellman's original book, music by Leonard (*West Side Story*) Bernstein,

59

lyrics by John (*The Golden Apple*) Latouche, Dorothy Parker, Stephen (*Follies*) Sondheim, and Richard Wilbur.

BACKGROUND: The 1956 production got some good reviews, received three Tony nominations, but won none, and lasted only 73 performances— but an original cast album would create a legion of admirers who for years sung the show's praises (and its score). *Candide* finally received its due through rewrites and Harold Prince's innovative 1973 production, nabbing eight Tony nominations, winning four awards. Many believe it would have won Best Musical had it been nominated in that category (the producer of *Raisin*, who had his own agenda and Best Musical aims, lobbied that it shouldn't), but it did receive a special Tony, and ran 740 performances.

STORY: A satire set in 1759 Westphalia, with Voltaire narrating. Candide believes his teacher, Dr. Pangloss, who says "everything happens for the best"— and then is put to the test throughout the show as he endures terrible misfortunes. Because he, an illegitimate child, loves Cunegonde, a well-born young woman, her father, the baron, and her brother, the vainglorious Maximilian, banish Candide from town. He's promptly abducted into the army, which attacks the baron's estate and kills all present but Cunegonde, who'll be used for the soldiers' pleasure. She goes from brothel to brothel until noticed by a rich Jew *and* a Grand Inquisitor of the Spanish Inquisition, who make her very happy. Candide and Pangloss also travel to Lisbon, but they're branded as heretics; Pangloss is hanged and Candide is horsewhipped. An old woman rescues Candide and leads him to Cunegonde. Her two paramours are furious, so, Candide to his horror, kills them. He and Cunegonde travel with the old lady to Cadiz, then Colombia, where they find that Maximilian and his former serving wench Paquette somehow survived and are being sold into slavery. They escape, though, and are given sanctuary by the Jesuits. Candide, Cunegonde, and the old lady leave on a ship but are attacked by pirates, who kidnap the women; Candide winds up in Montevideo, where he again meets Maximilian and Paquette. But when Candide tells Maximilian of Cunegonde's fate, the jealous brother chases Candide to kill him, but winds up being felled by a toppled statue. Candide and Paquette take off together and arrive in Eldorado, where they find gold—enough to take them back to Colombia, where they find the old lady—but discover that the pirates took Cunegonde to Constantinople to sell her. They sail to find her, but their boat sinks and they are stranded on an island. They are rescued and arrive in Constantinople, where they attend a banquet at which Cunegonde happens to be working as a dancing girl. Candide buys Cunegonde's freedom, then is surprised to see that Maximilian is still alive, albeit a slave; he buys his freedom as well. That's when they run into Pangloss, who also magically survived. They ask their old teacher for advice; he tells them that "only work makes life endurable." All agree and plan to work a farm—just as its cow falls over and dies. It's always something!

ASSETS: Arguably Bernstein's best score—and don't forget that he wrote the music for *West Side Story*. The book, formerly considered too heavy, has been lightened considerably and, if played with enough tongue in cheek, should delight. It's also a show that allows your low comics ample possibilities.

LIABILITIES: A costly show to do, given its immense cast and plethora of period costumes. Nor is the score easy to learn. And as the summary implies, a very difficult and circuitous story for many audiences; some don't get the irony of the piece and think the intended convolutions are too contrived.

RECOGNIZABLE SONGS: The overture, which functioned as the theme to "The Dick Cavett Show" in the 1970s.

WHO YOU'LL NEED: *Lead Singing Roles:* Voltaire, who also doubles as Pangloss, a Spanish governor, a host and a sage; Candide, the youthful and optimistic (tenor) lad; Cunegonde, the charming well-bred young girl (and the possessor of a stunning coloratura) whom he loves; Maximilian, her jealous, stunningly handsome, and egocentric brother; Paquette, their ample-bosomed but not wayward serving girl; an I've-seen-it-all old lady who has lost half of one buttock through accident. *Other Roles* (all meant to be doubled): Chinese coolie; soldier; priest; don; rosary vendor; sailor; lion; guest; huntsman; recruiting officer; don; agent; citizen; priest; sailor; eunuch; baroness; harpsichordist; penitent; steel drummer; baron; Grand Inquisitor; slave driver; captain; guest; Spanish don; servant; agent; sailor; recruiting officer; aristocrat; citizen; two penitents and prostitutes; soldier; agent; governor's aide; pirate; guest; two Bulgarian soldiers; aristocrats; fruit vendors; sailors; pygmies; cows; rich Jew; judge; man in black; citizen; pirate; botanist; guest; aristocrat; citizen; sheep; aristocrat; prostitute; lady with knitting; citizen; sheep: *Maximum, 85; minimum, 23.*

DESIGNATED DANCES: No choreographed "numbers," but musical staging throughout—and much chorus work—in no fewer than ten numbers.

SUGGESTED SETS: A few set pieces throughout to represent a classroom; an estate; various roads; a brothel; town squares; a slave auction block; a ship; a raft; a Jesuit rectory; a desert island; a farm.

COSTUMES: Eighteenth-century peasant wear and gentility finery; wigs; soldiers' uniforms; liederhosen; Renaissance teacher's costume; stylized underwear; religious vestments; traditional Orthodox Jewish garb; long dresses; nightgowns; Chinese coolie garb; pirate uniforms; costumes for two sheep, a lion, and a cow.

IMPORTANT PROPS: A pile of corpses; a pillory; chains and shackles; steel drum; harpsichord; a lifeboat; a statue of a saint, gold bricks; fruit.

PROVIDED INSTRUMENTATION: Two options: A full score and a partial (three reeds, two trumpets, trombone, percussion, violin, viola, cello, bass, piano, electric keyboard).

ADVERTISING AND MARKETING: During intermission, don't miss the opportunity to serve "Candide yams" and "Candide fruit."

SUGGESTIONS: Though Prince's production was environmental in scope— with some of the audience encircling the set, while others sat in the middle of it on stools—it's often been done (especially at New York City Opera) in a more conventional staging.

RESOURCES: Many recordings, including the original cast album, the 1974 revival cast album, the 1982 New York City Opera version, and the 1990 studio recording conducted and supervised by Leonard Bernstein; all are available on CD, cassette, and LP, with the last named also available on videotape and laserdisc; study guides.

RIGHTS: Music Theatre International.

CARNIVAL!

CREATORS: Book by Michael (*Hello, Dolly!*) Stewart, music and lyrics by Bob (*Take Me Along*) Merrill.

BACKGROUND: The 1961 musical opened to unanimously favorable reviews, received seven Tony nominations, won two awards, won the New York Drama Critics Circle Award as Best Musical, and ran 719 performances.

STORY: "The day before yesterday" in Southern Europe. Lili comes to a European carnival where her late father said she could always get a job from a friend of his—but she learns that he also has died. Still, she's attractive and winsome enough to attract and accept the attention of the carnival's vendor and Marco, its magician, not knowing that they have more salacious motives (the latter has a mistress, Rosalie, who is not thrilled with his attention to the young girl). Lili doesn't do well in her work and considers suicide, until talked out of it by a puppet—or, more accurately, by Paul, the puppeteer, once a dancer until an accident ruined his career. She becomes his assistant, and soon they and the puppets are the stars of the carnival. Paul falls in love with her, but she is still naively dazzled by Marco, and the two fight over her. Rosalie gets Marco a job with a better carnival, but Marco asks Lili to go with him. But by now, Lili has realized Paul is the better man, and decides to stay with him.

ASSETS: A lovely score, a tender book, and a musical that's quieter and more innovative than the average Broadway musical. If you have a young woman with a lilting soprano, there are few shows that will show her to greater advantage.

LIABILITIES: Just as *Barnum* is a tough show to do because creating a circus setting, finding a cast who can do the many stunts, and providing expensive costumes are difficult, so is *Carnival*, though not to such a great degree, because *Carnival* is about a fifth-rate carnival instead of a first-class circus. Still, this will be an expensive show to mount, and you will have to watch out for the tinges of melodrama in the book.

RECOGNIZABLE SONGS: "Love Makes the World Go Round."

WHO YOU'LL NEED: *Lead Singing Roles:* A waif (Anna Maria Alberghetti); a dour baritone puppeteer who can create voices for his hand puppets. *Supporting Singing Roles:* A slick and lusty magician; his long-suffering mistress (Kaye Ballard); the carnival owner; a puppeteer who plays a concertina; four roustabouts. *Other Roles:* A doctor; a cyclist; a dog trainer; a wardrobe mistress; a snake charmer; harem girls; a "bear"; a stilt-walker; an aerialist; a gypsy; a strongman; jugglers; clowns. *Maximum, 36; minimum, 29.*

DESIGNATED DANCES: A dynamic opening waltz for the company; a tango for Marco and the four roustabouts; a kick-line for the carnival performers; a ballet for the entire company which results in Lili realizing she is alone; much musical staging when setting up the carnival site.

SUGGESTED SETS: A carnival tent; its midway; puppet-booth stage; main office.

COSTUMES: Satiny European carnival costumes for ringmaster, clowns, and roustabouts (leotards and the like); simple suits for Lili and Paul; second-rate glamorous onstage costumes and offstage clothes for Rosalie, Marco, and the carnival owner.

IMPORTANT PROPS: Booths; banners and posters; a ladder and trapeze; a battered suitcase; a magic box into which swords can be thrust without injuring Rosalie; a puppet theater and puppets. "Have them made professionally," urges Thomas R. Stretton, who has directed the show in Philadelphia high schools. "They must look good."

SPECIAL EFFECTS: Marco does a few magic tricks: cigarette-magically-appearing-behind-the-ear stuff.

PROVIDED INSTRUMENTATION: Five reeds, two trumpets, two trombones, horn, two percussion, three violins, cello, bass and tuba, harp, guitar, accordion, piano-conductor. Also available with reduced instrumentation.

ADVERTISING AND MARKETING: Hold an actual carnival before the show, and sell your wares.

SUGGESTIONS: Insists Stretton, "Wonders happen just by adding a few strings of lights over the set in 'Yes, My Heart,' and by using helium balloons and 'choreographing' them in 'Beautiful Candy.' "

RESOURCES: The original cast album on CD, cassette, and LP; the movie *Lili* on which the musical is somewhat faithfully based.

RIGHTS: Tams-Witmark.

KISMET

CREATORS: Book by Charles Lederer and Luther (*Grand Hotel*) Davis, music adapted from Aleksandr Borodin by Robert Wright and George Forrest (who had collaborated on *Song of Norway*).

BACKGROUND: The 1953 production opened to good reviews, but during a newspaper strike, so theatergoers weren't able to read the news. Such stars as Helen Hayes made TV "talking-head" commercials in which they told how much they liked the show. By the time the newspapers came back, *Kismet* was on its way, winning five Tony awards—including Best Musical—and running 583 performances.

STORY: A day in ancient Baghdad. A clever poet and beggar comes to town and pretends to be a man named Hajj—who, he finds out, has an enemy named Jawan. Jawan kidnaps him, but fast-talking Hajj convinces him that he can find his lost son—and is given some gold to do it. This starts Hajj thinking about his own daughter Marsinah, who, we are shown, is being pursued by a much-in-demand caliph who, beseiged by females, adopts the guise of a gardener so that Marsinah will love him for himself. Meanwhile, back at the palace, the caliph finds that the evil wazir has Hajj before him; our hero has been arrested for suspicion of having stolen gold. Jawan, however, has also been captured, and he states that he gave Hajj the gold. Though the wazir discovers that he is Jawan's son, he sentences Jawan to death. He is about to do the same for Hajj when the caliph runs in to tell of his love, which infuriates the wazir. Hajj is employed to dispose of the caliph's new love, and when he finds it's Marsinah, he goes to her and insists she leave town. She doesn't want to obey, so Hajj decides the safest course is to put her in the wazir's harem, where she won't be noticed. The caliph is devastated when he cannot locate her and pleads with the wazir to find her. Eventually he discovers her in the wazir's harem, and is more devastated. Hajj kills the wazir, explains everything, and becomes emir of the city.

ASSETS: Hajj is a charismatic role, and if you've got the right baritone for it, you may have a show. The music has a great elegance, and the lyrics suit it surprisingly well.

LIABILITIES: Though the book is more than a bit convoluted, the bigger problem for you is that you'll need more money than Ali Baba and his forty Thieves had to do this show justice; it's very costume-and set-heavy.

RECOGNIZABLE SONGS: "Stranger in Paradise," "And This Is My Beloved," "Baubles, Bangles and Beads."

WHO YOU'LL NEED: *Lead Singing Roles:* A clever and charismatic baritone; his charming soprano daughter. *Supporting Singing Roles:* A handsome and strong (and strong-voiced) caliph; the heavy-set wazir, his sensuously beautiful main wife; a storyteller; a princess's handmaiden. *Other Roles:* The thief; a chief of police and his assistant; two palace guards; two princesses; a prosecutor; a widow; a chorus of beggars, merchants, dervishes, street dancers, sellers of baubles, bangles, and beads. *Maximum, 52; minimum, 37.*

DESIGNATED DANCES: A dance for the princess's handmaiden; a good deal of musical staging in three other numbers involving most of the company; some belly-dancing, too.

SUGGESTED SETS: Outside a mosque; a tent outside the city; a bazaar; a side street; a garden; palace interiors; a throne room; a ceremonial hall.

COSTUMES: Very *Arabian Nights*: Flowing robes; elaborate headdresses; plumes; dancing girl costumes; glorified rags; pantaloons; paneled skirts.

IMPORTANT PROPS: Torches; sacks of gold; bags of goods.

PROVIDED INSTRUMENTATION: Flute/piccolo, oboe/English horn, two clarinets, bass clarinet, bassoon, three trumpets, two horns, two trombones, tuba, four violins, viola, cello, bass, harp, percussion, piano-conductor. "But," warns Jim Hutchison of Honolulu's Diamond Head Theatre, "watch out for the revisions over the years that have caused the score and script not to match."

ADVERTISING AND MARKETING: "It's your kismet—that means fate—to see our *Kismet* on . . ."

SUGGESTIONS: If you're a racially mixed group, check with the licensers for the availability of *Timbuktu!*, a more authentically African version of the same story.

RESOURCES: The original cast album and a 1990 studio cast album on CD, cassette, and LP; the fairly faithful 1955 movie on videotape and laserdisc; the Edward Knoblock play on which the musical is somewhat faithfully based.

RIGHTS: Music Theatre International.

KISS ME, KATE

CREATORS: Book by Samuel and Bella Spewack *(who collaborated on Boy Meets Girl)*, music and lyrics by Cole *(Silk Stockings)* Porter.

BACKGROUND: Composer Jule Styne has become famous for his remark, "Musicals aren't written—they're *rewritten*," referring to all the work done on shows when they're out of town or in previews. But in its 1948 production, according to famed librettist Peter Stone *Kiss Me, Kate* "came into New York without a comma changed." It won the Tony as Best Musical, and ran 1,077 performances.

STORY: Late 1940s at the Ford's Theater in Baltimore. Fred Graham and Lilli Vanessi, once married, are now starring in a tryout of Shakespeare's *The Taming of the Shrew* in Baltimore. Though they've been divorced for a year, Lilli still seethes when she sees Fred pay a good deal of attention to Lois Lane, the nightclub chorine he's cast as Bianca. Lois, though, has a boyfriend—Bill—who's also in the cast, and owes gangsters ten grand, which they've come to collect. Lois is astonished to discover that Bill signed the IOU in Fred's name. Fred, though, is in Lilli's dressing room, where he overhears her phone conversation with her wealthy Georgian fiance

Harrison Howell. Nevertheless, the two are soon reminiscing about the times when they were struggling actors and in love. And when Fred's flowers for Lois arrive, his dresser, assuming they're for Lilli, gives them to her maid. Fred is furious when he finds out, because of the accompanying love note he'd written Lois. He approaches Lilli to explain the error, but she, flattered, says she'll keep it next to her heart and deposits it in her bosom without reading it before taking the stage in the scene where Petruchio within the show-in-a show meets Katharine. After Lilli reads the note, the scene takes on an additional meaning, as she hits, slaps, and bites him; he responds by taking her over his knee and spanking her. Afterward, Lilli immediately calls Howell and says she's leaving the show and will marry him—so Fred tells the gangsters that he'll have to close because of Lilli's leaving; they suggest (at gunpoint) to Lilli that she *not* leave. In fact, they become actors in the play to ensure that she not escape. She still tries to, but Fred encircles her with his whip. Howell later shows up (where he's recognized by Lois, who was once romanced by him—to the consternation of Bill), but infuriates Lilli when he doesn't believe that the two thugs in colorful costumes really prevent her from leaving. But the thugs find the debt is canceled when their boss has been deposed and disposed of. Lilli is now free to go, but she decides not to—realizing Fred is the man for her after all.

ASSETS: Great score, funny book, and an opportunity to showcase your two most dynamic—and egocentric—performers.

LIABILITIES: This show has not had a major revival in the forty years since the original Broadway production closed, and many think it's because much of the score is too operetta-ish for contemporary audiences. Does that include yours? And, on a much smaller note, be prepared for your customers to be distracted and start talking when they hear that your second female lead has the same name as Superman's girlfriend.

RECOGNIZABLE SONGS: "Another Op'nin', Another Show," "Wunderbar," "So in Love," "Too Darn Hot."

WHO YOU'LL NEED: *Lead Singing Roles*: One dynamic legit-voiced male Shakespearean star; one (soprano) female former Shakespearean star turned Hollywood movie queen. *Supporting Singing Roles*: A young song-and-dance man who's also a gambler; the nightclub chorine who loves him—and a few others; two comic gangsters who speak psuedo-elegantly; two *Taming of the Shrew* suitors; a stage manager; a dresser; a maid. *Other Roles*: A Southern straight-arrow; a banker; an angry taxi driver; a doorman; two messengers; a chauffeur; a chorus of at least three men, two women, and two young men. *Maximum, 54; minimum, 27.*

DESIGNATED DANCES: For the company, a dynamic opening number, a pavane, a beguine, a tarantella, and a finale; for Bill, a tender dance with a rose, a tap, and a flashy dance with male dancers; for Lois, a hornpipe; for Fred and Lilli, a waltz; for the gangsters, a soft-shoe.

SUGGESTED SETS: Baltimore's Ford's Theater backstage, in the alleys, and in two dressing rooms—a plain one for Fred and a much more elaborate one for Lilli; sets for the show-within-a show include a Paduan piazza; the dining room of Petruchio's house; the interior of Katharine's house.

COSTUMES: Rehearsal clothes; costumes worthy of a classical production of *The Taming of the Shrew* (medieval wear, gowns and dresses, tunics and tights); flashy gangster suits; doctor's, nurse's, taxi driver's, and trucker's uniforms.

IMPORTANT PROPS: Pay phone; chaise longue and poufs for Lilli's dressing room; a large pewter tankard to be banged against a rustic table; trays; bouquets; a whip; a string of sausages.

PROVIDED INSTRUMENTATION: Five reeds, three trumpets, horn, trombone, two violins, viola, cello, bass, percussion, harp, guitar-mandolin, piano-celeste, piano-conductor.

ADVERTISING AND MARKETING: Have girls or women named Kate sell kisses from a booth—Hershey's kisses, that is.

SUGGESTIONS: Because one character in the show is the busy and harried stage manager for the play-within-a-play, you might take him one step further during curtain calls by having him take the first call, and then noting on his clipboard every person who comes out to take a bow.

RESOURCES: The 1990 double-CD and cassette recording conducted by John McGlinn is the most complete representation of the score; the 1953 (reasonably faithful) movie (originally released in 3-D!) on videotape and laserdisc; Shakespeare's *The Taming of the Shrew*.

RIGHTS: Tams-Witmark.

THE MOST HAPPY FELLA

CREATOR: Book, music, and lyrics by Frank *(Guys and Dolls)* Loesser.

BACKGROUND: The 1956 production was a victim of the if-you-go-to-only-one-show-this-year syndrome—for it debuted forty-eight days after *My Fair Lady* opened to unprecedented raves, and that was the one show most theatergoers wanted to see. Nevertheless, a musical of this quality—with reviews almost as good as *My Fair Lady*'s—had to be a hit; it received six Tony nominations, won none, and ran 676 performances. A 1992 revival ran 232 performances.

STORY: Napa Valley in the late 1920's. Tony Esposito, an older and overweight Italian immigrant who owns a successful vineyard, falls in love from afar with a waitress. He leaves her a note; she responds and wants his picture, which he doesn't want to send. So he sends her a picture of his handsome foreman Joe, who's soon leaving his employ. But then Joe decides to stay a little longer, and when "Rosabella," as Tony has dubbed this woman, shows up to marry Tony, she's so devastated to find the truth—even after she learns that Tony has just had a near-fatal accident when he was en route to meet her—that she makes love to Joe. Some time later, Tony acknowledges that he's done a bad thing and sends for Rosabella's waitress friend Cleo, who soon falls in love with hired hand Herman. Eventually Rosabella comes to see that Tony is worth loving, but then discovers that she's pregnant; when she tells Tony, he's infuriated. But he realizes that he was the cause of her disappointment and forgives her as the curtain falls.

ASSETS: What a score! The book is quite tender, too, and you have two character parts—Cleo and Herman—ripe for good comedy.

LIABILITIES: Many more songs to learn than are in the average musical. (As Loesser enjoyed saying when asked if the show was an opera or a musical: "This is a musical comedy—with a lotta music.") Some do find the pregnancy resulting from one isolated night of love a little too contrived. And do you have a Tony, a sister, and three chefs who can sound convincingly Italian?

RECOGNIZABLE SONGS: "Standing on the Corner," "Joey, Joey, Joey," "Big D."

WHO YOU'LL NEED: *Lead Singing Roles:* A high, near operatic baritone for Tony; a lyric soprano for Rosabella. *Supporting Singing Roles:* A handsome foreman with a strong baritone; a comic seen-it-all waitress; the happy-go-lucky hired hand who loves her; three of his pals; Tony's realistic but dour sister; three enthusiastic chefs; a doctor; children. *Other Roles:* A cashier; a postman; a priest; a bus driver; a brakeman; a chorus of neighbors, waitresses, and workers. *Maximum,* 51; *minimum,* 16 (as were used in the 1992 Broadway revival).

DESIGNATED DANCES: A big production number for Tony and his neighbors; two struts for Herman, one with his three pals; a tarantella for the chefs; one hoedown for Herman, Cleo, and the neighbors, and another for Tony, Rosabella, and the neighbors.

SUGGESTED SETS: A restaurant; a main street of the Napa Valley; a barn; a front yard; a clearing; and a grape arbor.

COSTUMES: Waitress uniforms; cowboy boots and hats; laborers' work clothes; modest dresses; three chef hats and aprons; priest's cassock; arm and leg cast.

IMPORTANT PROPS: Coffeeshop equipment; cash register; checked tablecloths; table full of food; "Welcome, Rosabella!" banner; stretcher; rocking chair; wheechair; wrapped present with shawl inside; toolboxes and sawhorses; packing crates; a glue pot; wine barrels; a great many bunches of plastic grapes.

PROVIDED INSTRUMENTATION: Five reed parts, two trumpets, two trombones, three horns, harp, accordion, two violins, viola, cello, two basses, two percussion. In addition, the 1992 Broadway revival used two-piano orchestration that was sanctioned by Loesser himself.

ADVERTISING AND MARKETING: Have a "Most Happy Fella" contest in your community, asking people to nominate the most happy fella they know—and tell why he's so happy. The men whose stories most impress you can be invited to various performances, be given a free ticket, and be offered the opportunity to take a bow.

SUGGESTIONS: "Don't have contempt for joy," advises Scott Waara, who won a Tony as Herman in the 1992 production. One other note: Given that Tony spends much of the show in a wheelchair, this is a good role for a handicapped actor. The early and late scenes do call for an ambulatory Tony, but they could be restaged without too much inconvenience.

RESOURCES: The 1956 original cast album of the entire show and an abbreviated 1992 revival cast album on CD, cassette, and LP; the tape of the 1979 Broadway revival for the "Great Performances" TV series; Sidney Howard's play *They Knew What They Wanted*, on which the musical is very loosely based. And there's even an episode of "I Love Lucy" in which Lucy, Ricky, Ethel, and Fred all head out for a Saturday night performance of the show—only to find that Lucy bought tickets for the matinee that's just ended.

RIGHTS: Music Theatre International.

ON THE TWENTIETH CENTURY

CREATORS: Book and lyrics by Betty Comden and Adolph Green, music by Cy Coleman (who later collaborated on *The Will Rogers Follies*).

BACKGROUND: The 1978 production opened to mixed reviews, and star Madeline Kahn missed a number of performances and abruptly left the production. But acclaimed understudy (and future Tony winner) Judy Kaye took over, and the audience developed enough of a liking for her and the show to see it through 460 performances; it received nine Tony nominations and five awards.

STORY: 1930s on "The Twentieth Century, Ltd." from Chicago to New York. Theatrical producer-director Oscar Jaffee has fallen on hard times, so he tries to sign for his next production movie star Lily Garland, whom he gave her first break toward stardom when she was just Mildred Plotka. They had been lovers, which didn't work out, and a frustrated Garland had gone to California. Jaffee tries so hard to win back his leading lady—to the consternation of her current boyfriend Bruce Granit—and raises funds from a backer, Mrs. Primrose, who turns out to be "a nut." But Lily cannot resist by play's end.

ASSETS: A terrific score, a witty book, two fabulously large parts that offer a wide range for your performers.

LIABILITIES: There are some long stretches of book material between Oscar and Lily that never played as well as when read by Comden and Green in the show's backers' auditions. The operetta-pastiche score may be beyond some goups' vocal abilities.

WHO YOU'LL NEED: *Lead Singing Roles:* A dazzling theatrical force (John Cullum) with a strong baritone, a movie star (Madeline Kahn) with an elegant soprano. *Supporting Singing Roles:* A worrisome company manager, a sardonic press agent; a virile but vacuous leading man (Kevin Kline); a spinsterish religious fanatic, a successful young producer; a female doctor; a train conductor; four train porters. *Other Roles:* A fur-bedecked actress; a statesman; a maid; a secretary; a wardrobe mistress; a stage manager; a chorus of passengers, actors, and party guests. *Maximum, 47; minimum, 26.*

DESIGNATED DANCES: Four production numbers that involve much more musical staging than conventional dancing.

SUGGESTED SETS: A theater (with sets for both a Joan of Arc and a French Revolution production); train station; observation room; two drawing rooms; the front engine and caboose of the Twentieth Century Ltd.

COSTUMES: 1930s wear, including skirts and sweaters; a seductive negligee; elegant dressing gown; party clothes; Oscar's fedora and cape; costumes for the Joan of Arc production (knight armor), a biblical production, and a play about the French Revolution.

IMPORTANT PROPS: A French flag; a gun; flash cameras; a pitcher of water; a heart-shaped bouquet; eight-by-ten glossies of your Bruce Granit, and many stickers that state "Repent for the Time Is at Hand."

SPECIAL EFFECTS: Oscar's hat blown off by the wind when he tries to climb into the train from outside.

PROVIDED INSTRUMENTATION: Five reeds, two trumpets, two horns, two trombones, two percussion, three violins, viola, cello, bass, harp, keyboard-conductor.

ADVERTISING AND MARKETING: "These may be the last years of the twentieth century, but we've got a show to see that it goes out with a bang: *On the Twentieth Century,* opening on . . ."

SUGGESTIONS: The movie had a male "nut," and you could cast a "*Mister* Primrose."

RESOURCES: The original cast album on CD, cassette, and LP; the Ben Hecht-Charles MacArthur play *Twentieth Century,* on which the musical is fairly faithfully based, and a movie version of that play on videotape.

RIGHTS: Samuel French.

ROBERT AND ELIZABETH

CREATORS: Book and lyrics by Ronald Millar, based on Fred G. Moritt's idea, music by Ron Grainer.

BACKGROUND: The 1964 British musical opened to not-good reviews, but the public kept it running for 948 performances. A co-producer of the very different *Bye Bye Birdie* planned a Broadway production in the late 1960s, but couldn't raise the money, and as of this date, it still hasn't appeared on Broadway.

STORY: Victorian England. Edward Moulton-Barrett's six sons and three daughters are adults, but he rules them with an iron hand. He's especially intent on not allowing daughter Henrietta to even meet with her beloved Captain Cook. He even insists that the apple of his eye, his sickly daughter Elizabeth, whom for years he has confined to her room, each night drink a tankard of porter for medicinal purposes; she hates it, but she drinks it. Elizabeth does have one outlet—writing poetry, which has brought her to the attention of popular poet Robert Browning. He asks to visit, and she finally consents—on a day she knows her father will be out. (It's the same day that Henrietta brings Cook to meet Elizabeth, and announces she's marrying him.) Browning immediately tells Elizabeth that from her verses, he's fallen in love with her, which startles her, but not as much as his probing and inferring that her illness is psychosomatic. Elizabeth considers traveling to Italy with him—until her father forbids it—then decides she will go, after Browning encourages her to stand on her own two feet literally and figuratively. But she's still no match for her father, who banishes Browning from the house and later decides to move the family to the country. That's the straw that prompts Elizabeth to marry Browning and go with him abroad.

ASSETS: A riveting score that provides a stellar vehicle for a soprano who has ample opportunities to bring down the house with her songs; a good book, considering the parameters of its melodrama and operetta-like structure; the scenes between Elizabeth and her father crackle with conflict and excitement.

LIABILITIES: This is an *awfully* syrupy story that kids will especially loathe—seeing an era when children were so controlled by parents; the fact that two major characters have speech impediments may drive audiences to distraction; and Henrietta's beloved is so doltish that we are skeptical of their future happiness.

WHO YOU'LL NEED: *Lead Singing Roles:* A winsome female poet with a strong soprano; a handsome and confident male poet with a good baritone. *Supporting Singing Roles:* A very stern father; six brothers (one stutters); two sisters (one has a tendency to faint); their silly speech-impedimented cousin; her fiancé. *Other Roles:* A Cockney manservant; a famous actor; a supporting actor; a stage manager; a doctor; Londoners; buskers; policemen; friends and neighbors; an adorable dog. *Maximum, 40; minimum, 27.*

DESIGNATED DANCES: Musical staging for the opening; a scene representing play-rehearsal activity; a dress ball quadrille; two ballets (one that celebrates spring, another for Browning and Cook).

SUGGESTED SETS: Outside 50 Wimpole Street; its great hall (with mahogany, rosewood, and chandeliers); its garden; Elizabeth's room; Browning's study; a theater stage (with throne set), an arboretum; a railway station in London, and another in Florence. "Sets" representing a flower-shop and travel agency can be accomplished with a counter.

COSTUMES: Victoriana: high hats, morning coats, gloves; severe black costumes for the Barretts, a smoking jacket, negligee, overcoats, an attractive spring dress; fancy ball costumes; busker outfits, police uniforms.

IMPORTANT PROPS: A wheelchair, chestnut braziers, prayer books and Bibles, tea tray and service, a tankard of porter, floral bouquet, many gift boxes, dust-sheets, a bottle of pills, a cigar case.

PROVIDED INSTRUMENTATION: Five reeds, two trumpets, two horns, two trombones, two percussion, three violins, viola, cello, bass, harp, keyboard-conductor.

ADVERTISING AND MARKETING: "A show that Broadway hasn't yet seen but ran almost 1,000 performances in London is coming to town."

SUGGESTIONS: This is an excellent show to do in a small space because it is all about Elizabeth breaking free from that small room. At the end, pull away your set and expose a cycloroma of Italy behind them.

RESOURCES: The original cast album on cassette and LP; Rudolph Besier's *The Barretts of Wimpole Street*, on which the musical is faithfully based.

RIGHTS: Samuel French.

ALSO WORTH A LOOK

The Golden Apple
By Jerome Moross and John Latouch. This was one of the first shows (in 1954) to move from off-Broadway to on, where it won the New York Drama Critics Circle Award. But it proved to be too rarefied for Broadway audiences, and ran only 125 performances. Still, it is frequently revived because of its rich score. It's the Homeric legend transferred to the turn of this century in Washington state. Helen is still worth stealing, and Paris (a dancer who never speaks) does so in a hot-air balloon. In addition to that effect, you'll need 18 principal males and six principal females, all of whom must sing well—and often, for this is a "through-sung" musical (read: opera) with no book. But it's also charming and tuneful. Rights: Tams-Witmark.

"GOTTA
DANCE!"

Musicals That Feature Choreography

There was once a Broadway musical that dealt with producing a Broadway musical—called *A Broadway Musical*. One of its characters insisted that in any musical, "You gotta have dancing." And though *A Broadway Musical* played all of one official performance on Broadway before shutting its doors, there are many who think it's true: "You gotta have dancing" in a musical.

Of course, you also gotta have dancers—but if you do, here are some choreographically heavy shows worth investigating.

ANYTHING GOES

CREATORS: Revised book by Howard Lindsay and Russel Crouse (who later collaborated on *Life with Father*) from the book by Guy Bolton and P. G. Wodehouse *(who wrote the Jeeves novels)*; music and lyrics by Cole *(Kiss Me, Kate)* Porter.

BACKGROUND: When the 1934 Bolton-Wodehouse-Porter musical, concerning a shipwreck, was about to go into rehearsal, the S.S. *Morro Castle* sunk with a loss of 125 lives. Deciding it was not a time for a shipwreck musical, producer Vinton Freedley needed rewrites—but Bolton and Wodehouse weren't available. He hastily put together two writers—Lindsay and Crouse—who came up with a new book that wasn't ready during any rehearsals, and the cast only saw it during the tryout. But it was good enough for the production to get fine reviews and run 420 performances. It's since been an acclaimed 1962 off-Broadway hit (239 performances) and a Tony-winning 1987 revival (804 performances).

STORY: Billy Crocker must deliver information to his boss, who is about to leave for Europe on the S.S. *America*. Before the boat sails, Billy runs into old pal Reno Sweeny—an evangelist turned entertainer—and Hope, a young woman he's loved, who's sailing with her mother and, Billy's sorry to see, with Sir Evelyn, her fiancé. He decides to stow away and make Hope his own, and soon gets an extra passport from Moonface Mullins, Public Enemy Number 13, whose friend Bonnie is also making the trip. Billy keeps reminding Sir Evelyn that he has a proclivity to seasickness, and thus gets Hope alone. Later Billy asks Reno to seduce Sir Evelyn, and after she does, she decides that she likes him herself. Billy, meanwhile, is mistaken for Snake Eyes Johnson, which makes him a celebrity with the passengers and staff, but not with Hope. Billy eventually tells the truth, and chides the passengers for being so impressed with such a nefarious celebrity. He's put in the brig for his trouble, but soon escapes after a game of strip poker that wins him clothes that can disguise him. Reno dresses as a Chinese girl, one with whom Sir Evelyn is found in a compromising position—which means he must propose to her. Billy's boss becomes involved with Hope's mother, and Billy gets Hope as the curtain falls.

ASSETS: The most commonly licensed version is the 1962 Guy Bolton rewrite, which includes hits from other Porter shows; your audience almost always hears a familiar tune.

LIABILITIES: Young audiences tend to jeer at an era when a "girl" older than they must travel with a chaperone. There are also some stereotypical characterizations of Asians. As of this writing, the much-acclaimed 1987 book by John Weidman and Timothy Crouse is not available through licensers.

RECOGNIZABLE SONGS: "You're the Top," "It's Delovely," "I Get a Kick Out of You," "Anything Goes," "Let's Misbehave," "Blow, Gabriel, Blow."

WHO YOU'LL NEED: *Lead Singing Roles:* An ex-evangelist (Ethel Merman, Patti LuPone); a would-be Wall Street broker who can sing *and* be comic. *Supporting Singing Roles:* A comic public enemy who's distraught at only being Number 13; his good-natured moll; a lovely and unassuming heiress; her haughty mother. *Other Roles:* A high-class British gentleman; a bishop and his two converts (whom you may not want to label Chinese); at least four showgirl "angels"; sailors. *Maximum, 40; minimum, 22.*

DESIGNATED DANCES: Three major production numbers; a fox-trot for Billy and Hope; "The Heaven Hop" and a tap for Bonnie and the girls; some soft shoe for Billy, Reno, and Moon; an evangelical romp for Reno and company; much musical staging throughout.

SUGGESTED SETS: Deck of an ocean liner, with occasional scenes in stateroom cabins and its brig.

COSTUMES: Sailor suits and white uniforms for the staff, appropriate 1930s formal and casual wear for the passengers (halters and flared satin slacks for the women); knickers for Sir Evelyn; gowns for the entertainers; two parsons' suits; Chinese coolie outfits (if your converts are Asian); disguises for Billy including an old woman's garb and a fake beard made from a fur stole.

IMPORTANT PROPS: Floral bouquets; an armload of shoes; hats and canes.

PROVIDED INSTRUMENTATION: Four reeds, three trumpets, trombone, two violins, viola, cello, bass, percussion, guitar-banjo, piano-celeste; piano-conductor. Also available: Two reeds, trumpet, trombone, percussion, guitar and banjo, piano-celeste, piano-conductor.

ADVERTISING AND MARKETING: Take a leaf out of the book of the Barter Theater in Virginia, which has for years allowed theatergoers to barter their way into the theater: Have an "Anything Goes for Admission" performance—in which people can bring anything to the theater in exchange for admission. Much of what you accumulate could be given to homeless shelters and hospitals.

SUGGESTIONS: As director Jerry Zaks said when rehearsing his 1987 revival, "If your Sir Evelyn Oakleigh is too foppish and silly, Reno looks foolish for being interested in him." Play him straight.

RESOURCES: The 1962 and 1987 cast album on CD, cassette, and LP; the 1936 (fairly faithful) movie version; the 1956 movie bears virtually no resemblance to the show.

RIGHTS: Tams-Witmark.

THE BOY FRIEND

CREATORS: Book, music, and lyrics by Sandy (*Valmouth*) Wilson.

BACKGROUND: Importing a hit musical from England was not the norm in 1954—it had only been done a handful of times—but hit masters Cy Feuer and Ernest Martin decided to bring over this charmer which introduced Julie Andrews to American audiences. Though it received almost unanimous raves, it received not one Tony nomination, but ran for 485 performances.

STORY: A tongue-in-cheek look at the Roaring '20s on the French Riviera. Maisie, Dulcie, Fay, and Nancy—the girls at Madame Dubonnet's finishing school—are looking forward to getting boyfriends (madcap Maisie is especially interested in Bobby). Polly, though, is a bit more cautious, for she worries that any boy might only be interested in her for her father's money. When her father, Percival Browne, arrives, he finds the school's mistress, Madame Dubonnet, is an old flame. Tony, a messenger, then shows up with a package for Polly, and she's immediately smitten with him. (We'll later learn from Tony's parents, Lord and Lady Brockhurst, that he's given up a brilliant career and takes odd jobs to find himself.) Because he's just a messenger, Polly pretends to be a mere secretary, lest she and her money drive him away. When she lets him kiss her, his parents arrive on the scene—causing Tony to leave so abruptly and without explanation that he's inadvertently taken for a thief by the crowd. But Polly believes them, and now figures that Tony knew she was rich when he met her. Maisie and the girls are having better luck with Bobby and his friends; they've all received proposals, though Dulcie isn't sure—giving the randy Lord Brockhurst an opening to stake his claim, until his wife happens along. At a masquerade ball, though, all the deception is unraveled, and Polly and Tony are willing to forgive that each lied to the other, as they—and Percival and Madame Dubonnet *and* all the other boys and girls—wind up happily in love.

ASSETS: A fun score and a good enough book to sustain the parody. "And from a strictly business standpoint," said one theater's artistic director who begged not to be identified, "this three-act musical offers twice as many opportunities to sell refreshments during its two intermissions."

LIABILITIES: There's a great deal of camp in this show, and it's possible that your audience has camped out enough. (You can get around this if you simply play it as a 20s show.) The extreme animation, prancing, and preening was fun in the 1950s, when the Roaring Twenties were still within an audience's memory, but today's theatergoers may just find the show too silly.

WHO YOU'LL NEED: *Lead Singing Roles (both legit-voiced):* A sincere, well-bred young miss who takes herself seriously; her young admirer who is trying to hide his wealthy upbringing. *Supporting Singing Roles:* Four perfect young ladies from finishing school (one should be a "madcap"—Sandy Duncan played her in the 1970 revival—while another should be squeaky-voiced); an operatic finishing school headmistress who is fluent in French; a pompous millionaire father who does become more human; a monocled, randy lord and his austere lady; a maid who enjoys being the girls' surrogate mother. *Other Roles:* Two tango dancers; hotel guests; a waiter; a gendarme. *Maximum,* 30; *minimum,* 20.

DESIGNATED DANCES: A cakewalk opening; a Charleston for Maisie and Bobby; a waltz for Madame Dubonnet and Percival; a fox-trot for Polly and Tony; a kick-line to end act one, and a bouncy romp to begin act two; a soft-shoe for Tony; a production number for the maid and the boys; a prissy dance for Percy, augmented by a more joyful dance for the girls; a high-kick and toe dance number for Maisie and the boys; a boop-boop-a-doop number for Dulcie and Lord Brockhurst; a tango for two dancers; "The Riviera"—the movements of which are described in the song's lyrics; a Charleston finale.

SUGGESTED SETS: A drawing room in a finishing school; the beach; a cafe terrace.

COSTUMES: Garb worthy of the Roaring Twenties; flapper dresses; short skirts with unaccented bosoms; fringed French dresses; cloche hats; wigs with marceled dips; turbans and capes; dinner jackets; blazers and white flannels; old-fashioned swimwear; bandanas and bandeaux; costumes for a masquerade ball (including Pierrette and Pierrot costumes); maid, bellman, and messenger's uniforms; a yachting cap.

IMPORTANT PROPS: Hip flasks; many hatboxes and filled shopping bags; feather duster; a palm tree; floral bouquets; hassock; beach chairs (a few "sheltered" ones); umbrellas.

PROVIDED INSTRUMENTATION: Three reeds, two trumpets, two violins, percussion, bass, banjo, guitar, piano-conductor.

ADVERTISING AND MARKETING: "Anyone bringing a boyfriend to a performance gets him in for half-price."

SUGGESTIONS: After the success of *The Boy Friend*, Sandy Wilson wrote another musical which catches up with the same couples ten years later. Bet you can guess why it's called *Divorce Me, Darling*. It might be nice to play the two in repertory.

RESOURCES: The original cast album on CD, cassette, and LP; the 1971 greatly changed movie version on videotape and laserdisc.

RIGHTS: Music Theatre International.

A CHORUS LINE

CREATORS: Book by James Kirkwood (*who wrote the novel Some Kind of Hero*) and Nicholas Dante, music by Marvin (*They're Playing Our Song*) Hamlisch, lyrics by Edward Kleban.

BACKGROUND: In 1974, director-choreographer Michael Bennett, dancer Michon Peacock, and choreographer Tony Stevens invited fifteen of their dancer friends—and enemies—to discuss their backgrounds, lives, feelings, and need to dance. Eventually Bennett and other collaborators turned these discussions into a series of "workshops," where words, lines, speeches, songs, and dances were tried and retried; this new way of developing a musical led to the 1975 production that received raves, was nominated for twelve Tony

awards, won nine—including Best Musical—snared a Pulitzer Prize, and set
a record run of 6,137 performances.

STORY: A group of dancers are auditioned for an upcoming Broadway show
by Zach, its director-choreographer (whose voice is heard from the back of the
theater). Zach explains that because they'll be working together for a long and
intense period, he must be sure that he has the right four men and four women,
even though they will be cast in an anonymous yet precision-point chorus. So
he asks them to reveal themselves and listens as each divulges the story of his
or her life, loves, and ambitions. Zach then sends them offstage to learn some
steps—but asks one woman, Cassie, to stay. She's a dancer with whom he
once had a relationship, before she went to California, partly to escape him.
Now she's returned, not having had much luck there, and needs a job so much
that she's willing to return to the chorus. He's uncertain, but sends her off
with the others while he interviews Paul—a young effeminate Puerto Rican
whose professional dancing began with his work as a female impersonator.
When Paul recalls the effect this had on his family, he breaks down, and Zach
bounds onstage to comfort him. Then the auditioners return to show what
they've learned. At first, Cassie does have that extra sparkle that makes her
wrong for an anonymous chorus, which infuriates Zach—so Cassie adapts,
stating that she'd be honored to be part of an ensemble. She keeps trying, along
with everyone else; then Paul injures his knee and must be carried off. Zach
asks the auditioners what they'll do when they can't dance anymore, but each
proclaims that whatever happens, he or she won't be sorry to have tried. Zach
then makes his selections, as we see the eight winners savor their victory and
the nine losers walk away to deal with their defeat.

ASSETS: A most moving book, a much underrated score, and a cinematic
approach to a musical that made it look unlike any seen before. This is a
relatively inexpensive show to mount, because there's no elaborate set and
relatively few costumes. It's also a show that gives each performer at least one
moment to shine.

LIABILITIES: It's also a very cold show that makes its audience come to it;
because its characters speak frankly—and truthfully—some of your audience
may have a harder time embracing it than they would other shows.

RECOGNIZABLE SONGS: "What I Did for Love," "One (Singular Sensation)."

WHO YOU'LL NEED: *Lead Singing Roles:* A Puerto Rican woman who was
told she'd never make it in show business—and may never become a star—
but is content that she's tried. *Supporting Singing Roles:* an Italian-American
young man; a witty and attractive Buffalo native; an aggressive (and nearing
thirty) woman; a "different-looking" (read: not so attractive) woman; a young
woman who's still fantasizing about an ideal father; a young man who remembers his bout with gonorrhea; a young man who tells of an affair with a stripper;
a homosexual who's also the oldest of the bunch; a young black man who
almost became a teacher; a short Asian young woman who looks ageless (the

part has been played by non-Asians); a young woman who's danced so much in her home that she's ready for Broadway; a young woman who's opted for plastic surgery; a newly married at-ease man and his nearly hysterical, unable-to-sing wife; a young effeminate Puerto Rican man capable of sensitively delivering a long monologue about being a female impersonator. *Other Roles:* A chorus of about eight (or more) dancers who appear only in the first scene and are quickly eliminated. *Maximum, 30; minimum, 18.*

DESIGNATED DANCES: The long opening sequence where many dancers are eliminated (make the first steps purposely difficult, so that nobody looks too good—though by the end of the number, we should see the best dancers doing fairly well); a number that suggests ballet and includes some barre exercises; a lengthy montage about adolescence; a long and detailed solo for Cassie in which she shows what she's capable of; a tap combination; and a hokey, razzmatazz Vegas-style but nevertheless worthy-of-Broadway finale that concludes with a kick-line that never ends as the lights fade to black.

SUGGESTED SETS: Mostly a bare stage. Even the mirror units are optional. While the original production included an Art Deco–styled cycloramic design, you can use something else or nothing at all for the finale.

COSTUMES: First, the good news: For ninety-five percent of the show, the cast is in street clothes or dance leotards. Now the bad news: For the last number, your entire cast must be outfitted in identical costumes; the original production used the famous gold suits and top hats.

IMPORTANT PROPS: One dance bag; a live microphone over which Zach can be heard.

PROVIDED INSTRUMENTATION: Four reeds, three trumpets, three trombones, two percussion, harp, bass, guitar, keyboard, keyboard-conductor.

ADVERTISING AND MARKETING: "Broadway audiences had fifteen years to see *A Chorus Line*—but you've only got [how many days or weeks], starting on . . ."

SUGGESTIONS: Says Paul C. Norton, Associate Professor of Theatre Arts at Bay Path College in Longmeadow, Massachusetts, "Because the onstage performers tend to get breathless in some numbers, use swing dancers and/or a trained chorus on offstage mikes to augment them." And if you're doing this show at a high school, consider having an adult (perhaps you) play Zach; it'll lend a power to his role that another student wouldn't be able to deliver.

RESOURCES: The original cast album on CD, cassette, and LP; the 1985 (fairly faithful) movie version on videotape.

RIGHTS: Tams-Witmark.

42ND STREET

CREATORS: Book by Michael Stewart and Mark Bramble (who had collaborated on *Barnum*), music by Harry Warren, lyrics by Al Dubin (who wrote the score for the *42nd Street* movie).

BACKGROUND: After the 1980 production debuted, producer David Merrick announced to the cheering audience that director-choreographer Gower Champion had died earlier that day. Some cynics have suggested that the resulting headlines helped catapult the show to a 3,486-performance run, but they should be reminded that the show did receive seven Tony nominations, and won two—including Best Musical.

STORY: The 1930s on Broadway—*Dames at Sea* without the parody. Peggy Sawyer, a young hopeful from Allentown, arrives at auditions for producer-director Julian Marsh's new Broadway musical *Pretty Lady*—but too late. Billy, the show's romantic lead, likes the way she looks, and has Andy, the dance director, audition her. She's good, but there are no parts left, so Peggy leaves—forgetting her purse—and bumping into Marsh on her way out. He has been financially devastated by the Depression, so he's had to take a hundred grand from Abner Dillon—who's also the boyfriend of Dorothy Brock, an actress who will of course be starred in the show, even though her best days are behind her, and Marsh and Brock don't much get along. When Peggy returns for her purse, Maggie, the show's co-writer, takes her to lunch with three chorines; they teach her some dance steps. Marsh walks in, likes her, and says they can use an extra girl in the show; Peggy's hired. But things aren't going so well: Abner objects to Dorothy's love scenes and insists that she instead shake hands with Billy. It's only the start: Dorothy complains that she doesn't have enough to do, and turns out to have a lover, Pat, in addition to Abner. Julian insists (through strongarms) that Pat head to Philadelphia for a while, but Dorothy has Abner arrange for the show to try out in Philadelphia instead of Atlantic City. Then she gets drunk and frankly tells Abner about Pat, and Abner decides to withdraw his money—until the chorus kids talk him out of it. To make matters (much) worse, after a triumphant opening night in Philadelphia, Peggy bumps into Dorothy, who falls and breaks her leg. Marsh fires Peggy and decides to close the show, until the kids convince him to use Peggy in the lead. Marsh goes to the train station, where he and later the chorus urge her to return and take the role. She does, does well, and *Pretty Lady* winds up a Broadway hit. And perhaps Julian Marsh and Peggy Sawyer will become a couple as well.

ASSETS: A terrific score that not only will inspire your dancers to rise to the challenge, but also will have your audience tapping in their seats. And there's that wonderful moment when Julian, trying to convince Peggy to return to the show, can't believe that she'd opt for Allentown instead of "the two most glorious words in the English language—musical comedy."

LIABILITIES: It's hokey with a capital "H," and the sentiments that seemed to ring true in the mouths of 1930s screen actors are a bit arch for contemporary audiences. "And don't undertake this one unless you have a *lot* of backstage room for all the set pieces and the lightning-fast changes the chorus will do," says Melanie Larch of the Charleston (West Virginia) Light Opera Guild. "And dressers are a must."

RECOGNIZABLE SONGS: "Shadow Waltz," "You're Getting to Be a Habit with Me," "We're in the Money," "Lullaby of Broadway," "Shuffle Off to Buffalo," "42nd Street."

WHO YOU'LL NEED: *Lead Singing Roles*: An egocentric diva who's not as much of a star as she thinks she is; her naive and sincere understudy who must save the show; the show's innocently amorous tenor-voiced romantic leading man. *Supporting Singing Roles*: A producer-director (Jerry Orbach) who was once on top and is now struggling to return there; the nice guy and acerbic female who teamed to write the show; three chorus girls; a lover who must get out of town. *Other Roles*: A sugar daddy who's devoted to his fallen star; a dance director; a rehearsal pianist; a stage manager; two thugs; a doctor; a large chorus of tap dancers. *Maximum, 54; minimum, 23.*

DESIGNATED DANCES: Three enormous production numbers; an opening audition for the entire company; a waltz for Dorothy and the chorus; an audition for Peggy; a romp for Peggy, the woman author and three chorines; a love-scene dance for Dorothy and Billy; a soft-shoe for the show's authors; a lengthy ballet about the world of 42nd Street.

SUGGESTED SETS: On the stage of a 42nd Street theater and later a Philadelphia one; a Gypsy cafe; a leading lady's dressing room, and later Peggy's; a posh hotel suite; a honeycomb of the cast's dressing rooms; old-styled musical sets for *Pretty Lady*; Philadelphia's Broad Street Station.

COSTUMES: 1930s wear, simple for Peggy and the chorus kids, expensive and fancy for Dorothy, Julian, and the creative staff. Negligees; satiny costumes; top hats and tuxedos; flowing gowns, etc. for production numbers.

IMPORTANT PROPS: Peggy's good-luck scarf; her purse with a four-leaf clover and rabbit's foot inside; enormous replicas of dimes on which the dancers can dance to "We're in the Money."

PROVIDED INSTRUMENTATION: Five reeds, three trumpets, two trombones, bass, percussion, piano-conductor. There are optional parts for guitar-banjo and harp. Also available is a synthesizer part to eliminate the five reeds.

ADVERTISING AND MARKETING: "42nd Street comes to [your] Street on . . ."

SUGGESTIONS: Who's been the most devoted, dutiful, and talented female understudy in your company? Maybe it's time to reward her with a part like that of Peggy Sawyer. No question that she'll bring to the role the knowledge of what it's like to be an understudy—and it will make a good story for your local newspapers as well.

RESOURCES: The original cast album on CD, cassette, and LP; the 1933 movie on which the musical was fairly faithfully based.

RIGHTS: Tams-Witmark.

GRAND HOTEL

CREATORS: Book by Luther Davis, music and lyrics by Robert Wright and George Forrest (all of whom had collaborated on *Kismet*), additional music and lyrics by Maury (*Nine*) Yeston, and (uncredited) book help by Peter (*1776*) Stone.

BACKGROUND: Though the 1989 production was in good shape during its Boston tryout, some theatergoers were confused by its density—so director Tommy Tune brought in new writers to help the show become more accessible, leading to twelve Tony nominations, five awards, and 1,018 performances.

STORY: Life goes on—and so does death, disappointment, chicanery, thievery, illicit love, and even impending birth—in 1928 in Berlin's grandest hotel. We meet the baron now so destitute that he must charm innocent women like aspiring actress Flaemmchen and burglarize rooms—but he is a decent man who sees that Kringelein, a dying bookkeeper who now wants to have a fling before facing his impending death, gets a room at the hotel even though he's Jewish. One night, while the baron is stealing a necklace from the room of faded ballerina Grushinskaya, she appears; he at first tries to romance her, but soon loves her, to the consternation of devoted secretary Raffaela, who truly loves him, and to Flaemmchen, who felt she'd soon be a baroness. Flaemmchen sells herself to Preysing, a general director in the stock market, recently ruined after lying about a merger that fell through. Once she's in Preysing's room, she changes her mind, but he won't let her, and her screams alert the baron, who was robbing the adjoining room. They scuffle, and Preysing shoots and kills the baron. Kringelein, who'd made a good deal of money on a stock tip the baron gave him, offers to take Flaemmchen to Paris and take care of her baby with her.

ASSETS: A fascinating look at six people's lives, each of whom seems to impact on another, with markedly interesting consequences. A much-underrated score that has only recently been receiving its due.

LIABILITIES: To make the seamless story work and the show come alive will demand a great concept, vision, and much hard work. And it's still a dark story that's so fragmented many audience members have a hard time following it.

WHO YOU'LL NEED: *Lead Singing Roles:* A faded ballerina (Liliane Montevecchi); her assistant (Karen Akers); a dying bookkeeper (Michael Jeter); a (legit-voiced) baron who still wants to be noble despite his hardships; a most fetching typist who wants to be a movie star. *Supporting Singing Roles:* A desperate businessman and his adviser; a cynical doctor wounded in World

War I; a front desk clerk anxiously awaiting the birth of his child. *Other Roles:* A hotel manager; a washroom attendant; a menacing chauffeur; a doorman; four bellboys; four telephone operators; two ballet impresarios; two black entertainers; four scullery workers; a courtesan; a maid; a countess and a gigolo who weave throughout the action. *Maximum, 32; minimum, 19.*

DESIGNATED DANCES: There is constant movement throughout, but in addition to an opening production number, there is a fox-trot for the company that features the baron, Flaemmchen, and Kringelein; ballet exercise steps for Grushinskaya; a Charleston for Flaemmchen (and some steps for her while the blacks entertain); a polka for the company featuring Kringelein and the baron that leads into fancy footwork on that barre; and for the dancers a tango that borders on an Apache dance.

SUGGESTED SETS: Through the revolving door and into a grand hotel's sumptuous three-chandeliered red-carpeted lobby, ballroom, restrooms, and various guest rooms—which could all be suggested by a large, vast space.

COSTUMES: Matching elegant, Old World uniforms for the front desk clerk, bellmen, and maids; gowns and tuxes for guests; stevedore rags; a chauffeur's uniform; expensive coats with capes; mink and fake fur coats; ballerina outfit; toe shoes; a large opulent necklace; man-tailored woman's suit; a leg brace; boots, eye patch; camouflage suit; hats, including cloches, feathered numbers, turbans, and fezzes.

IMPORTANT PROPS: A ballet barre; a mirrored ball; luggage ranging from expensive to threadbare; a silver cigarette case, plenty of cigarettes and lighters; containers for jingling silverware; a cane; a syringe; a bouquet of red roses; towels; room keys; a stretcher; a mop and broom; a gun that can produce a loud shot; handcuffs; a chaise longue; many identical chairs.

PROVIDED INSTRUMENTATION: Four reeds, two horns, three trumpets, two trombones, two percussion, two violins, cello, bass, guitar-banjo, two percussion, two pianos.

ADVERTISING AND MARKETING: "It'll cost you less to stay at our *Grand Hotel* than at any other hotel in town. And you'll like our entertainment more, too."

SUGGESTIONS: Much of the action was originally positioned in the center of the stage—thus suggesting that the show could be done in a much smaller space.

RESOURCES: The original cast album on CD and cassette; the 1932 movie on which the musical was fairly faithfully based.

RIGHTS: Samuel French.

MY ONE AND ONLY

CREATORS: Book by Peter (1776) Stone and Timothy S. Mayer, music by George Gershwin, lyrics by Ira Gershwin (the Gershwins wrote much of the material for *Funny Face*).

BACKGROUND: After the 1983 production's first performance in Boston, star Tommy Tune apologized to the audience for what they'd just seen. But Tune was soon co-directing and had a bookwriter brought in; by the time the show opened on Broadway some weeks later, it gained fine notices, received seven Tony nominations, won three awards, and ran 767 performances.

STORY: It's 1927 in New York City and Billy Buck Chandler wants to be the first aviator to fly solo nonstop to Paris—especially after he meets Edythe Herbert, the third woman to swim the English Channel ("But," notes her manager, Prince Nicholas Erraclyovitch Tchatchavadze, "the first attractive one.") He just may do it if his crackerjack mechanic, the tomboyish Mickey, has her say. But when the Right Reverend Montgomery shows up and invites him to a party where Edythe will be, Billy accepts the invitation—as well as a session at Mr. Magix's Tonsorial and Sartorial Emporial, where he becomes elegant. Perhaps that's what makes Edythe notice and respond to him when she arrives at the party. This infuriates the prince; he blackmails Edythe by threatening to show the suggestive photographs she had taken when she was seventeen. When Billy just happens to sit next to her at a movie, she tells him that she's taken—but he kisses her and changes her mind. They discuss flying everywhere from New Jersey to Havana, but the prince has been following them and sabotages the plane. Billy and Edythe must land on a deserted isle. He's afraid now he'll never be first to Paris and get all that glory, but she tells him, "It's not what people think of you, it's what *you* think of you." Soon Prince Nikki arrives by boat to take her back, and though Billy is unhappy to see him—and unhappy that she's going off with him—he'll now get his chance to get to Paris. Before he does, though, he learns that Edythe has stowed away on a Moroccan-bound steamer. He decides to follow her, but comes to his hangar just in time to find Mickey arresting the prince; it turns out that she's a federal agent, and he's an impostor. Billy flies to Morocco and finds Edythe, just as the news that Lindbergh has made it to Paris comes over the wires. Actually, Billy passed Paris three days earlier, but didn't touch down, because he wanted to find Edythe—and "it's not what people think of you, it's what *you* think of you."

ASSETS: A classic score has found a funny book to complement it. An endearing show for fans of tap dancing.

LIABILITIES: There's a smarminess and profanity about some of the scenes and the language—a show in the 1920s could have never employed such language—but it may still not be right for you.

RECOGNIZABLE SONGS: "Soon," "S'Wonderful," "Strike Up the Band," "Nice Work If You Can Get It," "Funny Face," "How Long Has This Been Going On?"

WHO YOU'LL NEED: *Lead Singing Roles:* A demure but charming female swimming champion; the boyish young aviator who loves her (Tommy Tune). *Supporting Singing Roles:* His profanely wise-cracking female mechanic; a black reverend; an elegantly dressed older gentleman who can tap dance; a nefarious pseudo-Russian prince; six aquacade chorines. *Other roles:* Seven male dancers; a reporter; a policeman; a stage doorman; a train conductor; a housewife. *Maximum,* 39; *minimum,* 22.

DESIGNATED DANCES: Much tap dancing—for the ensemble in the opening and closing numbers; for Billy and the ensemble in two numbers; two numbers for Billy and Mr. Magix. In addition, there's a rhumba for the company; a harem girl dance; a "splash dance" for Billy and Edythe in a wading pool's worth of water.

SUGGESTED SETS: A train station; an airplane hangar; a barber's emporium; a Cuban-style nightclub; a movie theater; Central Park; a deserted beach; an aquacade; a Moroccan-style nightclub; an uptown chapel.

COSTUMES: 1920s flapper fashions for the women; everything from raccoon coats to tuxedos and high hats; priests' and bishops' robes; Cuban costumes; harem girl outfits; a bridal gown.

IMPORTANT PROPS: A propellered monoplane will be your biggest challenge, but you'll also need an open touring car; a barber's chair; flash cameras; bags and boxes; hats and canes; a bridal bouquet.

SPECIAL EFFECTS: Edythe goes to a movie, where projections show us her, Billy, and the Prince as performers; a small wading pool for the splash dance.

PROVIDED INSTRUMENTATION: Four reeds, two horns, three trumpets, two trombones, two percussion, two violins, cello, bass, guitar-banjo, two percussion, two pianos.

SUGGESTIONS: If you have a leading man who's taller than the chorus boys, don't miss the opportunity that Tommy Tune used in the original production: in the "High Hat" number, in which everyone was wearing high hats, he and the boys went behind a wall—and because of his height, you could still see his high hat dancing along.

RESOURCES: The original cast album on CD, cassette, and LP.

RIGHTS: Tams-Witmark.

ON YOUR TOES

CREATORS: Book by Richard Rodgers, Lorenz Hart, and George Abbott—who would later collaborate on *The Boys from Syracuse;* Music by Rodgers and Lyrics by Hart.

BACKGROUND: The 1936 production was a 315-performance hit that broke new ground with an innovative ballet; the 1954 revival was a 64-performance flop that was deemed hopelessly old-fashioned; the 1982 revival seemed *delightfully* old-fashioned, received five Tony nominations, won three—including Best Revival—and ran 505 performances.

STORY: Junior Dolan leaves his parents' vaudeville act to become a music professor. At a college some years later, he's especially proud of his students Sidney and Frankie (a girl); the former has written a ballet, while the latter has written a good love song (one that Junior doesn't realize is directed at him). Frankie's uncle knows Peggy, who backs the Russian ballet, so Sidney's going to get a chance—especially after prima ballerina Vera takes a shine to Junior. But Junior has come to love Frankie, and certainly doesn't endear himself to Vera when he must suddenly substitute in a ballet and almost ruins it. Sergei, the ballet's artistic director, is now so angry that he doesn't want to hear Sidney's ballet. And Junior is at odds with himself, because he's starting to think that Vera is for him. Peggy says she'll pull her money if Sidney's ballet is not performed, and it will be—along with Frankie's newest song, as American tap shoes meet Russian toe shoes. One problem remains: Vera has an admirer, Morrosine, who is so jealous that he intends to kill Junior in the middle of the ballet—so he keeps dancing until the police arrive. Junior decides on Frankie as Vera reconciles with Morrosine.

ASSETS: A wonderful score, not many set demands, and a show with so many parts of equal value that each of your principals will be able to convince himself and herself that he or she is the lead.

LIABILITIES: Did you read that plot synopsis? The 1982 acclaimed revival had production values and enough dazzling choreography to withstand Frank Rich's pan in the *New York Times*; your audience may be as bothered as he was by the archaic and impossible book. And while it's one thing to stage a good deal of dancing, it's another to tackle two full *ballets*.

RECOGNIZABLE SONGS: "There's a Small Hotel;" "Glad to Be Unhappy;" "Slaughter on Tenth Avenue."

WHO YOU'LL NEED: *Lead Singing Roles:* A sincere music professor who's interested in all his students; the (legit-voiced) young girl who loves and admires him. *Supporting Singing Roles:* Junior's vaudevillian mother and father; a young man who sings the ballad he's written; a Russian impresario; the female funder of the ballet company. *Other Roles:* The haughty and demanding prima ballerina; an intense music student with great classical ambitions; a jealous Russian suitor; two Russian comrades; four college students; two reporters; a stage manager; a doorman; a chorus of ballet dancers. *Maximum, 45; minimum, 21.*

DESIGNATED DANCES: A vaudeville routine for the Dolans; some soft-shoe for Junior and Frankie; a dance seduction between Vera and Junior; a production number that features tap and ballet for much of the company; two full ballets.

SUGGESTED SETS: A vaudeville stage and its dressing room; a college classroom; a prima ballerina's apartment; the opera house stage.

COSTUMES: Vaudeville costumes, with straw hats and canes; 1930s wear for college kids; unglamorous clothes for the Russians, though some smart fashions for Vera; Arabian Nights wear for the first ballet; and spangled outfits for the second.

IMPORTANT PROPS: A gun.

PROVIDED INSTRUMENTATION: Five reeds, horn, two trumpets, trombone, two percussion, three violins, viola, cello, bass, two pianos, piano-conductor.

ADVERTISING AND MARKETING: Get your posters in shops that sell ballet wear.

SUGGESTIONS: Play it eccentrically.

RESOURCES: The 1983 cast album on CD, cassette, and LP; the 1939 (somewhat faithful) movie.

RIGHTS: Rodgers and Hammerstein.

SWEET CHARITY

CREATORS: Book by Neil Simon (who wrote the comedy *Little Me*), music by Cy Coleman, lyrics by Dorothy Fields (who later collaborated on *Seesaw*).

BACKGROUND: The 1966 musical was one of the most anticipated of the season, especially after its fine Detroit and Philadelphia reviews—but it didn't quite live up to the promise, though with its large advance and Gwen Verdon in the lead, it ran 608 performances. But a 1986 Tony-winning revival vindicated the show as being better than anyone thought.

STORY: 1960s, New York City. Charity is a dance hall hostess who always picks the wrong man. To find a better one, she plans to attend a YMCA lecture—but gets stuck in the elevator with Oscar, who is claustrophobic. He is grateful to her for calming him, likes her a good deal, and asks to see her again. She agrees, though she tells him she works in a bank, fearing that the truth will scare him off. Oscar accidentally discovers the truth, but says it doesn't matter that she's danced with hundreds of men. However, after a few nights' sleep, he changes his mind and abandons Charity. That's when a Good Fairy enters Charity's life, and she's ready to believe that the apparition has the answers—until the Good Fairy turns around, displaying a sandwich board that advertises a new CBS series called "The Good Fairy."

ASSETS: A terrific score, an often funny book, and the chance to re-create some of the sparkling Bob Fosse dances.

LIABILITIES: The ending, and not only because it's downbeat, but also because the Good Fairy device comes out of left field. Also, the show has more sets than the average musical.

RECOGNIZABLE SONGS: "Big Spender," "If My Friends Could See Me Now"—thanks to a *Woman's Day* TV commercial.

WHO YOU'LL NEED: *Lead Singing Role*: A winsome and charming born loser. *Supporting Singing Roles*: Her two best friends; her gruff boss; her neurotic almost-husband; an Italian movie star (with grand baritone); his difficult girlfriend; his butler; a jazz musician with religious ambitions; his two biggest apostles. *Other Roles*: Young and old dance hall hostesses; a gigolo; policemen; a Good Fairy; a dog on leash (optional); a chorus of many Manhattanites in a variety of roles. *Maximum, 47; minimum, 23.*

DESIGNATED DANCES: Ironically enough, the number that displays the dance hall hostesses for the first time has no dancing in it at all, but after that, be prepared: Three energetic and trendy dances for the nightclub crowd; a frenetic jazz production number; an eleven o'clock number. Charity has an opening solo; a soliloquy dance; a hat-and-cane number; a stomp with her two girlfriends; a march with a mock-marching band.

SUGGESTED SETS: Central Park (your orchestra pit functions as a lake); a tacky dance palace; its locker room; outside and inside a trendy nightclub; Coney Island and its parachute jump; a Mexican restaurant with two adjoining booths; a YMCA lobby and its elevator; a movie star's posh apartment and Charity's more modest apartment.

COSTUMES: A basic black dress for Charity; contemporary wear; trendy finery for the nightclub denizens; sensuous dance hall hostess costumes; jazz musicians' clothes; marching band uniforms; policemen's uniforms; a Good Fairy gown.

IMPORTANT PROPS: A dance barre; a huge menu; telephones and a pay phone; champagne bottle; a birthday cake with candles; pop-up top hat and cane; a gift box containing a baby's snowsuit; a suitcase labeled "Almost Married"; a placard advertising "The Good Fairy" show; a transparent garment bag with zipper (very important for one of the show's best sight gags).

SPECIAL EFFECTS: Charity is twice thrown into the Central Park lake, and must emerge at least somewhat wet. Can you provide a working elevator that goes up at least one floor, and an amusement park parachute jump ride? (If not, see "Suggestions.")

PROVIDED INSTRUMENTATION: Two trumpets, two trombones, horn, three reeds, two violins, cellos, harp, drums, Fender bass, synthesizer, piano-conductor.

ADVERTISING AND MARKETING: Here's the most logical show for you to schedule a dress rehearsal or a performance from which all proceeds go to a favorite charity. Or print tickets with a space in which each theatergoer can write in the name of a charity, and indicate you'll donate a dollar to that fund for each ticket.

SUGGESTIONS: You needn't build an elevator or a parachute jump; if your two actors simulate motion, just three walls will suffice for the former, and a small car will do for the latter. The scene written for Charity's apartment could just as easily take place in the dance hall's locker room.

RESOURCES: The original cast album on CD, cassette, and LP; the fairly faithful 1970 movie on videotape; *The Nights of Cabiria* movie on which the musical is loosely based.

RIGHTS: Tams-Witmark.

THE TAP DANCE KID

CREATORS: Book by Charles Blackwell, music by Henry (*Dreamgirls*) Krieger, lyrics by Robert Lorick.

BACKGROUND: The 1983 production opened to not-great reviews, *but* received seven Tony nominations, won two awards, and found an audience for 412 performances. The authors didn't stop working on the show, and before the tour added four numbers, deleted one, and made other improvements for the musical's national and international tours.

STORY: 1980s, on Roosevelt Island, New York. William is a black upwardly mobile lawyer who keeps a stern grip on his family—making more decisions about their welfare than his wife Ginnie does. Of their two children, ten-year-old Willie is the apple of his eye, and William wants him to be a lawyer—not noticing that his fourteen-year-old daughter, Emma, is the one with legal ambitions. Willie instead takes after his mother (a former dancer), his Uncle Dipsey (a currently struggling dancer-choreographer), and his grandfather (an alcoholic vaudeville hoofer who never made it). When Dipsey gets a job choreographing in Buffalo, he asks Willie to join him. Ginnie isn't enthusiastic, and William is furious. Eventually budding lawyer Emma argues Willie's case with such authority that William must concede his son should make his own decision, but Willie, seeing that his father only has his best interests at heart, refuses to take the job.

ASSETS: A good score and, for the most part, a strong book. The fact that the family is black is handled matter-of-factly; only William's observations, such as "dancing is what they did on the plantation" would give the reader the hint that the family is black.

LIABILITIES: After he's been fighting all night for the right to dance and appear in a show, we can't believe that Willie would turn down the opportunity after he's come so far.

WHO YOU'LL NEED: *Lead Singing Roles:* A ten-year-old tap-dancing son; a director-choreographer uncle. *Supporting Singing Roles:* A stern lawyer father; a placating mother who has a profession; a fourteen-year-old overweight daughter. *Other Roles:* A leggy chorine girlfriend; a West Indian maid; a difficult dancer-actress, a techie, a teenage bully; a chorus of dancers and New Yorkers. *Maximum, 36; minimum, 17.*

DESIGNATED DANCES: Tap, more tap, and still more tap in no fewer than eight numbers. This includes some tap in high-top sneakers, some on ballet shoes with attached taps, and even some on roller skates. There's also stylized walking and movement representing how busy Manhattan is.

SUGGESTED SETS: A middle-class living room, dining room, bedroom, and terrace; a playground with slide and jungle gym; a rehearsal studio; a hotel ballroom, inside and outside a theater; a loft apartment.

COSTUMES: Contemporary street wear; rehearsal clothes; white tie and tails.

IMPORTANT PROPS: An old-fashioned show curtain (the glitzy one an audience sees during an overture); Walkman and headphones; onstage piano; sports bags; pay phone; feather duster.

PROVIDED INSTRUMENTATION: Two trumpets, two trombones, horn, three reeds, two violins, cellos, harp, drums, Fender bass, synthesizer, piano-conductor.

ADVERTISING AND MARKETING: Make a big deal of auditioning your ten-year-old boys, and get some local reporters and photographers to cover the auditions.

SUGGESTIONS: If you've listened to the show's cast album, don't assume that it faithfully complements the script; the writers did a great deal of work for a post-Broadway tour, and that's the script you'll receive.

RESOURCES: The original cast album on CD, cassette, and LP; the novel *Nobody's Family Is Going to Change* by Louise Fitzhugh, on which the musical was fairly faithfully based.

RIGHTS: Samuel French.

WEST SIDE STORY

CREATORS: Book by Arthur (*Gypsy*) Laurents, music by Leonard (*Candide*) Bernstein, lyrics by Stephen (*Company*) Sondheim.

BACKGROUND: The 1957 production is now regarded as a landmark and one of the most recognizable titles in the Broadway canon—so it will surprise you to learn that it received only five Tony nominations, and won only one (for choreographer Jerome Robbins). *The Music Man* was the big winner that year, and *Story* ran a comparatively short 732 performances; it was Hollywood's Oscar-winning movie version that put it in the classics category.

STORY: Romeo and Juliet updated to 1957: Now it's the white Jets against the Puerto Rican Sharks in New York City. Former Jet co-leader Tony, who's looking for more in his life than fights, goes to a dance at the urging of current Jet leader Riff and immediately falls in love with Maria, the very protected sister of Bernardo, the Sharks' leader. Bernardo's girlfriend, Anita, warns Maria that trouble is brewing. When a fight breaks out that Tony intended to stop, Bernardo kills Riff and Tony instinctively kills Bernardo. Maria, though devastated, stays by Tony, but her would-be suitor Chino eventually kills him in front of Maria and both gangs; as the curtain falls, the Sharks and the Jets come to realize that they must look for other solutions to solve their problems.

ASSETS: "In addition to that great score and poignant book," says Bert Silverberg, who's often directed the show in Rhode Island, "you'll find that high school boys who are reluctant to dance will respond if you tell them they can be Sharks or Jets. They'll like that, and will work very hard to live up to the tough-guy images—dancing all the way."

LIABILITIES: Says Jeffrey Dunn, who has directed many European tours of the musical, "Some productions play it as if everybody already knows the story before they come inside the theater. Whether your audience knows it or not, play it as if the story's being told for the very first time."

RECOGNIZABLE SONGS: "Maria," "Tonight," "I Feel Pretty," "Somewhere."

WHO YOU'LL NEED: *Lead Singing Roles:* A nubile and sweet Puerto Rican soprano girl, and the young Polish-American man who suddenly falls in love with her (he can be a lyric-baritone or a tenor); a fiery yet compassionate Puerto-Rican girl. *Supporting Singing Roles:* The brooding but still-capable-of-humor leader of the Sharks; the hot-headed leader of the Jets. *Other Roles:* Maria's jealous and crazed suitor; nine Jets; eight Sharks; five white girlfriends; six Puerto Rican girlfriends; a misunderstood and unaccepted tomboy; the long-suffering candy store owner capable of playing both comic and dramatic scenes; a very nervous social director; a detective and a police officer. *Maximum, 41; minimum, 23.*

DESIGNATED DANCES: For the company, the dance at the gym (which includes blues, a promenade, a mambo, a cha-cha, two challenge dances—

"and," says Dunn, "the Sharks and Jets must respond to them as challenges"); for the boys, the prologue, a school dance; a knife fight. ("Do not," cautions Dunn, "put knives in anyone's hands until they perfectly know and can execute the choreography. Even then, only let them work with plastic spoons for a while.") Some musical staging on the rumble; a huge-skirted romp for Anita and her friends; the "Somewhere" ballet.

SUGGESTED SETS: The New York streets, a backyard, a bridal shop, a gym; on a fire escape in an alley inside and outside a drugstore; under a highway, a bedroom.

COSTUMES: The Jets wear cool colors—blues and yellows—but the hotter Sharks wear reds and purples. All wear straight-legged jeans. ("Have each boy go out and buy his own," suggests Dunn, "so they'll all be different.") Sneakers should be black Converses. Each boy has a gang jacket—"though the Puerto Ricans have better ones," notes Dunn, "because their girlfriends sew for a living." Their clothes, too, are more flashy than the Jet girls'. Also a policeman's uniform; bridal veil for Maria; nicely fitting top hat for Tony.

IMPORTANT PROPS: Four or five lightweight bridal shop clothes dummies which are fully outfitted. ("Make certain," says Dunn, "that you establish in advance whether your costume or prop people will tend to the dummies; too often, one department will assume the other is taking care of it.") Switchblades; knives; guns.

PROVIDED INSTRUMENTATION: Five reeds, three trumpets, two trombones, two violins, cello, bass, guitar, piano, percussion, piano-conductor.

ADVERTISING AND MARKETING: Make a package deal with a school dance so that each event's patrons can get a discount.

SUGGESTIONS: "Many productions never give the show as it's written a chance," laments Dunn. "Instead, they restructure some of the scenes the way the movie was done. But the original structure is stronger than some directors think. Don't play with it."

RESOURCES: The original cast album on CD, cassette, and LP; the 1962 (somewhat faithful) movie on videotape; Shakespeare's *Romeo and Juliet*, which provided inspiration for the musical; a "Rehearscore" disc for Macintosh and IBM systems that eliminates the need for a rehearsal pianist; study guides.

RIGHTS: Music Theatre International.

ALSO WORTH A LOOK

Gentlemen Prefer Blondes

Isn't as much fun as the movie. There are some deadly Jule Styne–Leo Robin ballads that the film was smart enough to drop, and the Joseph Fields–Anita Loos book has a much less interesting romance for Dorothy. Still, there are "Bye, Bye, Baby," "A Little Girl from Little Rock," and "Diamonds Are a

Girl's Best Friend"—all sung by Lorelei Lee, who's so sure of herself and her gold digging that we admire the blatant nerve we wish we had. But replicating the decks and suites of the *Ile de France*, not to mention a suite in the Ritz, the Place Vendome, and the area near the Eiffel Tower can be costly. As for dances, prepare to choreograph a large cast in seven production numbers, some involving a kick-line, much tap dancing, some Charleston, and a few solo turns. Rights: Tams-Witmark.

Irma La Douce

Is the Marguerite Monnot-Alexander Breffort-Julian More-David Heneker-Monty Norman musical that features one woman—a prostitute with a heart of gold—who falls in love with a man who doesn't want her sleeping with anyone else. He adopts a disguise, becomes her customer, and insists on exclusivity; unfortunately, because he must pay her, he must take a second job to support the ruse, and he is soon so tired that their relationship greatly suffers. The piece is purposely fanciful—otherwise, wouldn't she recognize him from seeing him close up night after night?—and is a charmingly ribald fairy tale. But you'll need Parisian-inspired sets, costumes, and much Gallic choreography (including a ballet for penguins!). Rights: Tams-Witmark.

On The Town

Ran 463 performances back in the 1940s, but much of its charm had to do with its co-authors, Betty Comden and Adolph Green, being in the cast (no slight intended to composer Leonard Bernstein), and the marvelous Jerome Robbins choreography that dominated the night. Unless you have a Robbins in your neighborhood (and if you do, he or she won't be there much longer), you might consider another property, for this one seems to fail more often than not when revived. It's the story of three sailors who have one day in "New York, New York, a helluva town (the Bronx is up, and the Battery's down)," and spend most of it searching for the current Miss Turnstiles (a young woman featured on subway advertisements). Rights: Tams-Witmark.

Seesaw

By Michael Stewart, Cy Coleman, and Dorothy Fields, was in terrible trouble during its 1973 Detroit tryout, so producer Joseph Kipness gave a call to the up-and-coming Michael Bennett. "Whenever another Broadway show dies," Kipness told him, "Broadway dies a little more with it." Bennett responded to the call, took over as director, choreographer, and bookwriter, then replaced the leading lady and four other actors, and made *Seesaw* a respectable show. But the small story about Nebraska attorney Jerry Ryan and not-so-successful Broadway dancer Gittel Mosca, and their on-again, off-again relationship doesn't quite merge with the seven enormous production numbers that interrupt it. *Seesaw* offers a fine score and a terrific chance for a straight-arrow, good-looking, natively nonmusical male performer to be starred, but it's no work of art. Rights: Samuel French.

Singin' In The Rain

Routinely shows up on the list of the best movies ever made—and the Broadway version paled in comparison. For nonprofessionals, this won't be such a barrier—after all, any production you do will be fighting against the memory of a movie or Broadway production—but this one does have one seemingly insurmountable barrier which is, of course, all that rain. Yes, you can replicate a tinsel curtain, but is it worth it? Another problem: there is a movie sequence in which *your* principals must star; you could make it easy on yourself and use a camcorder, but the audience will know it's not a movie—so is there a film school in your area willing to help with this (time-consuming) sequence? And one last bugaboo: According to Joseph Patton, Resident Director-Choreographer with the Carousel Dinner Theater in Akron, Ohio, "Remember that all those wonderful numbers in the movie were filmed during many takes, and were cut and edited. You'll have no such advantage, and everyone's energy will be severely taxed." Rights: Music Theatre International.

Also See: *The Act; Anyone Can Whistle; Ballroom; Cabaret; Cats; Chicago; Dames at Sea; Follies; Good News!, Grease; Grind; Guys and Dolls; Half a Sixpence; Hello, Dolly!; La Cage aux Folles; Mack & Mabel; Meet Me in St. Louis; No, No, Nanette; Silk Stockings; Smile; Tenderloin; The Unsinkable Molly Brown; The Wiz; Wonderful Town.*

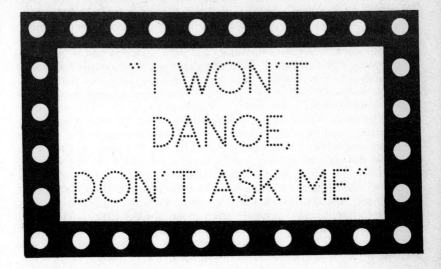

"I WON'T DANCE, DON'T ASK ME"

Musicals with Little Choreography

You've got a company who can act and sing, but when it comes to dancing—oh, brother. No fear; here are some musicals for which a choreographer is virtually expendable.

CITY OF ANGELS

CREATORS: Book by Larry (*A Funny Thing Happened on the Way to the Forum*) Gelbart, music by Cy (*Sweet Charity*) Coleman, lyrics by David (*The Goodbye Girl*) Zippel.

BACKGROUND: The 1989 production had such a complicated set that it couldn't go out of town. Traditionally, previewing in New York, where everyone can see your mistakes before they're ironed out, is a dangerous move—but not if you have a funny show that works, as this one did from the outset. Fine reviews, eleven Tony nominations, six awards—including Best Musical—and an 889-performance run followed.

STORY: The late 1940s in Hollywood. We feel as if we're watching a black-and-white 1940s film noir when the curtain goes up on Stone, a private eye (not only are the sets black, white, and gray, but Stone is too). He's just gotten plugged, and remembers what occurred that past week to make it happen. Flashback: The glamorous Alaura Kingsley hired him to find her stepdaughter, Mallory, child of her seventy-five-year-old husband who lives in an iron lung. Oolie, Stone's secretary, was resentful, and then, suddenly, on stage comes Stine, a young writer at his desk. (When he x's out words, Stone talks backward.) Stine writes detective novels, one of which has been bought for the movies; we've just watched a part of his screenplay. But when he brings the script to Buddy Fidler, a studio head, Stine's very frustrated to hear, "Flashbacks are a thing of the past." Yet he denies trouble when Gabby, his wife, who's also a writer, states that he's being driven crazy by Buddy and the studio. Sensing she doesn't respect him, Stine takes it out on his fictional Stone, having Stone remember the night he was a cop and found his girl, nightclub singer Bobbi, trying to sleep her way to the top. He scuffled with her big-shot paramour and accidentally killed him, which knocked him off the force. With Gabby back in New York, Stine comes on to Donna, a studio secretary on whom he patterns Stone's secretary, Oolie. Eventually even Stone, the detective character he's written, comes to life and shows him no respect. So Stine thinks of killing him off. It all ends with Stine and Gabby reconciling—and Stine and Stone also patching it up—when he walks away from the movie business.

ASSETS: A terrific score with pulsating jazz rhythms to which lyrics have been smoothly set. Almost every line in the script is either setting up a laugh or getting one. And there is the coup de theatre of simultaneously seeing two actresses each in their rooms each doing the exact gesture that the other is doing.

LIABILITIES: An expensive show, because you must have one set of sets, costumes, and props in black and white and one in color. It's also a show that primarily speaks to writers who have struggled long and hard, and may not be too interesting to much of your audience. There is some purposely didactic but still uncomfortable dialogue about Hispanics denied their rights. And some will be disappointed in the ending, when Stine essentially loses his battle, for he is denied the movie he so wanted.

WHO YOU'LL NEED: *Lead Singing Roles:* A tough-talking macho 1940s detective (a Humphrey Bogart type); a sensitive and slightly nebbishy writer. *Supporting Singing Roles:* Almost everyone in the black and white movie (listed first) has a real-life counterpart: a powerful studio exec/a dimwitted studio head who thinks he's brilliant; Stone's secretary/Buddy's secretary; a sultry torch singer/Stine's wife, also a writer; the stunning young wife who may want her elderly husband dead/Buddy's wife; her beautiful young stepdaughter/a starlet; a 1940s star-singer/a would-be movie star; a plainclothes police detective/a Mexican movie star. B&W only: a clean-cut and mellow-sounding quartet (two male, two female voices). *Other Roles:* A handsome twenty-year-old stepson/a movie star; a mountain of a man/a studio cop; his very small yet menacing partner/another studio cop; an iron-lung-bound invalid/a movie star; a madam/

a hairdresser; a police commissioner/a shoeshine boy; a reporter/an actor; a doctor/a barber; a detective's assistant/an actor; a porno vendor/an extra; a coroner/an extra; a hospital attendant/a cinematographer; an orderly/a composer. B&W only: a female extra. *Maximum, 45; minimum, 24.*

DESIGNATED DANCES: A tiny bit of movement from the Angel City Four; nothing else.

SUGGESTED SETS: We see either a black-and-white set or a color set, or both side by side. For black-and-white: The L.A. County Jail, its hospital, and its morgue; Stone's office; his studio apartment; a smallish jazz lounge; the streets of L.A.; a phone booth; a mansion, its plant-filled solarium, and its master bedroom; a recording studio; a room in a brothel. For color: A studio's sound stage; a Bel-Air mansion's garden and its study. For both side-by-side: Stone's office adjoining Stine's hotel room; Oolie's bedroom adjoining Donna's bedroom.

COSTUMES: In black-and-white: 1940s everyday streetwear; trenchcoats; policemen's, doctors' and orderlies' uniforms; facial bandages; woman's drop-dead dresses; working clothes; tennis outfit. In color: Late 1940s everyday streetwear; executive's bathrobe.

IMPORTANT PROPS: In black-and-white: An iron lung; a waist-high hospital table (gurney) on rollers; old-fashioned cathedral radio; microphones; big flash cameras and pistols; tennis racket; bedroom set; kitchen appliances; a buzzsaw; suitcases and their contents. In color: A typewriter; many telephones; Oscars; a camera crane and movie clapper boards; suitcases and their contents.

SPECIAL EFFECTS: Perhaps you can do something with video for the marvelous rear projection effects that had Stone walking in front of a movie of the streets of L.A. to great comic advantage. You'll also need your Stine to do some clever gymnastics as he escapes from being tied.

PROVIDED INSTRUMENTATION: Not set at press time.

ADVERTISING AND MARKETING: "Here's an easier way to travel to the *City of Angels*—by showing up at [name of theater]." Or could you work with a travel agency to sponsor a raffle for which the prize would be a trip to Los Angeles?

SUGGESTIONS: Who would you call to say you need an iron lung for a play? And who'd enjoy making that call? Maybe you could just use a wheelchair instead, for it'll be easier for you to get one. You'll lose some good laughs, but the show has plenty more.

RESOURCES: The original cast album on CD, cassette, and LP. Watch *The Maltese Falcon* to get a sense of *film noir*.

RIGHTS: Not set at press time.

DEAR WORLD

CREATORS: Book by Jerome Lawrence and Robert E. Lee, music and lyrics by Jerry Herman (the team that had recently collaborated on *Mame*).

BACKGROUND: The 1968 production was one of the first shows to postpone its Broadway opening umpteen times and play so many previews that theatergoers became suspicious about its worth—so it received more severe reviews and reaction than otherwise might have been. The show did receive two Tony nominations, winning one for its star, Angela Lansbury, and ran 132 performances.

STORY: Post-war Paris. A fanciful piece in which we meet Aurelia, the Madwoman of Chaillot. Once spurned by a man, she has since eccentrically spent much time at a cafe on the Left Bank of Paris. The cafe is threatened by "The President" and his evildoers who want to dislodge the valuable oil that's floating beneath it, and they enlist Julian, a young man with a troubled past, to plant a bomb there. But a deaf-mute prevents the scheme by knocking him out, and Julian's found by Nina, a lovely young lady. They fall in love, and Aurelia, remembering what it was to be young and in love, is charmed by them. Aurelia eventually makes certain that the enemies are destroyed—by tricking them into the sewers of Paris.

ASSETS: A very pretty score that showed another side of Herman's usually snazzy talent. The book is now more relevant than it was when the show opened, in that the president is involved in what amounts to a takeover. And it's often winsome (a garbageman complains that even garbage was once better than it is today).

LIABILITIES: How can a woman so out of touch with the world think she has an answer for every problem? Her anguish over her lost love makes her pathetic rather than sympathetic in our eyes. It's a fable, but audiences won't buy that the world's problems can be so easily remedied by simply tricking villians into a trap door and having them forever disappear. Is a woman who says, "Take the mouse out of the trap; I'm tired of feeding it," or "At each hour on the hour, all men's names automatically change," endearing or crazy? She seems to be hiding the truth from herself, and is conveniently schizophrenic.

WHO YOU'LL NEED: *Lead Singing Role:* The late-middle-aged and somewhat disheveled Madwoman of Chaillot (Angela Lansbury). *Supporting Singing Roles:* The equally eccentric Madwoman of the Flea Market; the more eccentric Madwoman of Montmarte, who is never without her invisible dog; a lovely young woman; the handsome young man who loves her; the town's chairman of the board, a prospector; a charming sewerman. *Other Roles:* A deaf-mute; a waiter; a doorman; a busboy; a juggler; a peddler. *Maximum,* 38; *minimum,* 22.

DESIGNATED DANCES: A "garbage dance" that occurs late in act one; a moment for a couple of tango dancers to shine.

SUGGESTED SETS: Most of the action is set in the Cafe Francis, so you should spend most of your dollars in making as pretty a French bistro as you can. Scene two occurs on the Seine riverbank, but you could use a scrim to obscure the cafe until you return to it in scene three. Build a turntable set, and you can then turn it around to show scene four's flea market—and act two, scene one's apartment where Aurelia lives. (Should you not want to do this, you'll still have ample time to set up Aurelia's apartment, for it appears only after intermission.) You might situate a heavily postered kiosk on one side of the stage for the opening scene, and then switch it to the other side for a subsequent scene. The second act also depends on a trap door device.

COSTUMES: From the not-fashionable, more bohemian Paris of yesteryear, long flowing dresses and gowns; boas; parasols; feather hats; gendarme costumes; expensive suits for the president and his staff; a miner's hat for the sewerman.

IMPORTANT PROPS: A chair on wheels to carry the villain around; a flower cart; a scooter; musical instruments and noisemakers for "One Person" number.

PROVIDED INSTRUMENTATION: Flute, two clarinets, oboe, two horns, two trumpets, trombone, violin, cello, bass, two guitars, percussion, drums, harp, concertina, two keyboards, piano-conductor.

ADVERTISING AND MARKETING: Considering that the title song tells about an ailing planet ("Someone has poisoned you, dear world . . . we're sick of having a sick world"), contact environmental-protection agencies and clubs, and ask them to sponsor a benefit, or do one for them.

SUGGESTIONS: Make Aurelia quietly mad, not adamant. Don't make her supercilious to those characters who (understandably) don't understand her. Avoid the tendency to make the villains nyah-hah-hah mustache twirlers. Send your cast into the auditorium for the rousing act one closer, "One person (can change the world)."

RESOURCES: The original cast album on CD, cassette, and LP; Jean Giraudoux's play *The Madwoman of Chaillot*, on which the musical is somewhat faithfully based and the 1969 movie version.

RIGHTS: Tams-Witmark.

EVITA

CREATORS: Book and lyrics by Tim Rice, music by Andrew Lloyd Webber (who collaborated on *Jesus Christ Superstar*).

BACKGROUND: The 1979 Broadway production was somewhat criticized for not being as strong as the London production from which it sprung, but audiences took to it, as did the Tony committee (eleven nominations, seven awards—including Best Musical), leading to a 1,567-performance run.

STORY: 1952 in Buenos Aires. On the day of Eva Peron's funeral, Che Guevara tells us about her life. She starts as Eva Duarte in rural Junin, seduces a nightclub singer, uses him to get to Buenos Aires, and works through men to become a model, broadcaster, and starlet. When she meets political comer Juan Peron, she attaches herself to him, to the consternation of the army and the aristocracy. She works on the lower classes to make certain they're behind her husband, and he wins the presidential election. That accomplished, she wants to enjoy Europe, and while Spain welcomes her, Italy and France don't, and she decides to avoid the previously scheduled England. She returns home, and supposedly works to help the lower classes, but most of her attempts are publicity stunts. While Peron's country is falling apart, so is Eva's health; she develops cancer and dies.

ASSETS: A riveting score with a satisfyingly theatrical and contemporary sound, and very few set demands. Nice parts into which your best young man and woman can sink their teeth.

LIABILITIES: A cold, hard-hitting, and seldom humorous show that offers many dark moments and precious few light ones. There's more music than in the average musical, meaning your cast has more to learn. (Don't forget that Patti LuPone found the role so difficult that she did not perform at matinees.)

RECOGNIZABLE SONGS: "Don't Cry for Me, Argentina."

WHO YOU'LL NEED: *Lead Singing Roles:* (Legit-voiced) Eva Peron (Patti LuPone), from a poverty-stricken girl of fifteen to a first lady at twenty-seven and invalid at thirty-three; Che Guevara, a radical who isn't reluctant to ask tough questions and who demands answers. *Supporting Singing Roles:* Eva's fat-cat and opportunistic husband; a smarmy nightclub singer; Peron's young mistress. *Other Roles:* A chorus of Argentinian citizens and children who play a myriad of roles. *Maximum, 37; minimum, 13.*

DESIGNATED DANCES: One production number for Eva and the Argentinians when she reaches Buenos Aires; another when the money keeps rolling in; some musical staging and marching in tempo on a few numbers.

SUGGESTED SETS: In and around Buenos Aires; the town square; a movie theater; a concert hall stage; Peron's flat and bedroom; on the balcony and inside of president's mansion; a tacky nightclub in a rural town.

COSTUMES: Late 1940s–early 1950s simple clothes for the underprivileged; formal clothes for the aristocracy; a dynamic gown and some glittering jewelry for Eva; fine bathrobes for her and Peron; military uniforms for the army and fatigues for Che; a South American nightclub outfit; a handsome fur stole and a more worn one.

IMPORTANT PROPS: Many political banners with Spanish slogans; a bevy of microphones; a battered suitcase.

SPECIAL EFFECTS: You can show the movie that the Argentinians are watching when Evita's death is announced.

PROVIDED INSTRUMENTATION: Flute, two clarinets, oboe, two horns, two trumpets, trombone, violin, cello, bass, two guitars, percussion, drums, harp, two keyboards, piano-conductor.

ADVERTISING AND MARKETING: "Evita seduced an entire nation. Can she seduce you? Come see, starting at . . ."

SUGGESTIONS: "Don't make Eva seem like a common tramp," advises Stan Barber, Artistic Director of the Pax Amicus Castle Theater in Budd Lake, New Jersey. "Make her a victim of not having options, as so few women had in those days. It makes the story that much stronger."

RESOURCES: The original cast album on CD, cassette, and LP. The 1981 TV movie *Evita Peron* with Faye Dunaway is also worth a look.

RIGHTS: Music Theatre International.

A FUNNY THING HAPPENED ON THE WAY TO THE FORUM

CREATORS: Book by Bert Shevelove (who directed the 1970 *No, No, Nanette*) and Larry (*City of Angels*) Gelbart, music and lyrics by Stephen (*Company*) Sondheim.

BACKGROUND: The 1962 production was dying during its out-of-town tryout, so Jerome Robbins came in to help director George Abbott; among his most important suggestions was to have an opening number that would let people unquestionably know they were seeing a comedy. Sondheim wrote "Comedy Tonight," which set the correct tone, and led to eight Tony nominations, six awards, and a 964-performance run.

STORY: Pseudolus, a slave in ancient Rome, will do *anything* to win his freedom—including prying a young virgin from her protector and the great warrior to whom she is promised because his young master has fallen in love with her from afar. Pseudolus lies, cheats, and bargains—nimbly and brilliantly—and wins the virgin for his master and freedom for himself.

ASSETS: A one-set show, a witty script that may be bawdy but is never vulgar (when you consider what "a purveyor of flesh" could have been called, it's a euphemism); in fact, for ancient Romans, the characters are pretty civilized.

LIABILITIES: Some audiences might be offended by the show's attitude toward women and its freewheeling sexuality that pervades the piece (though a recent production at Massachusetts's Concord-Carlisle High School brought down the house when one courtesan went wild wielding her whip). But in this age of AIDS, there is one sad note: When Pseudolus attempts to get the virgin from the pimp, he lies that she has the plague; once upon a time a straight line such as "Is it contagious?" answered by "Did you ever see a plague that wasn't?" was funny, but not now.

RECOGNIZABLE SONGS: "Comedy Tonight."

WHO YOU'LL NEED: *Lead Singing Roles:* An uninhibited, wily slave (Zero Mostel, or a Gene Wilder type). *Supporting Singing Roles:* His old henpecked master and battleaxe mistress; their innocent young adult son; a virginal young woman; a faithful and frantic servant; a very old distraught man whose eyesight is almost a memory; a "man-among-men" warrior; a "buyer and seller of courtesans." *Other Roles:* Six most bea-u-tiful courtesans; three "proteans"— "who," states the script, "do the work of 30." *Maximum, 25; minimum, 17.*

DESIGNATED DANCES: A bit of soft-shoe for the showstopping "Everybody Ought to Have a Maid"; some stylized steps (and bumps and grinds) for the courtesans when they're shown to a customer; a march for the soldiers. The chase sequence is virtually choreographed, too.

SUGGESTED SETS: The exterior of three houses (one should have a functional balcony) on a street in ancient Rome.

COSTUMES: Gowns and togas; wigs; laurel wreaths; provocatively skimpy outfits for the courtesans; three identical (and gauzy) female outfits for mistaken identity purposes.

IMPORTANT PROPS: A curtain that drops to the floor; an artificial leg; a ladder; juggling balls; a gong; money bags; cups of potions; a potion book; daggers; spears; vials; rings; baggage; parchments; flowers; a plaster bust of a woman.

PROVIDED INSTRUMENTATION: Five reeds, three trumpets, three trombones, percussion, three violins, viola, cello, bass, harp, two drums.

ADVERTISING AND MARKETING: "If the rest of Rome was anything like this, no wonder it declined and fell. Come see *A Funny Thing* . . ."

SUGGESTIONS: Given that the three "proteans" do the work of thirty, if you're looking to give a number of small parts to a number of people, you can find some here.

RESOURCES: The original cast album on CD, cassette, and LP. The (somewhat faithful) 1966 movie on videotape and laserdisc; the Roman comedies of Plautus from which the musical was adapted—including one called *Mostellaria*, most ironic since centuries later, Zero Mostel was the show's original leading man; a "Rehearscore" disc for Macintosh and IBM systems that eliminates the need for a rehearsal pianist.

RIGHTS: Music Theatre International.

A LITTLE NIGHT MUSIC

CREATORS: Book by Hugh Wheeler, music and lyrics by Stephen Sondheim (who later collaborated on *Sweeney Todd*).

BACKGROUND: The 1973 musical opened to very good reviews, received twelve Tony nominations, won six awards—including Best Musical—and ran 600 performances.

STORY: Middle-aged Fredrik, who has a grown son Henrik, has chosen Anne as his second wife. She is young—so young that even now, nearly a year after the wedding, she remains a virgin. This tempts Fredrik to seek out his old love, actress Desirée, who takes pity on his plight and is ready to bed him—when her current lover Carl-Magnus bursts upon the scene, and does not quite buy the innocent excuses Fredrik and Desirée give him. Carl-Magnus sends his own wife, Charlotte, to tell Anne of Fredrik's visit to Desirée. Anne is distraught, especially when Desirée convinces her mother, Madame Armfeldt, to invite Fredrik, Anne, and Henrik for a weekend in the country. When Carl-Magnus hears of it, he decides to go there as well. By the end of the play, Charlotte has tried to seduce Fredrik, Anne has run off with Henrik, and Fredrik has reunited with Desirée, the woman he's loved all along.

ASSETS: As Clive Barnes in the *New York Times* noted, "Good God—an adult operetta." Indeed; a charming score and witty book make for a most tasteful evening.

LIABILITIES: This is a highly elegant show, dealing with a strata of upper-crust society that could be alien to much of your audience. The music demands better voices than the average musical and is not easy to learn.

RECOGNIZABLE SONGS: "Send in the Clowns."

WHO YOU'LL NEED: *Lead Singing Roles:* A once-renowned but still-working actress. *Supporting Singing Roles:* Her not-so-innocent teenage daughter; her once-sensual but now profane mother; her long-ago lawyer-lover; his nubile (soprano) young wife; his pent-up adolescent son; a cocksure (baritone) dragoon; his long-suffering and demoralized wife (a Swoosie Kurtz type); two middle-aged maids; one precocious, sexually free younger maid. *Other Roles:* a butler; a (legit-voiced) chorus of two men and three women—or more. *Maximum,* 27; *minimum,* 17.

DESIGNATED DANCES: Three waltzes for everyone: one that opens the show; one in the middle of act two; one that closes the show. Some musical staging on the act one closer.

SUGGESTED SETS: Parlor and master bedroom with vanity table and bed; a local theater with stage boxes; Desirée's apartment with loveseat, dressing room screen, and hip bath; a country manse exterior, its master bedroom, its breakfast room, its dining room with a very long table and eight chairs, and its terrace, lawn, gardens, and neighboring birch-treed forest.

COSTUMES: Turn-of-the-century Scandinavian upper-class finery; negligees, nightshirts, nightcaps, nightgowns, and robes; parasols; fur pieces; a military uniform. "Don't kill yourself trying to get all-white costumes for the act one finale," urges David N. Matthews, Artistic Director of the Erie Playhouse. "They'll turn out to be different shades of whites and even creams."

IMPORTANT PROPS: Wheelchair; wigbox, suitcases; silver cigarette box; ball of silk; deck of cards; champagne bottles and flutes; trays with silverware and pitchers; candelabra and floral pieces; a sopping wet and balled-up suit; classical statues; croquet equipment; an onstage piano and cello. The original production included two automobiles for both couples' arrival at the country manse, but you could just have them walk on.

SPECIAL EFFECTS: A knife-throwing trick.

PROVIDED INSTRUMENTATION: Five reeds, three horns, two trumpets, trombone, percussion, celeste (piano), harp, three violins, viola, cello, bass, piano-conductor.

ADVERTISING AND MARKETING: "Send in your ticket requests for the 'Send in the Clowns' musical."

SUGGESTIONS: Play it light and with an airy quality; it is, after all, a musical souffle.

RESOURCES: The original cast album on CD, cassette, and LP; the somewhat faithful 1978 movie on videotape and laserdisc; the 1990 televised New York City Opera production; *Smiles of a Summer Night*, the movie on which the musical was fairly faithfully based; a "Rehearscore" disc for Macintosh and IBM systems that eliminates the need for a rehearsal pianist.

RIGHTS: Music Theatre International.

110 IN THE SHADE

CREATORS: Book by N. Richard Nash (based on his play *The Rainmaker*), music by Harvey Schmidt, lyrics by Tom Jones (who collaborated on *The Fantasticks*).

BACKGROUND: The 1963 production was one of many David Merrick musicals that year, and after this musical received decent reviews—and his *Hello, Dolly!* opened to exceptional ones—he lost interest in promoting it, and it closed after 330 performances.

STORY: Plain Lizzie's father and two brothers, Jimmy and Noah, worry that she's going to be an old maid because she shows her brainpower to men. This intelligence, though, allows Lizzie to see through Starbuck, the self-proclaimed "rainmaker" who comes to town and convinces everyone he can relieve the drought they're enduring. He also turns out to be the man that File, the local sheriff, is looking to arrest as a con man. File has been somewhat attracted to Lizzie, but he's been smarting from his wife's leaving him. Starbuck's attention and wooing of Lizzie, through which he convinces her she is desirable, however, galvanizes File to action, and by curtain's end, she has both men vying for her hand—and chooses the safe, reliable sheriff.

ASSETS: A glorious score and a solid book, with a final scene that will bring tears of joy to many watching the born loser who could never get a man suddenly having two from which to choose.

LIABILITIES: Lizzie's songs, written for a high soprano, can seem off-puttingly syrupy, but worse is the idea stressed through the show that a woman should fear remaining single. Contemporary audiences may well ask, "Why does she think she's nothing without a man?"

WHO YOU'LL NEED: *Lead Singing Role:* A strong soprano who is prettier than she thinks. *Supporting Singing Roles:* Her father who means well; her two brothers (one dumb, one no-nonsense); an attractive and slick con man (a Scott Bakula type); a moody but sensitive sheriff; a young female flibberti-gibbet. *Other Roles:* Cowboys; their wives and girlfriends. *Maximum, 28; Minimum, 13.*

DESIGNATED DANCES: Not much—because it's so hot that nobody much feels like dancing. The brothers and father have a few excited steps when Lizzie returns from a trip; the second act opening has a few ballet steps and a quick waltz; and Jimmy and his flibbertigibbet girlfriend have some excited steps.

SUGGESTED SETS: A open stretch of western land (wagon wheels, a western windmill, bales of hay); a train depot; the sheriff's office; a park with picnic tables; a modest western house.

COSTUMES: Western wear for men (vests, jeans, overalls, work pants, suspenders, bandanas, cowboy hats) and women (gingham dresses, aprons, a little red hat).

IMPORTANT PROPS: Cisterns; jugs; buckets; milk cans; picnic baskets; cakes; quilts and Indian blankets; hand fans to ward off the heat; fly swatters; a big bass drum and drumsticks; a can of white paint; lanterns; bags of feed; suitcases; umbrellas for the finale.

SPECIAL EFFECTS: A few firecracker effects; thunder and lightning—but your biggest challenge will be providing the rain that pours down at the end of the show.

PROVIDED INSTRUMENTATION: Five reeds, three horns, two trumpets, trombone, percussion, piano-celeste, harp, three violins, viola, cello, bass, piano-conductor.

ADVERTISING AND MARKETING: "No matter what the weatherman tells you, we're predicting that it'll be *110 in the Shade* next [week, weekend, month]—at least at [name of theater] . . ."

SUGGESTIONS: If you don't have the wherewithal to replicate the rain shower, have a tinsel curtain come down to represent the downpour. And if you don't want to build (or can't get) Starbuck's bright painted wagon for his big entrance, you can simply have him walk on, as he did in the 1992 New York City Opera production, and later change the lyric for Lizzie, from "You ride on your bright painted wagon," to "You ride into town like a cyclone."

RESOURCES: The original cast album on CD, cassette, and LP; N. Richard Nash's nonmusical play The Rainmaker in script and a (very faithful) 1956 movie version of *The Rainmaker* on videotape.

RIGHTS: Tams-Witmark.

Also See: *The Apple Tree; Company; The Cradle Will Rock; Do I Hear a Waltz?; How to Succeed in Business Without Really Trying; I Love My Wife; Little Shop of Horrors; The 1940's Radio Hour; No Strings; Pump Boys and Dinettes; Purlie; 1776; The Sound of Music; Sunday in the Park with George; Sweeney Todd, The Demon Barber of Fleet Street; They're Playing Our Song; Two by Two.*

"MEN!"

Musicals with Predominantly Male Casts

"Men!" complained Susan Johnson in *Whoop-up* (a 1958 flop musical we're *not* advising be revived), "tell them the truth, and they're off in a cloud of dust."

"At my school," said Peter Atlas of Concord-Carlisle (Massachusetts) Regional High School, "they're always around. I have many more boys trying out than girls." Maybe it's something in Concord's water (or its grapes)—or maybe it also happens in your town. Or maybe you're like the Worcester (Massachusetts) Firefighters Association, which every year has its firefighters do a show to benefit the relatives of those who have perished in the line of duty.

Whatever the case, if you have an abundance of men who are ready and willing to sing and dance, here are some musicals that will afford everyone a part.

THE BOYS FROM SYRACUSE

CREATORS: Book by George Abbott, music by Richard Rodgers, lyrics by Lorenz Hart (who all collaborated on *On Your Toes*).

BACKGROUND: The 1938 production ran a very-good-for-its-era 235 performances, and a movie was made, but *Boys* was pretty much forgotten until a 1963 off-Broadway revival ran 502 performances and reminded audiences just how much fun the musical was.

STORY: Ancient Greece. Antipholus of Ephesus has a slave named Dromio; Antipholus of Syracuse does, too. Though they are two sets of twins, neither knows of the other, and when the boys from Syracuse visit Ephesus, there is an evening of mistaken identity: Antipholus of Ephesus has grown bored with his wife, Adriana, but when she mistakenly confronts Antipholus of Syracuse, he does nothing to discourage the error—all the while really falling in love with Luciana, Adriana's sister. Finally the long-lost father of both Antipholuses shows up and sets things right, and all ends happily.

ASSETS: A fine score, and a still funny book with many juicy lines ("I wonder where people in hell tell each other to go"). A very democratic musical to mount, in that almost everyone has a moment to shine.

LIABILITIES: To really do it right, you'd have to have two sets of identical twins—one set handsome, one set comic—for if you cast two pairs of people who can easily be told apart, your audiences will lose respect for the characters' inability to figure out the mistaken identity. (Actually, they might anyway; this is a show where at least one of the four characters should say midway through act one, "Ohhhhh, I'll bet there's someone who looks just like me . . .")

RECOGNIZABLE SONGS: "This Can't Be Love," "Falling in Love with Love."

WHO YOU'LL NEED: *Lead Singing Roles:* Two tall identical-looking virile (baritone) men, two shorter identical-looking comic men who are their slaves; a sexually frustrated slave's wife; a forlorn well-born (soprano) wife; her charming (soprano) sister. *Supporting Singing Roles:* A duke; a sergeant; a goldsmith; a courtesan. *Other Roles:* A miserable wretch, a sorcerer; a tailor; a corporal; a merchant; his apprentice; five courtesans; three maids; three Amazons; two merchants. *Maximum,* 30; *minimum,* 20.

DESIGNATED DANCES: A pantomime dance for "Falling in Love with Love"; some steps for the courtesans' entrance; an act one finale ballet; a joyous dance for the brothers; some jitterbug steps for "Sing for Your Supper"—"which," notes Charles Fontana, who's directed the show for the armed forces, "has two encores written into the score. Make sure your rendition merits them."

SUGGESTED SETS: A town square; inside a lofty house; inside a brothel; a street outside.

COSTUMES: Tunics with pleated skirts; men's Roman gowns; shoulder drapes; burlap pantlegs; cloaks and hoods; women's gowns; Grecian dresses; aprons; wizard's outfit; courtesans' costumes; sandals; bobby helmet.

IMPORTANT PROPS: Herald trumpets; money bags; embroidery hoops; arm and leg chains; buckets; feather dusters; bowl of fruit; wine jugs and goblets; mallet and chisel; crystal ball; execution ax; police clubs and whistles.

SPECIAL EFFECTS: Smoke; magic tricks for the sorcerer (disappearing cane and handkerchief).

PROVIDED INSTRUMENTATION: Three reeds, two trumpets, trombone, percussion, two violins, cello, bass, harp, piano, piano-conductor.

ADVERTISING AND MARKETING: A twins-get-in-for-one-admission night is a must. In your community, are there any famous graduates from Syracuse University? Invite them to opening night, and get a local reporter to do a story on them and you.

SUGGESTIONS: "If the Dromios aren't good dancers," says Paul C. Norton, Associate Professor of Theatre Arts at Bay Path College in Longmeadow, Massachusetts, "stage their ballet as a Marx-Brothers-in-*Duck Soup* mirror movement."

RESOURCES: The 1963 off-Broadway cast album on CD, cassette, and LP; the 1940 (fairly faithful) movie; Shakespeare's A *Comedy of Errors*, on which the musical is based.

RIGHTS: Rodgers and Hammerstein.

DAMN YANKEES

CREATORS: Book by George Abbott and Douglass Wallopp, music and lyrics by Richard Adler and Jerry Ross (Abbott, Adler, and Ross had collaborated on *The Pajama Game*).

BACKGROUND: Less than a year after *The Pajama Game* opened, this new show by most of that hit's collaborators opened to fine reviews and settled in for a 1,019-performance run. One can only wish and wonder where Broadway would be today had Ross not died that winter.

STORY: 1950s, Washington, DC. Joe Boyd, a rabid fan of the woebegone Washington Senators baseball team, says he'll sell his soul to the devil to see his team beat the New York Yankees. Soon Mr. Applegate (read: the Devil) shows up to give him his wish, and sends a revitalized and renamed Joe Hardy to play on the Senators. But Joe discovers that the love of the wife he left behind is more important to him than seeing his team win the pennant. Not even Lola, Applegate's best temptress, can deter Joe from returning home, prompting Applegate to start rumors that Joe's really a banned Mexican League player. Lola, impressed with Joe's love for his wife, works against her boss, and good triumphs over evil by curtain's fall.

ASSETS: A zippy score and a book with a fascinating story line, with not too much inside baseball talk and terminology to distract nonfans. Many chances for your less talented and out-of-shape men to have big roles as ballplayers without looking awkward.

LIABILITIES: There are too many short scenes in the second act, and with all the set changing that it necessitates, the show often slows to a crawl. It's understandable why the movie chose to ignore Joe's two ballads. And it's sad that in the first scene Joe and his wife don't have more in common so we could really root for their getting back together.

RECOGNIZABLE SONGS: "(You Gotta Have) Heart," "Whatever Lola Wants," "Two Lost Souls."

WHO YOU'LL NEED: *Lead Singing Roles:* A devil of a song-and-dance man, his favorite homewrecker (Gwen Verdon), a superstar ballplayer. *Supporting Singing Roles:* A middle-aged overweight man (able to touch his toes, though); his wife; her sister (Jean Stapleton) and her best friend; a baseball manager; his five best ballplayers; a female two-sports reporter. *Other Roles:* The team's owner; the baseball commissioner; a postmaster; a guard; a male sports reporter; a teenage girl; two children; a chorus of baseball fans and nightclub denizens. *Maximum, 40; minimum, 26.*

DESIGNATED DANCES: Two solo spots for Lola; a mambo for her and a chorus boy; a number for her, Joe, and nightclub denizens; a soft-shoe and a hoedown for the ballplayers; much musical staging.

SUGGESTED SETS: A suburban-style home; around the offices, locker room, and dugout of Washington's Griffith Stadium; a hotel ballroom; the devil's garish apartment; a nightclub; the stately office of the baseball commissioner.

COSTUMES: 1950s street clothes and housedresses; a bathrobe; an exotic, erotic outfit for the devil's temptress; mambo costumes; formal dress wear; a team's worth of numbered Washington Senators uniforms, spiked shoes, and shin pads; a suit, red tie, and robe fit for a prince, for the Devil.

IMPORTANT PROPS: A black-and-white television; baseball gloves, bats and balls; hand fans.

SPECIAL EFFECTS: The Devil does have the ability to create a matchstick's worth of fire without benefit of match. Your transformation of Joes must be efficiently handled.

PROVIDED INSTRUMENTATION: Five reeds, two trumpets, three trombones, horn, four violins, viola, cello, bass, piano.

ADVERTISING AND MARKETING: "People called them the *Damn Yankees* long before Steinbrenner owned them. We'll show you why, in our production of *Damn Yankees*, opening on . . ."

SUGGESTIONS: While the Washington Senators for whom Joe Hardy sold his soul to the devil no longer exist, you may very well have a team in your region that is as woefully unsuccessful, be it major (Cleveland Indians) or minor. If so, ask the licensers if you might add some local color to your production by changing the team from the Senators to your town's also-rans.

RESOURCES: The original cast album on CD, cassette, and LP; the fairly faithful 1958 movie on videotape and laserdisc; Douglass Wallopp's novel *The Year the Yankees Lost the Pennant*, on which the musical is fairly faithfully based; study guides.

RIGHTS: Music Theatre International.

PAGEANT

CREATORS: Book and lyrics by Frank Kelly and Bill Russell, music by Albert Evans.

BACKGROUND: The 1991 off-Broadway production played a supper club, and stayed there for 441 performances.

STORY: Six male actors play female contestants—Miss Industrial Northeast, Miss Bible Belt, Miss Texas, Miss Deep South, Miss West Coast, and Miss Coastal Plain—all vie for the honor of becoming this year's Miss Glamouresse. At each pageant, five judges from the audience make their decision, and whoever is the people's choice is that night's winner.

ASSETS: A good enough score, sure, but a fantastic idea, very wittily done. (Miss Industrial Northeast is up front about not having "the luxury of a formal education"; Miss Texas generously spends time "working with the beauty-impaired.")

LIABILITIES: Your men must be convincing women—which is not an easy job. "It's not the piece of cardboard that hides your masculinity that does a man in," moans David LeDuca, who played all roles during much of the New York run. "It's that constantly standing and dancing on high heels."

WHO YOU'LL NEED: *Lead Singing Roles:* Seven men—one glitzy, pompadoured emcee, along with six contestants who can convincingly pass for women. One must play the accordion *and* roller-skate; one must be able to sing gospel and ring cowbells with his teeth; one must be able to twirl a rope; one must be a ventriloquist. (While the original company used the contestant who finished sixth to go offstage and then double as last year's Miss Glamouresse, you could cast two different men in these roles.) *Maximum,* 8; *minimum,* 7.

DESIGNATED DANCES: An opening number, two production numbers that involve little fancy footwork, and some roller-skating as well.

SUGGESTED SETS: Standard beauty pageant tinseled curtains; a mock-up of a spaceship; a booth in which the contestants can give their testimonials. The original production used pink and white as its theme and carried it through the sets.

COSTUMES: A sequined tux for your emcee; swimsuits, evening gowns, sashes with their titles, and beauty smocks for the contestants.

IMPORTANT PROPS: Because *Pageant* is sponsored by the mythical Glamouresse Beauty Company, there are fictitious products endorsed—such as Glamouresse Facial Spackle. So you'll need a tub that allegedly contains the goo, as well as an enormous powder puff; a hand-held vacuum cleaner; large hair rollers; a big aerosol hair spray can; jangly bracelets. Add to these a ventriloquist's dummy; a telephone; a bouquet of roses for the winner; signs the contestants can wear on their backs on which their judges' totals can be written and tallied.

PROVIDED INSTRUMENTATION: Four-piece piano combo.

ADVERTISING AND MARKETING: Let it be known that your first-row or ringside customers are given the responsibility of judging the pageant—and that you'll take reservations in advance for those who want to judge; you'll get some advance ticket sales that way.

SUGGESTIONS: Someday someone will produce *Pageant* with women in the roles—and audiences will enjoy it as the good parody of beauty pageants that it is.

RESOURCES: No cast album.

RIGHTS: Not set at press time.

PAINT YOUR WAGON

CREATORS: Book and lyrics by Alan Jay Lerner, music by Frederick Loewe (the authors of *My Fair Lady*).

BACKGROUND: The 1951 production had its troubles out of town, rectified them somewhat, opened to okay reviews, and ran 289 performances.

STORY: The California wilderness, 1853. Ben Rumson's daughter Jennifer finds gold on their land, and soon the town is named Rumson. Four hundred men arrive, many of whom have their eyes on Jennifer, the town's only woman. But she has great sympathy for Julio, who, because he's a Mexican, isn't welcomed by the other miners; she even offers to do his laundry. The other miners want Jennifer sent away, and Rumson is about to do just that when Jacob, a Mormon, arrives with Sarah and Elizabeth, his two wives. Since the town's got a woman shortage and Jacob has a surplus, he sells Elizabeth to

Ben for five hundred dollars. Jennifer is disgusted by this and runs away. A year later, Elizabeth is interested in rich miner Edgar Crocker, though Ben doesn't know it yet. Julio, having been discouraged by Jennifer's leaving, decides to prospect an area from which few have come back alive. Meanwhile, the town of Rumson is no longer yielding gold, and most miners have left for other places. Jennifer arrives home, much the educated and sophisticated lady after a stint at a finishing school, looking for Julio. He's eventually found, and Ben sells his wife (though she runs off with Edgar before the transaction can be completed), and heads for a new part of the country where he again hopes to strike gold.

ASSETS: A score that's beautiful and stirring, and some meaty parts for your lustiest and burliest actors.

LIABILITIES: A plot-heavy book that seems to have twists and turns for their own sake. The buying and selling of wives might have been funny once upon a time, but it no longer is. You'd think that Julio would go after Jennifer, not gold.

RECOGNIZABLE SONGS: "I Talk to the Trees," "They Call the Wind Maria."

WHO YOU'LL NEED: *Lead Singing Roles:* A crusty but adorable miner (Lee Marvin); his at first innocent but then sophisticated young daughter; the (tenor-voiced) Mexican miner who loves her. *Supporting Singing Roles:* An introspective miner (who should play banjo); a prospector and the fancy girl who loves him in her fashion; a doctor. *Other Roles:* A Mormon and his two wives, one of whom is feisty, the other more demure; a most pecunious miner; a savvy and experienced miner; a merchant; a saloon owner; a dude; a chorus of miners and fandango girls. *Maximum, 46; minimum, 20.*

DESIGNATED DANCES: A rousing opening; two more production numbers of standard Western influence; some square dancing and some can-can from the fandango girls.

SUGGESTED SETS: A Northern California hilltop; outside a general store; inside and outside Rumson's cabin; a saloon; inside Julio's cabin; digging sites; the town square.

COSTUMES: Forty-niners outfits; plaid shirts, overalls, and boots for the men; gingham dresses for Jennifer; Old West showgirl costumes for the fandango girls; severe black outfits for the Mormons; a lovely dress for someone who's just been to a finishing school.

IMPORTANT PROPS: A stagecoach; gold sacks; picks and axes; liquor bottles and glasses; bundles of laundry.

PROVIDED INSTRUMENTATION: Four reeds, horn, three trumpets, two trombones, two percussion, two guitars, two violins, two cellos, bass, electric piano, piano-conductor.

ADVERTISING AND MARKETING: If you have an old station wagon, or even a horse-drawn wagon, maybe now's the time to carefully paint it with all the information about your show, and let your cast members take turns driving and displaying it around town.

SUGGESTIONS: "Don't be surprised if the script Tams-Witmark sends you seems very different from your original cast album," advises John Pike, archivist for the Goodspeed Opera House in East Haddam, Connecticut. "The script is the revised version that Lerner readied for the post-Broadway national tour."

RESOURCES: The original cast album on CD, cassette, and LP; the barely faithful 1968 movie version on videotape and laserdisc.

RIGHTS: Tams-Witmark.

PROMISES, PROMISES

CREATORS: Book by Neil Simon (*The Goodbye Girl*), music by Burt (*Butch Cassidy and the Sundance Kid*) Bacharach, lyrics by Hal ("Do You Know the Way to San Jose?") David.

BACKGROUND: The 1968 production was in great shape its first weekend in Boston, opened to strong reviews, received eight Tony nominations, won two awards, and ran 1,281 performances.

STORY: 1960s, New York City. Chuck Baxter is an accountant who'd like to get ahead, so he allows his superiors to use his apartment to romance their mistresses. From afar, he loves Fran Kubelik, a cafeteria worker who is being taken to his apartment by Chuck's boss, Mr. Sheldrake. Baxter is temporarily disillusioned when he learns of Fran's trysts, but stays in love with her. She attempts suicide but survives and discards the powerful Sheldrake in favor of the more sensitive Baxter.

ASSETS: A rarity—the witty movie that was made better in a musical incarnation, and not only because it had a sound that Broadway had never heard—there was even a vocal quartet in the pit—but also because Neil Simon has Baxter address us directly and take us into his confidence; it's a terrific device that works charmingly. Here's a show about tired businessmen that doesn't pander to the tired businessman.

LIABILITIES: The idea that a woman in a liaison wouldn't go to a hotel is long gone. But more significantly, because the show has characters that sleep around and think nothing of it, the story has dated somewhat in this age of AIDS. (Lines about "raving sexpots" and rape don't help.)

RECOGNIZABLE SONGS: "Promises, Promises," "I'll Never Fall in Love Again," "Christmas Day," which has even had a few recordings as a holiday song.

WHO YOU'LL NEED: *Lead Singing Roles:* A charming but ambitious (baritone) accountant; a too-much-in-love (mezzo) waif. *Supporting Singing Roles:* A disapproving doctor; an icy personnel manager; a mortgage executive, a public relations man; a research executive, a claims investigator; an accounts receivable clerk; a mimeographer; a petty cash clerk; a barhopping woman looking for love. *Other Roles:* A bitter secretary, a sophisticated wife; a beefy brother; a telephone operator; a tootsie; a bartender; a waiter and waitress, a company doctor and nurse. *Maximum, 44; minimum, 21.*

DESIGNATED DANCES: A solo dance for Baxter; an all-out office party; a slow fox-trot for Baxter and the barhopper; a mock-dance for Baxter and the doctor; the illusion of people dancing while crammed together on a small dance floor.

SUGGESTED SETS: Offices (both lower-level glass cubicles and executive offices); an elevator bank; a lobby; the executive dining room; a Chinese restaurant; Madison Square Garden marquee; a seedy bar and a trendy one; a brownstone exterior and a modest apartment inside.

COSTUMES: Work clothes for men and women, including power suits for executives; restaurant worker uniforms; a London Fog raincoat; a gray homburg.

IMPORTANT PROPS: Office furniture, reclining chairs; Christmas decorations, a small tree, and a cardboard fireplace; a phone booth; a phonograph; a thermometer; an adding machine; a lady's compact; restaurant tables and chairs, a sundeck chaise; modest apartment furniture; a folding screen; empty liquor and milk bottles; a champagne bottle capable of making a loud shooting sound when popped; doctor's bag with stethoscope.

SPECIAL EFFECTS: Thunder and lightning.

PROVIDED INSTRUMENTATION: Four reeds, horn, three trumpets, two trombones, two percussion, two guitars, two violins, two cellos, bass, electric piano, piano-conductor.

ADVERTISING AND MARKETING: "Our *Promises, Promises* has a lot of promise. We promise. Promise us you'll come. If you don't, we promise you'll regret it."

SUGGESTIONS: Because of the aforementioned dated quality of a script that was written pre–sexual revolution and pre-AIDS, keep the show set in the late 1960s.

RESOURCES: The original cast album on cassette and LP; the 1960 movie *The Apartment*, on which the musical is (very faithfully) based.

RIGHTS: Tams-Witmark.

THE ROAR OF THE GREASEPAINT—THE SMELL OF THE CROWD

CREATORS: Book, music, and lyrics by Leslie Bricusse and Anthony Newley (who had recently collaborated on *Stop the World—I Want to Get Off*).

BACKGROUND: The 1965 production had already been produced for London, but shuttered during tryouts. The authors went back to work and mounted the show for America, where during the multi-city tryout, things seemed to be going so well that the album was recorded and released. But the show's reviews were only so-so, and of its six Tony nominations, it won none, and shuttered after 232 performances.

STORY: Power and the abuse of it, done symbolically and allegorically, with no time or place implied. Sir, representing the establishment, and Cocky, representing the downtrodden, continue to play The Game of Life. Sir always wins, so Cocky revolts—but is drawn back into the game when the new prize is a lovely young woman. She likes Cocky, but ultimately goes with Sir because he has more money. Cocky tries prayer, but when that brings no results, he takes out his displaced hostility by oppressing a black man—and wins for the first time. Sir, meanwhile, realizing that he needs Cocky to play the game, makes a few concessions and the two continue. The moral: The strong need the weak as much as the weak need the strong.

ASSETS: What a score—probably the last show to have not one, not two, not three, but *four* songs that much of the country had heard and liked before the show even opened. An inexpensive show to do, one for which whatever you have hanging around for costumes and sets might very well work.

LIABILITIES: A pretty banal book; saying that the downtrodden shouldn't be harassed is preaching to the already-convinced. (But if you feel your audience could use a little reminding...)

RECOGNIZABLE SONGS: "A Wonderful Day Like Today," "The Joker," "Who Can I Turn To (When Nobody Needs Me)?" "Feeling Good."

WHO YOU'LL NEED: *Lead Singing Roles:* A tyrannical buffoon; a meek and mild stooge (a Michael J. Fox type). *Supporting Singing Roles:* A smart-ass tomboy; a lovely ingenue; a gentle black man. *Other Roles:* A menacingly gigantic bully; a chorus of girls, or boys and girls, or young adults—or whatever you have. *Maximum, 21, Minimum, 6.*

DESIGNATED DANCES: For the kids, an opening strut; a Dixieland dance; a hat-and-cane number for Sir and Cocky; much musical staging throughout.

SUGGESTED SETS: A unit set of bleachers will work. "Or," says Christopher Catt, Artistic Director of St. Bart's Players in New York, "use a checkerboard motif—a checkerboard cyclorama, the stage painted as a giant checker-gameboard. Or simulate another kids' game, Chutes and Ladders."

COSTUMES: Glorified rags and ragged hats for most everyone.

IMPORTANT PROPS: A necklace full of religious and lucky charms (a crucifix, Star of David, four-leaf clovers, rabbits' feet, etc.) In fact, how about a small breakfast-sized box of Lucky Charms?

PROVIDED INSTRUMENTATION: Four reeds, horn, three trumpets, two trombones, two percussion, two guitars, two violins, two cellos, bass, electric piano, piano-conductor.

ADVERTISING AND MARKETING: "You'd expect a show with this title to be unusual, wouldn't you? Well—it is!"

SUGGESTIONS: Check with the licensers and see if they'll let you change Cocky's name. After all, if he's so meek, mild, and under Sir's thumb, the one thing he isn't is *cocky*. (His name is never used as a rhyme, so you don't have to worry about that.)

"This is a good show to experiment with various styles," says Catt. "I've had Cocky costumed as a harlequin, and it's worked very well."

RESOURCES: The original cast album on CD, cassette, and LP.

RIGHTS: Tams-Witmark.

THE ROTHSCHILDS

CREATORS: Book by Sherman Yellen, music by Jerry Bock, lyrics by Sheldon Harnick (Bock and Harnick collaborated on *Fiddler on the Roof*).

BACKGROUND: The 1970 production received decent reviews and nine Tony nominations, winning two awards for its leading and supporting actors, and ran 505 performances.

STORY: Meyer Rothschild, a Jew living in a walled-in German ghetto in 1772, understandibly seethes in anger every time schoolchildren taunt him, "Jew, do your duty!"—meaning that he must doff his hat and bow low to them. He knows that only money can change this situation so he sets out to get it, though his wife Gutele doesn't see the grand scope of his design. She does provide him with five sons, who are first his assistants in a coin business, then his business partners; soon they're loaning money to the prince, then to his cousin, the King of Denmark. But then Napoleon vanquishes the prince, and an aging Rothschild knows he'll have a difficult time getting back his loans. He instead sends the sons to various European cities to retrieve them and to continue in the banking business. Oldest son Nathan in London makes an almost critical yet understandable banking mistake, but he's soon the city's most successful trader—though he does take time out to meet, woo, and marry Hannah. He's soon approached by Prince Metternich to lend money to fight Napoleon, and agrees—if the Prince will lift his restrictions on the Jews and give them equal justice in the eyes of the law. Metternich agrees, Napoleon is destroyed—but the prince reneges on his promise. Meyer dies, but the sons make sure he does not die in vain: They work to undersell the bonds that the prince sells; it means risking their fortune, but they win and are accepted in court, and each is given the title of baron. At curtain's fall, court members doff their hats and bow low to them.

ASSETS: A musical about moneymaking would be a bore if we only had to root for people fattening their bankbooks, but the Rothschilds had greater aims, which is why it's such a good musical—not to mention a marvelous score.

LIABILITIES: A musical where two styles of costumes and sets—elegant and poverty-stricken—are necessary, thus doubling the costs. The second-act love story seems to be there simply because most musicals have a love story. And losing the powerhouse Meyer to old age in the second act is a shame.

WHO YOU'LL NEED: *Lead Singing Roles:* A won't-take-no-for-an-answer dynamic trader-salesman who ages into a patriarch (Hal Linden). *Supporting Singing Roles:* His easily satisfied but ultimately understanding (soprano) wife; five young sons and five counterparts as young men; a tender young woman who works for charity and marries a Rothschild; an unsympathetic ransom-taker; three vendors; three bankers. *Other Roles:* The humane Prince William of Hesse; his secretary; King Christian of Denmark; the imperious Prince Metternich; a general; a skeptic; a guard; three taunting Gentile schoolchildren; a chorus of store customers; court members, stockbrokers, and citizens. *Maximum, 46; minimum, 15.*

DESIGNATED DANCES: Court minuets; a joyous romp for Meyer and his sons after the prince allows them access to the King of Denmark; some musical staging.

SUGGESTED SETS: A grand European ballroom; the streets of the Frankfurt ghetto; in and around the Rothschild home; the London stock market; a treaty room in Aix-la-Chapelle.

COSTUMES: Late-18th-century wear, formal and elegant for the privileged, ragged and worn for other citizens; traditional Jewish garb (black hats and robes); courtier uniforms.

IMPORTANT PROPS: Vendors' carts; store merchandise.

PROVIDED INSTRUMENTATION: Five reeds, two trumpets, two horns, trombone, euphonium, two percussion, two violins, viola, cello, bass, harp, piano-conductor.

ADVERTISING AND MARKETING: "You don't have to be as rich as the Rothschilds to see our production of *The Rothschilds*, beginning on [date]. Tickets are only . . ."

SUGGESTIONS: In case you're wondering how such a large show can be done with fifteen people, Lonny Price's 1990 long-running off-Broadway production used the sons to double as the London stockbrokers. It's not the ideal solution, but the show's year-plus run indicates that it's an acceptable one.

RESOURCES: The original cast album on CD, cassette and LP; Frederick Morton's book *The Rothschilds*, on which the musical is fairly faithfully based.

RIGHTS: Rodgers and Hammerstein.

1776

CREATORS: Book by Peter *(Two by Two)* Stone, music and lyrics by Sherman ("See You in September") Edwards, who conceived the show.

BACKGROUND: The 1969 production was considered an unlikely bet. It's been alleged that during out-of-town tryouts, the authors eliminated the intermission to get people to stay until the final curtain. After constant reworking, the musical opened to raves, received six Tony nominations (including one for William Daniels, who, because of a billing technicality, was nominated in the Featured Actor category, and withdrew his name, correctly stating that his was a starring role), won three awards—including Best Musical—and ran for 1,217 performances.

STORY: The difficulties in getting thirteen colonies under Britain to break away from their mother country, spearheaded by John Adams. Because Adams has pleaded the case one time too many to the Congress in Philadelphia, Ben Franklin suggests that Richard Henry Lee from Virginia introduce the "resolution on independency," and Adams reluctantly agrees. But Dickinson, one-third of Pennsylvania's delegation, is a great opponent of independence (to the woe of fellow Pennsylvanian Benjamin Franklin); he makes a motion that the independency resolution be unanimous among the 13 colonies, assuming it never will be, as long as fellow Pennsylvanian Judge Wilson continues to be squarely in Dickinson's pocket. With only six in favor of independence, the fight appears hopeless—so Adams stalls proceedings by asking that a Declaration of Independence be written, one he soon insists that Thomas Jefferson write. But Jefferson isn't interested; he's been lusting for his wife, and just wants to go home to Virginia. Adams solves that problem by bringing Martha Jefferson to Philadelphia, and the declaration does get written. But it is hardly a triumph with the Southerners, because of a clause that states that slavery will be abolished. Though Adams stands firm, Franklin concedes that the slavery clause must go, or independence will be doomed. Adams and Jefferson very reluctantly agree, and the Southern states then vote for independence. Only Pennsylvania is the dissenter— Franklin for, but Dickinson and Wilson against—until it's pointed out to Wilson that if he votes for the measure, the majority will carry Pennsylvania but if he votes against the measure, he will forever be remembered as the man who prevented American independence. The meek man votes with the others, thus allowing the Declaration of Independence to be signed on July 4, 1776.

ASSETS: As critic Otis Guernsey said when naming *1776* one of the best plays of the 1968–1969 season, "When you entered the theater, you knew how it was going to turn out; after a half-hour, however, you weren't so sure." Indeed; during the early scenes, those against independence argue so vehemently that you may become convinced that there *is* no United States of America, and the bad news is now being broken to us as palatably as possible (meaning, through a musical). By emphasizing the human qualities of these historical heroes, Stone's book is arguably the best ever written for a musical.

LIABILITIES: During scene three, there is a full half-hour in which no song appears—probably the longest tuneless stretch in any musical ever produced. There is much important information here your audience must know, so concentrate on briskly directing this scene so that it doesn't drag and your audience doesn't doze. And you'd better have a dynamic actor to portray the indefatigable Adams.

WHO YOU'LL NEED: *Lead Singing Role*: Adams, an obnoxious and disliked—but powerful—agitator (William Daniels). *Supporting Singing Roles*: The crusty and sagacious Franklin; the hawkish and determined Dickinson; his bespectacled sycophantic colleague; the young and cocksure (legit-voiced) Rutledge; Richard Henry Lee, the egocentric aristocrat; a twenty-ish and lovely Martha Jefferson; a forty-ish and vibrant (mezzo) Abigail Adams; the preoccupied loner Sherman; the decent Livingston; a young dusty soldier. *Other Roles*: (Most function as the chorus) John Hancock, president of the Congress; the Delaware contingent of one ill patriot, one angry Scotsman, and one effete royalist; delegates from New Jersey (a lean and ascetic reverend), New Hampshire (learned and sincere), Rhode Island (alcoholic and aged), New York (foppish), Maryland (rotund), North Carolina (no mind of his own), Georgia (hawkish and cautious); an aging custodian and his young assistant; a pedantic secretary; a portrait artist. *Maximum, 27; minimum, 25.*

DESIGNATED DANCES: Not much: A military cakewalk for Adams, Franklin, and Lee; a bit of soft-shoe for Adams, Franklin, Jefferson, Sherman, and Livingston; a waltz for Martha, Adams, and Franklin; a minuet for the anti-independence forces.

SUGGESTED SETS: An early American chamber of Congress with several period tables, chairs, and desks.

COSTUMES: Late eighteenth-century wear, assembled so that the northern delegates wear plain linens and simple clothes in somber browns and blacks (Hopkins wears a Quaker suit), while the Southerners sport brocades of gold and green; two lovely full dresses for Martha and Abigail; simple clothes for the custodians; a Revolutionary War uniform for the soldier.

IMPORTANT PROPS: A tally board with the names of all the colonies that can have "yeas" and "nays" shifted at will; a day-by-day wall calendar with the dates May 8, June 7, 22, 28, 29, 30, July 1, 3, and 4; a Declaration of Independence for all to sign; riding crops, rifles; walking sticks; quill pens; inkwells; gavel; fly swatters; a painter's easel; wooden kegs; a music stand and violin.

PROVIDED INSTRUMENTATION: Four reeds, two trumpets, two horns, three trombones, percussion, harp, harpsichord, violin, viola, cello, bass, piano-conductor.

ADVERTISING AND MARKETING: Sell raffle tickets at the beginning of the show for the Declaration of Independence that will have just been signed by your cast; as patrons leave, the winning number can be posted.

SUGGESTIONS: You *must* have that tally board with the names of all the colonies and the shiftable "yeas" and "nays," as well as the day-by-day wall calendar, so that each audience member can see exactly how close or far away the vote is on independence. It's one of the reasons the movie didn't work nearly as well as the play—because the audience only got a fleeting glimpse of each date when the camera happened to pass by.

RESOURCES: The original cast album on CD, cassette, and LP; the very faithful 1972 movie on videotape and laserdisc (the latter has extra material cut from the film), featuring virtually all of the original Broadway cast.

RIGHTS: Music Theatre International.

SHENANDOAH

CREATORS: Book by James Lee Barrett (who wrote the movie on which the musical is based), Peter Udell, and Philip Rose (producer of *A Raisin in the Sun*), music by Gary Geld, lyrics by Udell (Geld and Udell had collaborated on *Purlie*).

BACKGROUND: The 1975 production started at the Goodspeed Opera House in East Haddam, Connecticut, where it picked up enough praise and financial support to move to Broadway; there it received decent reviews and six Tony nominations, winning for its leading man John Cullum and its book. These propelled it to a 1,050-performance run.

STORY: Charlie Anderson is a Virginia farmer, the father of six sons and a daughter, and a pacifist who won't take sides in the War Between the States. However, he is drawn into the conflict when his youngest son is abducted, and then must endure not only the loss of one son, but then the death of another son and the daughter-in-law who had just given birth to a girl. Charlie, though, looks to a better future for his granddaughter, and his optimism is rewarded when his abducted son returns home.

ASSETS: A flavorful country and western score, and a strongly written character and male role model in Charlie.

LIABILITIES: There are many lengthy book scenes (many that might have been turned into songs) that could slow down the action. Their being episodic doesn't help, either. The final scene, in which the abducted son returns and walks in on a crutch, has been known to get laughs from the cynical and unmoved audience members.

WHO YOU'LL NEED: *Lead Singing Role:* A virile (tenor-voiced) farmer and father of seven (John Cullum). *Supporting Singing Roles:* Six sons ranging from a young boy to a married man; a lovely daughter and daughter-in-law; a young black slave; a Confederate corporal with a glorious tenor voice. *Other Roles:* An ex-convict; a horse trader; three marauders; a chorus of Union and Confederate soldiers and officers; women churchgoers. "Because of the war," explains co-author-producer Rose, "the congregation is composed of more women than men—so," he says with a straight face, "if you don't have enough women, dress the male chorus members as women." *Maximum, 39; minimum, 25.*

DESIGNATED DANCES: An opening march for the soldiers; a raucous hoedown for the sons; a stomp for Charlie; a high-kick romp for the daughter-in-law and the (newly freed) slave; stylized movement of fighting and killing.

SUGGESTED SETS: The Anderson farmhouse, its bedrooms, and surrounding grounds with split-rail fences; outside and inside a church (with pews); a farmyard with a stone well; a wooded area; a country road with split-rail fences.

COSTUMES: 1860s rustic wear; suede vests; workpants; burlaps and tweeds; suspenders; boots; full skirts; petticoats; pantalettes; corselettes; aprons; shawls; Sunday clothes; wedding wear for bride and groom; a slave's ragged clothes; a preacher's outfit; train engineer's uniform; Union and Confederate soldiers' uniforms; two pads representing different stages of pregnancy.

IMPORTANT PROPS: Early American furniture; a tombstone; a tree stump; barrels, crates, nail kegs, and buckets; water dipper; rocking chair; porch settee; oil lamps; liquor jugs; fishing poles and bait boxes; hymnals; a patchwork quilt; wool spools; wedding garlands; knives; rifles; a crutch; a "baby."

SPECIAL EFFECTS: Sounds of a chugging steam train and its whistle; a church organ.

PROVIDED INSTRUMENTATION: Flute/piccolo, bassoon, two clarinets, two trumpets, two horns, trombones, percussion, three violins, viola, cello, bass, harp, guitar-banjo, harmonica, piano-conductor.

ADVERTISING AND MARKETING: "You don't have to go to Shenandoah to see *Shenandoah*. It will play . . . ."

SUGGESTIONS: Says Melanie Larch of the Charleston (West Virginia) Light Opera Guild, "Seek out the help of any Civil War re-creation groups in your area. Not only can they help you with the historical elements, but they may also find you some men to flesh out the opening number."

RESOURCES: The original cast album on CD, cassette, and LP; the 1965 movie on which the musical is somewhat faithfully based.

RIGHTS: Samuel French.

ALSO WORTH A LOOK

The First

Tells the story of Jackie Robinson's breaking baseball's color line in 1947, thanks to Branch Rickey, who was determined to find a Negro League ballplayer who just couldn't fail. It hurts the story a bit that we know he'll make it—and that's one of the reasons that the 1981 Broadway production lasted only 37 performances. Baseball fans will enjoy hearing such vintage baseball names as Pee Wee Reese, Eddie Stanky, and Clyde Sukeforth. Your cast can include as many as forty-eight men and twelve women, or as few as twenty men and five women. The book is by Joel Siegel, better known as a critic, music by Bob Brush, better known as the producer of TV's beloved *The Wonder Years,* and the lyrics by Martin Charnin, who turned the *Annie* comic strip into a smash. Rights: Samuel French.

Zorba

By Joseph Stein may not measure up to the *Zorba the Greek* novel or film, but it has one of John Kander and Fred Ebb's best scores. If you have a strong capable actor who can handle the yeoman chores with the proper humor and sense of experience—and you aren't disturbed by the prospect of a doleful show that's supposed to be life-affirming—consider it. "But," says Paul Roberts, who directed the show for the Winthrop (Massachusetts) Players, "if you want to be truly authentic to the Broadway production and to Greek heritage, you should have an actor who can pick up a table with his teeth." Rights: Samuel French.

Also see: *Anything Goes; The Apple Tree; Assassins; Baker Street; Barnum; Ben Franklin in Paris; Big River; Cabaret; Camelot; The Cradle Will Rock; Falsettoland; The Fantasticks; A Funny Thing Happened on the Way to the Forum; Golden Boy; Guys and Dolls; The Happy Time; Irma La Douce; Jesus Christ Superstar; Li'l Abner; Little Me; Man of La Mancha; March of the Falsettos; Oliver; On the Twentieth Century; Pacific Overtures; South Pacific; The Tap Dance Kid; Three Guys Naked from the Waist Down; Top Banana; Two by Two; West Side Story; The Wiz; The Wizard of Oz; Working.*

"WHERE ARE THE MEN?"

Musicals with Predominantly Female Casts

"Where are the men?" the shipbound female ensemble moaned in *Anything Goes*. "They may very well have been speaking about the community theaters I've headed," quips Susan Copeland, who's helmed a few in Tennessee. "Many men simply don't realize how much fun it is to become part of a musical. Nor," she adds with a wink, "do they know it's an excellent way to meet young women."

But if you can't convince men to join your group, you'll need to investigate shows with predominantly female casts.

"A"...MY NAME IS ALICE

CREATORS: Conceived by Joan Micklin Silver and Julianne Boyd.

BACKGROUND: The 1984 New York production was part of the American Place's Women's Project, and did so well at that theater that it moved to the Village Gate for a 232-performance run.

STORY: A revue of songs, poems, and monologues about the female experience, ranging from a working, high-achieving mother, to two sisters who realize how important they are to each other after their men have left them. Songs include one about three housewives thoroughly enjoying a male strip joint, and sketches include one about a construction worker commenting on a woman's "gazoombas," prompting her to ask about his "wogabongo," which embarrasses and puts him squarely in his place.

ASSETS: A good deal of wit, some nifty music, a chance to do a show with social significance, and an opportunity for your women stars to show their versatility, playing 1960s group singers and most everything else.

LIABILITIES: Not having an original cast album makes learning the songs a little more difficult for a cast. Some of the language and situations may be too frank for some audiences.

WHO YOU'LL NEED: *Lead Singing Roles:* One mature and earthy thirtyish black woman; one sexy but neurotic twentyish white woman; one twentyish high-energy black dancer; one fiftyish motherly but mischievous white woman; one thirtyish cosmopolitan white woman. (You could also use a different actress for each character.) *Maximum, 44; minimum, 5.*

DESIGNATED DANCES: Some musical staging in the opening and closing; a solo tap for your designated dancer.

SUGGESTED SETS: None per se—a desk; a table; three chairs; a bench on an empty stage.

COSTUMES: Contemporary wear, as well as a hairdresser's cape; "little old lady's" shoes and stockings; four basketball uniforms; French beret and slit skirt; construction hard hat.

IMPORTANT PROPS: Highchair; a pig made from a Clorox bottle; binoculars; four basketballs; construction worker's lunchbox; hubcap.

PROVIDED INSTRUMENTATION: Reed, percussion, piano-conductor.

ADVERTISING AND MARKETING: Allow anyone named Alice to attend free—or, if you feel that's a bit too generous, free with any paid admission.

SUGGESTIONS: There are parts for "Howard," "Stanley," and "Workman" where you don't need to use women, if you have a few men who'd like to be in the show.

RESOURCES: No cast album.

RIGHTS: Samuel French.

FIRST IMPRESSIONS

CREATORS: Book by Abe (*Guys and Dolls*) Burrows, music and lyrics by Robert Goldman, (who produced the movie *One Flew over the Cuckoo's Nest*), Glenn Paxton, and George Weiss.

BACKGROUND: The 1959 production opened to nice out-of-town reviews, but perhaps New York's critics were expecting the musicalization of *Pride and Prejudice* to be better than it was. They also didn't much like Hermione Gingold as the mother of the Bennet brood. Only 84 performances later, the show was gone.

STORY: Early 19th century England. Mrs. Bennet, a British provincial, is very upset that her husband intends to leave his money to male cousin Collins instead of their five daughters, but is encouraged when she hears that two eligible gentlemen, Bingley and Darcy, are moving to her neck of the woods. However, Elizabeth, her eldest (and strongest and wittiest) daughter, is disgusted by her mother's obvious machinations. At a dance, Elizabeth decides not to be impressed by Darcy, who is equally unimpressed by impoverished and untitled Elizabeth; Bingley, however, is interested in Elizabeth's sister Jane. Once Elizabeth learns that the mysterious Captain Wickham is an enemy of Darcy, she decides to seem interested in him. Mrs. Bennet, meanwhile, makes certain that Jane takes a horseback ride in the rain to visit Bingley—so that she'll catch cold and be forced to stay there a while. Elizabeth, embarrassed by the ruse, eventually visits her, where she's encouraged by Bingley to play the piano and sing; Darcy now finds himself more interested in her. Most interested in her, though, is the newly arrived Collins—whose attention pleases Mrs. Bennet, who sees it as a way for the family's money to stay in the family. But Elizabeth has no interest in Collins, especially when Darcy soon drops his guard and expresses his admiration for her. She responds, and all is progressing, until Darcy overhears Mrs. Bennet bragging about Jane's winning over Bingley. It prompts Darcy to remember his station, abandon Elizabeth, and influence Charles to break with Jane. Collins marries another, and Darcy eventually comes around to tell Elizabeth he's missed her—but she cannot forgive his prejudice to her and Wickham, and especially his coming between Bingley and Jane. When Darcy makes it up to Wickham, even providing him with money so that he can marry Elizabeth's sister Lydia—and Bingley returns to Jane—Elizabeth finally forgives Darcy, and they unite.

ASSETS: A pleasant score and a much wittier book than has been alleged, with incisive dialogue and characterizations of a leading lady and leading man who are verbally well-pitted against each other. There's even some contemporary relevance when Mrs. Bennet bemoans that the country "has more women than men."

LIABILITIES: Many sets and costumes that must reflect the elegance of that era. Those in love with the Jane Austen masterpiece often are chagrined that the musical doesn't live up to it. There isn't much contemporary youth appeal, either.

WHO YOU'LL NEED: *Lead Singing Roles:* A headstrong and intelligent young woman who won't apologize for who she is; a stuffy young gentleman who eventually comes to appreciate that her personality is more important than her background. *Supporting Singing Roles:* A meddlesome mother (a Charlotte Rae type), her four other daughters (a "perfect" one, a shy one, a pragmatic one, and a young one); a lovesick and foppish cousin; a dashing gentleman. *Other Roles:* A henpecked but opinionated husband; a grande dame aunt and her daughter, an almost-dashing best friend and his sister; a local lady; her lofty husband; their unattractive daughter; a sincere captain; two lieutenants; three butlers. *Maximum, 42; minimum, 23.*

DESIGNATED DANCES: A polka; a mazurka; a minuet; a waltz; a dance for Bingley and Jane; a good deal of musical staging.

SUGGESTED SETS: Outside and inside a modest British house; a stately British home; a road with a tall hedge; a garden; a street with shops.

COSTUMES: Early-nineteenth-century finery; full dresses and petticoats; morning coats; cloaks; wedding gowns; tuxedos; dresses and suits.

IMPORTANT PROPS: A harp; a wicker traveling case; a hatbox; horse heads; a carriage; a bow and arrow; portraits of nobles (though these could be suggested fourth-wall).

PROVIDED INSTRUMENTATION: Five reeds, two horns, two trumpets, two trombones, two percussion, three violins, two violas, two cellos, bass, harp, keyboard, piano-conductor.

ADVERTISING AND MARKETING: "We're doing a musical about a poor family trying to marry off five daughters. No, it's not *Fiddler on the Roof*—it's *First Impressions,* opening on . . ."

SUGGESTIONS: Take a chance on this one; it's quite underrated.

RESOURCES: The original cast album on LP; Jane Austen's *Pride and Prejudice* on which the musical is faithfully based.

RIGHTS: Samuel French.

HIGH SPIRITS

CREATORS: Book, music, and lyrics by Timothy Gray and Hugh *(Make a Wish)* Martin.

BACKGROUND: The 1964 production received decent enough reviews during its three out-of-town stops, but director Noel Coward asked Gower Champion to come in and help. The musical opened to adequate reviews, garnered seven Tony nominations, and won none, because Champion's other show that year—*Hello, Dolly!*—won most of them. Nevertheless, the musical ran 375 performances.

STORY: The present, in rural England. Mystery novelist Charles Condomine and his second wife Ruth have invited Madame Arcati, a local medium, to dinner so that she can conduct a seance, which will be research for Charles's new book. Who shows up at the seance but the spirit of Elvira, Charles's deceased first wife—of whom Ruth is rather jealous. Trouble is, only Charles can see or hear her, which makes Ruth assume he's playing a joke on her, or that he's gone mad. But Charles eventually convinces Ruth that he's not bonkers after getting Elvira to move some flowers to another part of the room. Ruth then becomes more jealous—and has reason to be: Elvira eventually fools with Charles's car so that he'll get into an accident, perish, and join her. Except it's Ruth who winds up driving the car and dying—thus giving Charles *two* reappearing deceased spouses. They decide to ask Merlin the Magician for the hemlock that killed Socrates, and put it in a brandy decanter. After Madame Arcati visits and gets rid of the spirits, she and Charles toast with the brandy, and join Elvira and Ruth in the other world.

ASSETS: A fine score, a witty book, fat parts, and—with minimal sets, costumes, dancing, and cast demands—an inexpensive show to mount.

LIABILITIES: It's a rather "small" play that doesn't really lend itself to a musical—though if you have a small space, you'll be able to make this liability work for you. You may not like the drug references, either.

RECOGNIZABLE SONGS: Should we count Petula Clark's "You'd Better Love Me," which sold millions of copies in the 1960s? Perhaps not; people were buying the record for what was on the other side: "Downtown."

WHO YOU'LL NEED: *Lead Singing Roles:* A sparklingly witty and mischievous first wife. *Supporting Singing Roles:* A charming if slightly daffy—but happy—medium (a Charlotte Rae type); a consternated husband (a Kevin Kline type); his coolly jealous and lovely wife. *Other Roles:* A very nervous maid who desperately wants to please; a doctor; a typically English married couple; students of mysticism. *Maximum, 31; minimum, 8.*

DESIGNATED DANCES: For Elvira, two solo vamps and one production number; for Madame Arcati and her students, one production number.

SUGGESTED SETS: The nicely furnished Condomine living room; a road to their house; a coffee house; a posh nightspot.

COSTUMES: Contemporary wear—though you'll have to decide if you'll set the show in the 1930s when the play took place, the 1960s when the musical took place, or now. One filmy cloudlike garment for Elvira, and later one for Ruth. Eccentric clothes for Madame Arcati and her followers; a maid's uniform.

IMPORTANT PROPS: A stationary bicycle; a crystal ball; a Ouija board and planchette; a suitable and sturdy table on which to conduct a seance; a vase of flowers; a brandy decanter; a phonograph and a record that represents Charles and Elvira's favorite song.

SPECIAL EFFECTS: During the seance, the table should move about from below and fall over with a crash. Vases fly and doors open on their own accord. There's also a pre-recorded song. And, in the original production, Elvira flew à la Peter Pan.

PROVIDED INSTRUMENTATION: Five reeds, two horns, two trumpets, two trombones, two percussion, three violins, two violas, two cellos, bass, harp, keyboard, piano-conductor.

ADVERTISING AND MARKETING: "Here's a way to get your fill of *High Spirits* without having a hangover in the morning." (Which brings up a good point: Is it possible, in your community or situation, to ask a liquor company to advertise in your program, or to sponsor an intermission bar with their "high spirits"?)

SUGGESTIONS: If you have the resources to have your Elvira fly, by all means do so—but this is not so important to the action; after all, she doesn't fly in *Blithe Spirit*, the play on which the musical is based.

RESOURCES: The original cast album on CD and LP; Noel Coward's play *Blithe Spirit*, in script and in its movie version.

RIGHTS: Tams-Witmark.

HOW NOW, DOW JONES

CREATORS: Book by Max Shulman (*who wrote the short story collection The Many Loves of Dobie Gillis*), music by Elmer Bernstein (*who wrote the score for the movie The Man with the Golden Arm*), lyrics by Carolyn (*Little Me*) Leigh.

BACKGROUND: The 1967 Broadway production fired movie director Arthur Penn on the road and brought in eighty-year-old George Abbott to direct, and despite Clive Barnes's *New York Times* review calling the show "How to Try at Business Without Really Succeeding," it received six Tony nominations, won one for supporting actor Hiram Sherman, who'd already left the production by that time, and played 220 performances.

STORY: 1967, New York. Kate Montgomery, who announces the Dow-Jones on the radio each day is in love with the financially obsessed Herbert, who says he won't marry her until the Dow Jones average hits 1,000. She meets Charley, an unhappy loser, and winds up bedding him in a one-night stand. Then, pregnant and needing a husband, she announces that the Dow has hit

1,000 so that Herbert will marry her. When her lie. is discovered, Americans pull their money from the market, which begins a financial panic that's stopped in the nick of time when Wall Street's greatest tycoon and trader puts enough money into the government. Kate and Charley then find each other and marry.

ASSETS: A tuneful score, terrific lyrics, and built-in appeal for those interested in money. Some might also be amused by the benign male-bashing (men are perceived as being far less interested in love than in their careers).

LIABILITIES: Would anyone on Wall Street change buying and selling patterns on the basis of one broadcast? As William Goldman wrote about the show in *The Season*, "Not one financial expert in all these 50 states thinks to himself, 'Hmmm, a little odd; no sign of even a boomlet, and here's the biggest recorded stock increase in the history of the world.'. . . No. Everyone goes crazy and starts buying everything, and the country is on the verge of financial ruin. With a plot like that, are you surprised there was a little trouble out of town?"

RECOGNIZABLE SONGS: "(Will Everyone Here Kindly) Step to the Rear?"

WHO YOU'LL NEED: *Lead Singing Roles:* A pretty woman who announces Dow Jones averages; the adorably hapless man with whom she falls in love (Tony Roberts). *Supporting Singing Roles:* A best girlfriend; the preoccupied magnate whose mistress she becomes; and—most important—a bunch of housewives who like to invest in the market, and have the musical's showstopper. *Other Roles:* A career-minded boyfriend; an upwardly mobile wife; a senator; a doctor; the most powerful man on Wall Street; some tycoons; brokers; onstage musicians (very optional) for the nightclub band. *Maximum*, 52; *minimum*, 31.

DESIGNATED DANCES: Some musical staging for the first- and second-act openers; two ballets, one to represent a night on the town, one a Wall Street panic; the titanic "Step to the Rear" production number.

SUGGESTED SETS: Wall Street and its private offices; a restaurant, bar, and nightclub; one modest Manhattan living room and bedroom; apartment furnished with leopard skins; one Queens middle-class living room.

COSTUMES: Contemporary white-collar work and leisure clothes; upper-middle-class suburban dresses; many pairs of horn-rimmed glasses; one torn brassiere. The original production had a stylized second-act opening in which everyone wore white costumes, but you don't need it.

IMPORTANT PROPS: Plenty of office furniture; telephones; tables and chairs (for office, restaurant, and home); cups and saucers; beer mugs; bags of groceries; mobile garbage can; picture of oil wells; graph charts; dozens of *Wall Street Journals* and tabloids; live mikes; pennants; tickertape; a stretcher; wicker wheelchair; an elegant cane.

SPECIAL EFFECTS: An (optional) electronic dollar sign.

PROVIDED INSTRUMENTATION: Five reeds, two horns, two trumpets, two trombones, two percussion, three violins, two violas, two cellos, bass, harp, keyboard, piano-conductor.

ADVERTISING AND MARKETING: "Wall Street comes to [name of your] Street when *How Now, Dow Jones* opens at . . ."

SUGGESTIONS: Of course the Dow hit 1,000 long ago (on December 7, 1972—five years to the day after this show's opening), but you can adjust your figure to the Dow's next big goal, or keep it in the late '60s.

RESOURCES: The original cast album on cassette and LP.

RIGHTS: Samuel French.

NINE

CREATORS: Book by Arthur Kopit (who wrote the play *Oh Dad, Poor Dad . . .*) from a Mario Fratti translation, music and lyrics by Maury (*Grand Hotel*) Yeston.

BACKGROUND: The 1982 musical opened to nice enough reviews just before Tony voters went to the polls; it was the show on their minds, and they gave it twelve Tony nominations. It won five awards—including Best Musical—and ran 739 performances.

STORY: The present, at a spa near Venice. Famed film producer Guido Contini has a wife, Luisa, but plenty of girlfriends, too, especially his favorite mistress, Carla. He's under contract to start a new movie, but his personal life is getting in the way—so much so that he doesn't even know what movie he's making (his French producer reminds him it's a musical). He still has problems with his leading lady, Claudia, who damns him as a Casanova—which gives him an idea for his movie: *Casanova*. The subject matter does not please Luisa, or Claudia, who gives up the role. Carla nags Guido to divorce his wife and marry her, and when he refuses, she leaves him. He considers suicide but goes on, and realizes his love for his wife is the solution to his problems, and has been all along.

ASSETS: A nifty score in a show that can showcase many of your female performers.

LIABILITIES: Some audiences won't find a man's incessant womanizing (and lying) very funny. The score isn't easy to sing.

WHO YOU'LL NEED: *Lead Singing Roles:* A handsome, dynamic internationally known Italian movie director (Raul Julia). *Supporting Singing Roles:* His brave but long-suffering wife; his sensuous and uninhibited mistress; his stunning leading lady; his somewhat disgusted mother; a young buxom woman who seduced him when he was very young; a flamboyant French movie producer; a masked henchwoman; four German women; Guido as a boy of nine. *Other Roles:* Seven Italian women; a gondolier; "Our Lady of the Spa", young Guido's three schoolmates. *Maximum, 26; minimum, 14.*

DESIGNATED DANCES: Seven production numbers, including the long musical version of *Casanova.*

SUGGESTED SETS: A white-tiled spa on which many little tiled "settees" are positioned, with a cyclorama of Venice in the background.

COSTUMES: In the original production, there was much fanciful black wear for everyone, with some classically glamorous costumes for the *Casanova* sequence, and white exotic lingerie for the women—but you don't have to adhere to this scheme.

IMPORTANT PROPS: Many tambourines; a gondola; an elaborate telephone; an enormous feather boa; an orchestra baton.

PROVIDED INSTRUMENTATION: Five reeds, two horns, two trumpets, two trombones, two percussion, three violins, two violas, two cellos, bass, harp, keyboard, piano-conductor.

ADVERTISING AND MARKETING: You can have endless variations on the "nine" motif—a raffle in which there are nine winners of nine free tickets; kids of nine get in free. Start the show at nine so people can eat their dinners, or even do some open rehearsals at nine in the morning.

SUGGESTIONS: A show that needs a spectacular look to succeed.

RESOURCES: The original cast album on CD, cassette (the most complete version), and LP; 8½, the movie on which the musical is fairly faithfully based.

RIGHTS: Samuel French.

NO, NO, NANETTE

CREATORS: Book by Otto Harbach and Frank Mandel, music by Vincent (*Hit the Deck*) Youmans, lyrics by Irving ("Swanee") Caesar and Harbach.

BACKGROUND: Boston sports fans point to this show as the beginning of the end of the Red Sox. Wanting to produce the musical, then-owner Harry Frazee sold Babe Ruth to the Yankees to get the financing. Show freaks, though, think it was worth it. The original 1925 production ran a then-amazing 321 performances; a 1925 London production ran 665 performances; these spawned a 1930 movie and a 1940 remake. A wildly successful 1971 revival received six Tony nominations, won two awards (and would have won Best Revival had that category been instituted then), and ran 861 performances.

STORY: Nanette gets a proposal from current beau Tom, but wants to taste the Roaring Twenties before she settles down. Her Bible-salesman guardian Jimmy Smith would be worried, if he wasn't having a problem with three young lovelies who are threatening to blackmail him. He calls his lawyer, Billy, who tries to send Jimmy to Philadelphia so Billy can use Jimmy's Atlantic City house. Billy's wife, Lucille, trusts him; Jimmy's wife, Sue, also trusts him. But everyone winds up in Atlantic City, and Billy is soon blamed for Jimmy's sins. Eventually all is explained and forgiven, and it all works out happily.

ASSETS: Great score, fun characters, a delightful *homage* to a long-past era. And there are three acts, which gives you twice as many intermissions to sell refreshments, souvenirs, and raffle tickets.

LIABILITIES: Though some young people decide to love the show, many think it's stupid and inconsequential.

RECOGNIZABLE SONGS: "I Want to Be Happy," "Tea for Two."

WHO YOU'LL NEED: *Lead Singing Roles:* A young woman who's wild for the 1920s but tame for today; her straight-arrow young beau; her mother's cosmopolitan best friend; the friend's snazzy lawyer husband. *Supporting Singing Roles:* Nanette's two guardians; three beautiful showgirls who claim to be in love. *Other Roles:* A long-suffering maid; a chorus of thirty-five who are described as "Nanette's friends." *Maximum, 53; minimum, 18.*

DESIGNATED DANCES: For Lucille, a production number that showcases her; for Billy, a solo dance and one with two showgirls; for Sue, a tap number involving virtually all of the company and an eleven o'clock production number; for Lucille and Billy, much musical staging on each of the two finalettos and the finale.

SUGGESTED SETS: Only three (one for each act): Jimmy's sumptuous townhouse (with poufs); the garden of an Atlantic City bungalow; its living room.

COSTUMES: 1920s wear; loud argyle-style sweaters; pin-stripe jackets; dresses with sashes far below the waist; college wear; tam o'shanters; old-fashioned bathing suits; sailor caps; lifeguard outfits; a maid's uniform; showgirl costumes; tap shoes for everyone.

IMPORTANT PROPS: Many hatboxes, giftboxes, and shopping bags; ukeleles for everyone; giant beach balls which four of your chorines should "ride" by simply walking on them and staying on the top, should you care to risk it.

PROVIDED INSTRUMENTATION: Five reeds, three trumpets, two trombones, horn, percussion, guitar, banjo, ukelele, two violins, viola, cello, bass, piano-conductor.

ADVERTISING AND MARKETING: "See the show that was so good that its producer sold Babe Ruth to the Yankees to get the money to put it on." Serve tea for two at intermission.

SUGGESTIONS: "There's a tendency to play the show as camp," laments Carol Lucha-Burns, Chairman of the Theater Department at the University of New Hampshire, "but you must stress the honest relationships between the people. It will make the show that much better."

RESOURCES: The original 1971 cast album on CD, cassette, and LP; the 1930 and 1940 movie versions bear little relationship to this show.

RIGHTS: Tams-Witmark.

NUNSENSE

CREATORS: Book, music, and lyrics by Dan Goggin.

BACKGROUND: The 1985 off-Broadway musical opened very quietly, but soon won the award of Best Musical from the Outer (out-of-town) Critics Circle, and, as of this writing, is still running in New York, and has had over three hundred productions worldwide.

STORY: The present, in New Jersey. The Little Sisters of Hoboken have endured a calamity—fifty-two members of their order died when eating botulism-packed vichyssoise—and the surving nuns had only enough money to bury forty-eight of them (because the Mother Superior bought a VCR). The survivors have decided to raise the money by doing a show at their Mount Saint Helen's School Auditorium; it's a show that proceeds from the ridiculous to sublime, especially in an act concocted by Sister Mary Amnesia, so dubbed because she can't remember her real name. By show's end, though, the sister remembers that she was once Sister Mary Paul—who, it turns out, was the big winner in the Publishers' Clearing House Sweepstakes—and can furnish the money to bury the dead.

ASSET: "People just get the biggest kick out of seeing nuns in funny situations," says Julie J. Hafner, who's played all the roles for the New York company. "And it's the amateur musical for all seasons," insists Charles Fontana, who directs for the armed forces. "In fact, this show glorifies the amateurish; production values shouldn't be high, and your orchestra can be a single piano."

LIABILITIES: This ain't no Pulitzer Prize winner, and while the first-act situations are fun, the second act only offers more of the same, which does make it wearing. "And," adds Fontana, "the 'poppers' sequence—in which one nun inhales some 'Rush' and laughs hysterically—might baffle middle America." So might the song that celebrates theatrical understudies; will your audience know who Bibi Osterwald and Lenora Nemetz are? Lastly, you may find that some of your audience won't appreciate nuns saying "hell" and "ass," or having an occasionally irreverent observation (though many nuns who've attended enjoyed this irreverence).

WHO YOU'LL NEED: *Lead Supporting Roles:* An overweight but quick-witted nun; a kind and ready-to-party nun; a streetwise nun; a childlike nun who can at least attempt to do some ventriloquism; a nun who originally wanted to be a star. *Maximum-minimum, 5.*

DESIGNATED DANCES: Song-and-dance steps; tap dance; kick-line; even flamenco—but none of it need be slick; they're supposed to look amateurish.

SUGGESTED SETS: While the original production took place on the set of the just-concluded eighth-grade production of *Grease*—complete with posters of James Dean, Elvis, and Marilyn Monroe; jukebox, soda fountain, bedroom set, and a banquette of beauty parlor chairs with dryers overhead (which, turned around, display the "Greased Lightning" car mock-up)—"you can," says author Goggin, "do it in a setting as nondescript as a church basement, or even the school gym." It's also fun to deck the walls with some hand-drawn signs for a school's bingo night, bake sale, pep rally, dance, and student council elections.

COSTUMES: Nuns' habits; wimples; bib collars; orthopedic black shoes; crucifixes; oversized rosary beads. Ideally, the musicians should be attired as religious brothers and sisters. In addition, you'll need a bathrobe and fluffy slippers; a chef's hat; aprons; ballet toe shoes; tap shoes; a Carmen Miranda fruit headpiece.

IMPORTANT PROPS: Statues of Mary and Joseph; St. Christopher's holy cards; a mock-up of a *Baking with the BVM* cookbook; a ventriloquist's puppet dressed as a nun; maracas; kitchen equipment (bowl, whisk, egg carton, spoon); an umbrella; a movie screen; a bouquet of lilacs; an exercycle; a bottle of Rush poppers; those "frog-clickers" that nuns use to demand silence.

SPECIAL EFFECTS: The sound of an electric school bell will be easy enough, but you'll also need to have a movie parody of "Gunsmoke"—called "Nunsmoke," of course—and a series of old-time silent movie title cards, which ends with a picture of your Mother Superior in a provocative bathing suit.

PROVIDED INSTRUMENTATION: Three reeds, percussion, keyboard-conductor.

ADVERTISING AND MARKETING: Can you do better than the original ad campaign that boasted "*Nunsense* is habit-forming"?

SUGGESTIONS: Why not do a production of *Nunsense* right after a production of Grease? That way you can stage two shows on the same set.

RESOURCES: The original cast album on CD, cassette, and LP.

RIGHTS: Samuel French.

QUILTERS

CREATORS: Book by Molly Newman and Barbara Damashek, music and lyrics by Damashek.

BACKGROUND: The musical was developed at the Denver Center Theater Company, and made it to off-Broadway in a 1984 production. Even though it lasted only 12 performances, it has been a fine attraction for many of the nation's regional theaters.

STORY: A family album of America's pioneer women as defined by the quilts they made—from their first quilts through the ones they made for baptisms, schoolwork, birthday gifts, hope chests, childbirth, and getting their children through their fear of the dark. The women endure a fire that destroys the quilts, then survive and rebuild their homes, their lives, and their quilts.

ASSETS: A charming score and a tender book that nevertheless shows us how difficult life was for pioneers. You'll admire these women who show strength and resolve in the face of tremendous adversity.

LIABILITIES: No original cast album to help your cast learn their songs. Some male theatergoers may think it doesn't speak to them, and may come muttering to and from the theater. If your audiences prefer a standard song-and-dance show, look elsewhere. Some will also object to a scene in which a mother of eleven wants an abortion and goes through with it. And perhaps most difficult of all, you'll have to come up with seventeen quilts.

WHO YOU'LL NEED: *Lead Singing Roles:* Seven actresses; most of the time, one actress plays a mother of six, while the other six play her daughters, but there is a good deal of doubling throughout the musical. *Maximum, 42; minimum, 7.*

DESIGNATED DANCES: An opening production number; a bit of folk and square dancing; a waltz.

SUGGESTED SETS: An empty stage with a log cabin and fences.

COSTUMES: Pioneer wear; gingham skirts; flannel dresses; peplummed blouses; vests; jumpers; camisoles; bloomers; aprons; pregnancy pads; smocks; sunbonnets; bust binders; overalls; long-johns; boots.

IMPORTANT PROPS: Hoops to suggest a Conestoga wagon; hand puppets; sawhorses; tubs; stools; sewing baskets; seventeen quilts.

SPECIAL EFFECTS: Sounds of baby crying; driving blizzard; train whistles.

PROVIDED INSTRUMENTATION: Piano-conductor.

ADVERTISING AND MARKETING: Given that "quilt" is now a term that can be associated with the quilt that memorializes the victims of AIDS, do some performances as AIDS benefits.

SUGGESTIONS: A good show for a black-box theater.

RESOURCES: General information on quilts can be found in: *New Discoveries in American Quilts* by Robert Bishop, *American Quilts and Coverlets* by Bishop and Carleton L. Stafford, *Letters of a Woman Homesteader* by Elinore Pruitt Stewart, *Our Homes and Their Adornments* by Almon C. Varney.

RIGHTS: Dramatists Play Service.

SMILE

CREATORS: Book and lyrics by Howard (*Little Shop of Horrors*) Ashman, music by Marvin (*A Chorus Line*) Hamlisch.

BACKGROUND: The 1986 production received lukewarm notices from critics, who felt it lost the satirical bite of the movie on which it was based. After 48 performances, it was gone—"but *Smile*," says Ken Mandelbaum in *Not Since Carrie*, his landmark book on Broadway failures, "was perhaps the most underappreciated musical of the '80s, and it is highly recommended to stock and amateur groups."

STORY: 1980s, Northern California. Robin, an innocent state finals contestant for the Young American Miss pageant, is rooming with Doria, a perpetual and savvy beauty contest entrant. They and all their rivals are coached by feisty Brenda, who still isn't over losing the pageant eighteen years ago, and naive husband Bob, who believes in her and the pageant. Contestant Doria urges fellow contestant Robin to "use" her dead father for sympathy votes, but Robin doesn't want "orphan points." After a while, she's not so sure; Maria, a Mexican girl, does a confident cooking demonstration while singing and dancing, and is cited for Outstanding Achievement in Individual Talent. This infuriates contestant Shawn, and when she catches Brenda and Bob's son and a friend in the girls' room secretly taking pictures of nude girls, she enlists them to get one of Maria. When it's put in with the other slides and shown to the SRO audience on pageant night Maria is devastated and leaves, and Bob is crushed even before he discovers his son is responsible. But Brenda won't be defeated, and makes an impassioned *apologia* that gets her a promotion to the National Committee. Shawn wins the contest, Robin goes home, and Doria goes searching for the next beauty pageant.

ASSETS: A terrific score, a strong book, and a chance to make a wry comment on family values.

LIABILITIES: You'll have to have enough fetching and attractive young girls who look as if they'd have a chance to win a Young American Miss pageant. And your community may not want to see the slide of the nude Maria. (See "Suggestions.")

WHO YOU'LL NEED: *Lead Singing Roles:* Robin, a charming and sincere brunette young woman; Doria, a savvy but decent blond young (mezzo) woman. *Supporting Singing Roles:* The not overly pretty, not overly talented, not overly smart eventual winner (who does a ventriloquist act); a Mexican-American girl who revels in her heritage; a Valley Girl; her confidante; ten other contestants (one doubles as last year's Young American Miss); the female powerhouse who runs the beauty pageant and her very sincere husband; the game show host who's emceeing the pageant; the no-nonsense director-choreographer. *Other Roles:* A randy young teenager and his best friend; the national chairman of the Young Miss Foundation; two mothers; two judges; a reporter/photographer. *Maximum, 32; minimum, 18.*

DESIGNATED DANCES: Heavy: A routine on a ramp; an open-the-parasols-to-music number; an aerobics-oriented routine; an exit dance for the losers; much musical staging.

SUGGESTED SETS: A campus building of Santa Rosa Junior College—its multipurpose room/gymnasium where rehearsals are held; the auditorium where the pageant itself takes place; the dormitories upstairs (ideally, on a second level of the stage); the cafeteria; various offices.

COSTUMES: Contemporary wear; white gowns; old-fashioned "ice-cream parlor" outfits with parasols; a white leotard-and-tights outfit; a Gay Nineties costume" a yellow-smile-face T-shirt; a sequined tux jacket; tiaras for the winner and runner-up; name tags; sashes with the names of the cities from which the girls hail.

IMPORTANT PROPS: A rolling staircase; a podium; numbered tables; lobby photo/poster of the emcee, Elks and Rotary logos; Mexican hand-painted clay bowl; cheerleader pom-poms; bamboo poles; flaming fire batons; coffee urn and styrofoam cups; a ventriloquist's dummy; a Bible; rosary beads; flower arrangements; two calla lillies; slide projector; cameras; candles; suitcases; pillows for all the girls to fight (which unleash flying feathers).

SPECIAL EFFECTS: Flashbulbs; a ramp that encircles the orchestra (important to the plot); a video of the national chairman explaining the pageant; slides of the various contestants; the nude slide.

PROVIDED INSTRUMENTATION: Five reeds, three trombones, three horns, two trumpets, two keyboards, two cellos, violin, guitar, bass, drums, percussion, piano-conductor.

ADVERTISING AND MARKETING: Get ads from all the photographers in your community; have them display your *Smile* posters in their studios.

SUGGESTIONS: If you don't want to show Maria in the buff, place the slide projector centerstage facing fourth wall, and have everyone on stage react when they look out and "see" it.

RESOURCES: Though an original cast album was taped after the show's closing, it has not yet been commercially released; the 1975 movie *Smile* on which the musical was loosely based.

RIGHTS: Samuel French.

THE UTTER GLORY OF MORRISSEY HALL

CREATORS: Book by Nagle Jackson and Clark (*You're a Good Man, Charlie Brown*) Gesner, music and lyrics by Gesner.

BACKGROUND: All right, we'll be perfectly honest about this: The Broadway production opened May 13, 1979, and closed May 13, 1979—but this musical is nevertheless a natural for a production in a girl's private school.

STORY: "Now or yesterday" at an English Girls' School. Headmistress Julia Faysle wants Morrissey Hall to be highly regarded among Britain's girls' boarding schools, but a journal of education publishes an article that suggests otherwise. Faysle bears down on the girls, eventually resulting in student ringleader Felicia Carswell's imagination running wild—she thinks they're going to be sold into white slavery, and convinces others it's true. The girls go on a hunger strike, frustrating Faysle even more, and matters escalate until there is—literally—a full-scale war in which the girls shoot arrows, then guns, then cannons that they've acquired through mail order. Faysle retreats into her office, where she escapes reality by perusing her pressed flowers—and when they are threatened, oh, does she retaliate. By play's end, we see the school's previous headmistress pay a visit, discover the war, and comment to Faysle that it's not unlike the one that Faysle herself conducted when she was a student at Morrissey Hall. The war ends, as we come full circle, as an adult Ms. Carswell comes to teach at the school.

ASSETS: For an audience that enjoys laughing at English stiff-upper-lip behavior, an abundance of opportunities. Your student audience will be very interested to hear what goes on in the principal's office, and will love seeing the kids get the better of the teachers. Their parents and teachers may very well nod in sad recognition and empathize at the uphill battle that's involved in dealing with teenagers.

LIABILITIES: Where will you get the warfare equipment? As for the show itself, the headmistress is too weak a character, and while we can laugh at her being overwhelmed by screaming teenagers, we can't respect her for incompetently retreating. The score isn't for everyone, as it is very British flavored in that stately-halls-of-England way.

WHO YOU'LL NEED: *Lead Singing Role*: A frazzled headmistress (a Holland Taylor type). *Supporting Singing Roles*: Her secretary; a chemistry teacher; an English teacher; a dance teacher; a gym teacher; a music teacher (who functions as the musical director); twelve girl students around seventeen years of age. *Other Roles*: A former headmistress, a new teacher; a custodian; a boy student from another school; a salesman. *Maximum, 30; Minimum, 22.*

DESIGNATED DANCES: A razzmatazz strut for Faysle and the English teacher; dancing class calisthenics; a gallop; a ballet for the girls; a solo ballet of grace and grandeur for the dance teacher. In addition, when the bell rings, the girls are virtually choreographed to move as a huddled unit as they crowd through the corridors to get to their next class.

SUGGESTED SETS: A Gothic-style girls' school depicted on a unit set: A headmistress's office; her secretary's office; a reading room; dorm rooms (ideally on a second level); a portrait of a previous headmistress overwhelming all.

COSTUMES: British teachers' suits and hats; girls' school uniforms; gym suits; caps and gowns; one boy's school uniform, and one man's business suit; St. George and dragon suits, costumes by which three girls can represent flowers; war-surplus wear (helmets, ammunition vests and belts, yellow gloves and armbands).

IMPORTANT PROPS: Desks; chairs; telephones; filing cabinets; pot of flowers; plant sprayer; a can of film; a book of pressed flowers; a wall sconce; a large blanket, an enormous trunk capable of housing a boy; an amusement park bumper car; incense pots; holy water sprinklers; large crucifixes; a bullhorn siren; a megaphone; a microphone; binoculars; sawhorses, a Tarzan-type swing-rope that must support a person; shorter ropes; bicycle chains; riding crop; ax; machine guns; blunderbuss; torch; a cannon; travel posters; a sign that says "Head Monstress."

SPECIAL EFFECTS: An electric school bell; shooting arrows that land perilously near the headmistress; a battle scene in which half the set is destroyed—and can be repaired for your next performance.

PROVIDED INSTRUMENTATION: Five reeds, three trombones, three horns, two trumpets, two keyboards, two cellos, violin, guitar, bass, drums, percussion, piano-conductor.

ADVERTISING AND MARKETING: Take radio ads that furtively ask, "Ever wonder what happens behind the scenes at a girls' school?"—before adopting a light-hearted tone for "Then come to our musical, *The Utter Glory of Morrissey Hall* on (date)."

SUGGESTIONS: If you're in a school where girls wear uniforms, use them as the Morrissey Hall uniforms; they'll bring down the house.

RESOURCES: The original cast album on LP; *The Belles of St. Trinian's* movies which inspired the musical.

RIGHTS: Samuel French.

Also See: Annie; Applause; Ballroom; Bells Are Ringing; The Best Little Whorehouse in Texas; The Boy Friend; Bridgadoon; Cats; Dear World; Do I Hear a Waltz?; Fiddler on the Roof; Follies; 42nd Street; Gigi; The Grass Harp; Hello, Dolly!; I'm Getting My Act Together and Taking It on the Road; I Remember Mama; The King and I; A Little Night Music; Meet Me in St. Louis; Milk and Honey; The Music Man; Over Here; The Rink; The Secret Garden; 70, Girls, 70; She Loves Me; The Sound of Music; Sweet Charity; The Threepenny Opera; Working.

"KIDS!"

Musicals for Grade School and Junior High Students

"Kids!" sang Paul Lynde as harried father Harry McAfee in *Bye Bye Birdie*, "I don't know what's wrong with these kids today." Nothing that putting them in a musical won't cure. Here are some musicals worth examining if you have a number of talented kids you want to show off to good advantage. ("Though," urges David N. Matthews, Artistic Director of the Erie Playhouse, "double-cast kids whenever you can—because kids often get sick and can't go on the way adults will.")

I REMEMBER MAMA

CREATORS: Book by Thomas *(Annie)* Meehan, music by Richard *(The Boys from Syracuse)* Rodgers, lyrics by Martin *(The First)* Charnin and Raymond *(Baker Street)* Jessel.

BACKGROUND: The 1979 production may have been too old-fashioned for Broadway; but it also didn't help that the director-lyricist, choreographer, one actor, and one actress were fired. After opening to one good review, Richard Rodgers's final musical ran only 108 performances—but has found a happy home at many community theaters and high schools.

STORY: Katrin, now an author, remembers her family in San Francisco circa 1910: Papa, a carpenter; her three sisters and one brother; but most of all Mama, the rock on whom the kids rely emotionally. Mama's sisters also rely on her—especially Trina, who at forty-three has found a man—an undertaker—to marry her, and hopes that her sister will help convince their Uncle Chris to let her marry. (She can't; Uncle Chris won't accept a Swede and a Methodist, given that Chris is Norwegian and Lutheran). But the biggest problem is that Papa has been laid off, and eventually leaves for Norway because he's offered a job there. Mama still keeps the family together, elicits an okay for Trina from Uncle Chris before he dies, and even gets writing advice for Katrin (in exchange for a recipe) from a famous author. Papa, meanwhile, missing his family too much, returns home, just before Katrin sells a story that pays enough to keep the family together in America.

ASSETS: A pleasant score and sincere book; a show for *almost* the entire family (today's teens might not much like it because it's *so* pro-parent).

LIABILITIES: Those who consider Rodgers's *The Sound of Music* too sticky-sweet will feel that that musical is *Assassins* compared to this one. What's more, Uncle Chris's prejudice may have been a subject for comedy in less enlightened times, but not now.

WHO YOU'LL NEED: *Lead Singing Roles:* A kind and endearing mother who must comfortably sing one song in Norwegian (an Ellen Burstyn type); her patient but not henpecked husband. *Supporting Singing Roles:* Their dutiful thirteen-year-old son; their twelve-year-old daughter who loves to play the piano; their seven-year-old daughter who loves her cat (which you'll also need); their fifteen-year-old daughter who loves her impending womanhood; a thirty-year-old author who narrates and doubles as their sixteen-year-old daughter who wants to be a writer; three aunts; the undertaker who loves one of them; a tyrannical uncle; a famous female author. *Other Roles:* An outcast wife; the landlord's rent collector; a doctor; a nurse; a chorus of seamen. *Maximum, 35; minimum, 15.*

DESIGNATED DANCES: Not many—two Norwegian folk dances for the entire family; a ragtime and cakewalk for Uncle Chris, the children, and some seamen; a romp for the children while laundry is being hung to dry.

SUGGESTED SETS: The kitchen (with ice box and wood-burning stove); dining room; parlor (with upright piano); back porch of a turn-of-the-century San Francisco Victorian house; a hospital; a posh hotel lobby; a room at a ranch.

COSTUMES: 1910 poor-but-clean fashions; a white party dress; a black suit for the undertaker; seamen's uniforms; longshoremen's wear; doctor and nurse uniforms; a suit befitting a successful female author.

IMPORTANT PROPS: A covered dish; a crate of oranges; firewood; bouquets of flowers; lilies; baskets of laundry; a wicker suitcase. While an automobile is indicated in two scenes, it isn't necessary.

PROVIDED INSTRUMENTATION: Two flutes, oboe, two clarinets, bassoon, three horns, two trumpets, trombone, tuba, two percussion, three violins, viola, cello, bass, harp, piano, piano-conductor.

ADVERTISING AND MARKETING: "Do you remember Mama in the movies or on TV? We do—and we'll keep you remembering her in our musical version of *I Remember Mama*, beginning on . . ." If you schedule this show for May, you can have a Mother's Day tie-in.

RESOURCES: A not-quite-original cast album is available on CD, cassette, and LP; the original John Van Druten play on which the musical was loosely based; the "Mama's Bank Account" short stories on which the play was based; and the movie version of the play available on videotape. You may even be able to find kinescopes of the "Mama" TV series that was popular in the early 1950s.

RIGHTS: Rodgers and Hammerstein.

THE ME NOBODY KNOWS

CREATORS: Adapted by Robert H. Livingston and Herb Schapiro, music by Gary William Friedman, lyrics by Will Holt and Schapiro.

BACKGROUND: The 1970 off-Broadway production was so successful that after 208 performances it transferred to Broadway, where it received five Tony nominations, won none, and played 586 performances.

STORY: 1970s, New York City—or now. A collage of poems and stories taken from the school writings of underprivileged children, ages seven through eighteen, who live in Manhattan, the Bronx, Harlem, and Bedford-Stuyvesant, set to music. They tell of their fears and frustrations, not in anger, but in sorrow. Heroin, prejudice, and alcoholism are subjects they know and talk about.

ASSETS: A very tuneful pop-rock score complements some very moving sentiments. A inexpensive show to mount, for it's very light on sets and costumes.

LIABILITIES: It's a revue format, and because each kid has a chance to shine, you may find your cast competing to see if one number can be better than the next—thus hurting the humanity of the show. There's also more music to learn than in the average musical.

RECOGNIZABLE SONGS: "Light Shines (All over the World)."

WHO YOU'LL NEED: *Lead Singing Roles:* Six boys and six girls, ages twelve to twenty, some black, some Hispanic, some white. *Maximum, 20; minimum,* 9.

DESIGNATED DANCES: Some contemporary steps in four production numbers.

SUGGESTED SETS: A collage to represent that which is not so glittering about city life.

COSTUMES: Contemporary street wear—none of it of expensive quality.

IMPORTANT PROPS: None to speak of.

PROVIDED INSTRUMENTATION: Reed, trumpet, trombone, cello, bass, guitar, drums, piano-conductor.

ADVERTISING AND MARKETING: Arrange to perform at City Hall and government functions; aside from exposure, you also gain an opportunity to show the lawmakers your inner-city concerns.

RESOURCES: The original cast album on cassette and LP; *The Me Nobody Knows*, a collection of poems assembled by Stephen M. Joseph on which the musical is faithfully based.

RIGHTS: Samuel French.

OLIVER!

CREATORS: Book, music, and lyrics by Lionel *(Blitz!)* Bart.

BACKGROUND: The 1963 production—a then-rare London musical import—was publicized so well by producer David Merrick during its West Coast tryout that even bad reviews wouldn't have been able to stop it. But the reviews were good; ten Tony nominations and two awards followed, as did a 776-performance run.

STORY: Victorian England. Orphan Oliver Twist infuriates Bumble, the parish beadle, when he asks for a little more gruel—so Bumble rids himself of the problem by selling Oliver to an undertaker. Oliver runs away and hooks up with Fagin and his band of young thieves. He enjoys their attention and particularly likes Nancy, the oppressed girlfriend of Sikes, the district's bully. But then Oliver is caught by the authorities—just for looking guilty—and is placed in the care of an old gentleman. Fagin fears he'll blow the lid on his operation, so he and Sikes send Nancy to get Oliver. She captures him, but

Bumble endeavors to return him to his elderly benefactor (for a price, of course). Nancy realizes that the street life is not for Oliver and sabotages Sikes, so he kills her—but he's shot dead as well. Oliver returns to his benefactor, and Fagin is out of business.

ASSETS: A memorable score, a solid book—and though the Dickens novel on which it is based is over 150 years old, it is still relevant, for it is in a sense a latter-day musical version of *Goodfellas* that tells about a young man who is seduced by the glamour of the underworld.

LIABILITIES: The characterization of Fagin has often been accused of being anti-Semitic, and thus may offend some of your audience. And are we supposed to applaud after a song in which a man teaches boys to steal?

RECOGNIZABLE SONGS: "Consider Yourself," "As Long As He Needs Me."

WHO YOU'LL NEED: *Lead Singing Roles:* A conniving ne'er-do-well, his defeated-by-life female compatriot who has a legit belt voice (a Patti LuPone type); his prize young pupil who knows the score; an innocent orphan who learns from him. *Supporting Singing Roles:* A bumbler; a widow he lusts after; a confident base (*and* bass) bully; a streetwise young girl; an old married couple; two maids; a benefactor. *Other Roles:* An undertaker; a good-sized chorus of workhouse orphans, young thieves, and Londoners. *Maximum, 52; minimum, 24.*

DESIGNATED DANCES: Three large production numbers; much musical staging on three other numbers.

SUGGESTED SETS: In and outside the orphanage workhouse; an undertaker's shop; a tavern; a green.

COSTUMES: Mid-nineteenth-century glorified rags for everyone.

IMPORTANT PROPS: Bench dining-tables; a bucket of gruel; bowls and crude cutlery; wicker baskets and trays full of strawberries; balloons; modest suitcases; coffins; a pub sign.

PROVIDED INSTRUMENTATION: Two options here. Full orchestration for four reeds, two horns, two trumpets, two trombones, two violins, viola, cello, bass, two percussion, piano-conductor, or reduced orchestration for four reeds, horn, trombone, violin, cello, bass, two percussion, piano-conductor.

ADVERTISING AND MARKETING: "Consider yourself at home for *Oliver*, at . . ." At intermission, sell pretzels—but call them "Oliver Twists."

SUGGESTIONS: The show is usually directed as a good-time musical comedy—which it really isn't—so you might try a very Brechtian approach.

RESOURCES: The original cast album on CD, cassette, and LP; the very faithful 1968 movie on videotape and laserdisc; Charles Dickens's novel *Oliver Twist*, on which the musical is somewhat faithfully based.

RIGHTS: Tams-Witmark.

SNOOPY!!!

CREATORS: Book by Charles M. Schulz Creative Associates, Warren Lockhart, Arthur Whitelaw (one of the producers of *You're a Good Man, Charlie Brown*), and Michael L. Grace; music by Larry Grossman, lyrics by Hal Hackady (Grossman and Hackady collaborated on *Minnie's Boys*).

BACKGROUND: The 1983 production opened off-Broadway to adequate reviews and ran 152 performances, but has been widely produced in non-professional theaters.

STORY: The world according to Snoopy—and other lovable characters from the *Peanuts* strip: Peppermint Patty worries about her big nose, Linus waits for the Great Pumpkin; Charlie Brown remembers his adorable little puppy who grew up to be Snoopy; they all wish they knew when they were "young" what they know now. The beagle, meanwhile, feels he needs a change, resists the thought that he's a dime-a-dozen and aims to be a great writer; that doesn't quite happen, but he does get a promotion to head beagle.

ASSETS: A bright enough score that complements those characters who are still known and loved by much of the world. Kids know how to play these characters they've seen endless times on TV. And it's an inexpensive show to do.

LIABILITIES: This semi-sequel to *You're a Good Man, Charlie Brown* doesn't live up to the original, and those familiar with it may very well be disappointed.

WHO YOU'LL NEED: *Lead Singing Role:* Snoopy (who could be played by a female). *Supporting Singing Roles:* Charlie Brown; Sally Brown; Lucy; Linus; Peppermint Patty. *Other Role:* Woodstock (a mute bird). *Maximum-minimum,* 7.

DESIGNATED DANCERS: Three production numbers for the entire company, a soft-shoe strut for Snoopy.

SUGGESTED SETS: Five all-purpose blocks, a big doghouse.

COSTUMES: Outfits that closely resemble what the kids wear in the comic strip.

IMPORTANT PROPS: A large cardboard red heart (which can separate into two pieces); a stop sign; a ladder; a coat-hanger sculpture; a sandwich sign;

baseball caps and gloves; green catcher's mitt; a moon; tree branches; five pumpkins; dark glasses; a sand pail; a photo album; an Easter basket and five colored eggs; a dog collar; a water dish; straw hat and cane; (prop) typewriter; hand puppets (one is a *Jaws* shark); a snowman; "The Doctor Is In" booth and sign; Linus's blanket.

PROVIDED INSTRUMENTATION: Guitar, bass, two percussion, keyboard, keyboard-conductor.

ADVERTISING AND MARKETING: Go to card shops and try to convince the managers to allow you to hang your poster (featuring a likeness of Snoopy, of course) near their Snoopy cards and merchandise.

SUGGESTIONS: Woodstock could fly in if you have the capability.

RESOURCES: The original cast album on CD, cassette, and LP; dozens of Charles Schultz cartoon books featuring the beloved beagle. You might also investigate *You're a Good Man, Charlie Brown*—though you may wind up deciding to do that show instead.

RIGHTS: Tams-Witmark.

THE SOUND OF MUSIC

CREATORS: Book by Howard Lindsay and Russel Crouse (who wrote *Life with Father*), music by Richard Rodgers, lyrics by Oscar Hammerstein II (who had just collaborated on *Flower Drum Song*).

BACKGROUND: The 1959 production, the last Rodgers and Hammerstein collaboration (Hammerstein died eight months after the opening), received almost all-positive reviews and seven Tony nominations. It won four awards— tying with *Fiorello!* for Best Musical—and saw star Mary Martin beat out Ethel Merman's performance in *Gypsy* for the Best Actress award ("You can't buck a nun," the Merm was heard to say). The show remained for 1,443 performances.

STORY: Late 1930s, Austria. Postulant Maria is not considered nun material by her superiors, and is given a temporary assignment caring for the seven children of Captain Von Trapp, who's become an unhappy martinet since his wife's death *and* since his beloved Austria seems to be succumbing to the Nazi regime. While the children attempt to drive crazy their new governess, Maria wins over Liesl, the oldest, when she promises not to tell the captain about the girl's love for delivery boy (and Nazi sympathizer) Rolf. Maria then completely charms the other children when she teaches them to sing. When the captain's friend Max, a music impresario, hears them, he books them into a nearby festival. Though the captain is reluctant to allow his children to perform, his fiancée Elsa encourages him to let them. The captain's inability to see the

Nazi reality scares Elsa away from marriage—although the captain has slowly been falling in love with Maria because of the wonderful job she's done with his children. They marry, but do not quite live happily ever after; the captain turns down a commission with the Nazis and becomes their enemy. He, Maria, and the children try to escape after appearing at the festival. They're caught by Rolf, but because of his love for Liesl, he allows them to escape. They are traveling over the mountains to Switzerland at the play's end.

ASSETS: *Dramatics* magazine reports this is one of the most performed titles by stock, college, and amateur groups throughout the country. A magnificent score and, despite the many it's-too-sugar-coated complaints about the book, a solid and witty libretto. And think of how many tickets you'll sell to all the children's parents, grandparents, sisters, cousins, and aunts.

LIABILITIES: This is an expensive show to do, and not only because your seven kids have no fewer than five separate sets of costumes; such sites as an abbey, a villa, and the Austrian hillsides demand a type of scenic grandeur that will be difficult to reproduce convincingly.

RECOGNIZABLE SONGS: "The Sound of Music," "My Favorite Things," "Do-Re-Mi," "Sixteen Going on Seventeen," "Climb Ev'ry Mountain," "Edelweiss."

WHO YOU'LL NEED: *Lead Singing Role:* A (legit-voiced) novice who's at first a flibbertigibbet, a will o' the wisp, and a clown—but later becomes a strong woman. *Supporting Singing Roles:* A stern captain who becomes humanized; his baroness fiancée; his impresario friend; his seven children (boys of eleven and fourteen; girls of five, seven, nine, thirteen, and sixteen-going-on-seventeen); a Mother Superior with strong soprano voice; three nuns; a young boy who becomes a Nazi but is too young to realize the implications. *Other Roles:* A German officer; an admiral; a baron; a postulant; a butler; a housekeeper. *Maximum,* 43; *minimum,* 22.

DESIGNATED DANCES: A march; a dance for Rolf and Liesl; a folk dance for the captain and Maria; a waltz for all.

SUGGESTED SETS: An abbey with altar and stained glass windows; its main office, corridors, cloister, and garden; a villa's exterior, living room, terrace, and bedroom with a brass bed; a mountainside; a concert hall.

COSTUMES: For the children, white sailor uniforms for boys and similar skirted outfits for girls; party clothes; concert outfits; nightgowns and pajamas; costumes that have the identical fabric of one room's curtains—because the plot has Maria making play outfits for the kids from them. Also captain's military uniforms and Nazi uniforms; 1930s Austrian finery and folk costumes for most of the cast; butler's and housekeeper's uniforms; for Maria, a postulant outfit with petticoats underneath; an unbecoming dress and hat; a couple of modest dresses; a wedding gown with myrtle wreath.

IMPORTANT PROPS: Milk pails on a shoulder yoke; a pitchpipe and two shrill whistles; a carpetbag; a guitar; a bicycle; an eiderdown comforter; a bolt of material; tea tray with cakes; giftboxes; pistol.

PROVIDED INSTRUMENTATION: Two orchestrations available. Reduced for flute, oboe, clarinet, horn, trumpet, trombone, violin, viola, cello, bass, percussion, guitar, piano, piano-conductor. Large for all of the above, plus bassoon, tuba, harp, an extra horn, trumpet, trombone, three extra violins.

ADVERTISING AND MARKETING: "Instead of hearing some rap singers, how about hearing some Trapp Singers? See *The Sound of Music* on . . ."

SUGGESTIONS: "Don't neglect the captain's character," advises Stan Barber, Artistic Director of the Pax Amicus Castle Theater in Budd Lake, New Jersey. "He's got some serious choices here about all he's about to lose by giving up his house and home. And make Elsa a real option—a charming and lovely woman—for it's more dramatic for the captain to have a real dilemma there, too."

RESOURCES: The original cast album on CD, cassette, and LP; the fairly faithful 1965 movie on videotape and laserdisc; the book *The Trapp Family Singers*, by Maria Augusta Trapp, on which the musical is fairly faithfully based.

RIGHTS: Rodgers and Hammerstein.

THE WIZARD OF OZ

CREATORS: Book by Frank Gabrielson, music by Harold Arlen, lyrics by E. Y. Harburg (Arlen and Harburg later collaborated on *Jamaica*).

BACKGROUND: Everyone loves the classic 1939 movie so much that it was adapted for stage presentation in the 1960s. Though this version has never played Broadway, it's played most everywhere else.

STORY: How can we put this? Girl hates home, girl leaves home, girl wants home back, girl gets home.

ASSETS: Of course there's that classic score, but the real pull is the charming story in which everyone is out for everyone else: "What about that heart you promised the Tin Man?" booms the Scarecrow to the Wizard—not, "Hey, where's the brain you promised *me*?"

LIABILITIES: It's an expensive show to do.

RECOGNIZABLE SONGS: "Over the Rainbow," "Ding, Dong—the Witch Is Dead," "We're Off to See the Wizard."

WHO YOU'LL NEED: *Lead Singing Roles*: A frightened but brave young girl; Scarecrow; Tin Man; Cowardly Lion (the latter three, of course, double as Kansas farmhands in the first and last scenes). *Supporting Singing Roles*: A good witch; a chorus of crows; a bunch of Munchkins (little kids) including the mayor, the barrister, two city fathers, the coroner, three Lullabye Leaguers, and the Lollipop Guild. *Other Roles*: The Wicked Witch of the West (who doubles as Miss Gulch), a would-be professor (who doubles as the Wizard of Oz), a palace guard, three apple trees, six flying monkeys; a chorus of Emerald City denizens, and an adorable little dog. *Maximum, 63; minimum, 30.*

DESIGNATED DANCES: A celebration from the Munchkins; a strut for Dorothy and Scarecrow, later adding Tin Man and Cowardly Lion to the parade; a march for them and much of the company; a celebration for everyone once the Wicked Witch is dead.

SUGGESTED SETS: A road and farm in Kansas; a yellow brick road; the merry old land of Oz; the witch's castle.

COSTUMES: Ah, there's the rub! Scarecrow, Tin Man, and Cowardly Lion need not look exactly like the famous trio in the movie, but audiences seem to be more pleased when they do. In addition, there are some stylized costumes for the Munchkins; uniforms for the flying monkeys; a beautiful gown for the Good Witch and an ugly one for the Wicked Witch; plain farm wear for Dorothy and the Kansas residents; a pair of ruby slippers.

IMPORTANT PROPS: Farm implements; a medicine show wagon; a house on top of a dead witch's legs; a broomstick.

SPECIAL EFFECTS: A tornado; a trap door to get rid of the Wicked Witch when she's melting.

PROVIDED INSTRUMENTATION: Two flutes, oboe, two clarinets, bassoon, three horns, two trumpets, trombone, tuba, two percussion, three violins, viola, cello, bass, harp, piano, piano-conductor.

ADVERTISING AND MARKETING: "Be thankful your very young children can't read this, because they'd be pestering you forever to take them to see *The Wizard of Oz* at our theater. But we're letting you know so you can get tickets for them and you in advance, and give them a delightful surprise."

SUGGESTIONS: Would your community enjoy even more *The Wiz*, a 1975 more contemporary sounding version?

RESOURCES: The best version is the 1987 London revival cast album on CD, cassette, and LP; the 1939 classic film on videotape and laserdisc on which the musical is very faithfully based.

RIGHTS: Tams-Witmark.

YOU'RE A GOOD MAN, CHARLIE BROWN

CREATORS: Book, music, and lyrics by Clark Gesner (though Gesner originally used the pseudonym "John Gordon" as bookwriter so it wouldn't appear that he'd done everything).

BACKGROUND: The 1967 production became an instant off-Broadway smash and ran 1,547 performances.

STORY: A typical—i.e., difficult—day in the life of Charlie Brown. His kite won't do what he wants it to, he makes the final out in a baseball game he could have won, he doesn't have the nerve to talk to that little red-haired girl, and he finds that few kids like him—but by show's end, Lucy comes up to Charlie Brown and asserts, "You're a good man, Charlie Brown."

ASSETS: *Dramatics* magazine reports this is one of the most performed titles by stock, college, and amateur groups throughout the country. It's very inexpensive, and kids understand it because they've so often seen the characters on *Peanuts* TV specials.

LIABILITIES: Some object that the musical's treatment is far less sophisticated musically than the TV specials; there jazz is used, while here "baby music" is.

WHO YOU'LL NEED: *Lead Singing Roles:* Charlie Brown; Snoopy (who could be played by a female); Lucy. *Supporting Singing Roles:* Linus; Patty; Schroeder. *Maximum-minimum,* 6.

DESIGNATED DANCES: Two marches for the company; a solo strut for Charlie Brown; a big vaudeville-inspired eleven o'clock number for Snoopy.

SUGGESTED SETS: The show traditionally has been done with brightly painted building blocks that serve to become a bench, a rock, a desk, and Snoopy's doghouse.

COSTUMES The same T-shirts and dresses seen in the comic strip.

IMPORTANT PROPS: Those aforementioned building blocks; an enormous dogfood bowl; a miniature grand piano; an oversized lunch bag; Linus's blue blanket; a jump rope; a TV; a batch of valentines; Lucy's "The Doctor Is In" booth; a tree with one leaf on it—which falls off; baseball bats and gloves.

PROVIDED INSTRUMENTATION: If you're in a small space (as the original production was), use the bass-percussion-flute-and-piano orchestration; if you're in a large theater, you might consider the full orchestration: Five reeds, two trumpets, trombone, horn, two violins, cello, bass, percussion, guitar, piano-celeste, piano-conductor.

ADVERTISING AND MARKETING: Interesting, isn't it, how Charlie Brown used to be the star of *Peanuts*—but over the years he's been superseded by a beagle? It's gotten to the point where licensing agents now describe this show as "the fabulous Snoopy musical." Maybe you should, too.

SUGGESTIONS: Another good show for very young children, for they won't be overtaxed by the short scenes. They'll also look cute when reciting such good dialogue.

RESOURCES: The original cast album on CD, cassette, and LP; the 1973 TV version.

RIGHTS: Tams-Witmark.

Also See: *Annie; Babes in Arms; Big River; Bring Back Birdie; Bye Bye Birdie; Cats; Godspell; Gypsy; Into the Woods; Li'l Abner; Peter Pan; The Roar of the Greasepaint—The Smell of the Crowd; Starlight Express; Stop the World—I Want to Get Off; The Wiz.*

"YOU ARE 16 GOING ON 17"

Musicals for High Schoolers

If you run a high school drama club—or if you're the head of a community house that wants to bring adolescents off the streets and involve them in a healthier activity—here are some musicals that you and the teens will enjoy producing and performing.

BABES IN ARMS

CREATORS: Rewritten book by George Oppenheimer, based on Richard Rodgers and Lorenz (*Pal Joey*) Hart's original, music by Rodgers, lyrics by Hart, for stock and amateur productions.

BACKGROUND: The 1937 production featured many genuine teenagers, and the critics were as charmed as the audiences at how well they did with one of the best Rodgers and Hart scores, allowing a 289-performance run.

STORY: The 1978 Oppenheimer version takes place "the day before yesterday" on Cape Cod. It's about teenage Valentine and his friends including buxom

Terry and comic Gus, who allow themselves to be overworked and underpaid at a summer theater in return for the chance to put on Val's revue for bigshot Steve Edwards. Susie believes in Val, but he feels she's just a kid—and prefers the sophisticated Jennifer, who's worked professionally, thanks to an ambitious stage mother who wants her in egotistical Lee Calhoun's new play. But when theater owner Fleming wants to extend Calhoun's play an extra week—thus canceling the kids' revue—the kids sabotage his worthless play. It's eventually divulged that Steve is Susie's brother, and all works out as the kids get to do their show—triumphantly.

ASSETS: A fine score, and, if you have the kids who are young and enthusiastic enough to believe what they're saying, this can be a good time.

LIABILITIES: While the original version was surprisingly ahead of its time in tackling the subject of prejudice, this version is a silly view of a theatrical era long-past—if it ever existed at all.

RECOGNIZABLE SONGS: "Where or When," "Babes in Arms," "I Wish I Were in Love Again," "My Funny Valentine," "Johnny One Note," "The Lady Is a Tramp."

WHO YOU'LL NEED: *Leading Singing Roles:* An ambitious young song-writer; the slightly younger and adorable girl who loves him. *Supporting Singing Roles:* A young actress with a burgeoning figure and a personality (and legit voice) to boot; a boy who's all thumbs; a throw-herself-into-it worker. *Other Roles:* The apprentices—an athletic and handsome boy, a girl who's sensitive about the braces on her teeth, a teen muscleman, a baby-faced youngster trying to grow up, a preppie; a buffoonish Southern playwright; the all-business theater owner; his struggling female partner; an agent who's also a good big brother; a stage mother; a press agent who functions à la the stage manager in *Our Town*, but with far less to do. *Maximum, 37; minimum, 18.*

DESIGNATED DANCES: A march and an eleven o'clock number for the entire company; a ballet for Terry, Gus, and the apprentices; three other production numbers.

SUGGESTED SETS: Inside and outside a Cape Cod summer theater; a barn; an inn bedroom; a country road.

COSTUMES: 1930s wear for kids; for the girls, linen dresses, print dresses, shirtwaist dresses, evening dresses, playsuits, slacks, tiaras, and jewelry; for the boys, worsted suits, seersucker suits, blazers and slacks, Bermuda shorts, chinos, blue jeans, khaki shorts.

IMPORTANT PROPS: Paint pails and brushes; hammers and nails; saws; ladders; lanterns; a breakaway statue; a tea service, a filled Coke cooler; a soft drink booth. For the ballet: fencing foils; dueling pistols; jeweled guitar; megaphone; camera-take board; oversized Oscar.

PROVIDED INSTRUMENTATION: Four reeds, two trumpets, trombone, percussion, violin, viola, cello, bass, piano, piano-conductor.

ADVERTISING AND MARKETING: Ask people to bring baby food or equipment to the theater in exchange for a free ticket or a discount, then donate the proceeds to charity.

SUGGESTIONS: You can play the show as if you totally believe it, or campily as if you believe none of it; don't mess with Mister In-Between.

RESOURCES: The most complete recording is a 1990 studio cast CD and cassette. There is a hardly faithful 1939 movie on videotape.

RIGHTS: Rodgers and Hammerstein.

BIG RIVER

CREATORS: Book by William Hauptman, music and lyrics by Roger ("King of the Road") Miller.

BACKGROUND: The 1985 production was the big hit during a weak season, nabbing ten Tony nominations, winning seven awards—including Best Musical—and running 1,005 performances.

STORY: Mid-1800's on the Mississippi. Huck Finn tells us his real story—of an abusive father and the domestication imposed by a widow and a spinster—so he bolts for his freedom, soon meeting up with slave Jim, who's escaped to win his own freedom. As they raft down the Mississippi, they meet "the King" and "the Duke," who use their royalty (and Huck and Jim's naivete) to live royally on the raft. At one port, all but Jim go ashore to put on a show and earn some money; when Huck returns, he plays a trick on Jim, pretending to be a slave hunter, which hurts and infuriates Jim. Huck does what was then unthinkable: he apologizes to a black. At the next port, the con men hear that a rich family has suffered the loss of their patriarch and pretend to be his just-arrived heirs. It's too much for Huck, who returns the money. Mary Jane, the deceased's daughter, asks him to stay with her, but he feels a responsibility to Jim. When he returns, a tarred-and-feathered Duke says that he sold Jim for forty dollars. Huck is determined to free Jim and, with the help of Tom Sawyer, does just that. Huck and Jim separate; Huck will go west to avoid further domestication and Jim will head north to find his freedom.

ASSETS: A perky score with a charming if irrelevant song that praises hogs; a show in which boys' natural qualities can be charmingly used; a country-western score by a pop song writer.

LIABILITIES: A clumsy book in which the second act doesn't soar nearly as much as the first; in fact, the second half of the first act doesn't soar as much as the first part of the first act. Blacks are often referred to by a historically accurate but offensive and pejorative word.

WHO YOU'LL NEED: *Lead Singing Roles*: A charming young adult man who prefers freedom to domestication; an older strong black (bass-voiced) slave who becomes his friend. *Supporting Singing Roles*: A dypsomaniac father (John Goodman); an aunt; an instigating friend; an actor who pretends to be a duke; a preacher who pretends to be a king; a didactic widow; a strange woman; a female gospel singer. *Other Roles*: A judge; a counselor; a sheriff; an Englishman; a slaveowner; a young fool; a Mark Twain lookalike; three boys; male and female slaves; townspeople; tarts; loafers; onstage musicians (optional); a "body" to lie in state in a coffin. *Maximum, 44; minimum, 20.*

DESIGNATED DANCES: Musical staging on the opening number; some rustic soft-shoe; a few hoe-down dances.

SUGGESTED SETS: An enlarged frontispiece disclaimer that *Huckleberry Finn* not be taken too seriously; a nice dining room; rural Missouri fields; a lean-to; an island; a ferry stop; a moveable log raft that Huck and Jim negotiate down the river.

COSTUMES: Late nineteenth-century Midwest finery and shabby clothes; calico dresses (including one for Huck); denim overcoats; garish prostitute clothes; fanciful actors' costumes (including one hermaphroditic one with wig and breasts); a tarred-and-feathered costume; women's black mourning clothes.

IMPORTANT PROPS: A moonshine jug; candles; pipes; a bag of gold; a cot, stretcher, and blanket; a stool, sofa, table, and chairs; a coffin; a trunk; a wagon full of cotton; water bucket and dipper; tin pot; a lantern on a stick; logs; raftpoles; a canoe; spyglass; horseshoe; skunk; large catfish; artificial cabbages and tomatoes; an edible chicken; an "Alas, poor Yorick"–sized skull; bottle of whiskey; a crowbar; hickory sticks; leg chains; a hammer and chisel; switches; whips; knives; wooden swords; revolvers; shotguns.

SPECIAL EFFECTS: Thunder and lightning; fog; rain; sounds of birds, dogs, gunshots, and cannons; lights of St. Louis in the background.

PROVIDED INSTRUMENTATION: Woodwind, trumpet, tenor trombone, percussion, guitar, bass, piano, piano-conductor, and—for onstage musicians—violin, harmonica, guitar.

ADVERTISING AND MARKETING: First, learn what your community feels about *The Adventures of Huckleberry Finn*—some don't approve of it—and adjust how much you'll stress *Big River*'s source material.

SUGGESTIONS: An onstage band of country-western musicians is a good touch. The river can be played fourth-wall. A nice show to be done in an arena setting with the slightest suggestion of sets. The act-one curtain isn't as powerful as most, so you can eliminate the intermission to good effect.

RESOURCES: The original cast album on CD, cassette, and LP; Mark Twain's novel *The Adventures of Huckleberry Finn.*

RIGHTS: Rodgers and Hammerstein.

BRING BACK BIRDIE

CREATORS: Book by Michael Stewart, music by Charles Strouse, lyrics by Lee Adams (the same team that did *Bye Bye Birdie*).

BACKGROUND: This 1981 musical, the much-awaited sequel to the enormously popular *Bye Bye Birdie*, told what happened twenty years after Conrad Birdie's disastrous appearance on "The Ed Sullivan Show." It was judged too silly, closed after 4 performances, and received a single Tony nomination for star Chita Rivera, who didn't win.

STORY: New York City, 1980. Conrad's been gone for twenty years, but English teacher Albert and wife Rosie are offered twenty thousand dollars if they can locate him and get him to appear on the Grammys. Rosie is more preoccupied with her teenage daughter and son; Jenny's ready to move out and live with her boyfriend, while Albert Jr. is a guitar freak. Albert enlists Detective Mtobe's help, and he gets a lead that Birdie may be in Arizona. They—and the reluctant Rosie—travel to Tucson to bring back Birdie, and find in a watering hole Albert's longlost mother—as the bartender. (She's still insulting Spanish Rosie, as she did in *Bye Bye Birdie*.) Meanwhile Jenny, unknown to her parents, takes off with a "Sunny"—read: Moonie—and young Albert joins a rock group. Albert, Rosie, and Mom travel to Bent River Junction, where they meet the mayor of the town—whom they recognize as a very overweight and bilious Birdie. They convince him to play a gig at a nearby stadium, where he bombs; the kids prefer a punk-rock group called Filth. When Rosie discovers the guitarist of the punkers is young Albert, she's infuriated and heads for home—but Albert's delighted to be back in show business. Mamma's glad to be pulling Albert's strings again, and introduces him to "Rose II"; the middle-aged Albert responds to the sweet young thing and asks Rosie for a divorce. But after he sees that Rosie is merely insulted, not devastated, and plans her own romance, he appreciates her more. Birdie refuses to appear on the Grammys—he's got political ambitions that would be injured if he rocked'-n'-rolled on TV. Mamma pulls back, even admitting *she's* Spanish; Jenny finds a new boyfriend, and Albert Jr. returns home to his happy parents.

ASSETS: While the musical can't compare with its illustrious predecessor, it is an enjoyable show for not-too-demanding audiences who might be intrigued by what happened to Albert, his mother, Rosie, and Conrad.

LIABILITIES: Would you believe that Albert's mother, who decried Spaniards every step of the way in *Bye Bye Birdie*, eventually admits that she's Spanish? That's the level of the book's wit. And those interested in how Kim and Hugo made out won't find any mention of them here.

WHO YOU'LL NEED: *Lead Singing Roles:* A more mature Albert (Donald O'Connor) and Rosie (Rivera). *Supporting Singing Roles:* Their winsome teenage daughter and their slave-to-music teenage son; a Nigerian private detective; an Elvis impersonator of the later years; Albert's bossy mother. *Other Roles:* A New Age religious leader, a sexy but sweet young woman; a Native American squaw and brave; a tourist and her husband; three reporters; a waiter; a house manager; a cameraman; a bag lady; a street cleaner; a porter; a guard; boys who form the rock group; two teenagers who are "Sunnies"; a chorus of girlfriends, Birdie fans, and stagedoor Johnnies. *Maximum, 46; minimum, 21.*

DESIGNATED DANCES: Two solo spots for Rose, another with a chorus; an Elvis number for Birdie; two production numbers for the kids; a fox-trot for Albert and Rosie.

SUGGESTED SETS: A darkened office; a modest Forest Hills house; a bus terminal in New York and another in Arizona; a Western nightclub; a mayor's office; the stage of a stadium; a New Age religious compound; a locker room; a motel room; a TV studio; the Grammy Awards stage.

COSTUMES: Contemporary wear, though the kids' clothes should be wildly more colorful than the adults'; choir robes; saffron robes for the New Age religious believers; Western cowboy wear; lycra, spandex, and punk-pink wigs for your rock group; a large gold lamé jumpsuit for Birdie.

IMPORTANT PROPS: Filing cabinets; guitars and tambourines; a box of Cheer detergent and bottles of Joy and Yes dishwashing liquid; beer cans that overflow when opened; a lockable closet.

PROVIDED INSTRUMENTATION: Four reeds, horn, three trumpets, two trombones, percussion, three violins, cello, guitar-banjo, bass, piano-conductor.

ADVERTISING AND MARKETING: *"Bye Bye Birdie* was such a success that we're going to bring back Birdie—Conrad, that is—in the sequel to the smash hit, *Bring Back Birdie."*

SUGGESTIONS: If you do two musicals a year, you might consider doing *Bye Bye Birdie* first, then following it with *Bring Back Birdie*, using your same leads for the sequel.

RESOURCES: The original cast album on LP.

RIGHTS: Tams-Witmark.

BYE BYE BIRDIE

CREATORS: Book by Michael (*Hello, Dolly!*) Stewart, music by Charles Strouse, lyrics by Lee Adams (who later collaborated on *Applause).*

BACKGROUND: The 1960 production was the surprise hit of the season, receiving eight Tony nominations, winning four awards—including Best Musical—and running 608 performances.

STORY: 1960, New York City. Conrad Birdie is about to be drafted, so Albert Peterson—his producer-songwriter-manager—faces ruin. Albert's longtime girlfriend Rosie comes up with an idea for a contest—one of his fans will give Birdie "one last kiss" on "The Ed Sullivan Show." The winner is Kim McAfee from Sweet Apple, Ohio, but her steady boyfriend Hugo Peabody is furious. So is Albert's mother, who follows him and the entourage to Ohio to make sure he doesn't marry Rosie. And so is Kim's father, who is ready to prevent Kim from appearing until Albert offers him a spot on the Sullivan show. He makes an ass of himself on nationwide TV, but that's eclipsed by Hugo's rushing onstage and punching Conrad. Both Rosie and Kim are fed up with their men, and each bolts. Eventually, Kim and Hugo reconcile and Albert tracks down Rosie; despite his mother's protests, he decides to marry her.

ASSETS: *Dramatics* magazine reports this is one of the most performed titles by the country's stock, college, and amateur groups. With Elvis Presley now on a stamp, there'll always be interest in this show about a 1950s rock star. Add to this the nostalgia of "The Ed Sullivan Show," the continuing generational war—not to mention a very good book and score—and you've got a hit.

LIABILITIES: Albert gives Rosie a good deal of a-woman's-place-is-in-the-home talk in the second act, which, during the 1991 Tommy Tune revival, prompted some audience members to hiss. After delivering these lines, Tune looked directly at the audience and said mock-apologetically, "Hey—it's 1959." The audience loved it.

RECOGNIZABLE SONGS: "Kids," "Put on a Happy Face," "A Lot of Livin' to Do"—and "We Love You, Conrad," which some audience members who were teens in 1964 will remember as the "We Love You, Beatles" chant.

WHO YOU'LL NEED: *Lead Singing Roles:* A music publisher who should have been an English teacher (Dick Van Dyke); his secretary and fiancée (Chita Rivera). *Supporting Singing Roles:* A charismatic Elvis Presley type; his adoring teenage girl fan; her jealous boyfriend; her harried father (Paul Lynde); her mother; and her little brother. *Other Roles:* The quintessential overprotective mother; a small-town mayor; his sexually repressed wife; a barkeep; a voluptuous woman; a chorus full of female teenagers to love Conrad. *Maximum, 45; minimum, 22.*

DESIGNATED DANCES: A dance for Albert in which he's joined by an unhappy teen; a march for most of the company; three Elvis-inspired numbers for Birdie, one of which the teens join; a fox-trot for Rosie and Albert; for Rosie, a solo tango, a dream ballet with the dancers, and a romp with some Shriners.

SUGGESTED SETS: A modest office; an Ohio home; railroad stations in New York and Ohio; a courthouse; a theater stage; a roadside retreat; a suburban nightspot; an erector-set structure on which the kids can carry on a musical telephone conversation.

COSTUMES: 1960s suits and dresses, more stylish for the Manhattanites than for the Ohioans; clothes typical of teens; a mink coat for Albert's mother; waiters' and bartenders' outfits; Shriners' fezzes; a military uniform; a few elaborate gowns; a posh bathrobe—"and do have a gold lame suit for Conrad," pleads original costume designer Miles White. "It's all I ever saw him in."

IMPORTANT PROPS: Filing cabinets; a mock-guillotine on which Rosie imagines Albert beheaded; many telephones with long, long cords.

PROVIDED INSTRUMENTATION: Four reeds, horn, three trumpets, two trombones, percussion, three violins, cello, guitar-banjo, bass, piano-conductor.

ADVERTISING AND MARKETING: There's a lyric that insists that Conrad Birdie's habit is "making fudge"—so whip up a batch of the chocolate stuff, label it "Conrad Birdie's Fudge," and sell it during intermission.

SUGGESTIONS: If you do two musicals a year, you might consider doing *Bye Bye Birdie* first, then following it with *Bring Back Birdie*, using your same leads for the sequel.

RESOURCES: The original cast album on CD, cassette, and LP; the barely faithful 1963 movie version on videotape and laserdisc.

RIGHTS: Tams-Witmark.

DO BLACK PATENT LEATHER SHOES REALLY REFLECT UP?

CREATORS: Book by John R. Powers, music and lyrics by James Quinn and Alaric Jans.

BACKGROUND: While the 1982 Broadway production lasted only 5 performances and received no Tony nominations, this show has had a good deal of success in many regional productions, and should score in your town as well.

STORY: Growing up Catholic in Chicago in the 1950's, from grammar school through high school. Second-grader Eddie likes Becky, a heavyset girl, though he can't admit it to his friends. Becky's weight makes her miserable, which causes Sister Lee to take pity on her and give her the great honor of crowning the Blessed Virgin Mary's statue at the May procession. By the time the kids reach high school, Becky's lost weight and Eddie has grown to love her—and though Becky loves him, too, she instead decides to become a nun. Years later, though, Eddie hears that Becky's left the convent, and he plans to make her his again. A nice collage of memories of sitting through twelve years of Catholic education: grammar school (memorizing of catechism questions, the routine corporal punishment the nuns and priest administer), junior high (girls are told to pull down their skirts past their knees; boys are recruited to become priests), and high school (the very veiled sex education; at dances, they're to "leave room for the Holy Ghost").

ASSETS: A bouncy score, some clever lyrics, and situations bound to make those who attended parochial schools moan with recognition, while making kids who didn't sorry-grateful that they didn't. If your group consists mostly of kids, they'll already have a head start on understanding their characters. The character of Sister Lee is especially strong, for while she is at first characterized as a mean old crone, we see she is capable of great empathy.

LIABILITIES: Clever as it is, the show could be more clever. Non-Catholics won't be nodding their heads and laughing with recognition when they hear terms such as "mission money," and may feel left out. In fact, will they even understand the title, which refers to the nuns' fear that boys will see girls' panties reflected in their shiny shoes?

WHO YOU'LL NEED: Kids who can go from second-graders to high school seniors, with Eddie and Becky also able to play adults. *Lead Singing Roles:* A sincere and polite boy; his girlfriend who has a good deal of baby fat during grade school but loses it. *Supporting Singing Roles:* Two wise-guy (but paper-tiger) friends and a nondescript fellow student; a goody-goody smart girl; two whining girls; one no-nonsense priest. *Other Roles:* Four nuns; a school secretary. *Maximum, 14; minimum, 13.*

DESIGNATED DANCES: Dances typical of a school dance (fast dances, slow dances, and the bunny hop); a joyous solo dance for Eddie; a solo jig for Sister Lee; one major production number in which girls and boys stomp in oversized patent leather shoes.

SUGGESTED SETS: A school office; a second-grade classroom; a church; a playground with jungle gym; a high school gym; a porch; an athletic field.

COSTUMES: Catholic school uniforms; gym suits; 1950s wear for grammar school kids; early 1960s wear for high schoolers; fat padding for Becky; priest cassocks; traditional nuns' habits—and most important and challenging, oversized patent leather shoes.

IMPORTANT PROPS: A pitchpipe; a whistle; frog-clickers; jump rope; basketball; football; baseball bats; missals; diplomas; lunchboxes; a large statue of the Blessed Virgin Mary; a garland of flowers with which to crown her.

PROVIDED INSTRUMENTATION: Two reeds, two trumpets, trombone, cello, bass, guitar, percussion, drums, piano-conductor. (If you have an organ, so much the better for some church sounds.)

ADVERTISING AND MARKETING: You might try, "If you liked *Nunsense*, you'll love this"—though, truth to tell, it may be more accurate to say that many who loved *Nunsense* might *like* this. You might also try to sell those T-shirts that blare, "I survived Catholic schools."

SUGGESTIONS: If you're up for it, you might consider casting freshmen and sophomores for the first act, and have juniors and seniors perform the second act.

RESOURCES: The original cast album on CD, cassette and LP; the John R. Powers book that inspired the musical.

RIGHTS: Samuel French.

DOONESBURY

CREATORS: Book and lyrics by Garry Trudeau, from his comic strip, music by Elizabeth (*Runaways*) Swados.

BACKGROUND: There were high hopes for the 1983 production, but the musical couldn't match the expectations. It received no Tony nominations and closed after only 104 performances.

STORY: Early 1980's, in a house in "Walden." Mike Doonesbury is the type of guy who writes out on index cards his marriage proposal to J.J., who has no idea he's as interested as he is. She becomes quite angry with him, in fact, because he's invited her mother, who abandoned her during a 1970s I've-got-to-find-myself spree, to stay for the weekend. But Mike convinces J.J. to abandon her hard feelings, and that's when she falls in love with him.

In addition, the other famous Trudeau characters are in the midst of college graduation. Mark wants to be a radio talk show host, B.D. wants to play for the Dallas Cowboys, Zonker wants to be the resident tanning director for his Uncle Duke's new condominium complex, which was supposed to be a court-ordered drug rehabilitation center. Almost everyone gets almost everything he wants.

ASSETS: In addition to a great built-in name recognition with the beloved comic strip characters, you have a funky score, some clever lyrics, and a book with many lines that have the satiric sting of the comic strip. There are also many endearingly wry perceptions—"You know what we forgot to do while we were college students? Go to Europe and buy Eurailpasses and sew patches on our knapsacks and stay in filthy two-dollar youth hostels and get drunk at all of Hemingway's favorite cafes."

LIABILITIES: The show was meant to be topical, so it now has many dated references to Ronald Reagan's press conferences; though, truth to tell, with very minor revisions, they could apply to any politician. More difficult to fix will be the 1980s mentality that pervades the piece—from lines like "Real estate is ringing everyone's bell these days," to "We've got to thank the Big Gip for bringing 'making it' back in style," to a song called "It's the Right Time to be Rich" and many drug references.

WHO YOU'LL NEED: *Supporting Singing Roles* (as you'd expect from a bunch of college seniors living in a commune): A decent but socially graceless guy; a radio talk show host; a dim-witted football player; a latter-day hippie; his scheming uncle; two devoted girlfriends; a feminist mother; her bitter daughter. *Other Roles:* A television correspondent; a provost. *Maximum-minimum,* 11.

DESIGNATED DANCES: One spirited dance and a 1950s shoo-op for the kids; one rhythmic boogie for all (the television correspondent needn't be good at the boogie; in fact, he's supposed to be inept); a short rap strut and breakdance steps for Mark, a dance for Duke and Zonker called "Pas de Duke."

SUGGESTED SETS: A communal house, its back porch, and its nearby puddle; a Los Angeles courtroom; a campus radio station; a graduation platform. All should mirror Trudeau's style.

COSTUMES: 1970s college student clothes; preppie regalia; a football helmet; pajamas; army fatigues; tool apron; hard hat; gas mask; five graduation caps and gowns; sunglasses, hats, and visors for fanciful hand puppets of a cactus, daisy, daffodil, and orchid.

IMPORTANT PROPS: A screenless TV; hand mikes; telephones; many index cards; a refrigerator; swivel chair; folding chairs; couch and floor pillows; an automatic weapon; a pistol in a holster; a tape measure; snorkeling gear; a briefcase; a diaper bag; a "baby"; a casserole; doughnuts; orange juice; a beer-can pyramid; serving spoons; spatula; cereal bowls; plates; flash camera; diplomas; a plant mister, and those aforementioned hand puppets of plants.

SPECIAL EFFECTS: Duke drives an onstage bulldozer into the house and knocks down walls. You could get by without the bulldozer, but the walls should come tumbling down.

PROVIDED INSTRUMENTATION: Reed, trumpet/flugelhorn, trombone, cello/percussion, guitar, bass, drums, two keyboards, piano-conductor.

ADVERTISING AND MARKETING: "If you enjoyed reading *Doonesbury* this morning, see it on stage tonight at . . ."

SUGGESTIONS: The Broadway production used a bench on which the actors not then performing would sit in full view of the audience. Sometimes they'd sing backup to the songs, other times they'd just watch what was happening.

"But don't feel," advises Swados, "that the bench must be retained in your production."

RESOURCES: The original cast album on CD, cassette, and LP; the myriad *Doonesbury* comic book collections.

RIGHTS: Samuel French.

GOOD NEWS!

CREATORS: Book by Laurence Schwab and Buddy DeSylva, music by Ray Henderson, lyrics by Lew Brown and DeSylva (who all collaborated on *The George White Scandals*).

BACKGROUND: The 1927 production was such a celebration that even the ushers were garbed as collegians and coeds; the orchestra was not in place before the show, but ran down the aisles and then entered the pit. Of course, it was the terrific score and great reviews that kept the show running for a then-monstrous 551 performances.

STORY: 1920s, at a private college. Tom, the star football player at Tait, may flunk astronomy and be ineligible to play in the big game. Pat, the girl he impulsively promised to marry one night—and who plans to hold him to it—is nevertheless too busy with sorority duties to coach him, so she has her cousin Connie do it. Connie helps, but Tom still doesn't pass. However, the prof's a football fan, so he tells Connie he'll pass him. Connie and Tom fall in love, and eventually Pat lets Tom off the hook so that Connie and Tom can marry, right after he wins the big game. There are also many eternal-triangle subplots that are just as convoluted and of course work out just as happily.

ASSETS: Good score and some fun nonsense; kids always enjoy playing slightly older kids, and this show gives them the chance to get some previews of coming attractions of the most enjoyable aspects of campus life.

LIABILITIES: The show is corny with a capital "C," and not merely because no professor would tell a student that he's passing her boyfriend (and give the unjustifiable reason why). One example of the corn out of dozens: A beefy football player bursts into the benchwarmer's room looking for his girlfriend, who's hiding under the bed. When she inadvertently says something, the star player asks, "What was that?" and the scrub adopts a falsetto voice in hopes of convincing the intruder that he actually said something. And the star believes him.

RECOGNIZABLE SONGS: "The Best Things in Life Are Free," "Just Imagine," "Button Up Your Overcoat," "You're the Cream in My Coffee," "The Varsity Drag," "Good News," "Keep Your Sunny Side Up," "Life Is Just a Bowl of Cherries."

WHO YOU'LL NEED: *Lead Singing Roles:* A good-looking and good-natured star halfback; a demure sorority sister. *Supporting Singing Roles:* A beefy running back; a benchwarmer; a meek but eager freshman; one calculating sorority sister; two male seniors (one heavyset, one thin); two female students. *Other Roles:* An astronomy professor; a football coach; a trainer; a large chorus of boy and girl cheerleaders; an onstage marching band; a dog. *Maximum,* 45; *minimum,* 23.

DESIGNATED DANCES: Plenty of soft-shoe; duets; a march; energetic production numbers—especially "The Varsity Drag," in which your cast will spend a lot of time "down on its heels and up on its toes."

SUGGESTED SETS: The Tait College quadrangle; one of its dormitory rooms (with working window shade); outside its sorority and fraternity houses; outside its football stadium; on its gridiron; in its locker room; a boathouse (optional).

COSTUMES: 1920s college wear; football, cheerleader, and band uniforms; pajamas (at least one pair should be loud).

IMPORTANT PROPS: A 1920s jalopy with detachable running board and fenders; beds; framed pictures; a salt shaker; a coal bin with coal; picnic paraphernalia and sandwiches; a rubbing table; locker room benches; Ace bandages; a baseball bat; a lacrosse stick; a horseshoe; megaphones; pom-poms; balloons and pennants (ideally with a big "T" or "Tait" emblazoned on each).

SPECIAL EFFECTS: Your biggest challenge will be the football game, which is accomplished by actors running on treadmills. Many schools bells also sound.

PROVIDED INSTRUMENTATION: Flute, clarinet, B ♭ cornet, trombone, drums, two violins, viola, cello, bass, piano-conductor.

ADVERTISING AND MARKETING: Make up one-page newspapers that are headlined *Good News!* and feature stories about your cast, the production, and the impressive history of the show, then distribute them all around town.

SUGGESTIONS: If yours is a school with a heavy tradition of football, schedule your performances the days just before the big game.

RESOURCES: No commercially released original cast album, but the soundtrack of the 1947 movie will be somewhat helpful, as will its videotape and laserdisc.

RIGHTS: Samuel French.

HENRY, SWEET HENRY

CREATORS: Book by Nunnally Johnson (who wrote the screenplay of *The World of Henry Orient,* on which the musical is based), music and lyrics by Bob *(Carnival)* Merrill.

BACKGROUND: The 1967 production was the first musical reviewed by Clive Barnes when he became critic of the *New York Times*; he asserted that show music must have a more contemporary sound than this traditional show cared to give. It lasted 84 performances, received two Tony nominations, and won neither, but offers good opportunities to non-professionals.

STORY: 1960s, New York. Valerie and Gil, two female teenage students at the prestigious Norton School in Manhattan, while in Central Park happen upon a distinguished man named Henry trying to seduce a very nervous woman named Stella—who becomes more nervous when she notices the kids. When the girls are taken to a concert the following week, they discover that the amorous man is avant-garde composer Henry Orient. Val immediately "falls in love," Gil offers to help her win her man, and the two make Orient the focus of their lives. They find his address and head out to see him—hounded by Natalie Kafritz, a schoolmate who's promised two boys that they could have dates with the girls. To get rid of Kafritz, they say that Val is an addict and Orient is her pusher—but all that does is send Kafritz to the police. Thus, when Henry is ready to make love to the nervous Stella, and the shade is pulled, the cops begin their drug bust, and arrest Val as well. Her distrustful mother, learning all about the Orient plan, calls Henry for his side of the story, and winds up meeting with him. The girls hear about this and rush to his house to tell *their* side of the story—just as he's escorting Val's mother inside to make love. Val's mother lies to her husband, but he can tell what's going on, and decides to end the marriage, promising Val that he and she will have a better relationship from now on. By the end of the show, Kafritz's dates have shown up for Val and Gil, and they begin relating to real boys.

ASSETS: A fun score and book—the first-act curtain is a surefire howler—with plenty of opportunities for schoolgirls to shine.

LIABILITIES: Those who know the movie on which the musical is based won't be as pleased by this effort. And the second act begins with a scene involving hippies that demands you keep the show in the late 1960s.

WHO YOU'LL NEED: *Lead Singing Role*: An extroverted young girl. *Supporting Singing Roles*: Her introverted best friend; an eccentric and randy pianist (Peter Sellers); the bubble-headed married woman he wants to romance; a young but street-smart and matchmaking student. *Other Roles*: A mother and father whose marriage is crumbling; a well-adjusted mother; a police captain and two cops; a prim teacher; an usherette; Val as an adult; girl and boy prep school students. *Maximum, 51; minimum, 28.*

DESIGNATED DANCES: For the girl students, an opening march and a waltz; two production numbers for most of the company; a semichoreographed sequence for one of Orient's avant-garde pieces, in which human bodies are used as musical instruments.

SUGGESTED SETS: A New York City street; the Central Park Zoo; Washington Square; a concert hall; a luncheonette; a cocktail bar; a locker room;

telephone booths; a suave apartment and the exterior of its building; bedrooms; a living room.

COSTUMES: An oversized mink coat for Valerie; school uniforms for both boys and girls; contemporary wear; tuxedo for Orient; policemen's outfits; hippie clothes.

IMPORTANT PROPS: School lockers; telephones, pay phones.

PROVIDED INSTRUMENTATION: Five reeds, three trumpets, two horns, three trombones, two percussion, two violins, viola, three celli, bass, harp, guitar, piano-conductor.

ADVERTISING AND MARKETING: Try sending your candy sellers through the community selling "O. Henrys" and promoting the upcoming production at the same time.

SUGGESTIONS: It's a small story that can benefit from a modest production.

RESOURCES: The original cast album on LP; the 1964 movie *The World of Henry Orient* on which the musical is fairly faithfully based.

RIGHTS: Samuel French.

INTO THE WOODS

CREATORS: Book by James Lapine, music and lyrics by Stephen Sondheim (who collaborated on *Sunday in the Park with George*).

BACKGROUND: The 1987 production opened to mixed reviews, but was nominated for ten Tonys, won three awards, and ran 765 performances.

STORY: A fairy tale about a baker and his wife who are childless, but learn from a witch that they will conceive—*if* they bring her a cow as white as milk, a cape as red as blood, hair as yellow as corn, and a slipper as pure as gold. After meeting Jack (of Beanstalk fame), Little Red Riding Hood, Rapunzel, and Cinderella, they get what they want. So does that foursome—but still all the characters somehow aren't satisfied. Then they must fight a seemingly undefeatable enemy before they can live somewhat happily ever after, and find much meaning as a result of their fight.

ASSETS: A good score that complements a fun idea—bringing together all those fairy tale characters we've known and loved some time in our lives; audiences enjoy seeing them all thrust together.

LIABILITIES: The second act shows the darker side of fairy tales and their characters; many of them are maimed or killed—and while there are fascinating and haunting observations, audiences tend to enjoy Act One much, much more than Act Two. Sondheim's fast-paced music and lyrics are hard to learn and more difficult to perform.

WHO YOU'LL NEED: *Lead Singing Roles:* A witch who's at first ugly and later beautiful (a Cher type); a simple baker who wants to be master of his household; his wife who suspects he's better off with her help; a (soprano) Cinderella. *Supporting Singing Roles:* A tart-tongued Little Red Riding Hood; a wolf; a simple-minded but sincere Jack and his long-suffering mother; Rapunzel; Cinderella's mother; her henpecked father, insensitive stepmother, and two mocking sisters; her vain prince-suitor; Rapunzel's equally vain prince-suitor; a narrator who may (or may not) double as a "mysterious man." *Other Roles:* A grandmother, a steward, the voice of a female giant; Snow White and Sleeping Beauty, who are walk-ons at the end of the show. *Maximum, 23; minimum, 19.*

DESIGNATED DANCES: A hop-skip-and-jump prance for the entire company at the opening, the finaletto, and the finale; a vaudeville-like turn for the wolf; some musical staging on two other numbers.

SUGGESTED SETS: The first scene in each act takes place in three houses (Cinderella's, Jack's, and the Baker's), which needn't be elaborate; the rest of the evening is spent in the dark, tree-filled woods.

COSTUMES: Male and female peasant outfits; a witch's cape, hat, and fright wig; a baker's toque; gowns suitable for a royal festival; a wolf outfit (exposed genitalia optional); nightgowns; epauletted uniforms and boots worthy of princes; one cape that's red and another made of wolf's fur; a shock of long blond hair; two fancy "gold" slippers, sunglasses appropriate for blind girls.

IMPORTANT PROPS: A horse-drawn carriage; a bed with quilt covers for Grandma; a basket; a table with cloth; a lantern; gold harp; walking sticks; a mobile of birds; a suitcase; a "baby"; some hunting knives; and a cow as white as milk on wheels.

SPECIAL EFFECTS: Flying the bird mobile from above; fog; thunder and lightning; the distorted electronic voice of a giant, the sound of heavy footsteps; a giant's falling to earth.

PROVIDED INSTRUMENTATION: Flute/piccolo, clarinet, bassoon, two horns, trumpet/piccolo trumpet, percussion, piano, synthesizer, two violins, two viola, cello, bass, piano-conductor.

ADVERTISING AND MARKETING: Plan to raffle off some golf clubs at intermission, and advertise it as "Win some woods at *Into the Woods.*"

SUGGESTIONS: A 1992 production at Concord-Carlisle (Massachusetts) High School situated center a very large fairy tale book whose pages were turned to reveal every setting from Grandma's house to Rapunzel's tower. It also cast an actor to play Jack's cow, and the school's principal as the menacing female giant.

The scene in which the witch changes from an ugly harridan to a beautiful woman must be accomplished quickly. The original production gave Bernadette Peters, who'd been playing the ugly witch, much more time by having another performer come out in her witch costume while she stood behind a tree, ready to emerge in all her beauty. The audience didn't notice, because by then they'd come to accept that that woman in the black cape and ugly makeup was Peters. Do the same; it's easier.

RESOURCES: The original cast album on CD, cassette, and LP; the very faithful 1990 TV version on videotape and laserdisc, Grimm's fairy tales; a "Rehearscore" disc for Macintosh and IBM systems which eliminates the need for a rehearsal pianist; videocassette interviews with the creators.

RIGHTS: Music Theatre International.

LI'L ABNER

CREATORS: Book by Norman Panama and Melvin Frank, music and lyrics by Gene de Paul and Johnny (Top Banana) Mercer.

BACKGROUND: The 1956 production received mostly good reviews, got three Tony nominations, won two awards, and ran 696 performances.

STORY: A typical day in Dogpatch, USA, in the 1950s. Daisy Mae wants to get married; L'il Abner wants to go fishin'. Both plans take a back seat to the big news emanating from Jubilation T. Cornpone Square: Their town, Dogpatch, has been deemed the most useless in the country, and will be home for atomic bomb testing. Most everyone's happy, but Abner's mother, Mammy Yokum, doesn't want to move and insists that they all look for something in the town that makes it unique. She decides on Yokumberry Tonic, whose daily spoonsful have made L'il Abner the outstanding physical specimen he is. When the juice makes a Dogpatch visitor look like Charles Atlas, Washington's General Bullmoose becomes interested for his own ends, and is angry when Abner won't accept his offer of a million dollars for the tonic formula; Abner plans to donate it to the government. Meanwhile, Daisy Mae is hoping that she can land Abner on Sadie Hawkins Day, when women chase men; Abner agrees to be caught so that she won't have to marry Earthquake McGoon, but the general's "ward," Appassionata von Climax, catches him instead. Soon after, it's disclosed that Yokumberry Tonic has one problem: It makes a boy strong, but it virtually kills his interest in romance. The tonic may be a failure, but it frees Abner from Appassionata; Earthquake, not thrilled with Daisy Mae's relatives, withdraws, and the town is spared when the statue of Jubilation T. Cornpone is lifted for removal, and a letter from "A. Lincoln" is discovered that designates Dogpatch a national shrine because of its role in the Civil War.

ASSETS: Dramatics magazine reports this is one of the most performed titles by stock, college, and amateur groups throughout the country. A bouncy score with terrific lyrics; as for that book, it may have been written to be topical in a now-long-gone era, but it still is relevant to our time, when we're expressing more concern about having a nuclear plant in the neighborhood.

LIABILITIES: You've got to have the right type of strong, muscular, and handsome boys to pull this one off; they're not always the easiest to lure into a musical production.

RECOGNIZABLE SONGS: "Jubilation T. Cornpone."

WHO YOU'LL NEED: *Lead Singing Roles:* A beefy, strong, sincere but not so bright young Southern stud; the innocent and well-built young woman who truly loves him (a Donna Dixon type). *Supporting Singing Roles:* A loud and good-natured marriage broker; Abner's dominating mother and his henpecked father; an efficient scientist; a conservative and corrupt army general. *Other Roles:* The general's curvaceous young "ward"; a dimwitted would-be suitor; a weird man with an evil eye; lab assistants; women and wives of Dogpatch; some well-built boys who needn't be very talented but should look good in swimsuits. *Maximum, 40; minimum, 18.*

DESIGNATED DANCES: Five production numbers in which everyone stomps around the stage (though your boys will be barefoot, and that could wear on them; be prepared for injuries).

SUGGESTED SETS: Not only in mythical Dogpatch, USA (with its cabins, fishing hole, town square, and various roads) but also in Washington, D.C. (a government laboratory, the Oval Office, and a general's office and mansion).

COSTUMES: While duplicating Al Capp's drawings is the ideal, you can get by with more conventional hillbilly duds.

IMPORTANT PROPS: An enormous statue for the town square; obstacles to be put in the path for the Sadie Hawkins Day race; fishing poles, lab equipment.

PROVIDED INSTRUMENTATION: Five reeds, three trumpets, three trombones, two violins, viola, cello, bass, percussion, guitar-banjo, piano-conductor.

ADVERTISING AND MARKETING: *"L'il Abner* may no longer be found in your local newspaper, but it can be found on your local stage on . . ."

SUGGESTIONS: While much of the topical humor has of course dated, you still can get by with it—if you make Dogpatch *so* in the dark that it is only now learning about nuclear bombs, et al.

RESOURCES: The original cast album on CD, cassette, and LP; the faithful 1959 movie on videotape and laserdisc; the Al Capp comic strips available in a myriad of collections.

RIGHTS: Tams-Witmark.

MERRILY WE ROLL ALONG

CREATORS: Book by George Furth, music and lyrics by Stephen Sondheim (who collaborated on *Company*).

BACKGROUND: The 1981 production, after a long and troubled preview period, opened to bad reviews; the usually feisty producer Harold Prince decided that a fight wasn't winnable—and by closing after only 16 performances, he created a mystique about the show that many have since revived.

STORY: 1980. When rich-and-famous producer-composer Franklin Shepard is asked to return to Lake Forest High School to be the graduation speaker, he doesn't know what to tell them. Inside, he's reminiscing about his life—last year's party after his not-so-good movie opened and everyone lied and said how good it was; a few years earlier when he cold-shouldered his oldest and dearest friend and collaborator Charley, who was only approaching him because their mutual friend Mary asked him to. And so Shepard goes back through time, as he recalls when Charley embarrassed him on national TV for being more interested in money than art; when he betrayed his wife and his producer by having an affair with the producer's wife; when he had his first musical hit with Charley; when they played the show's big hit song at a party that gave impetus to the production; when they were struggling in small nightclubs—all the way back to when Frank, Charley, and Mary were on the roof of their building and began a life that then seemed so full of promise—but didn't turn out the way Franklin Shepard expected it to.

ASSETS: Sondheim's warmest score, one of his easiest for nonprofessionals to maneuver; enough good parts to satisfy your young actors.

LIABILITIES: A story that deals with moral and business corruption of writers doesn't always interest audiences; its being told backward doesn't allow for a conventional climax.

RECOGNIZABLE SONGS: "Good Thing Going."

WHO YOU'LL NEED: *Lead Singing Roles:* A famous but shallow producer-composer; a sincere but alcoholic best woman friend writer; a sincere and always right playwright-lyricist. *Supporting Singing Roles:* A savvy theatrical producer; his ostentatious wife; a simple and wronged wife; a piano accompanist; a female auditioner. *Other Roles:* Shepard as an adult; a smarmy TV talk show host; a young reporter; two Midwestern parents; a headwaiter, waiter, waitress, and bartender; a photographer; a soundman; a valedictorian; an interior decorator; a rock star; a movie star; party guests. *Maximum, 39; minimum, 28.*

DESIGNATED DANCES: Much musical staging for the opening number, which is reprised in fits and starts four other times; a jitterbug to end the first act; a nightclub ditty with modest choreography; a number for the three principals involving moveable typing tables.

SUGGESTED SETS: A high school gymnasium; a posh California house; a Beverly Hills cocktail lounge; a talk show set in a TV studio; a Central Park West apartment; outside a New York City courthouse; outside Broadway's Alvin Theatre; a Sutton Place apartment; a Greenwich Village nightclub; a cold-water flat, a producer's office; a rooftop on 100th Street.

COSTUMES: The original production began previews with a sweatshirt motif on which everyone's occupation or role in the show was stated in block letters—"Producer," "Best Pal"—though the waitress's shirt said "Unemployed Actress." As previews progressed, this motif was dropped in favor of clothes representative of the eras in the show (1957–1980).

IMPORTANT PROPS: Typewriters on roller-mounted typing tables; a grand piano and an upright; cassette tape recorder.

PROVIDED INSTRUMENTATION: Five reeds, three trumpets, trombone, tuba, horn, three cellos, electric bass, guitar, two keyboards, two percussion, piano-conductor.

ADVERTISING AND MARKETING: "It started the careers of Tony winners Jason *(Seinfeld)* Alexander and Tonya *(Jelly's Last Jam)* Pinkins and Tony nominee Liz *(Baby)* Callaway. How many future Tony nominees and winners will you see in our production of *Merrily We Roll Along?*" If you do use the costume motif of branding each sweatshirt with an occupation, don't miss the chance to create ones that say "Audience Member" and put them on sale.

SUGGESTIONS: While the original production used kids, subsequent productions have used adults. In other words, if the book and score appeal to you, don't be hemmed in by casting.

RESOURCES: The original cast album on CD, cassette, and LP; the Kaufman-Hart play of the same name on which the musical was very loosely based.

RIGHTS: Music Theatre International.

RUNAWAYS

CREATORS: Music and lyrics by Elizabeth Swados (who later wrote the music for *Doonesbury).*

BACKGROUND: The 1978 production opened off-Broadway, where it seemed right at home, and played 76 well-attended performances, then moved to Broadway, where it had a tougher time selling tickets. It received five Tony nominations, won none, but did survive 267 performances.

STORY: The present in the inner city. What drives kids to run away from home? Some of them are abused, some watched their parents abuse each other; some left after a divorce, some ran away from orphanages. Some are adamant, some have regrets, some try alternative religions. Some are victims—and some are perpetrators—of rape and violence; some state they have no heroes, while others muse that they're really the sons and daughters of famous people. They eat food from garbage cans, shoplift, become prostitutes or junkies, break windows in frustration, dream of revenge. And some of them die—but not before all of them plead with their parents and society, "Let me be a kid again."

ASSETS: A message worth hearing, a score with a distinct sound, and an opportunity for some of your kids to relearn how lucky they are, and for others to reflect on their own difficulties and realize they're not alone in their problems.

LIABILITIES: Swados's music is considered by some listeners to be difficult and unmelodic. Some communities will find the street-smart and stark realism too much to take.

WHO YOU'LL NEED: *Supporting Singing Roles:* Twenty-eight kids, ranging from thirteen to twenty-one, half of them male, half female, including two boys and girl who are also fluent in Spanish; a violinist. *Other Roles:* A deaf-mute and an interpreter.

DESIGNATED DANCES: No formal choreography, but much street stepping; a basketball "dance."

SUGGESTED SETS: City streets with fences and barriers; bleachers and benches.

COSTUMES: Contemporary teen clothes in varying states of raggedness; a frock coat; red tap shoes; some safari hats.

IMPORTANT PROPS: A Lego-block skyscraper; dolls; basketball and hoops; a toy piano, helicopter, alligator, robot, and rifles; Silly String; skateboards; suitcases; balloons; spray paint; a bag of "pot."

PROVIDED INSTRUMENTATION: Two reeds, two trumpets, percussion, drums, string bass, guitar, piano-conductor.

ADVERTISING AND MARKETING: Contact some runaway shelters and halfway houses and do free performances for them.

SUGGESTIONS: The cast calls for a hearing-impaired youth who signs, and while you could have a hearing actor play this part, don't lose the opportunity to find a hearing-impaired actor, so that your cast can learn from him or her.

RESOURCES: The original cast album on cassette and LP.

RIGHTS: Samuel French.

Also See: The Boys from Syracuse; Cats; A Chorus Line; Cinderella; Dames at Sea; A Day in Hollywood/A Night in the Ukraine; Diamond Studs; The Fan-

tasticks; *The First*; *A Funny Thing Happened on the Way to the Forum*; *Godspell*; *Grease*; *Guys and Dolls*; *Hair*; *Half a Sixpence*; *How to Succeed in Business Without Really Trying*; *It's a Bird . . . It's a Plane . . . It's Superman*; *Jesus Christ Superstar*; *Joseph and the Amazing Technicolor Dreamcoat*; *Little Shop of Horrors*; *Minnie's Boys*; *The Music Man*; *Oklahoma!*; *Once on This Island*; *Once upon a Mattress*; *Pippin*; *Pump Boys and Dinettes*; *Return to the Forbidden Planet*; *The Roar of the Greasepaint—The Smell of the Crowd*; *The Rocky Horror Show*; *Smile*; *Snoopy!!!*; *Starmites*; *Sugar*; *West Side Story*; *Where's Charley?*; *The Wiz*; *The Wizard of Oz*; *You're a Good Man, Charlie Brown*.

"HOW DO YOU DO, MIDDLE AGE?"

Musicals with Parts for Middle-Aged Performers

Midway through the first act in *The Girl Who Came to Supper*, Jose Ferrer's Prince Regent of Carpathia came to terms with his advancing years by singing "How Do You Do, Middle Age?" If you have a preponderance of performers for whom this could be a theme song, you might cast them in one of the following shows for your next production.

COMPANY

CREATORS: Book by George Furth, music and lyrics by Stephen Sondheim (who later collaborated on *Merrily We Roll Along*).

BACKGROUND: During the show's 1970 tryout, the last song indicated that getting married meant living "happily ever after in hell"—which wasn't what some audiences (consisting of many wives and husbands) wanted to hear. So the authors did a 180-degree turn and wrote a new song that said, despite the difficulties, getting married meant "being alive." It made the pill a less bitter one to swallow, for the production then received thirteen Tony nominations, won six awards—including Best Musical—and ran 702 performances.

STORY: The present in New York City. Bobby is a single guy whose friends have all married. Some have divorced, one couple is in the process of splitting, others grin and bear it. And yet every one of them wants him to get married, which, he decides by evening's end, may not be a bad fate.

ASSETS: A very truthful look at marriage, one with which honest audiences will agree—that one is "sorry-grateful" about the entire experience. The heavily synthesized score brought a new sound to Broadway that may still sound new if your audiences are accustomed to a traditional Broadway sound. There is a perception that the show must be dated, since it's almost a quarter-century old, but this isn't true: The issues over which the five couples struggle, and the ways they harass, emasculate, and humiliate each other are still what many see when they visit "those good and crazy people," their married friends.

LIABILITIES: How will your audience react to the pot-smoking sequence? And more than one audience has been driven to distraction by the chant of "Bobby, Bobby baby, Bobby bubi," etc. "And it's bothersome," complains Stan Barber of the Pax Amicus Castle Theater in Budd Lake, New Jersey, "that none of his friends ever suggests that he may be homosexual. Were the authors too frightened to risk that?"

WHO YOU'LL NEED: *Lead Singing Role:* One attractive approaching-middle-age single (Dean Jones). *Supporting Singing Roles:* six principal males and eight principal females—all of whom had better be able to maneuver Sondheim's difficult lyrics, but especially a flibbertigibbet who can sing a mile a minute and a "tough broad" (Elaine Stritch). *Other Roles:* Four female offstage singers. *Maximum, 18; minimum, 14.*

DESIGNATED DANCES: Not demanding: Michael Bennett's choreography was famous for making nondancers appear comfortable doing their snazzy best with top hats and canes without worrying about perfection. But there's a famous "Tick-Tock" dance representing a sexual experience that must be sensuously danced by an attractive woman. A karate match between one married couple involves some choreographic moves.

SUGGESTED SETS: The original look included several levels that represented many contemporary New York apartments. You can do it in one small space, changing furniture to represent each apartment. A bar will be necessary to simulate a nightclub.

COSTUMES: Though pictures of the original production will suggest very 1970s styles, the show has not dated and can be set in the present—allowing your cast to wear ordinary street clothes. You'll also need a female flight attendant's uniform; a wedding dress; a groom's tuxedo; a few waiters' and waitresses' uniforms.

IMPORTANT PROPS: A birthday cake with thirty-five candles; umbrellas for all (ideally, each a different color); a toaster; liquor bottles and glasses; "joints" and a bag of "grass."

SPECIAL EFFECTS: The sound of telephones ringing and their busy signals, and some voice-overs.

PROVIDED INSTRUMENTATION: Five reeds, three trumpets, two horns, two trombones, three violins, two cellos, electric keyboard/piano-conductor, two guitars, bass, two percussion—and parts for four female pit voices.

ADVERTISING AND MARKETING: "Won't you keep us company at *Company*?" Also give a program ad discount for this show to any firm that actually has the word "company" in its official business title.

SUGGESTIONS: Considering that the "Tick-Tock" dance represents the sexual encounter between the stewardess and Bobby, why not try it as a dance for two?

RESOURCES: The original cast album on CD, cassette, and LP; the 1970 documentary of the taping of the original cast album.

RIGHTS: Music Theatre International.

DO I HEAR A WALTZ?

CREATORS: book by Arthur Laurents, music by Richard Rodgers (who'd just written music and lyrics for *No Strings*), lyrics by Stephen Sondheim (who'd just collaborated on *Anyone Can Whistle* with Laurents).

BACKGROUND: This show, the first after Oscar Hammerstein's death for which Rodgers took on a lyricist, was 1965's most anticipated musical—given that Laurents and Sondheim had already written *West Side Story* and *Gypsy*. But Sondheim's acerbic style didn't match Rodgers's lush romantic sensibility, and the two never made much of a secret that they didn't get along. The show received only three Tony nominations, won none, and ran 220 performances.

STORY: 1960s, Venice. Leona Samish, a single American tourist, takes her first trip abroad to Venice, where lovers, she notes, abound. It makes her feel wistful, especially when she goes to her *pensione* and finds that the other guests that week are two married couples (the young Eddie and Jennifer, the middle-aged McIlhennys). The next day in a glass shop she's attracted not only to a goblet, but also to the handsome shopowner, Renato DiRossi; when she says she'd like a pair of the goblets, he responds that he'll try to find another for her. He later does, and asks her out—but she wonders if he's a fortune-hunter. She's convinced of it when she sees that the McIlhennys found a goblet just like hers, so DiRossi admits they're very common in Venice. Then she discovers he's married, and she breaks the date. Later she finds that Eddie is cheating on his wife with Fioria, the *pensione* owner, and she further berates DiRossi with some displaced hostility for not respecting the institution of marriage, but he pooh-poohs that and urges her to "take the moment" with him. She's mollified when DiRossi shows up with a beautiful necklace for her and he later asks her to stay in Venice. She's tempted, but the mood is shattered when she discovers that he doesn't have enough to pay for the necklace—she makes up the balance—and then learns he received a commission for selling it. Leona drowns her sorrows and hurtfully discloses the Eddie-Fioria affair to Jennifer. A sadder-but-wiser Leona prepares to return to America after having loved not too wisely or too well, but is now more determined than ever to find love.

ASSETS: A very fine score and bittersweet book. It's not an expensive show to do, because the cast isn't very large, nor are the set and costume demands overwhelming. There isn't much dancing, but what there is—when Leona and DiRossi finally give in for the big second-act waltz—is thrilling.

LIABILITIES: The fact that a handsome necklace from a handsome stranger puts Leona in a romantic mood is problematic. And this sweet, sentimental musical might cause some to fall asleep.

RECOGNIZABLE SONGS: "Do I Hear a Waltz?"

WHO YOU'LL NEED: *Lead Singing Roles:* An American secretary in her late thirties; the Italian (tenor) shopowner who may or may not be in love with her (Sergio Franchi). *Supporting Singing Roles:* A savvy *pensione* owner; an attractive young couple who pretend their marriage is happy; a middle-aged couple on a very scheduled itinerary; the *pensione* maid who "no understand" English. *Other Roles:* A young glassware shop clerk; a man on a bridge; a female American tourist; a young but shrewd Venetian boy who makes a living as a guide. *Maximum, 33; minimum, 18.*

DESIGNATED DANCES: Not much: Some musical staging for the opening, and that wonderful swirling waltz for our two lovers.

SUGGESTED SETS: All around Venice—a piazza; a *pensione*; its garden; a Venetian glassware shop.

COSTUMES: Contemporary wear; gondolier outfits; maid's uniform. Be prepared to make an outfit you can spare for Leona, for it must be soaked wet after she falls into a canal (offstage).

IMPORTANT PROPS: Gondolas; eighteenth-century Venetian goblets; a garnet necklace; elaborate tea and liquor services; balloons.

PROVIDED INSTRUMENTATION: Four reeds, two trumpets, three trombones, percussion, four violins, two violas, two cellos, bass, harp, guitar/mandolin, piano-conductor.

ADVERTISING AND MARKETING: Create a radio ad for the listener to hear a few seconds of "The Blue Danube Waltz" before asking, "Do you hear a waltz? You can hear others beginning on . . ."

SUGGESTIONS: See if you can get the licensers to allow Eddie and Jennifer to sing the original version of "We're Gonna Be All Right"—far more acerbic, witty, and interesting (it contains an extra verse)—that was revised before the out-of-town tryout.

RESOURCES: The original cast album on CD, cassette, and LP; the 1955 movie *Summertime*, on which the musical is faithfully based, and the Laurents play *The Time of the Cuckoo*, available on videotape.

RIGHTS: Rodgers and Hammerstein.

IS THERE LIFE AFTER HIGH SCHOOL?

CREATORS: book by Jeffrey Kindley, music and lyrics by Craig *(Working)* Carnelia.

BACKGROUND: The 1982 musical, having had a difficult preview period in New York during which the director was replaced, opened to mixed reviews, received no Tony nominations, and ran 12 performances—but has much fine writing in it.

STORY: The present—at a suburban high school. The trials and tribulations of going through high school—and how the problems we encountered there still bother us and affect our lives—especially in the face of a reunion.

ASSETS: A marvelous score by Craig Carnelia, musical theater's best-kept secret, enhances situations with which your audience will immediately identify. The show has a built-in appeal with that title, but most of all, with few sets and costumes, and props, it's a very inexpensive show to produce, and a natural for a high school auditorium stage.

LIABILITIES: Of *course* there is life after high school—and still wondering and worrying about events that happened years and years ago makes these characters seem rather neurotic.

WHO YOU'LL NEED: *Supporting Singing Roles:* Five men and four women who aren't defined by character names, but by their own; an ensemble show *Maximum*, 35—*minimum*, 9.

DESIGNATED DANCES: No choreography as such, but one number about beer in which three men must weave; another about marching bands in which everyone marches.

SUGGESTED SETS: A bare stage with school lockers.

COSTUMES: Contemporary street clothes.

IMPORTANT PROPS: Beer cans; musical instruments in their cases; banners proclaiming a high school reunion; tables and chairs.

PROVIDED INSTRUMENTATION: Two guitars, two cellos, bass, drums, percussion, piano, piano-conductor.

ADVERTISING AND MARKETING: Invite many of your town's most illustrious high school graduates to your opening, proving that there *is* life after high school—and make this a media event.

SUGGESTIONS: There's a big number about marching bands called "Thousands of Trumpets" for which you can order parts for twenty-four band musicians. But if you can't provide that many, order the prerecorded tape with a marching band sound from the licensers.

RESOURCES: The original cast album on CD, cassette, and LP; Ralph Keyes's docu-novel on which the musical is loosely based.

RIGHTS: Samuel French.

LA CAGE AUX FOLLES

CREATORS: Book by Harvey Fierstein (*who wrote the play Torch Song Trilogy*), music and lyrics by Jerry (*Hello, Dolly!*) Herman.

BACKGROUND: The 1983 production opened to raves in Boston, and nothing could stop it from steamrolling onto Broadway, where it received equally good critical notices, nine Tony nominations, six awards—including Best Musical—and ran 1,761 performances.

STORY: The present, in St. Tropez. George and Albin are lovers; the former is a nightclub owner, while the latter is a female impersonator and stage-named Zaza, the star of the club, who gets cheers every time he performs and then tears off his wig. But George did have a straight adventure at one point, and it produced a son, Jean-Michel, who was raised by George and Albin. Jean-Michel has been very comfortable with his home life—until now. Seems he's met Anne, the daughter of a most conservative couple, and he wants to bring Anne and her parents to meet his father and mother, but *not* Albin. When George breaks the news to Albin, the latter is furious and hurt, but he later agrees to dress as a man and be "Uncle Al" when Anne's parents arrive. But when Jean-Michel's mother cancels, Albin seizes the opportunity to pretend he is she. They all go to a nearby club, where "Zaza" is asked to entertain; he does, and after the wild applause, makes the mistake of tearing off his wig. Anne's parents are mortified, but Anne stands up for her rights, and all ends happily.

ASSETS: A bouncy score, a very funny and yet touching book. A show that takes a great many risks, and enlightens an audience about another kind of love.

LIABILITIES: Very expensive to stage. And you will still find some audience members who'd rather not see a musical in which the leading men are lovers.

RECOGNIZABLE SONGS: "I Am What I Am," "The Best of Times Is Now."

WHO YOU'LL NEED: *Lead Singing Roles:* A man who can be a flamboyant female impersonator; his virile, handsome, caring, and patient lover (a John Forsythe type). *Supporting Singing Roles:* "Their" attractive twenty-ish son; a nightclub owner; two very conservative parents; a female-impersonator maid; a chorus of 12 Cagelles (the original production cast two women among the male Cagelles so that the audience could enjoy guessing which was which). *Other Roles:* A lovely and winsome twenty-ish girlfriend; some nightclub personnel; a chorus of eight St. Tropez townspeople. *Maximum, 41; minimum, 23.*

DESIGNATED DANCES: An opening number for the Cagelles; one production number for Albin and the Cagelles; another for Albin and some nightclub patrons; one pleasant interlude for Jean-Michel and Anne; some musical staging on two other numbers.

SUGGESTED SETS: A glitzy nightclub stage with two production number sets; Zaza's flamboyant dressing room; a very elaborate and femininely designed living room of an apartment; a charming cafe; the beach of St. Tropez; another nightclub.

COSTUMES: Many nightclub costumes; a French maid's outfit (worn by a man); European contemporary wear; many baubled, bangled, and beaded costumes; shoes. Laments David N. Matthews, artistic director of the Erie Playhouse, "Women's shoes in men's sizes are very hard to come by. We ended up dealing with a transvestite shop in New York, which was very expensive."

IMPORTANT PROPS: A fully-stocked makeup table for Albin; a working trapeze; a dressing screen; many tables and chairs; an oversized feather duster.

PROVIDED INSTRUMENTATION: Five reeds, three trumpets, two horns, two trombones, drums, two percussion, four violins, cello, bass, guitar/banjo, harp, accordion/electric keyboard, keyboard-conductor.

ADVERTISING AND MARKETING: "You may have seen the movie *La Cage aux Folles*, or its sequel, *La Cage aux Folles II*, or *its* sequel, *La Cage aux Folles III*—but you haven't seen *La Cage aux Folles* at all until you've seen our musical version of *La Cage aux Folles*."

SUGGESTIONS: Says Joseph Patton, Resident Director-Choreographer with the Carousel Dinner Theater in Akron, "The men you have as your female impersonators can't just play themselves in drag. It won't work unless they are totally serious about their work. What's more, your two lead males must be comfortable with being a loving couple. If they're secure, your audience will follow."

RESOURCES: The original cast album on CD, cassette, and LP; the 1978 movie on which the musical was very faithfully based.

RIGHTS: Samuel French.

ON A CLEAR DAY, YOU CAN SEE FOREVER

CREATORS: Book and lyrics by Alan Jay (*My Fair Lady*) Lerner, music by Burton (*Finian's Rainbow*) Lane.

BACKGROUND: The 1965 production opened overlong on the road, replaced leading man Louis Jourdan with newcomer John Cullum—giving him his big break—limped in to mixed reviews, received three Tony nominations, won none, and ran 280 performances.

STORY: The present, in New York City. Daisy Gamble goes to Dr. Mark Bruckner to hypnotize her so she can stop smoking. He becomes more interested in her self-proclaimed ESP powers—which she soon shows him are genuine— but the real astonishment comes when, under hypnosis, Daisy reveals her past life as Melinda Wells, an elegant eighteenth-century woman. Once Daisy's out of her trance, Mark asks her for a date so that he can learn more about Melinda; Daisy, unaware of Melinda, assumes he's interested in her, which excites her—for her current boyfriend Warren just isn't that interesting to her. When Mark again puts Daisy under hypnosis, he learns of Melinda's past with Edward Montcrieff, a handsome man who rescued her from a lascivious would-be suitor. Soon Mark is the toast of the psychiatric world with his published findings on Melinda—but one day Daisy arrives early for an appointment, discovers a tape recording session Mark made with her, and finds out that she's the Melinda who has made Mark famous. She's crushed that Mark has been using her, which sends her back to Warren. Now that Mark's lost Daisy, he realizes he's in love with her, and, knowing that she has ESP, continually thinks of her until she returns to him. He apologizes, and they wind up together.

ASSETS: A fascinating idea for a musical, and a powerhouse role for an actress, who must be convincing as an all-thumbs working-class neurotic and an elegant and haughty to-the-manor-born goddess. Interestingly enough the pressure on one to stop smoking is now of even more interest than it was when *Clear Day* premiered in 1965.

LIABILITIES: With two eras to cover, this is a heavy set and costume show. And can we really believe that Mark loves Daisy for herself, or is he still planning to use her?

RECOGNIZABLE SONGS: "On a Clear Day, You Can See Forever," "What Did I Have That I Don't Have Now?"

WHO YOU'LL NEED: *Lead Singing Roles:* An addle-headed contemporary young woman who can also play an elegant eighteenth-century lady (a Faith Prince type); the intense (baritone) psychiatrist who loves one of them. *Supporting Singing Roles:* A very level-headed boyfriend; an eighteenth-century British nobleman; a (tenor) rakish ne'er-do-well; Daisy's four friends. *Other Roles:* Four eighteenth-century acquaintances; three psychiatrists; six students; a secretary. *Maximum, 49; minimum, 21.*

DESIGNATED DANCES: Three production numbers involving much of the eighteenth-century cast; one involving Daisy and her friends; another involving Warren and Daisy's friends.

SUGGESTED SETS: A New York psychological clinic, its solarium, its director's office; an apartment building rooftop; the airport. You'll also need a few period pieces to suggest the eighteenth-century scenes in Melinda's mind.

COSTUMES: Not only contemporary business and casual clothes, but also eighteenth-century finery for the nobles and their servants.

IMPORTANT PROPS: A potted plant that can "grow" as the evening progresses; many well-stocked bookcases; rooftop patio furniture.

PROVIDED INSTRUMENTATION: Two violins, viola, cello, bass, flute, piccolo, clarinet, bass clarinet, oboe, English horn, two horns, three trumpets, two trombones, two percussion, celeste, harpsichord, piano-conductor.

ADVERTISING AND MARKETING: "No matter what the weather's like, we'll give you a clear day—starting on [date] when we present *On a Clear Day, You Can See Forever.*"

SUGGESTIONS: Daisy's boyfriend Warren sings a song in which he tells us he's actually looking forward to turning sixty-five so he can retire and get the many benefits his company offers. Some productions have made Warren do a silly, frenetic dance while he's giving the information, but the song will be more witty and the character more interesting if you simply have him deliver his diatribe in a calm, rational, and offhand way.

RESOURCES: The original cast album on CD, cassette and LP; the (fairly faithful) 1970 movie on videotape and laserdisc.

RIGHTS: Tams-Witmark.

THE PAJAMA GAME

CREATORS: Book by George *(Fiorello!)* Abbott and Richard Bissell, music and lyrics by Richard Adler and Jerry Ross (Abbott, Adler and Ross later collaborated on *Damn Yankees).*

BACKGROUND: The 1954 production opened in Boston to a bad review from Elliott Norton, the dean of drama critics, but most other critics disagreed, as did Tony voters—who tabbed it Best Musical—en route to a 1,063 performance run.

STORY: 1950s, in a Midwestern town. Sid Sorokin has bluffed his way into a superintendent's job at a pajama factory, but makes a bad first impression on his boss, Mr. Hasler, and on Babe, the head of the union's grievance committee, after he shoves a lazy worker. Sid and Babe are mutually attracted, but she's wary of getting involved with management, because she and the union have been pressing for a raise. When it becomes apparent Hasler is stringing the employees along, Babe sabotages the production line, and Sid must fire her. But he decides to romance Hasler's secretary, Gladys, to get the key to the company books—and once he does, he learns that the raise was figured into the budget six months ago. Armed with this information, he strongarms Hasler into giving the raise, which makes Babe again love him.

ASSETS: A good score, a well-constructed book, and a number of meaty character parts for actors who seldom get a chance to shine in other musicals.

LIABILITIES: Sid Sorokin is a dinosaur by contemporary standards. He's a superintendent who thinks nothing of coming on to a co-worker ("You're the cutest grievance committee I've ever had to deal with"), and his way of dealing with employees ("Personally, I think a little physical punishment is good for people once in a while") won't endear him to today's audiences. As for Babe (what an anachronistic name for a woman!), she's easily duped into believing she's won when Hasler agrees to give the raise, but doesn't press the retroactive issue—which she should, considering that Hasler's been pocketing that allocated money for six months.

RECOGNIZABLE SONGS: "Hey, There," "Steam Heat," "Hernando's Hideaway."

WHO YOU'LL NEED: *Lead Singing Roles:* A feisty (tenor) superintendent (a Hal Linden or Ted Danson type); his union-bound love. *Supporting Singing Roles:* A wily female bookkeeper; the comical time-study man who loves her; a randy union president (a Walter Matthau type); two office workers who can take part in a company show; a hefty secretary. *Other Roles:* Babe's good-natured father; the austere company president; some female pajama sewers and male factory helpers; two kids. *Maximum, 35; minimum, 18.*

DESIGNATED DANCES: A good deal, mostly involving Gladys, who dances with two chorus boys in "Steam Heat" and with almost everyone in the "Hernando's Hideaway" tango for the cast, and does a vampy dance with the union president (who also cavorts in a reprise with a factory worker); the time-study man has a rubber-legged solo, a soft-shoe with a secretary, and a brief dance with two sewers; two other production numbers; a dream ballet; a finale that's a musically staged fashion show.

SUGGESTED SETS: A pajama factory, its desk-filled main office; picnic grounds with tables and/or blankets, and a path leading to those grounds; a meeting hall.

COSTUMES: 1950s Midwest wear; picnic wear; play suits; bathing suits; gaudy pajamas for all; two baseball uniforms for the kids; three stylized black suits and derbies; a railman's uniform; a guardian angel's outfit.

IMPORTANT PROPS: Many sewing machines; a stopwatch; a necklace with a key on it; a dictaphone; a garment truck; a toolbox; a typewriter; bundles and boxes of pajamas; beer bottles; a petrified flying bat (or something equally arcane); a stamp album; a ledger book; a banner to proclaim the picnic; a knife-board with outline of person.

SPECIAL EFFECTS: One of the most endearing moments occurs when Sid sings a memo to himself on the dictaphone ("Hey, There"), and then plays it back and sings counterpoint to it—so you'll have to make this tape. You'll also have to accomplish two knife-throwing sequences and a small factory explosion, and create a pair of pajamas that will split at the seams when worn.

PROVIDED INSTRUMENTATION: Five reeds, three trumpets, three trombones, four violins, viola, cello, bass, guitar, percussion.

ADVERTISING AND MARKETING: "One night, a Hollywood producer saw an unknown Shirley MacLaine play Gladys in *The Pajama Game*—and signed her to a contract. To all producers: come see our Gladys, [her name], in our production of *The Pajama Game*, beginning on . . ."

SUGGESTIONS: You must stage it as a period piece, though some audiences won't want to be reminded of this sexist era in American labor.

RESOURCES: The original cast album on CD, cassette, and LP; the faithful 1957 movie version on videotape and laserdisc; *7½ Cents*, the Richard Bissell novel on which the musical is very loosely based; a "Rehearscore" disc for Macintosh and IBM systems that eliminates the need for a rehearsal pianist.

RIGHTS: Music Theatre International.

Also See: *Anyone Can Whistle; Applause; The Apple Tree; Baby; Baker Street; The Baker's Wife; Ballroom; Bells Are Ringing; Ben Franklin in Paris; Bring Back Birdie; The Cradle Will Rock; Dear World; Donnybrook; The Education of Hyman Kaplan; Fiorello!; Follies; Gigi; Golden Rainbow; Grand Hotel; The Grass Harp; Guys and Dolls; Hello, Dolly!; High Spirits; I Can Get It for You Wholesale; I Do, I Do; The King and I; Kiss Me, Kate; Les Miserables; A Little Night Music; Mame; Man of La Mancha; Marry Me a Little; Me and My Girl; Milk and Honey; The Music Man; 110 in the Shade; On the Twentieth Century; Over Here; Rags; 1776; Show Boat; Silk Stockings; Something's Afoot; Starting Here, Starting Now; Sweeney Todd; Take Me Along; The Threepenny Opera; Walking Happy; What About Luv; Woman of the Year; Working; Zorba; The Zulu and the Zayda.*

"THANK GOD
I'M OLD!"

Shows That Don't Depend on Young Casts

"Thank God, I'm old," sang Joice Heth in *Barnum*, in which she pretended to be 160 years old. If you're in a group of senior citizens, you may or may not quite agree—but you will be glad to find musicals in which you and your colleagues can perform.

BALLROOM

CREATORS: Book by Jerome Kass, music by Billy Goldenberg, lyrics by Marilyn and Alan ("What Are You Doing for the Rest of Your Life?") Bergman (who had all collaborated on the *Queen of the Stardust Ballroom* television musical on which this musical is based).

BACKGROUND: The 1978 Broadway production was Michael Bennett's first musical after his *Chorus Line* megahit, and could have never lived up to that achievement. Because both critics and audiences were disappointed that the ace wasn't trumped, the show ran only 116 performances, received eight Tony nominations, and won one for choreography.

STORY: The present, in the Bronx. Bea Asher is a widow who, despite opening a bric-a-brac store with her sister-in-law, has languished since her husband's death over a year ago. A waitress she's come to know urges her to drop by the local ballroom and get back into life. Bea reluctantly does, and finds that she likes the people there—especially Al Rossi, a mailman, who makes her again feel good about herself. Soon they are a couple, to the consternation of her family, who have depended on her to mourn her husband and babysit the grandchildren. And even when Al admits to Bea that he is married and must stay married, she keeps seeing him and going to the ballroom, despite her family's protestations—because by this time the wonderful friends she's made in the ballroom are becoming her family. By the end of the show, she's become the new Queen of the Stardust Ballroom, and will take her happiness where she can find it, realizing that fifty percent of Al is better than a hundred percent of most other men.

ASSETS: An easy show to mount, for the costume and prop demands are minimal. A bouncy score and charming and witty dialogue for the characters who come to the Stardust Ballroom. They may not be today's idea of "beautiful people," but they attain beauty when they dance and enjoy themselves. In fact, they *are* beautiful people in the way they love and support each other. Says co-choreographer Bob Avian, "It was great to see those older dancers become kids again when they danced." So too it will be for you and your cast. As one character says, "Who says we're only entitled to one prom?"

LIABILITIES: A dull unmusical beginning; a show with no youth appeal; too many songs are sung by the bandstand singers and too few by the principals. And since it takes Al so long to admit he has a wife—and then he never divulges just why he won't divorce her—he seems unworthy of our Bea.

WHO YOU'LL NEED: *Lead Singing Roles:* A timid, recently widowed middle-aged woman (Dorothy Loudon); one male and one female band singer. *Supporting Singing Role:* An Italian-American mailman. *Other Roles:* A married daughter; grown son; intrusive sister-in-law; long-suffering brother-in-law; best friend; three women customers; the outgoing Queen of the Stardust Ballroom; a number of couples who are comfortable dancing all night long. *Maximum, 43; minimum, 21.*

DESIGNATED DANCES: There's plenty of dancing. Your cast will need to learn the cha-cha, fox-trot, hustle, Lindy, merengue, rhumba, samba, tango, and waltz. And while you'll want them to be good, they will be believable and adequate if they do as well as any middle-aged folk do on the dance floor.

SUGGESTED SETS: A bric-a-brac shop; a ballroom with banquettes; inside and outside Bea's house.

COSTUMES: What middle-aged Bronx men and women would wear to a ballroom—suits, paisley jackets, jersey dresses, sparkle dresses, wrap dresses. At the finale, everyone wears evening gowns and tuxes, but you needn't go all-out—as long as you've saved their best clothes for this occasion. Formal wear for your male and female band singers; a waitress uniform; raincoats; a pair of man's pajamas; a tiara.

IMPORTANT PROPS: A glitter ball; plastic or glass glasses, bar drinks; cake; assorted bric-a-brac; a Scrabble game and a dictionary.

PROVIDED INSTRUMENTATION: Four reeds, three trumpets, horn, three trombones, two percussion, three violins, two cellos, bass, harp, guitar, piano-conductor.

ADVERTISING AND MARKETING: "If you aren't much of a dancer, this may be your favorite *Ballroom* of all time. In fact, if you're an inveterate or veteran dancer, this may *still* be your favorite *Ballroom* of all time. For on [date], [name of theater] is presenting *Ballroom* . . ."

Visit your local ballroom and put up posters advertising your show. In fact, you might want to visit your local ballroom to *cast* your show.

SUGGESTIONS: If you have access to a ballroom, you might want to try to stage the musical there. And one other very small point: the reigning Queen of the Stardust Ballroom is named Pauline Krim—and there's something about that funny-sounding name that makes the honor a silly one.

RESOURCES: The original cast album on CD, cassette, and LP; the *Queen of the Stardust Ballroom* TV movie on which the musical is fairly faithfully based, on videotape.

RIGHTS: Samuel French.

FOLLIES

CREATORS: Book by James Goldman (who wrote the play *The Lion in Winter*), music and lyrics by Stephen (*Company*) Sondheim.

BACKGROUND: The 1971 production may have lost the Best Musical Tony to *Two Gentlemen of Verona*, but it did win seven out of its eleven nominations; it was, however, a most expensive show to run. It did make it through an impressive 521 performances—breeding a legendary core of followers who talk about it to this day.

STORY: 1970s, at Weismann's about-to-be-demolished theater. Phyllis and Sally were Follies girls courted and wed by Ben and Buddy (though Ben also played with Sally's affections); now it's many years later, and they're attending a Follies reunion before the theater in which they performed is razed. Each marriage is in disarray, and Sally still longs for Ben, who is interested, albeit in a one-night stand. Sally, though, has had that before with Ben; she is already fantasizing marriage—especially after Buddy admits to having a mistress—and tells her. Buddy doubts Ben will love Sally. He's right; Ben's never loved anybody, and doesn't know how, and Phyllis is ready to divorce him. But in the end, each couple stays together and decides to tough it out.

ASSETS: One of the great scores of all time, brilliantly evoking the composers and lyricists of yesteryear; fat parts that should be able to accommodate the talents of almost everybody in your company; a fascinating device by which we watch both generations and their different dreams and conclusions.

LIABILITIES: The most expensive show you may ever produce; even if you had to costume only the older group, you'd spend a fortune—but you must double those expenses to costume the young performers. As for the show, watching two couples assess and reassess their marriages may make you want to throw up your hands and say, "Oh, if you're so unhappy, why don't you just stop complaining and do something about it?" And do we believe that they'll really love each other now after this one night of insight?

RECOGNIZABLE SONGS: "Broadway Baby," "I'm Still Here," "Losing My Mind."

WHO YOU'LL NEED: *Lead Singing Roles:* A still-dazzling former showgirl who's now a middle-aged woman; her diplomat-businessman husband; a middle-aged but still pert and pretty Phoenix housewife; her very animated and chatty oil-businessman husband. *Supporting Singing Roles:* Young, innocent, and idealistic performers who parallel the four principals; a former show biz couple who now own a store; a fiftyish French chanteuse; a white-haired tenor; a distinguished opera prima donna and her young counterpart; a couple whose specialty was novelty numbers; a razzmatazz "Broadway Baby" of yore and her young counterpart; a tart survivor who's still here with her own TV series; a woman who's convinced to try dancing one more time—if everyone else will; showgirls to represent The Spirit of First Love, The Spirit of Young Love, The Spirit of True Love, The Spirit of Pure Love, The Spirit of Romantic Love, and The Spirit of Eternal Love. *Other Roles:* A former impresario, a pair of older ballroom dancers and their young counterparts; a major-domo, a chauffeur; a four-piece onstage band; other former Follies showgirls and their young counterparts. *Maximum, 51; minimum, 33.*

DESIGNATED DANCES: Plenty. Six production numbers, including one of the great showstoppers in history, "Who's That Woman?," in which the young ghost chorines mirror the dance that the elders remember and do; a bolero for the ballroom dancers; a dance soliloquy for Buddy; much musical staging for three other numbers.

SUGGESTED SETS: The inside of a theater with a great deal of construction scaffolding and two gaudy *Follies* sets.

COSTUMES: Elaborate, some black-tie and white-tie formal wear and gowns for the reunion's attendees (or at least some fine clothes for the others); the ghosts of the girls are dressed in black-and-white showgirl costumes with feathered headdresses; sashes that indicate what years the alumnae appeared in the Follies; hats and canes.

IMPORTANT PROPS: A staircase; a wheelchair, a small car that Buddy is strapped onto in his Follies number.

PROVIDED INSTRUMENTATION: Five reeds, horn, three trumpets, three trombones, violins, viola, cello, bass, harp, guitar, percussion, piano-conductor.

ADVERTISING AND MARKETING: "Mr. Dimitri Weismann requests the pleasure of your company at a reunion of all who appeared in his *Follies*, on . . ."

SUGGESTIONS: A 1975 production at Philadelphia's LaSalle University put in an intermission just after "I'm Still Here"—and had all the characters stay on stage at a large table, chatting and eating.

You *could* try mounting a vest-pocket, fewer-cast-members *Follies*; after all, it is believable, especially if you set the show in the present, that only a few Weismann girls would be around.

RESOURCES: The most complete recording is *Follies in Concert*, on CD, cassette, and LP; a documentary of that 1985 presentation on videotape and laserdisc.

RIGHTS: Music Theatre International.

MY OLD FRIENDS

CREATORS: Book, music, and lyrics by Mel Mandel and Norman Sachs.

BACKGROUND: The 1979 production opened off-Broadway and did well enough for 100 performances, encouraging its producers to move to Broadway. But the small show soon found itself out of its league, received only one Tony nomination, and closed after 53 performances.

STORY: Peter Schermann moves to a retirement home and is dissatisfied with conditions there—mostly because the female executive director is insensitive and runs everyone's life. She even keeps the piano locked—but Peter opens it so his new friend Heloise can entertain everyone. The executive director relocks it, but things look brighter at the home after a resident writes a letter that gets her fired. But then Peter, a lifelong carpenter, is condescendingly treated by the home's carpenter, and were it not for his infatuation with Heloise, he might leave. When one resident dies, Peter concludes that life is short, and he must leave. He convinces Heloise to go with him.

ASSETS: A charming and sensitive look at growing older from people who are endearing in their resistance to being old. It realistically deals with the pros and cons of living the retirement home lifestyle; the residents may bicker with one another, but they also support one another. There are some clever songs, especially one in which Peter details his medicines, one in which a resident fantasizes a sexual liaison with a nurse, and another in which all the residents write to their children.

LIABILITIES: Peter is too quick to fall in love with and propose to Heloise. And while this may seem to be an ideal show to do in a retirement home, it really isn't—because the musical suggests that its inhabitants would be better off leaving the home and living on their own.

WHO YOU'LL NEED: Sixty-ish performers. *Lead Singing Roles:* A virile leading man; a charming lady who seems to be the home's youngest senior citizen. *Supporting Singing Roles:* An ex-vaudevillian; a nattily dressed senior citizen; a portly man; a Hispanic man; a black woman; an eccentric woman. *Other Roles:* An executive director; a carpenter; an authoritative female voice-over. *Maximum, 15; minimum, 11.*

DESIGNATED DANCES: A fox-trot and waltz for Peter and Heloise; a "dance" where everyone does some steps while sitting down; a mambo for everybody.

SUGGESTED SETS: Technically, we're in and around a retirement home virtually all evening, with the final scene set in a carpentry shop—but the musical was written for the setting to be abstract. Including a staircase with a loose post would be a boon, though.

COSTUMES: Contemporary street clothes; a carpenter's overalls; an arm sling.

IMPORTANT PROPS: Most of them are mimed (including a bicycle and a piano), but you will need two microphones (one stand-up and one hand-held); a coffee urn; some tables and chairs; a toolbox; a Phillips screwdriver; a dictaphone; a deck of cards; a cane; Christmas party decorations. In addition, for the carpentry scenes, you'll need some new pieces of wood, pieces to depict a rocking horse and bench in progress; as well as a finished rocking horse and bench, and a nicely crafted wooden sign that says "Peter Schermann, Carpenter."

PROVIDED INSTRUMENTATION: Bass, piano, piano-conductor.

ADVERTISING AND MARKETING: "Bring your old friends to meet *My Old Friends.*"

SUGGESTIONS: Play it with energy, or the point of the show will be lost.

RESOURCES: No cast album.

RIGHTS: Samuel French.

70, GIRLS, 70

CREATORS: Book by Fred Ebb and Norman L. Martin, adapted by Joe (*Cabaret*) Masteroff, music by John Kander, lyrics by Ebb (who had recently collaborated on *Zorba*).

BACKGROUND: The 1971 production was judged to be one too many about older performers—for *No, No, Nanette* and *Follies* had recently opened to strong reviews; it ran 36 performances, and later received a Tony nomination for leading actress Mildred Natwick.

STORY: The present, in New York City. Things are pretty poky at the rundown Sussex Arms Retirement Home, especially since Ida left; she knew she was dying, and decided to move into the Waldorf and take one last fling at life. One day Ida returns, looking great and swathed in fur. She confesses about a new life that started when she was waiting to buy a thermometer and the clerk treated her rudely—so she took it. Pleased with the results, she's continued to shoplift—which explains the fur. Soon she and her friends decide that if they become a gang of thieves, they'll be able to buy the hotel and make it a nicer place to live. They're doing fine for a while, but are about to get caught when Ida tells them to leave, and she'll stay behind to be arrested. Actually, she knows she's going to die—and does. As two of the other residents get married, she "returns" and urges the audience to enjoy their lives while they may.

ASSETS: A lively score, and a chance for senior citizens to show how much ooomph they still possess.

LIABILITIES: Well, we *are* talking about stealing, and while it's supposed to be harmless and adorable, it really isn't. The story goes all over the place in the second act. And where are you going to get all these furs which some audience members won't want to see?

WHO YOU'LL NEED: *Lead Singing Role*: A charming older woman who's inadvertently become a thief (an Angela Lansbury type). *Supporting Singing Roles*: A big black elder mama; a grandmother and her bellhop grandson; a jazzy pianist; a former store detective who's now the gang's lookout; a former safecracker who's gone straight and the senior citizen with whom he's fallen in love; an ex-vaudevillian hotel clerk; two feisty old women. *Other Roles*: A detective and a policeman. *Maximum, 34; minimum, 13.*

DESIGNATED DANCES: Five production numbers for the company; a strut for the mama and one feisty woman; another for the bellhop and his grandmother; some musical staging on two more numbers.

SUGGESTED SETS: A rundown Manhattan hotel; a fur shop; Bloomingdale's Fur Department; the vault room of the Arctic Cold Storage Company; the International Fur Show at the New York Coliseum.

COSTUMES: A drop-dead dress for Ida, inexpensive street clothes for the rest; policemen's uniforms.

IMPORTANT PROPS: Minks, ermines, and other furs; an oversized and seemingly uncrackable safe; many television sets; a piano on wheels; sticks of dynamite; chandeliers; a large blackboard and pointer; a large crescent moon on which Ida can perch.

PROVIDED INSTRUMENTATION: Four reeds, three trumpets, horn, three trombones, two percussion, three violins, two cellos, bass, harp, guitar, piano-conductor.

ADVERTISING AND MARKETING: You could, of course, offer free admission to any "girl" who's seventy—but you may be better off offering a prize to the seventieth "girl" who walks through the door.

SUGGESTIONS: See if you can get the music for a most fetching song—"I Can't Do That Anymore"—which was added to the 1991 London production; it's a guaranteed showstopper.

RESOURCES: The original cast album on CD, cassette, and LP; Peter Coke's play *A Breath of Spring*, on which the musical was loosely based, and the movie *Make Mine Mink*, which inspired the musical.

RIGHTS: Samuel French.

ALSO WORTH A LOOK

TAKING MY TURN

This is from Robert H. Livingston, Gary William Friedman, and Will Holt—the authors of *The Me Nobody Knows*, which brought dignity to the stories of underprivileged youth; here, the intention is to bring the same dignity to the problems of the aged who live in retirement homes. You'll only need four men and four women to perform this earnest musical. Rights: Samuel French.

"COMEDY TONIGHT"

Musicals Out for Laughs

"I've been selling tickets over the phone for TeleCharge for five years now," says Jeff Ludwinowicz, "and it still amazes me how many, many customers call up and say, 'What's the funniest show you've got tickets for?' There's no question in my mind that most people want to laugh when they go to the theater."

If your audiences are typical of TeleCharge customers, here are some musicals guaranteed to deliver the laughs.

DAMES AT SEA

CREATORS: Book and lyrics by George Haimsohn and Robin Miller; music by Jim Wise.

BACKGROUND: This 1968 spoof of 1930s movies opened very quietly off-Broadway, but partly through the help of new star Bernadette Peters, it became a minor sensation that stayed around for 575 performances.

STORY: 1930s, New York City. Ruby gets off the bus to take Broadway by storm, and in the first of many tongue-in-cheek incidents, immediately gets a chorus job. She has lost her suitcase, however, but it's soon delivered by Dick, a sailor who wants to write for Broadway. Mona, the show's star, is taken by him, while Luckey, his buddy, catches the eye of Joan, the lead dancer. Ruby gets Dick back, but there's a bigger problem: The theater has been sold, so the show must take place on the sailors' ship, helmed by Captain Courageous, who used to date Mona. When Mona makes another play for Dick, everyone gets her seasick so Ruby can take her role and become a star. Afterward, everyone gets married.

ASSETS: A zippy score with a nice sense of humor, and a book that includes as many *homages* to the musical movies of the 1930s as could possibly be included.

LIABILITIES: To those with no knowledge of or affinity for 1930s movie musicals—and it must be assumed that their legion is growing every day—this will seem an idiotic and pointless show.

WHO YOU'LL NEED: *Lead Singing Roles:* A sunny ingenue anxious for a chance (Peters); her adoring sailor. *Supporting Singing Roles:* His buddy; their captain; a demanding star actress; a good-natured but wisecracking chorine; a harried producer–director–theater owner. *Maximum, 7-minimum, 6.*

DESIGNATED DANCES: Much, for there's musical staging in virtually every song—everything 1930s, Fred Astaire and Ginger Rogers; shadow dances; tap; a waltz; a locomotion dance; a beguine for Mona and the captain; two rousing act finales; an equally rousing act two opening; a twirl-your-umbrellas production number for all.

SUGGESTED SETS: The first act takes place backstage at a 42nd Street theater, the second occurs on the deck of a battleship.

COSTUMES: Quintessential 1930s wear; satin-lapeled outfits; long gloves; ballet tutus; sleeveless V-neck pullover sweater; regulation sailor whites with bell bottoms for both men and women; officer whites with epaulets; three wedding dresses; ragged hat and coat; a man's bathrobe for Mona; naval uniforms for the captain and his sailors; rehearsal togs; Oriental robes; rain slickers; wedding outfits; tap shoes for all.

IMPORTANT PROPS: A small onstage piano and stool; giant ticker-tape machine; a ladder; cellophane umbrellas; an Oriental idol; Chinese gong and lanterns; walking stick; perfume atomizer; mops and pails; a telescope; bouquets and flowered hoops; battered suitcase; a Baby Ruth.

SPECIAL EFFECTS: Sounds of a loud explosion; sets that shake and bricks that fall as a result of it; a follow-spotlight for shadow dances.

PROVIDED INSTRUMENTATION: Two reeds, trumpet, three violins, bass, percussion, piano, piano-conductor.

ADVERTISING AND MARKETING: If there's a naval port nearby, get some of its personnel to be involved—as "technical advisers," as honorary captains, or even become a chorus to back up the big numbers. You'll certainly expand your audience potential, and you'll have a chance for a nice feature in the newspaper.

SUGGESTIONS: Is there any chance that you could mount the show on a ship? Don't rule it out until you've checked.

RESOURCES: The original off-Broadway cast and recent London revival cast albums on CD, cassette, and LP; the fairly faithful 1974 TV version.

RIGHTS: Samuel French.

A DAY IN HOLLYWOOD/A NIGHT IN THE UKRAINE

CREATORS: Book and lyrics by Dick Vosburgh, music by Frank Lazarus, additional music and lyrics by Jerry (Hello, Dolly!) Herman.

BACKGROUND: The 1980 production opened to strong reviews, received eight Tony nominations, won two awards—one of them for choreographer Tommy Tune—and ran 588 performances.

STORY: The first act is a revue that celebrates movies—especially dancing in movies. The 1980 production used above the stage a small "ankle-stage," whose curtain lifted simply to show the "famous feet" of various stars; we could tell that up there were Charlie Chaplin, Sonja Henie, Tom Mix, Judy Garland's ruby-slippered Dorothy, Dracula, Al Jolson, and Mickey and Minnie Mouse just from their feet. The second act is "the Marx Brothers movie that the Marx Brothers never made," a musical very loosely based on Chekhov's The Bear, in which Serge B. Samovar (read: Groucho) comes to collect money from widowed Mrs. Pavlenko (read: Margaret Dumont) whose husband owed him—and winds up marrying her. In addition, the Harpo and Chico characters help Mrs. Pavlenko's highborn daughter marry her impoverished writer-lover, despite her mother's protests.

ASSETS: A Day in Hollywood would be a sharp, smart, tuneful revue even without the "ankle-stage," but becomes inspired by its innovative use. A Night in the Ukraine is perfectly and unquestionably in tune and style with the Marx Brothers' movies we know and love. (Groucho dictates a letter to Chico, who has a hard time with it; Harpo enacts charades to get his meaning across to Chico.)

LIABILITIES: The first act has nothing to do with the second, which may annoy some audiences who prefer one linear story all night long. It's not easy to emulate the physical comedy for which the Marxes were famous. (The licensers have determined that you may produce A *Night in the Ukraine* without A *Day in Hollywood*—but you cannot produce A *Day in Hollywood* without A *Night in the Ukraine*. Go figure.)

RECOGNIZABLE SONGS: A medley of "Ain't We Got Fun," "Too Marvelous for Words," "On the Good Ship Lollipop," "Louise," "Beyond the Blue Horizon."

WHO YOU'LL NEED: *Lead Singing Roles:* The ensemble of six all have the chance to sing and dance for the first act while two others will only be seen from their knees down; in the second, they must portray Groucho; Chico; Harpo; Zeppo; Margaret Dumont; an ingenue; a maid; a manservant. But there are other demands: Chico must play the piano in his namesake's inimitable way; Harpo must be an excellent mime, though harp-playing isn't necessary (the licensers will provide you with a tape); the Margaret Dumont type has a saxophone solo in the first act. *Maximum, 12; minimum, 6.*

DESIGNATED DANCES: Heavy in the first act, especially for the otherwise least-featured performers on that "ankle-stage"; a frenetic solo dance for a female during "Sleepy Time Gal," which is meant to totally play against the lyric; a tap number for the six principals while their arms are intertwined. Virtually none in the second act: just some solo Groucho-esque moves.

SUGGESTED SETS: For the first act, six doors with portholes representing the lobby of Grauman's Chinese Theater, with the "ankle-stage" above. For the second, an opulent pre-Revolutionary Russian villa.

COSTUMES: For the first act, 1930s movie usher uniforms with epaulets and white gloves for your six principals—as well as ice skates, cowboy boots, ruby slippers, Mickey and Minnie Mouse shoes. "For the second act," says Vosburgh, "a good look at any Marx Brothers movie should show you what you need—though," he adds, "look at the earlier movies rather than the later ones."

IMPORTANT PROPS: For the first act, an onstage grand piano; a Hollywood clapper board; a cardboard cutout of Nelson Eddy; a clarinet, ukelele, saxophone, and melodica. For the second act, a bicycle; dueling pistols; and, for Harpo's coat, a horn, a watering can, a baby doll, a stethoscope, a doctor's hammer, a rubber chicken, and a banana that, once unpeeled, can be zipped back up.

PROVIDED INSTRUMENTATION: Three pianos.

ADVERTISING AND MARKETING: Hold a raffle at intermission, with the prize being "A Day in Hollywood." (We of course wish that you can sell enough tickets to also give a trip for "A Night in the Ukraine.")

SUGGESTIONS: While Harpo was played by a woman in the original production, you could cast a man, and give the first-act songs assigned to her to another woman in the cast.

Try to replicate the "ankle stage" above the action, but if you can't, then have your appropriately-shod actors stand in the wings, put their feet out for all to see, and get the desired effect that way.

RESOURCES: The original cast album on CD, cassette, and LP; such Marx Brothers movies as *The Cocoanuts*, *Animal Crackers*, *Horsefeathers*, *Monkey Business*, *Duck Soup*, and *A Night at the Opera*.

RIGHTS: Samuel French.

LITTLE ME

CREATORS: Book by Neil Simon (who wrote the comedy *The Odd Couple*), music by Cy *(The Will Rogers Follies)* Coleman, lyrics by Carolyn *(How Now, Dow Jones)* Leigh.

BACKGROUND: The 1962 Broadway production starred Sid Caesar in seven roles, opened to strong reviews, received ten Tony nominations, but won only one for Bob Fosse's choreography, and ran a disappointing 257 performances.

STORY: 1960s on Long Island. Belle Poitrine, a Zsa Zsa Gabor type of pseudo-star (who has no idea how funny she is), reminisces about her life—growing up on the wrong side of the tracks while yearning for Noble Eggleston. His mother forbids a relationship between them because Belle has no wealth, culture, or social position, so Belle sets out to get all three. She gets money from Mr. Pinchley, the town's miser, who takes a shine to her after she points out that he's got some good in him deep down inside; she gets culture from a stint with international French entertainer Val DuVal; she gets social position after becoming a Hollywood star—but by this time, Noble has lost everything and is on the wrong side of the tracks himself. Belle doesn't care, and reunites with him as the curtain falls.

ASSETS: A terrific score with most witty lyrics, and a laugh-a-minute book. And, as the 1992 production at Manhattan's York Playhouse proved, there's a way to do it with as few as seven actors by doubling, tripling, and then some.

LIABILITIES: The excellent Patrick Dennis novel on which the musical is based was really a sly parody of the memoir of an untalented would-be legend, but the authors chose instead to emphasize Sid Caesar's roles—which took away from Belle's story.

RECOGNIZABLE SONGS: "On the Other Side of the Tracks," "Real Live Girl."

WHO YOU'LL NEED: *Lead Singing Roles:* A terrific comic who can play a rich snob, an eighty-eight-year-old banker, a great French entertainer, an unfit-for-duty soldier, a European movie director, the Prince of Rosenzweig, and a rich snob's son (a Billy Crystal type); the ample-bosomed ingenue, who's smitten by him no matter how many other men she meets. *Supporting Singing Roles*: The mature ample-bosomed heroine; a big-city gambler; the intimidated son of a multimillionaire; two seedy vaudeville bookers; a prince's attache. *Other Roles*: A biographer; a butler; two nurses; two secretaries; a newsboy; a defense lawyer; a preacher; a German officer; a general; a courier; a steward; a production assistant; a low-class mother and a high-class one; a young preppie couple; a granddaughter; a lowlife young adult. *Maximum, 36; minimum, 7.*

DESIGNATED DANCES: "The Rich Kids' Rag"; some vaudeville steps; a male dance solo; an ensemble waltz; a big number for the entire cast.

SUGGESTED SETS: The high-class and low-rent districts of Venezuela, Illinois; a banker's office; a jail cell; a vaudeville stage; a Chicago nightclub; a bunker in France; a ship; a Hollywood soundstage; a casino in Rosenzweig; a Southampton mansion.

COSTUMES: A glitzy gown for the older Belle; a dress made from flour sacks for young Belle; a whorish dress for Belle's mother, overalls; old-fashioned knickers; jodhpurs, petticoats, fancy finery for rich kids, pin-checked suits for the vaudeville promoters; a glittery outfit for Val DuVal; a sweater with an H (for Harvard) on one side and a Y (for Yale) on the other; tuxedos for club scene; a "pregnant" dress for Belle; World War I doughboy and German Hun uniforms; 1920s flappers' outfits for ladies; a nurse's uniform; flier's goggles; white naval captain uniforms; widow's weeds; formal prince costume; Egyptian costumes.

IMPORTANT PROPS: Picnic baskets; trash barrel; candelabra; a wheelchair (ideally an old-fashioned wicker one); a baby doll; a roulette wheel; director's chairs.

PROVIDED INSTRUMENTATION: Three reeds, two trumpets, two trombones, percussion, drums, three violins, viola, cello, harp, two guitars, Fender bass, keyboard, piano-conductor.

ADVERTISING AND MARKETING: "Neil Simon's first musical is one of his best. Come see *Little Me* on . . ."

SUGGESTIONS: While Sid Caesar played seven roles in the original, James Coco and Victor Garber split the chores in the 1982 revival. Closer, but not yet right; how about casting seven men in the roles, and make it Belle's show—as it should have been all along?

RESOURCES: The original cast album on cassette and LP; the Patrick Dennis novel on which the musical is rather loosely based.

RIGHTS: Tams-Witmark.

ONCE UPON A MATTRESS

CREATORS: Book by Jay Thompson, Marshall Barer, and Dean Fuller, music by Mary Rodgers, lyrics by Barer.

BACKGROUND: The 1959 production opened off-Broadway, made a star of Carol Burnett, moved to Broadway, received two Tony nominations—for Burnett and for Best Musical—won neither, and ran 470 performances.

STORY: A fifteenth-century kingdom suffers under a curse that can't be broken until "The mouse has devoured the hawk." To make matters worse, nobody in the kingdom, declares its wicked Queen Aggravain, can marry until her son Prince Dauntless finds a princess worthy of him and they marry. Actually, the queen—who totally dominates her son and her mute husband, King Septimus—doesn't want her son to marry, and always gives each princess an impossible-to-pass test. This causes a problem for Lady Larken and Sir Harry, who *have* to get married, what with a little visitor on the way. Harry leaves the kingdom in search of a suitable princess, but all he finds is Princess Winnifred, a most awkward young woman whose nickname is Fred, who makes her entrance after having swum the moat. Aggravain is repulsed, but Prince Dauntless is so impressed that she swam the moat that he falls in love. So Aggravain sets up a most impossible-to-pass test: Winnifred will sleep on twenty mattresses under which one pea will be placed; if she can feel that pea while trying to sleep, she has the sensitivity of a real princess and will deserve Dauntless. But the court jester and its minstrel discover the plan, and counteract it by placing much junk under the mattresses so that Winnifred won't be able to sleep. The next morning, when she enters bleary-eyed and exhausted, Aggravain is furious, but Dauntless is thrilled, and when his mother objects, he tells her to be quiet. The mouse has devoured the hawk; the queen is struck dumb and King Septimus can suddenly speak ("And," he insists, "I have a lot to say"). Both couples marry and live happily ever after.

ASSETS: *Dramatics* magazine reports this is one of the most performed titles by stock, college, and amateur groups throughout the country. No surprise; it boasts a good score and an excellent and witty book and lyrics, and is a show for the entire family.

LIABILITIES: A heavy costume show.

WHO YOU'LL NEED: *Lead Singing Roles:* An ungainly princess (Carol Burnett), and the meek and tied-to-his-mother's-apron-strings prince who thinks she's the bees' knees. *Supporting Singing Roles:* A handsome knight and the (soprano) lady-in-waiting who's waiting for him; a loud and dominating queen; a minstrel; a wizard; the court jester who plays the palace. *Other Roles:* A meek king who does not speak until the end of the show (when he gives a line that always gets applause), but must be good at miming what he's trying to say; a chorus of ladies-in-waiting and knights. *Maximum*, 30; *minimum*, 10.

DESIGNATED DANCES: Three production numbers; a solo soft-shoe for the court jester; a purposely-difficult-to-do mock-dance called "The Spanish Panic" for the entire company.

SUGGESTED SETS: A throne room; a great hall; a gallery; a courtyard; a corridor; a dressing chamber; the wizard's room; the green; the bedroom in which there will be a toweringly tall series of "mattresses" on which our princess can rest.

COSTUMES: Fairy-tale styled fifteenth-century garb for all; colorful court costumes; gowns for ladies-in-waiting; page-boy outfits (and one into which Lady Larken can fit); one soaking wet dress for Winnifred (and its exact double that can later be torn to shreds); a wizard's outfit.

IMPORTANT PROPS: Large drinking tankards; an enormous bed with mattress after mattress piled upon it, jousting equipment; a lute; a helmet; a large spiked ball; a couple of lobsters; clunky pieces of bric-a-brac that can be put between the mattresses.

PROVIDED INSTRUMENTATION: Flute, oboe, clarinet, bass clarinet, two trumpets, trombone, horn, percussion, three violins, viola, two cellos, bass, harp, guitar, piano-conductor.

ADVERTISING AND MARKETING: Make sure you hit all the mattress stores in your area to display your posters, or even ask them to donate a mattress or two that you can raffle.

SUGGESTIONS: Play it with the same sense of savvy that the *Peanuts* comic strip gives its characters; this is, after all, a pretty fractured fairy tale.

RESOURCES: The original cast album on cassette and LP; the 1960 and 1965 TV productions.

RIGHTS: Rodgers and Hammerstein.

SOMETHING'S AFOOT

CREATORS: Book, music, and lyrics by James MacDonald, David Vos, and Robert Gerlach, additional music by Ed *(Broadway Jukebox)* Linderman.

BACKGROUND: Though the 1976 production lasted only 61 performances on Broadway, the musical has been a staple of nonprofessional theaters everywhere.

STORY: A spoof of the British whodunit set to music. It's 1935, and seven people are invited for a weekend in the country at a British estate, but once they arrive at the estate, they are killed off one by one. Miss Tweed, a sleuth with a number of theories, turns out to be no Jessica Fletcher, and there aren't many survivors by the musical's final curtain.

ASSETS: A nicely crafted old-fashioned score buttresses a funky book that has many surprises, while happily leaving its biggest surprise for the end.

LIABILITIES: A highly technical show that demands an unusually high number of special effects. What's more, there's no original cast album, so your cast will have a tough time learning the material, unless you hire a pianist and a singer or two to record the score for them.

WHO YOU'LL NEED: *Lead Singing Role:* A tweedy and rotund amateur female detective. *Supporting Singing Roles:* An ingenue; the juvenile she comes to love. *Other Roles:* A grande dame; a family doctor; an elderly colonel; a dissolute nephew; a saucy Cockney maid; a Cockney caretaker; a butler. *Maximum-minimum, 10.*

DESIGNATED DANCES: A march that leads to a kick-line; some soft-shoe for most of the cast.

SUGGESTED SETS: An entrance hall of a lord's country estate in the Lake District of England—with a chandelier overhead and an enormous vase near the staircase.

COSTUMES: Traveling clothes; dressing gowns; and evening dresses in a 1935 British style, as well as a pith helmet; maid and butler uniforms; rowing togs; mackintoshes; a long muffler.

IMPORTANT PROPS: Suitcases; wicker baskets; elaborate furniture and dustcovers; liquor tray; decanters; and cart; a chamber pot; lanterns; golf clubs; a doctor's bag and stethoscope; a knapsack; a shotgun; pistols; spears; blowgun; dart; fireplace poker; garden shears; Ovaltine; a cucumber sandwich; a necklace; a shrunken head; a feather duster; an easel and canvas; a gramophone; many telephones.

SPECIAL EFFECTS: Many—an explosion; an electrocution; a dart from a blowgun; gas that hisses through a telephone; a falling chandelier; a breakaway railing; lightning; smoke. Sounds of thunder; wind; rain; clock chimes; birds; offstage clatter.

PROVIDED INSTRUMENTATION: Two reeds, trumpet, trombone, two percussion, bass, guitar-banjo, piano-conductor.

ADVERTISING AND MARKETING: "We'll tell you right now—the butler didn't do it. But who did in the musical whodunit *Something's Afoot?* Find out on . . ." And don't miss the chance to put your posters in every shoe store in town.

SUGGESTIONS: In your program, when you list the songs of the show, don't list who sings them—for if you do, your audience will be able to infer who's going to survive until the end of the show.

RESOURCES: Although Agatha Christie's novel *And Then There Were None* (a/k/a *Ten Little Indians*) is not the official source of *Something's Afoot*, it did provide enough inspiration that your cast will learn something about the style being parodied by reading it.

RIGHTS: Samuel French.

SUGAR BABIES

CREATORS: Conceived by Ralph G. Allen and Harry Rigby (who produced the musical *Irene*), sketches by Allen based on traditional material, music by Jimmy *(Four Jills in a Jeep)* McHugh, lyrics by Dorothy *(Sweet Charity)* Fields and Al *(Cain and Mabel)* Dubin, additional music and lyrics by Jay Livingston and Ray Evans (who collaborated on the song "Que Sera Sera") and Arthur Malvin.

BACKGROUND: The 1979 production was an immediate popular success, and didn't need to win any of its eight Tony nominations to run 1,208 performances.

STORY: A revue that celebrates and glamorizes the age of burlesque—the ribald sketches, the lofty torch songs, the Oriental and fan dance strips, and the song and dance done by the cops, tootsies, nurses, acrobats, con men, hootchy-koocthy girls, and bubble dancers.

ASSETS: It's fast, funny, and tuneful, and gives everyone in your company a chance to get a hand for doing something.

LIABILITIES: One of the more expensive shows for costumes and props—many of which are one-of-a-kind items that can't be faked. Some audiences will be offended by the nonstop barrage of double entendres.

RECOGNIZABLE SONGS: "Don't Blame Me," "Exactly Like You," "I'm in the Mood for Love," "I Can't Give You Anything but Love," "On the Sunny Side of the Street."

WHO YOU'LL NEED: *Lead Singing Roles:* A top banana (Mickey Rooney); a prima donna (Ann Miller). *Supporting Singing Roles:* A juvenile (who needn't be so young); a soubrette; a barbershop quartet. *Other Roles:* A candy butcher; two character men; a straight man; a second comic; an eccentric; chorus boys; a female ensemble of Sugar Babies. *Maximum,* 52; *minimum,* 20.

DESIGNATED DANCES: Heavy—high-kick production numbers; fan dances; pelvic thrusts; locomotion train effect; tap dance for prima donna and boys; ballet of female "statues" that come to life when faun kisses them; patriotic finale; the "Sugar Babies Bounce."

SUGGESTED SETS: A "Gaiety Theater" proscenium arch; modest pieces representing a shabby hotel lobby; a train; a schoolroom; scrim with ads for local businesses; a Statue of Liberty drop.

COSTUMES: Bright-colored tux and tails; red-white-and-blue costumes for the finale; a bra from which a full-length evening gown front descends; breakaway dress; foot bandage; fringes; dickeys; long-johns, feather boas; baggy pants; net stockings; feathered hats; hats with schooners on top; a naval commander's hat; wedding day tux and gown; negligees and nightgowns; party dresses; policeman's coat; schoolmarm dress; pigtail wigs; garish dress and wig for man; kilt; a faun outfit; a Statue of Liberty costume; belly dancer outfit; tuxedos; bowler hats; purses; judge's robe and British wig; minstrel show red velvet tuxes; top hats; tights; skimpy duds and flesh-colored tights for your Sugar Babies.

IMPORTANT PROPS: An upright piano mounted on bicycle wheels; large baggage cart with expensive luggage; knives; a whip; rocking chair; glitter ball; teacher and students' desks; flashlights; swings; garters that can be freely thrown to the audience; mallet-sized gavel; balloons; a knife-board with a man's silouette on it; three sticks with eight, ten, and twelve fish on them; a very large light bulb; a bicycle with reinforced handlebars on which your prima donna sits; enormous ostrich-feather fans; many swings; seltzer bottles; songbooks; fishing pole; cafe tables and chairs; a ridiculously sized hypodermic needle; tambourines and banjos; candy—especially Sugar Babies—that can be sold.

SPECIAL EFFECTS: Sounds of sirens, gunshots, and birds twittering; black light.

PROVIDED INSTRUMENTATION: Five reeds, three trumpets, horn, three trombones, two percussion, three violins, cello, bass, harp, guitar-banjo, piano-celeste, piano-conductor.

ADVERTISING AND MARKETING: "Use real ads on your scrim," says the show's conceiver Ralph G. Allen, "and make some extra money by selling space on the curtain to local firms—ideally ones in business back in the days of burlesque."

SUGGESTIONS: Says Allen, "Producers should feel free to reassign the parts. One actor needn't play all the roles assigned to Mickey Rooney, if a different division of responsibilities would better suit the personalities of the cast and circumstances of the production."

RESOURCES: The original cast album on CD, cassette, and LP.

RIGHTS: Samuel French.

THEY'RE PLAYING OUR SONG

CREATORS: Book by Neil (*Promises, Promises*) Simon, music by Marvin (*A Chorus Line*) Hamlisch, lyrics by Carole ("Arthur's Theme") Bayer Sager.

BACKGROUND: The 1979 production received only four Tony nominations, and won none of them, for *Sweeney Todd* was the big winner that year—but audience response (and smaller operating expenses) helped to keep the musical running almost twice as long (1,082 performances) as the Sondheim classic.

STORY: The present in New York City. Vernon Gersch is an Oscar-winning songwriter and Sonia Walsk has had one hit record—though you'd never know he is the more successful partner when they try collaborating; she's sure of herself and he's insecure. Despite her kookiness (or perhaps because of it), Vernon falls in love with her, which causes problems in their working relationship. Only a separation makes them realize how much they love and need each other.

ASSETS: Fine score, funny script, likeable characters, and a show that isn't very expensive to mount.

LIABILITIES: The script abounds with lines such as "There's a problem with the middle eight bars," and you'll have to wonder how much interest your audience will have in the worries and cares of two professional songwriters.

WHO YOU'LL NEED: *Lead Singing Roles:* An attractive but neurotic successful male songwriter who ideally can play piano (a Jerry Seinfeld type); a up-and-coming eccentric female songwriter (Lucie Arnaz, or a Kirstie Alley type); each should sing in a pop style. *Supporting Singing Roles:* Each has three alter egos who function as back-up singers. *Maximum,* 8; *Minimum,* 2.

DESIGNATED DANCES: Not much; slow sensual rock; one solo dance for each lead.

SUGGESTED SETS: Vernon's Central Park West apartment; his studio; Sonia's small and shoddy apartment; a trendy nightclub; a beach house; a recording studio.

COSTUMES: Vernon wears expensive contemporary casual clothes, but it's a running joke that Sonia routinely wears costumes from shows as diverse as *The Cherry Orchard* and *Pippin.* (You could have her wear odds and ends and then pick a show that fits what she wears. And in a couple of scenes, she wears "normal" clothes.) But however you costume your leads, you'll have to quadruple the job for two of the scenes—because each character's three alter egos wear exactly what Vernon and Sonia do. In addition, pajamas; robes; nightgowns; knitted leg warmers; man's winter coat; four hospital gowns.

IMPORTANT PROPS: An onstage handsome grand piano; a foreign convertible with a hood that opens; a tape recorder; an Oscar; a shoulder bag; a leather portfolio; suitcases; wine bottle; a leg cast; a cane; restaurant tables and chairs; sofas and armchairs; overnight bag and tennis racket; a bicycle; potted plants; blender; grandfather clock; a gift-wrapped box; four toy pianos. "And go to any lengths to get those toy pianos," insists Charles Fontana, who directs for the armed forces. "No matter how badly the show is going, a solid rendition of the piano number, 'Fill in the Words,' will win back the audience—*if* the pianos are in tune."

PROVIDED INSTRUMENTATION: Three reeds, two trumpets, two trombones, percussion, drums, three violins, viola, cello, harp, two guitars, Fender bass, keyboard, piano-conductor.

ADVERTISING AND MARKETING: "A musical written by Neil Simon, and you know what that means—laughs galore in *They're Playing Our Song,* opening . . ."

SUGGESTIONS: Says Joseph Patton, Resident Director-choreographer of the Carousel Dinner Theater in Akron, "It's fun to cast the alter-egos in ethnic pairs—with blacks, Asians, Hispanics—which gives opportunities and an integrated cast." Of course, you can always cast your leads as ethnics, and use a WASP as an alter ego, too.

RESOURCES: The original cast album on CD, cassette, and LP.

RIGHTS: Samuel French.

THREE GUYS NAKED FROM THE WAIST DOWN

CREATORS: Book and lyrics by Jerry Colker, music by Michael Rupert (the actor best known for portraying Marvin in *March of the Falsettos* and *Falsettoland*).

BACKGROUND: The 1985 off-Broadway production opened to moderate reviews and ran 166 performances.

STORY: 1980s, New York City. Nice-guy comic Ted meets angry comic Phil and very gifted if wacko Kenny while all are performing at a club. They team up, and even though unreliable Kenny walks off during their big "Tonight Show" audition, Ted and Phil make it appear part of the act and get the gig anyway. There they're a hit, and although Kenny doesn't "wanna be no superstar," the three sign to do a sitcom. Then they discover they'll be playing undercover (and dressed-in-drag) policemen. Should they sell out or do the comedy that suits them best? Can they, once the critics and public stereotype them? Phil decides he can; Kenny can't deal with any of it and commits suicide; and Ted returns to his small-club comedy roots.

ASSETS: A good show to do at a comedy club, for it merges the world of stand-up (still very popular as of this writing) and musical theater.

LIABILITIES: Guys struggling to reach the top—and the pitfalls that occur when they reach it—make for a pretty predictable story.

WHO YOU'LL NEED: *Supporting Singing Roles:* Three comedians in their twenties: one amiable (Scott Bakula, or a Jerry Seinfeld type); one angry; and one off-the-wall nihilist. *Maximum-minimum,* 3.

DESIGNATED DANCES: Minimal, with a few stabs at production numbers.

SUGGESTED SETS: A black box that can become nightclub (a variety of signs indicate that they're in various places: The Komedy Klub East, The Last Stand-up, the Funny Farm, etc.); a television studio.

COSTUMES: Street clothes; sneakers of varying colors; admiral's coat with braid; bicorn hat; kneepads; print boxer and leather shorts; breakaway pants; Mexican vest; white dinner jacket; Hawaiian shirts; silver sequin dress; baseball jacket; pirate's hat; monk's robe; football shoulder pads; wigs (curly dark, blond, and "Bob Dylan"); three full policewomen uniforms.

IMPORTANT PROPS: It's often been said that comedy stems out of tragedy, and a look at what you'll need here proves it: a bullwhip; a syringe; a plastic ax; a gun; a noose; a black hood; airline oxygen masks; airsickness bags. But you'll also need a microphone; tape recorder; basketball; guitar; harmonica; champagne bottle; tote bag; boom box; stuffed cat; Mickey Mouse ears. Most difficult will be the three marionettes that should be made to resemble your three comedians. And while Martin *(Annie)* Charnin insists, "You can't do a revue without stools," it's true of this show, too: three short ones, three tall ones.

PROVIDED INSTRUMENTATION: Two reeds, trumpet, guitar, bass, drums/xylophone, keyboard, keyboard-conductor.

ADVERTISING AND MARKETING: "This is an ad for our musical called *Three Guys Naked from the Waist Down.* Come see if there's truth in advertising."

SUGGESTIONS: If you have three comedians whose humor is much in the style of the three here, see if you can insert some of their routines in addition to or in lieu of the existing material.

RESOURCES: The original cast album on CD, cassette, and LP.

RIGHTS: Samuel French.

Also see: *Bells Are Ringing; The Best Little Whorehouse in Texas; Chicago; City of Angels; Do Black Patent Leather Shoes Really Reflect Up?; Doonesbury; Drat! the Cat!; A Funny Thing Happened on the Way to the Forum; Grease; Guys and Dolls; How to Succeed in Business Without Really Trying; I Love My Wife; Li'l Abner; Little Shop of Horrors; Minnie's Boys; Nunsense; Promises, Promises; The Rocky Horror Show; Snoopy!!!; Sugar; Top Banana; What About Luv?; You're a Good Man, Charlie Brown.*

"PUT ON YOUR SUNDAY CLOTHES!"

Musicals That Rely Heavily on Costumes

Have you a working arrangement with a local theater that is generous with its costumes? Do you know a seamstress who can take what seems like Eliza Doolittle's guttersnipe outfit and, after a few hours' work, turn it into what seems like her gown for the Embassy Ball? If so, here are some shows that will greatly display the assets you have at your disposal.

BAKER STREET

CREATORS: Book by Jerome (*The Apple Tree*) Coopersmith, music by Raymond (*I Remember Mama*) Jessel, lyrics by Marian Grudeff.

BACKGROUND: The 1965 production was greatly hyped by its Barnumlike producer, Alexander H. Cohen, who erected onto the theater a new facade featuring an animated Holmes, Moriarty, and other assorted Baker Street types. But the production did not live up to such hoopla. Only four Tony nominations resulted, and one award for sets—and the show lost virtually all of its money after a 313-performance run.

STORY: 1897, London. Sherlock Holmes is trying to retrieve a client's love letters to actress Irene Adler. But Professor Moriarty stole them, and when Sherlock and Irene go to the villain's lair to retrieve them, Holmes is captured and set next to a time bomb—and need we tell you that he manages to work his way out, with a little help from his teenage Baker Street Irregulars?

ASSETS: Good lyrics, nice score, and Holmes does not appear at all odd when he sings. Add to this that there are legions of Sherlock Holmes fans, ranging from the Baker Street Irregulars to those who fondly recall a few Arthur Conan Doyle stories; all would have an inherent interest in this show.

LIABILITIES: It's an awfully confusing story. Actually, Moriarty wants to kill Holmes not because of the letters, but because the detective has found out that he's putting a bomb in the midst of the Queen's jubilee. The romance seems to be there merely because all musicals up to that time had had a love story. Your cast will also be asked to affect convincing British and Cockney accents.

RECOGNIZABLE SONGS: "A Married Man," recorded by Richard Burton shortly after his first marriage to Elizabeth Taylor.

WHO YOU'LL NEED: *Lead Singing Roles:* Sherlock Holmes; a legit soprano actress of great charm. *Supporting Singing Roles:* The amiable Dr. Watson; the malevolent Moriarty; a maid; as many young adult urchins—Baker Street Irregulars, as they're called—as you care to have. *Other Roles:* A bumbling inspector; a handsome captain; a large menacing man; three killers; policemen; guardsmen; a landlady; dancing girls; two stagehands who are also spies; a doctor; a flag vendor; an American couple; friends and well-wishers. *Maximum, 46; minimum, 22.*

DESIGNATED DANCES: A music hall production number; two impromptu dances for the Irregulars; a dance through London's underworld; a big eleven o'clock number featuring almost everyone.

SUGGESTED SETS: Outside and inside 221B Baker Street; a London street; an alley; onstage, backstage, and the dressing room at the Theatre Royal; Irene's digs; Moriarty's ship (though it could be his apartment); the streets of the London underworld (you needn't have such specific sets as a cafe, opium den, or Turkish bath; a bare stage will do); the White Cliffs of Dover (ditto). One scene in which Holmes travels in a horse-drawn carriage needn't take place there; he could simply be pacing.

COSTUMES: Holmes's famous deerstalker cap, cape, and briar pipe; late nineteenth-century London wear; an Anglican deacon costume; a captain's uniform, Native American costumes for dancing girls; mourning clothes for many; underworld disguises for Holmes and Irene to make them look lower-class; ragged clothes for a beggar and a drunk.

IMPORTANT PROPS: *Much* Victoriana; an elaborate time bomb; two practical makeup tables; a chemistry table; bookcases with books; glass-bell display case; a silhouette of Holmes; a wall safe; a Buddha; blackboard with mathematical formulas on it; cameras and a tripod; a picture of Queen Victoria; an Oriental gong; two coffins; a police whistle; a doctor's bag; champagne glasses; mounds of very large jewelry pieces.

SPECIAL EFFECTS: Smoke and fog; sounds of Big Ben, horses' hooves and carriage, pistol shots, a hurdy-gurdy; voice-over for Moriarty.

PROVIDED INSTRUMENTATION: Three violins, viola, cello, bass, flute, oboe, clarinet, three trumpets, two horns, two percussion, harp, organ-celeste, piano-organ conductor.

ADVERTISING AND MARKETING: "Want to see some other lethal weapons? Come to [name of the street on which your theater is] and see *Baker Street*, the Sherlock Holmes musical."

SUGGESTIONS: Yes, Irene's songs are written for a soprano, but her style of singing seemed old-fashioned even in 1965—so you might consider a recitation approach. While you're at it, try playing Irene as less elegant; make her younger and sexier. She'll make Holmes seem more human, too.

RESOURCES: The original cast album on LP; Arthur Conan Doyle's stories "The Adventure of the Empty House," "A Scandal in Bohemia," and "The Final Problem."

RIGHTS: Tams-Witmark.

BEN FRANKLIN IN PARIS

CREATORS: Book and lyrics by Sidney *(Dylan)* Michaels, music by Mark Sandrich.

BACKGROUND: The 1964 production opened to moderate notices and was easily overlooked in the wake of heavy competition. Though Robert Preston gave a bravura performance—one of his finest—he wasn't even nominated for a Tony (Sammy Davis, Tommy Steele, Cyril Ritchard, and winner Zero Mostel were); a nomination for Best Book was all the show could muster; it ran 215 performances.

STORY: If someone wrote a sequel to *1776*, this might be it. After signing the Declaration of Independence, Franklin goes to France to enlist aid for the Revolutionary War. He romances Countess Diane, a close confidante of Louis XVI, but has a tough time convincing her to use her influence. By curtain's end, he has, and America receives French aid.

ASSETS: To write Ben Franklin, a star-quality role if there ever was one, is no easy task, but Michaels was up to it, writing with great warmth, wit, and humanity, and providing his hero with an unforgettable monologue in the penultimate scene. The very good music includes two showstoppers.

LIABILITIES: Some will view Ben as sexist. ("And you are drunk with power, Madame; 'tis unfeminine.") The show's operetta quality damaged its Broadway run, and could be less appreciated over a quarter-century later. Though the book deals with matters as significant as those in 1776, it isn't as riveting.

WHO YOU'LL NEED: *Lead Singing Roles:* A charismatic elder statesman; his (soprano) former love who is now close to the King of France; *Supporting Singing Roles:* Two grandsons (ages seven and seventeen); a young French girl. *Other Roles:* Louis XVI; his advisers; the successful playwright Beaumarchais; a British ambassador; a British spy; a painter; monks; sailors; ladies and gentlemen of the French and Spanish courts. *Maximum, 47; minimum, 20.*

DESIGNATED DANCES: Not much—an "army ballet" and a swirling waltz for Franklin and his grandson's girlfriend (and everyone else). Franklin and his elder grandson join first the younger grandson and then Beaumarchais in a couple of numbers.

SUGGESTED SETS: A dock; a Paris street; a park; a winery; Ben's house; Countess Diane's *maison*; the Pont Neuf; the Left Bank; an outdoor cafe; the Spanish Embassy; the Throne Room at Versailles. The original production used a balloon with gondola that flew over the action, but this is not altogether necessary to a successful production.

COSTUMES: Late eighteenth-century plain and fancy American wear; gowns, fans, and finery for the French court; velvet breeches; a fine wig; monks' robes; an apron; and, for Ben's infirm leg, a large cast. "Try keeping it unautographed," said Preston throughout the run.

IMPORTANT PROPS: A Franklin stove; a rocking chair; a printing press; a spinning wheel; a bicycle *without pedals.* In addition, there is a wine vat the size of a hot tub; a bookseller's cart with books; divans; loveseats; a silver *objet d'art*; bundle of straw; an easel; a blueprint; baggage, suitcase, lightning rods; kites; and bifocals.

SPECIAL EFFECTS: Thunder and lightning.

PROVIDED INSTRUMENTATION: The instrumentation is hard to find, according to many musical directors. "But," says Thomas R. Stretton of Cheltenham, Pennsylvania, "the publisher has it contained on microfilm and can print it out."

ADVERTISING AND MARKETING: If you've recently produced 1776 at your theater and had a strong Ben Franklin, here's a show where you can showcase him once again. If you're really ambitious, do both in rep; at least you'll get twice as much out of your costumes.

SUGGESTIONS: The authors admit that Ben Franklin was in his seventies when he took the trip to Paris, but suggest that he be played as a man in his fifties, so as not to seem as much of a dirty old man.

RESOURCES: The original cast album on LP.

RIGHTS: Samuel French.

BRIGADOON

CREATORS: Book and lyrics by Alan Jay Lerner, music by Frederick Loewe (who later collaborated on *My Fair Lady*).

BACKGROUND: The 1947 production was the third for the Lerner and Loewe team who had written a promising musical called *The Day Before Spring* four years earlier. But they found it difficult to find a producer for *Brigadoon*, until Cheryl Crawford took on the task. Her faith in the pair resulted in the show receiving a Tony for Best Dance Direction (as choreography was called in those days) and a 581-performance run.

STORY: While in Scotland, Tommy, engaged to a young woman he's not sure he loves, and Jeff, a cynical alcoholic in the making, find Brigadoon, a town not on any map. Tommy also finds Fiona, with whom he falls in love, but then discovers that the town and its people come to life only once every hundred years—and will be destroyed if one of its inhabitants leaves. Harry, in love with Fiona's sister Jean, who is marrying Charlie, decides to break the spell, but is accidentally killed by Jeff as he is departing. Although Tommy wants to stay, Jeff convinces him to return to his fiancée and New York. Back home, Tommy sees he's made a mistake and returns to find Brigadoon again; he does, because his love for Fiona is so strong.

ASSETS: A terrific score, a well-written and witty book, with very well-defined characters; good name recognition.

LIABILITIES: It's an awfully sentimental tale by today's standards, and two lovers' primarily being attracted on the basis of looks doesn't help. The Scottish words—such as "braw," "lea," "bairn," "dinna," and "winna"—and their appropriate accents may prove problematic to your actors—not to mention your audiences, which may spend much of the time turning to one another and asking, "What did he say?"

RECOGNIZABLE SONGS: "The Heather on the Hill," "Almost Like Being in Love."

WHO YOU'LL NEED: *Lead Singing Roles* (both legit-voices): A virile and perceptive American; a savvy Scottish maiden. *Supporting Singing Roles:* A demure sister, a pompous father; a bridegroom-to-be, a man-hungry maiden. *Other Roles:* A world-weary American who doesn't sing but has much dialogue (and often steals the show); a milk seller, a weaver and his unhappy son, a schoolmaster; a barkeep, a chic and severe New York woman; townspeople, bagpipers and experts in traditional sword dancing (lest your actors inadvertently hurt themselves). *Maximum*, 42; *minimum*, 20.

DESIGNATED DANCES: A wedding feast with traditional Scottish dances, sword dances, and country dances.

SUGGESTED SETS: A forest; a road; a town square with booths and carts; a shed; two modest Scottish homes; a churchyard; a swank New York City bar. "And because that bar comes between two scenes in the Brigadoon village," says Thomas R. Stretton, who has directed the show in Philadelphia high schools, "you must completely conceal it—ideally by a scrim—so that the complete contrast can be made."

COSTUMES: Contemporary casual wear for the two men; fanciful period Scottish dress for everyone else: waistcoats and kilts; woolens and plaids. "And get the correct plaids," insists David N. Matthews, managing director of the Erie Playhouse. "There's always going to be someone Scottish in the audience who'll yell 'foul' if you mess up."

IMPORTANT PROPS: Two rifles; baskets of cloth swatches; jugs of ale; fishing poles with fish hanging from them; a parchment; a rocking chair; a trunk; a large Bible.

PROVIDED INSTRUMENTATION: Two violins, viola, cello, bass, flute/piccolo, oboe, two clarinets, bassoon, horn, three trumpets, trombone, percussion, piano-celeste, piano-conductor.

ADVERTISING AND MARKETING: "They say that Brigadoon comes around only once every one hundred years. We're happy to say that this is the year in . . ."

SUGGESTIONS: When Tommy gives the milk seller some money for milk, the townspeople are so consternated by the coin and its recent date that Jeff blithely asks, "What did you give him, a hunk of uranium?" Very topical in 1947, but not what would come to mind now. The line used in the 1980 Broadway revival—"What did you give him, a Susan B. Anthony dollar?" still could be used.

RESOURCES: The 1992 cast album on CD and cassette is the most complete; the 1954 movie on videotape and laserdisc.

RIGHTS: Tams-Witmark.

CAMELOT

CREATORS: Book and lyrics by Alan Jay Lerner, music by Frederick Loewe (who collaborated on *My Fair Lady* and *Gigi*).

BACKGROUND: The 1960 Broadway production had everyone hoping for—or expecting—another *My Fair Lady* from the team that had delivered that smash their last time out. With director Moss Hart having a heart attack and Lerner and Loewe also falling sick, it's a wonder the overlong show came in at all, but it did, limping in to mostly ho-hum reviews. Come Tony time, it received five nominations and won four awards—though the one for Richard Burton as Best Actor was the only major award. Not until the nation saw a good chunk of the musical on "The Ed Sullivan Show" did patrons start lining up at the box office to keep the show running for 873 performances.

STORY: 1138, England. Arthur is very scared about the prospect of marrying Guenevere, the bride who's been arranged for him. But when he happens to meet her in the forest—she does not know who he is—he is charmed by her. She likes him, too, and is relieved when she discovers he will be her husband. Arthur grows through her love, and conceives of the idea of a round table at which knights who practice chivalry will sit. Lancelot of France, a most ego-centric knight, is one of the first to respond to the cause. Guenevere doesn't like him initially, but after a jousting match in which he seemingly brings a man back from death—and vanquishes all challengers—she begins to fall in love with him. Lancelot becomes enamored of her, and though Arthur can see what's coming, he feels powerless to stop their love. When Lancelot is in Guenevere's bedroom, Arthur's illegitimate son, Mordred, a born mischief-maker, breaks in and has Guenevere arrested for treason. But Arthur helps the two to escape and muses on the fall of Camelot as the curtain drops.

ASSETS: A fine score and often compelling book; the last scene, in which Arthur tells about the end of Camelot, now has an extra power with audiences who remember the John F. Kennedy era. If you're looking for a show for a large outdoor presentation, here's one big enough to fill your dimensions.

LIABILITIES: In addition to being an expensive show to mount, there's that unhappy ending. It's believable that Guenevere could be impressed with Lancelot when such an egocentric sincerely prostrates himself before her, but what makes her crave him—that he brought a severely wounded knight back from seeming death, or that he just took out three guys in a joust? If it's the latter, she's not very regal, and the message of the show becomes "You gotta be a jousting hero to get along with a beautiful girl." Guenevere doesn't grow much from the girl who's so self-absorbed that she wants men to "cause a little war" for her, and the creators might have been better off if they had found something more right for Guenevere than a convent.

RECOGNIZABLE SONGS: "Camelot," "How to Handle a Woman," "If Ever I Would Leave You."

WHO YOU'LL NEED: *Lead Singing Roles:* The decent King Arthur (Richard Burton); the lovely (mezzo) Queen Guenevere (Julie Andrews). *Supporting Singing Roles:* The stern-jawed Sir Lancelot (Robert Goulet); three cocksure knights; Arthur's illegitimate ne'er-do-well son; the voice of a spirit. *Other Roles:* An aged Merlin the Magician; Morgan Le Fey; three ladies; two pages;

a herald; a young boy; Pellinore, an old and doddering knight, and his sheepdog; various knights; nymphs; ladies of the kingdom. *Maximum, 48; minimum, 30.*

DESIGNATED DANCES: A series of jousts for the knights; a brief hornpipe for Arthur and Guenevere; a "Persuasion" ballet for Mordred, Morgan Le Fey, and nymphs; some musical staging on two other numbers.

SUGGESTED SETS: A castle; its towers, great hall, royal box, and various rooms; nearby hilltops and countrysides.

COSTUMES: Twelfth-century garb; a wizard's tall hat and robes; rusty armor; chain mail; the formal clothes that the friends and relatives of the king and queen wear to a parade, festival, joust, and knighting; outfits for the half-animal, half-human nymphs of Morgan Le Fey's forest.

IMPORTANT PROPS: A telescope; a lance; a monocle; wine decanter; scroll; backgammon set; baskets of candy; dressing tents; banners for a parade, festival, joust, and knighting; flowers; tapestry; easel.

SPECIAL EFFECTS: Fog.

PROVIDED INSTRUMENTATION: Two violins, viola, cello, bass, flute-piccolo, oboe-English horn, two clarinets, bassoon, three horns, three trumpets, two trombones, percussion, guitar-lute-mandolin, harp, piano conductor. Also available is a condensed orchestration of eleven or twelve pieces.

ADVERTISING AND MARKETING: "Come and we'll tell you all about the scandal in England's Royal Family—of 1138."

SUGGESTIONS: If you eliminate Pellinore, you also don't have to have a dog.

RESOURCES: The original cast album on CD, cassette, and LP; the 1968 fairly faithful movie version on videotape and laserdisc; T. H. White's novel *The Once and Future King*, on which the musical is loosely based.

RIGHTS: Tams-Witmark.

CANTERBURY TALES

CREATORS: Book by Martin Starkie and Nevill Coghill, music by Richard Hill and John Hawkins, lyrics by Coghill.

BACKGROUND: Although the show was a smash hit in England (admittedly a more indigenous site for this classic tale), the 1969 Broadway production, despite four Tony nominations, and one win for costumes, managed only 121 performances.

STORY: Geoffrey Chaucer, at the Tabard Inn with a bunch of pilgrims on their way to the shrine of Thomas à Becket in Canterbury, recounts the tales told by the group on their journey. The Miller's Tale involves an old carpenter who makes the mistake of marrying a young lovely who's admired by a young man; the Steward's Tale is about a corrupt miller whose two daughters are seduced no matter how much he tries to prevent it; the Merchant's Tale is about an old man whose young wife meets her lover in a secret garden to which her husband assumes he has the only key; the Wife of Bath's Tale concerns the age-old riddle, "What do women want?" The knight suggests it's not dominance, but love and respect that each married partner gives the other. All agree—just as they're reaching their destination.

ASSETS: A good enough score, and a pleasant Cliff Notes version of the famed tales.

LIABILITIES: The show is in rhyme, which can be very wearing on an audience. It's also a show that the English tend to appreciate more because its source material is generic to them. Its ribald quality may make it inappropriate for more rarefied communities.

WHO YOU'LL NEED: *Supporting Singing Roles:* Chaucer; his host; the Wife of Bath; a miller; a cook; a merchant; a knight; a steward; a prioress; a (soprano) nun; a priest; a clerk at Oxford; a squire; a friar; a pardoner; a summoner; a sweetheart—all of whom play various roles in the four tales told. *Maximum, 46; minimum, 18.*

DESIGNATED DANCES: Much is done in a latter-day rock style; three production numbers, including a "mug dance."

SUGGESTED SETS: The Tabard Inn; an orchard; a chapel; a garden; Canterbury Cathedral. If you're interested in replicating one of the more charming aspects of the original production, you'll have flats on which many varieties of food are painted—and you'll set them in front of your assembled cast to indicate a feast in front of them.

COSTUMES: Fourteenth-century garb; long full dresses; a scholar's robes; tunics; tights; cleric's robe; nun's habit; wedding dress; nightcaps and gowns for the husbands.

IMPORTANT PROPS: Many, many mugs—and long flats on which will be painted all the food and drink that will adorn a table; similarly, there are flats to be painted as beds, which are placed in front of a couple and represent them in bed.

PROVIDED INSTRUMENTATION: Three trumpets, horn, two trombones, two guitars, bass, two percussion, piano-conductor.

ADVERTISING AND MARKETING: "Fourteenth-century Pilgrims had to travel for four days to hear the *Canterbury Tales;* we'll give them to you in one fun-filled musical evening, beginning on . . ."

SUGGESTIONS: There's a tendency for non-professionals who deal with rhyming verse to make it very sing-song. Watch for this—and nip it in the bud.

RESOURCES: The original cast album on LP; Geoffrey Chaucer's *Canterbury Tales* on which the musical is loosely based.

RIGHTS: Music Theatre International.

HALF A SIXPENCE

CREATORS: Book by Beverley Cross, music and lyrics by David *(Irma La Douce)* Heneker.

BACKGROUND: Tommy Steele, once the Elvis Presley of London, starred in the 1965 Broadway production, after having wowed the West End in this pleasant musical. His personal notices were excellent, and though the musical won none of its nine Tony nominations, he propelled the show to a 511-performance run.

STORY: 1900, England. Arthur Kipps may only work in a fabric shop for the stern Mr. Shalford, but he does have his friends—including Chitterlow, an aspiring playwright, and Ann, his down-to-earth childhood sweetheart. As a token of his eternal love for her, Arthur breaks a sixpence, keeps half, and gives her the other. Soon he hears that much more money might come his way via an inheritance, but he thinks nothing of it, and goes to a woodworking class that his boss demands he attend. The teacher is Helen Walsingham, and Arthur is dumbstruck by her beauty and breeding. He becomes far more dumbstruck when he discovers that his inheritance will be twelve hundred pounds a year. He quickly invests some money in Chitterlow's play, and a great deal more with Helen's broker-brother. When Helen discovers he has money, she becomes interested in him, so Arthur impulsively proposes to her at a party—where Ann happens to be a servant. She is devastated that Arthur has thrown her over, and he, eventually tiring of Helen and her mother's incessant attempts to gentrify him, cancels the engagement and marries Ann. Nevertheless, the two aren't very happy, because Arthur feels he should strive for the upper classes, while Ann is content where she is. It becomes a moot point when they discover that Helen's brother has bolted with Arthur's fortune, and they are destitute—that is, until Chitterlow's play opens to raves and will make Arthur yet another fortune. But he's smarter this time around, and appreciates his marriage more than his money.

ASSETS: An effervescent score, and a chance for a real star turn for your strongest leading man.

LIABILITIES: Your cast must affect convincing British and Cockney accents. And if you want to do a musical about a young Cockney man who comes into money, you're much better off with *Me and My Girl*—in which the leading man doesn't betray his love. After all, some audiences won't like Arthur for so quickly forgetting his girl and acting uppity.

WHO YOU'LL NEED: *Lead Singing Roles:* A winning shop boy who strikes it rich *and* ideally can play the banjo; his demure girlfriend. *Supporting Singing Roles:* Three apprentices; his imperious boss; his playwright friend. *Other Roles:* A high-class young lady; her brother and mother; a floorwalker; a cheeky maid; a photographer; two reporters; two students; two customers; four shopgirls. *Maximum, 47; minimum, 24.*

DESIGNATED DANCES: No fewer than five production numbers, as well as a soft-shoe for Arthur and Ann.

SUGGESTED SETS: A dry goods store; a promenade; a pub; a street; a classroom; a lighthouse site; an elegant party setting; a solarium; a kitchen; a photographer's studio; a parlor; a pier; a building site; a bookshop—but the vast majority need only be suggested.

COSTUMES: Turn-of-the-century Victorian British wear; apprentice clothes; white trousers; striped trousers; knickerbockers; morning coats; blazers; tuxedo with opera cloak; checked caps; bowlers; top hats; deerstalker hats; straw boaters; dresses with high white collars; blue-and-white sailor dress; maid's uniform; bride's gown.

IMPORTANT PROPS: Folded draperies; flash camera on tripod; old-fashioned bicycle, ornate tea service, strings of patio lights and two halves of a sixpence.

PROVIDED INSTRUMENTATION: Three violins, viola, cello, bass, flute, oboe, clarinet, three trumpets, two horns, two percussion, harp, organ-celeste, piano-organ conductor.

ADVERTISING AND MARKETING: Find out the current rate of exchange for half a sixpence in American money, and advertise that you're charging that modest sum to attend a dress rehearsal.

SUGGESTIONS: The first-night audience was dazzled by Tommy Steele all performance long, but was especially charmed during "If the Rain's Got to Fall," when his straw boater hat fell off—and a bit later in the number, a chorus boy retrieved it and Frisbeed it over to him. Except that it wasn't an accident, but a well-planned piece of stage business that was done every performance. It has become part of the *Half a Sixpence* mystique, and when the American Dance Machine revived the number in one of their programs, they included the "mistake." It's up to you if you want to do it, too.

RESOURCES: The original cast album on LP; the rather faithful 1967 movie; H. G. Wells's novel *Kipps*, on which the musical is loosely based.

RIGHTS: Samuel French.

LITTLE MARY SUNSHINE

CREATOR: Book, music, and lyrics by Rick Besoyan.

BACKGROUND: The 1959 off-Broadway production opened with no stars, an unknown writer, and an advance sale of $8.70—but got raves and ran 1,143 performances.

STORY: Early 20th century rustic Colorado. Spoofing the endearingly silly conventions of operetta. Captain Jim of the Forest Rangers loves demure Little Mary; Corporal Billy loves the not-so-sure Naughty Nancy, and retired General Oscar Fairfax finds Mme. Ernestine. All ends deleriously happily.

ASSETS: A fun score, a just-right approach to the material, and a charming return to the way musicals were when they didn't need to be anything more than a pleasant operetta.

LIABILITIES: The stereotyped Indian (with his Me-like-firewater vocabulary). And as audiences have aged and have had no real connection with operetta, many of the jokes may be lost on them.

WHO YOU'LL NEED: *Lead Singing Roles:* A soprano Little Mary (a Julie Hagerty type); a tenor Billy; a baritone Big Jim. *Supporting Singing Roles:* A randy maid; a contralto former opera prima donna; a retired diplomat. *Other Roles:* An Indian chief; his malcontent son; an Indian guide; a chorus of six forest rangers and six young ladies in finishing school. *Maximum, 30; minimum, 13.*

DESIGNATED DANCES: A waltz, a soft-shoe, and the like—most of which the script describes as "a few simple steps"—plus a mistaken-identity scene that has some musical staging.

SUGGESTED SETS: The Colorado Inn; the garden nearby; a "primrose path"; the point lookout; in front of a teepee; a bedroom. But you could get by with as little as a one-set drop (and a schlocky one at that) of the Colorado Inn exterior.

COSTUMES: Six forest ranger uniforms; six girls' finishing school outfits (crinolines galore); three Indian outfits, including a long feathered headdress; a maid's uniform; villain's black cape.

IMPORTANT PROPS: Croquet equipment; swings that hang from a tree; party lanterns; old-fashioned camera on tripod; goatskin bag; teepee; Indian blanket; tomahawks; sheets knotted into an escape rope; a jewel case with necklaces and bracelets; a dressing screen; a big forty-eight-star American flag.

PROVIDED INSTRUMENTATION: Flute, oboe, bassoon, two clarinets, two trumpets, two French horns, trombone, percussion, two violins, viola, cello, bass, harp, piano-conductor. Also available is a two-piano arrangement.

ADVERTISING AND MARKETING: Sell orange juice—the "Sunshine drink"—during intermission.

SUGGESTIONS: As Besoyan always stressed, "It is absolutely essential to the success of the musical that it should be played with the most warmhearted earnestness. There should be no exaggeration in costume, makeup, or demeanor, and the characters, one and all, should appear to believe throughout in the perfect sincerity of their words and actions."

RESOURCES: The original cast album (and the London cast album, on which there is additional material not found on the off-Broadway album) on CD, cassette, and LP. Preprinted posters available from licenser.

RIGHTS: Samuel French.

THE SECRET GARDEN

CREATORS: Book and lyrics by Marsha Norman (who wrote the play 'Night, Mother), music by Lucy Simon.

BACKGROUND: The 1991 production marked one of the first almost-all-women teams to write, produce, and direct a musical. Their efforts resulted in seven Tony nominations, three awards, and a 656-performance run.

STORY: Mary Lennox's parents die, and she must live with her hunchbacked Uncle Archibald. He's been reclusive since the death of his wife, which occurred during the birth of their son. The sickly boy, now secluded, stays out of view because he knows his father blames him for his mother's death. Mary eventually brings father and son together.

ASSETS: "Seventy percent of theater tickets," said producer Heidi Landesman, "are bought by women. We knew they'd like this show." So will your female audience.

LIABILITIES: Mary is such a brat that she could be called the anti-Annie. There is an issue of whether Archibald should send the girl to school or just let her stay and walk around the garden. Should there be any doubt? There is very little humor, the score is rather dull, and much of this material is turgid.

WHO YOU'LL NEED: *Lead Singing Roles:* A strong-willed pre-teen young girl; her handsome but hunchbacked (baritone) uncle. *Supporting Singing Roles:* His stern doctor-brother; his sickly young son; a no-nonsense housekeeper; a perky chambermaid; her upbeat brother; an old gardener. *Other Roles:* A "ghost" chorus that includes the hunchback's soprano wife, the girl's parents, an Indian fakir, and a few others. *Maximum, 34; minimum, 16.*

DESIGNATED DANCES: Only a swirling waltz and two production numbers.

SUGGESTED SETS: Decorate your proscenium arch with flowers and drapes and transform it into a Victorian dollhouse. As for the interiors, much of the original production used oversized picture frames to suggest some rooms, which used furnishings and not flats; a dead-center door against the back wall led to the secret garden. And it included very large moss-embellished garden sculptures of a peacock, swan, owl, and wren—which, when put together, interlocked and became one wall. There were two different secret gardens, the first one elaborate and the second one more so with cherubs adding to the fauna and flora.

COSTUMES: Victorian formal dress clothes; gowns; mourning clothes; smoking jacket; Indian fakir outfit; sari; uniforms for train conductor and the military (replete with medals and sashes); gardening clothes; leather apron. If you have the resources to dress almost everyone in white for the second-act opening, so much the better.

IMPORTANT PROPS: A brass bed; a rocking horse; a schooner model; Victorian tables; chairs; a chaise longue; a leather fauteuil; an ottoman; ornate couches; end tables; a teapot and tea set; an old-fashioned flash camera on a tripod; a steamer trunk with drawers; a candelabra with lit candles, hand lanterns; hurricane lamps; doctor's bag; walking stick; birthday cake; red scarves; wheelbarrow; garden shears; rows of potted plants; plant atomizer; watering can; sacks of seeds; a very large key.

SPECIAL EFFECTS: Smoke to represent a dollhouse on fire; fog; sound of child crying; echo effects for the ghosts' dialogue.

PROVIDED INSTRUMENTATION: Not set at press time.

ADVERTISING AND MARKETING: "The secret is out—*The Secret Garden* is coming to town on . . ."

SUGGESTIONS: You should duplicate the original production's cross-section of the dollhouse that hung on the back wall. It included miniatures of what was in the mansion's actual rooms: the bed, rocking horse, chaise longue, schooner model, table and chair. Whenever your characters are in a certain room of the house, have a corresponding light go on in the cross-section's room.

RESOURCES: The original cast album on CD and cassette; the Frances Hodgson Burnett novel on which the musical is loosely based, and its 1949 movie and 1987 TV-movie.

RIGHTS: Samuel French.

TENDERLOIN

CREATORS: Book by George Abbott and Jerome Weidman, music by Jerry Bock, lyrics by Sheldon Harnick (the team that had just written *Fiorello!*)

BACKGROUND: Late 19th century, New York. The 1960 production couldn't live up to the Pulitzer Prize winning *Fiorello!*, received three Tony nominations, won none, and ran 216 performances.

STORY: Late 1800's, New York City. The Reverend Dr. Brock is determined to close down the city's Tenderloin—the seat of vice and prostitution. Tommy Howatt, who sees no problem with the district, pretends that he's on Brock's side, but really isn't. He falls in love with Laura, a debutante who thinks there's some good in him. He tricks the preacher into visiting a brothel, ostensibly so the preacher can learn which of the police are on the take, but really so Tommy can get a picture of Brock that will later be doctored to look as if Brock participated in the debauchery. When the case goes to trial, Tommy admits what happened, and while he doesn't wind up with Laura, he emerges a better person. Brock succeeds in closing the district, but finds himself so unpopular that he must move to Detroit, which is fine with him, because he has work to do there as well.

ASSETS: A terrific and tuneful score.

LIABILITIES: A heavy set and costume show with a weak act-one finale. Cynical New Yorkers found Brock a bit of a pain for being so adamant in battling the girls, which may or may not be a problem for your community.

RECOGNIZABLE SONGS: "Artificial Flowers"—but don't expect it to sound like the Bobby Darin hit of yesteryear; here, it's a slow-tempoed art song.

WHO YOU'LL NEED: *Lead Singing Roles:* A driven preacher; a double-agent young man; a charming debutante. *Supporting Singing Roles:* Her magnate uncle; three seen-it-all prostitutes. *Other Roles:* A society beau; a *nouveau riche* country yokel; a police lieutenant; an inspector; a seedy photographer; madams and prostitutes; drunks; swells; pickpockets; policemen; parishioners, choirmaster; choir. *Maximum, 60; minimum, 27.*

DESIGNATED DANCES: Most of the company is involved in three production numbers; a march; a pantomime with some leapfrogging; a "horse race" on which Tenderloin women ride the shoulders of their men; "a dance of orgiastic proportions."

SUGGESTED SETS: Inside and outside a church; a parish house; a police station; an opulent Fifth Avenue house; a brothel; a courtroom; on a beach with cabanas; Central Park.

COSTUMES: Turn-of-the-century clothes; cheap and flashy plaid suits for the Tenderloin denizens; Prince Albert coats; white tie and tails; plus-fours; hats; canes; gloves; pocketbooks; long dresses for the swells; bathing suits; cowboy hats.

IMPORTANT PROPS: A pulpit; many suitcases; a camera on a tripod; a tea set; champagne; beer bottles and glasses; a velvet ring box with an enormous diamond ring; beach chairs and blankets; seashells; hobby horses; riding crops; a piece of embroidery; some little black books.

PROVIDED INSTRUMENTATION: Three violins, viola, cello, bass, three saxes, three clarinets, two horns, two trumpets, two trombones, percussion, harp, guitar-banjo, organ-celeste, piano-conductor.

ADVERTISING AND MARKETING: Put your *Tenderloin* posters in meat markets and butcher shops around town, and convince their owners to advertise in your program.

SUGGESTIONS: Noted Shakesperean actor Maurice Evans played Brock in the original production, but you can cast a much younger man who could play the role less sternly and righteously. He'll emerge as a good man instead of a sobersides.

Instead of directing the show as a conventional musical comedy, you might reconceive it with a Brechtian *Threepenny Opera* approach.

RESOURCES: The original cast album on LP; the Samuel Hopkins Adams novel on which the musical was somewhat faithfully based.

RIGHTS: Tams-Witmark.

WALKING HAPPY

CREATORS: Book by Roger O. *(Pippin)* Hirson and Ketti *(Look Homeward, Angel)* Frings, music by James Van Heusen, lyrics by Sammy Cahn (who had recently written the score for the movie *Robin and the Seven Hoods*).

BACKGROUND: The 1966 production opened to adequate reviews, received six Tony nominations, won none, and lasted 161 performances.

STORY: 1880s, England. Henry Horatio Hobson owns a boot shop, but spends most of his time in the pub, confident that his eldest daughter Maggie can effectively run Hobson's. Maggie, though, has come to resent her father's taking her for granted—but is even more incensed when he tells her that because she has reached age thirty, her chance at love and marriage has passed. Thus, when a customer comes in the store and insists on learning which of the employees made her shoes—because she's never seen any finer—Maggie takes note of that bootmaker, Will Mossop, and decides to make him her husband and business partner. Will is reluctant—he doesn't love her—but she's so strong-willed and he's so weak that he gives in. Eventually he and Maggie set up a shop, and Hobson, threatened by a drunk-and-disorderly lawsuit, comes to realize he needs both of them more than he ever cared to admit. Once Will agrees to return to the shop *Mossop* and Hobson's, though, Maggie says she's leaving him, because she knows he doesn't love her, and a loveless marriage turned out to be not enough for her. But Will has come to love her for all that she's done to improve his life and make him happier, and the two settle down to a much better life than before.

ASSETS: Have you a very talented actor who doesn't have a standard leading man voice and good looks? Here's a chance to showcase him in a role that depends on his being slight of build and spirit—at least until the end of the show.

LIABILITIES: A book-heavy show with an average score, resulting in a musical that's not as good as the play and movie on which it's based. Your cast will also be asked to affect convincing British and Cockney accents.

WHO YOU'LL NEED: *Lead Singing Roles:* A meek and mild bootmaker; the no-nonsense strong-willed woman who decides to use and love him. *Supporting Singing Roles:* A pompous and often inebriated boot shop owner; his two other pretty young daughters; his three drinking buddies; a temperance worker; an overweight bootmaker; a thrown-over girlfriend and her angry mother; a chorus of bar patrons, townspeople, etc. *Other roles:* Two young suitors; two young ruffians; a barkeep; an upper-class customer; a footman; a customer; a boy to give out handbills. *Maximum, 40; minimum, 14.*

DESIGNATED DANCES: A clog dance for the chorus; a box dance for Will, his former fiancée, her mother, and chorus; two production numbers for Hobson, one a dream ballet which he does with four "devils"; two solo dances for Will, one of which—the title song—leads to a big production number for the chorus.

SUGGESTED SETS: A London pub; the main floor and downstairs of Hobson's bootery; Mossop's bootery; a park, a street, and an alley in the poorer part of town; the sitting room of an upper-class house; outside and inside a warehouse, which includes a chute.

COSTUMES: Late-nineteenth-century British industrial town wear; checkered and plaid waistcoats; bowler hats; vests; boots and spats; long dresses with lace fronts; bonnets; four devils' costumes.

IMPORTANT PROPS: Shop signs; many beer steins; box of brass rings; shoe stands and hammers; bags of grain that can be split open; a wedding cake; valises.

SPECIAL EFFECTS: A trap door for Will to emerge from the basement when summoned by foot stomps.

PROVIDED INSTRUMENTATION: Three violins, viola, cello, bass, three saxes, three clarinets, two horns, two trumpets, two trombones, percussion, harp, guitar-banjo, organ-celeste, piano-conductor.

ADVERTISING AND MARKETING: "Run, don't walk, to *Walking Happy*."

SUGGESTIONS: Choose this one if you have a talented-yet-unassuming-looking actor who can't play traditional leading man roles.

RESOURCES: The original cast album on LP; the play and two film versions of Harold Brighouse's play *Hobson's Choice*, on which the musical is somewhat faithfully based.

RIGHTS: Samuel French.

ALSO WORTH A LOOK

Cinderella

Originally produced as a television special in 1958 (with Julie Andrews) and again in 1965 (with Lesley Ann Warren), is available as a stage production—and boasts as good a score as any that Richard Rodgers and Oscar Hammerstein II wrote for the stage. It's still a story of girl meets prince, girl loses shoe, girl gets prince—with some pithy observations from the King and Queen, as well as those wicked stepsisters.

Your only real problem will be that some kids, most young adults, and even some older adults won't want to go near anything called *Cinderella*. Rights: Rodgers and Hammerstein.

Gigi

This was the 1958 movie that Alan Jay Lerner and Frederick Loewe wrote after *My Fair Lady*, and was produced on Broadway on 1973. It does have a marvelous score—"Thank Heaven for Little Girls," "The Night They Invented Champagne," "Gigi," and "I Remember It Well" are all excellent—but there is something a little creepy about a family so intent on selling its young lovely girl. Rights: Tams-Witmark.

Plain and Fancy

A 1955 musical about two city folk who visit Amish country and inadvertently play havoc with the residents' old-fashioned virtues and values; was "for a while," as reported by Steven Suskin in his book *Opening Night on Broadway*, "an amateur-group favorite, but within a decade it seemed hopelessly tame and creaky"—and a bit condescending to the Amish. It also has as its second-act opening the not-easy task of building a barn. Rights: Samuel French.

Seven Brides for Seven Brothers

"This," according to Joseph Patton, Resident Director-Choreographer with the Carousel Dinner Theater in Akron, "is very difficult to do, not only because you need so many accomplished singers and dancers, but also because the song added for your leading lady—"One Man"—means that your leading lady must also belt, which she didn't have to do in the movie." Rights: Music Theatre International.

A Tree Grows in Brooklyn

George Abbott, Betty Smith, Arthur Schwartz and Dorothy Fields based this on Smith's novel, it received pretty strong reviews when it opened in 1951, but couldn't last more than 272 performances. Many have surmised that the production occurred too soon after the much-acclaimed 1945 movie, which won't be a problem for you. Now that the glorious score is again available on CD and cassette, you might investigate it—and after hearing it, with its moving ballads, tuneful production numbers, and uproarious comedy songs, you may want to schedule it right away for your theater. Rights: Samuel French.

Where's Charley?

This may have been written by George Abbott (the author of *Fiorello!*, *The Pajama Game*, and *The Boys from Syracuse*) and Frank Loesser (the composer-lyricist of *Guys and Dolls*, *The Most Happy Fella*, and *How to Succeed in Business Without Really Trying*), and did run nearly two years—but you must remember that the 1948 production opened to more bad reviews than good, and that Ray Bolger was the one reason the public kept coming. Yes, it has a fine score, but today it might consternate audiences who'll spend much of their time wondering why nobody can figure out that the oversized woman with a youthful face is really an Oxford University student. There's not much youth appeal, either, as kids hate to see people older than they having to worry about having a chaperone around at all times. Your cast must also effectively portray British accents. Still, if you've got the right comedian who can be at ease in a long dress and can get the audience to sing along with him on "Once in Love with Amy," you may have a show. Rights: Music Theatre International.

Also See: *Annie Get Your Gun*; *Barnum*; *The Boy Friend*; *Candide*; *Carousel*; *Dear World*; *First Impressions*; *Follies*; *42nd Street*; *George M!*; *Grind*; *Happy New Year*; *Hello, Dolly!*; *Here's Love*; *Into the Woods*; *The King and I*; *Kiss Me, Kate*; *La Cage aux Folles*; *Les Miserables*; *A Little Night Music*; *Mack & Mabel*; *Mame*; *Me and My Girl*; *Meet Me in St. Louis*; *The Music Man*; *My Fair Lady*; *My One and Only*; *No, No, Nanette*, *No Strings*; *Oklahoma!*; *Once upon a Mattress*; *Peter Pan*; *Robert and Elizabeth*; *1776*; *Show Boat*; *Sugar Babies*; *Sunday in the Park with George*; *Sweeney Todd, The Demon Barber of Fleet Street*; *Take Me Along*; *The Threepenny Opera*; *The Wiz*; *The Wizard of Oz*.

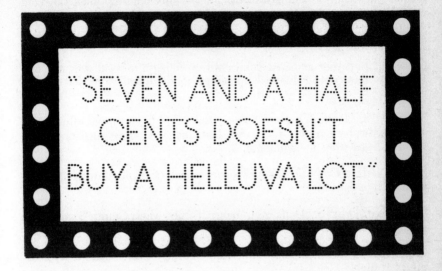

"SEVEN AND A HALF
CENTS DOESN'T
BUY A HELLUVA LOT"

Musicals That Can Be Done on a Small Budget

What's happenin' all over? I'll tell you what's happenin' all over—high schools don't have the enrollment they used to.

As for the economy, Mrs. Lovett in *Sweeney Todd* says it best: "Times is hard." Or at least it often seems that way for a theater company.

So maybe you should—or must—consider a small cast show. Here are some of the better bare-bones choices:

DON'T BOTHER ME, I CAN'T COPE

CREATORS: Book, music, and lyrics by Micki *(Working)* Grant.

BACKGROUND: The 1972 Broadway production—a series of spirited songs—opened quietly, but because of its ability to provide a joyous evening (and because its simple costs kept expenses to a minimum), it racked up 1,065 performances.

STORY: "This is a 'hymn to us,' " says director Vinnette Carroll. "How the black man, who's come a long way, must continue moving forward." But it doesn't shy away from citing his frustrations—unfit housing, unemployment woes, dull jobs, etc.

ASSETS: A moving score, to-the-point lyrics, and a timely message.

LIABILITIES: If your audience comes out expecting a musical with plot and characters, they could go home disappointed, for this is really a concert evening of songs.

WHO YOU'LL NEED: *Lead Singing Roles:* Six black singers—three men and three women. *Other Roles:* Six black dancers—three men and three women. *Maximum, 18; minimum, 9.*

DESIGNATED DANCES: Your six dancers will be involved in eleven modern-jazz type dances.

SUGGESTED SETS: "Don't overproduce it," says Micki Grant. "Two ladders should be sufficient."

COSTUMES: "Contemporary American clothes," stresses Carroll. "No costumes as such."

IMPORTANT PROPS: Handfans are all you'll need—though the original production gave them to everyone in the audience.

PROVIDED INSTRUMENTATION: Alto saxophone, guitar, bass, drums, piano-conductor.

ADVERTISING AND MARKETING: "Feel like you can't be bothered or that you can no longer cope? Have we got a show for you!"

SUGGESTIONS: "Black pride and dignity must be stressed so that the 'tongue-in-cheek' sequences read the way they were written rather than as minstrel turns," says Carroll.

RESOURCES: The original cast album on LP and cassette.

RIGHTS: Samuel French.

THE FANTASTICKS

CREATORS: Book and lyrics by Tom Jones; music by Harvey Schmidt (who later collaborated on *I Do, I Do*).

BACKGROUND: The authors enjoy telling the story of their opening on May 3, 1960, when Jean Kerr, wife of *New York Herald-Tribune* drama critic

Walter Kerr, removed the gum from her mouth before the show began and deposited it in her *Playbill*. They were then horrified, but have since been mollified by the three-decade-plus off-Broadway run.

STORY: Anytime, anyplace. Boy falls in love with girl next door; their parents are thrilled by the prospects of their uniting, but know that if they sanction the union, the kids will automatically rebel, kids being what they are. Nevertheless, when the kids do get together, they find real life to be humdrum and disappointing. They also find through a series of struggles that the world is cruel and that they can find strength in each other, and appreciate their love as the musical ends.

ASSETS: A fine score and tender book; one of the most-produced musicals of all time (as of this writing, more than eleven thousand productions in more than three thousand U.S. cities and towns).

LIABILITIES: Not much happens in the second act, but there's a bigger problem in the first: When the show was written, "rape," though not a joy-inducing term, was not the red-flag word it is today—and "It Depends on What You Pay" incessantly mentions it. Nevertheless, the authors wrote a new song to replace this one for the show's thirtieth anniversary tour, so you might try to have the licenser give it to you.

RECOGNIZABLE SONGS: "Try to Remember," "Much More," "Soon It's Gonna Rain."

WHO YOU'LL NEED: *Lead Singing Roles:* A virile narrator; a juvenile male lead; an ingenue. *Supporting Singing Roles:* Their two fathers. *Other Roles:* Two hammy actors; a mute. *Maximum,* 8; *minimum,* 7.

DESIGNATED DANCES: A bit of stylized movement; a vaudeville turn for the fathers; some flamenco steps for the narrator; a mock swordfight.

SUGGESTED SETS: Just a bare stage; a few poles; a wooden bench; a banner that states *The Fantasticks* in Harvey Schmidt's distinctive purple penmanship.

COSTUMES: Casual street clothes, as well as a fanciful hat and cape; a Native American outfit; a doublet; a red scarf; a ratty wig; a winter scarf.

IMPORTANT PROPS: A cardboard moon that can be turned around to be the sun; a carpetbag; a biology book; a watering can; a bow and arrow; small tree branches; wooden-stick "swords"; a long gray China silk cloth; a necklace; torn red silk strips to represent fire; a mask on a stick.

PROVIDED INSTRUMENTATION: Harp, bass, drum, piano.

ADVERTISING AND MARKETING: "It's been running in New York since 1960; now it's your chance to see what the excitement's about."

SUGGESTIONS: A nice show for a black-box theater—and a not-so-nice one for a big auditorium, for it depends on intimacy. And you could make one or both fathers mothers.

RESOURCES: The original cast album on CD, cassette, and LP; the 1965 TV version; Edmund Rostand's play *Les Romanesques*, on which the musical is loosely based; a "Rehearscore" disc for Macintosh and IBM systems that eliminates the need for a rehearsal pianist.

RIGHTS: Music Theatre International.

I DO, I DO

CREATORS: Book and lyrics by Tom Jones, music by Harvey Schmidt (who earlier collaborated on *The Fantasticks*).

BACKGROUND: Having David Merrick produce while Mary Martin and Robert Preston are starring in your musical certainly doesn't hurt, and this 1966 musical racked up six Tony nominations, a win for Preston as Best Actor, and a 560-performance run.

STORY: 1890's–1940's, New York. The history of a marriage from the first night of the honeymoon, through the birth of a son and daughter, middle-aged blues, the empty-nest syndrome, all the way to a positive assessment of the institution by evening's end.

ASSETS: The fattest possible parts for a man and woman; of the nineteen songs, "He" figures in all but four, while "She" sings in all but three. What's more, the songs are very good. And your older audiences will chuckle with recognition as they see their lives onstage.

LIABILITIES: Not much youth appeal in this show. (Said Canadian playwright Larry Fineberg, "If this is what married life is all about, then I'm staying single.") It's a more demanding costume show than at first meets the eye because it covers so much time and changes of style.

RECOGNIZABLE SONGS: "My Cup Runneth Over."

WHO YOU'LL NEED: *Lead Singing Roles:* Two star-quality performers who can not only carry a show, but can also convincingly play newlyweds, a middle-aged couple, and senior citizens. *Maximum, 4-minimum, 2.*

DESIGNATED DANCES: There's musical staging throughout, as well as a soft-shoe for Him (very soft, for He doesn't wear any shoes during it), and some ballroom, waltz, and a chance to polka.

SUGGESTED SETS: A large four-poster bed (on rollers or a turntable) is the focal point of a bedroom that has turn-of-the-century decor in the first act and 1930s in the second.

COSTUMES: Turn-of-the-century clothes; formal wedding wear; a striped flannel nightshirt and a pink silk nightgown; a pregnancy pad; a bird-of-paradise plumed hat; pajamas; festive paper hats. More contemporary street clothes as the play progresses.

IMPORTANT PROPS: A cowbell; a crib; two makeup cases with makeup to age the performers (onstage); many children's toys (dolls, rocking horses, tricycle, etc.), toy instruments.

PROVIDED INSTRUMENTATION Four reeds, two trumpets, trombone, two horns, violin, viola, cello, bass, two percussion, two pianos, harp.

ADVERTISING AND MARKETING: "Any couple who is celebrating an anniversary during our run of *I Do I Do* will get in free on that night. Any couple getting married on any day during our run of *I Do! I Do!* will also get in free—though we're assuming that they'll have better things to do."

SUGGESTIONS: If you're a theater that counts a family in its membership— husband, wife, grown son, and daughter—consider casting the kids in the first act and their parents in the second.

RESOURCES: The original cast album on CD, cassette, and LP; a TV version with Hal Linden and Lee Remick on videotape; Jan de Hartog's play *The Fourposter*, on which the musical is faithfully based.

RIGHTS: Music Theatre International.

JACQUES BREL IS ALIVE AND WELL AND LIVING IN PARIS

CREATORS: Music and lyrics by Jacques Brel, English lyrics and additional material by Eric Blau and Mort Shuman.

BACKGROUND: The 1968 off-Broadway production was one of the first four-person, let's-feature-a-songwriter cabaret revues. It was also one of the best, which explains its 1,847-performance run.

STORY: A cabaret revue of Jacques Brel's best and most haunting songs.

ASSETS: A tart collection of songs and lyrics; a chance for your performers who are singers first and actors second to get their feet wet in a theatrical production.

LIABILITIES: A plotless night, with none of the dramatic impact of watching a character go through a crisis and emerge from it.

RECOGNIZABLE SONGS: "Sons," "Amsterdam," "If We Only Have Love."

WHO YOU'LL NEED: *Supporting Singing Roles:* Two males and two females—though you could use as many as eighteen performers and split the score among them.

DESIGNATED DANCES: No choreography as such, but much musical staging on most of the numbers.

SUGGESTED SETS: A bare stage, with the effects set by lighting.

COSTUMES: Casual contemporary street wear for the men and elegant gowns for the women; a soldier's outfit and steel helmet.

IMPORTANT PROPS: A rifle.

PROVIDED INSTRUMENTATION: Piano (double celeste), electric guitar (doubles mandolin, acoustic guitar), bass (doubles electric bass), precussion.

ADVERTISING AND MARKETING: "No, Jacques Brel is no longer alive and well and living in Paris, but his memory and songs live on—in *Jacques Brel Is Alive and Well and Living in Paris*, which we're presenting on . . ."

SUGGESTIONS: Though the lyrics are in English, the Gallic nature of the piece remains—so cast actors with a feel for matters French.

RESOURCES: The original cast album on CD, cassette, and LP; the 1975 movie that kept the songs and added some stunning visual images.

RIGHTS: Music Theatre International.

ROMANCE/ROMANCE

CREATORS: Book and lyrics by Barry (*Olympus on My Mind*) Harman, music by Keith (*Onward, Victoria*) Herrmann.

BACKGROUND: The 1988 production made its way from off-off-Broadway to the Main Stem (albeit at Broadway's smallest theater), garnered five Tony nominations, and ran 297 performances.

STORY: Two one-act musicals: the first is about Alfred and Josefine, members of the late-nineteenth-century Vienna upper class, who each decide to go incognito to meet someone who'll fall in love with the person and not the money and station. After they find each other and fall in love, they worry about how to tell the truth, but eventually do, to each other's great surprise.

In the second act, we're in the contemporary New York Hamptons, where Sam and Barb have taken a summer share with their best friends, married Monica and Lenny. Sam and Monica are best friends, and both have fantasized about sleeping with each other. One night, while their mates are asleep, they discuss the possibilities, and even go as far as to leave the house—only to immediately return without going through with it. They'll remain faithful, and continue fantastizing.

ASSETS: A charming score and solid book (with one big mistake, detailed below).

LIABILITIES: "Though this show can be done on a shoestring," says Ronald Crepeau, a Colorado freelance director, "you will have to find laces for *both* shoes." In other words, because you have two one-acters, you'll need two sets, and two sets of costumes. On the artistic side, it's painful to see Alfred and Josefine, upon discovering the truth about each other, cynically sneer, "I never did trust him/her." Too bad they just didn't fall into each other's arms and laugh at their good fortune.

WHO YOU'LL NEED: *Lead Singing Roles:* A charming baritone man (Scott Bakula); an equally charming alto woman. *Supporting Singing Roles:* One supporting tenor actor and one supporting soprano actress who can dance well together in Act One, and play comic octogenarians in Act Two. *Maximum, 8; minimum, 4.*

DESIGNATED DANCES: For the first act, some musical staging, two waltzes for the supporting players, polka for everyone; for the second, some octogenarian soft-shoe.

SUGGESTED SETS: For the first act, a man's bedroom and a woman's boudoir, a country inn, and the streets of Vienna; for the second, a New York City skyline, a Hampton beach house with kitchen unit, deck rails, and screen door.

COSTUMES: For the first act, sumptuous evening clothes for all, as well as old pants, a hunting jacket, and hat for your male lead; a peignoir, tea gown, calico frock straw hat, and parasol for your female lead; a maid's uniform. For the second act, trendy summer apparel (especially white outfits); pajama bottoms; windbreaker; and clothes befitting two octogenarians.

IMPORTANT PROPS: For the first act, a suitcase; carpetbag; walking stick; pocket watch; for the second, a shoulder bag; squash racket; laptop computer; box of Pampers; baby clothes; pint of ice cream; wine bottle; ice bucket; jump rope; headphones; beach towels; cane.

PROVIDED INSTRUMENTATION: Two reeds, trumpet/piccolo trumpet, keyboard-synthesizer, drums/percussion, bass, piano-conductor.

ADVERTISING AND MARKETING: "*Romance/Romance*—so nice, we named it twice. So nice, you may want to see it twice. Come, starting on . . ."

SUGGESTIONS: Although Scott Bakula and Alison Fraser played the leads in both acts, you can certainly give four people the opportunity to play the leads, one pair supporting the other in each act.

RESOURCES: The original cast album on CD, cassette, and LP; the two short stories, Arthur Schnitzler's *The Little Comedy* and Jules Renard's *Pain de Menage*, on which the musicals are loosely based.

RIGHTS: Samuel French.

STOP THE WORLD—I WANT TO GET OFF

CREATORS: Book, music, and lyrics by Anthony Newley and Leslie Bricusse (the authors of *The Roar of the Greasepaint—The Smell of the Crowd*).

BACKGROUND: David Merrick produced this 1962 import musical for—are you ready for this?—$75,000. With such a low overhead, Anthony Newley's galvanic performance, three hit songs plugging the show, five Tony nominations (and a win for supporting actress Anna Quayle), it ran 556 performances.

STORY: The life of the average man, here a Brit called Littlechap, from birth, quick marriage to the boss's daughter, fast fatherhood, infidelity—and his long-suffering wife.

ASSETS: A fine score, and a thought-provoking book that effectively touches on the most identifiable facets of human life. The circus-styled conceit still seems innovative.

LIABILITIES: As Jean Kerr, who wrote the play *Mary, Mary*, once said, "I do not wish to see a musical comedy performed on bleachers in which the leading man wears clown-white make-up." We've seen many more bizarre sights (and musicals) in the last thirty years, but you must wonder if your audiences will share Kerr's opinion.

RECOGNIZABLE SONGS: "Gonna Build a Mountain," "Once in a Lifetime," "What Kind of Fool Am I?"

WHO YOU'LL NEED: *Lead Singing Roles:* An egomaniac (Anthony Newley); his sweet and long-suffering wife who affects German, Russian, and English accents. *Supporting Singing Roles:* Their two twin daughters (they needn't be identical); a young son; a chorus. Note: in a way, some of your musicians are characters, too for they must play notes that represent voices. *Maximum, 30; minimum, 6.*

DESIGNATED DANCES: Much stylized mime, but no production numbers and only a modicum of musical staging during birth sequences.

SUGGESTED SETS: One set of bleachers, with a tunnel emerging from it.

COSTUMES: The original production used overalls, stylized rags, or anything else that strikes your fancy. In addition: a wedding veil and a pregnancy pad.

IMPORTANT PROPS: Campaign signs; a cane; medals and scrolls of honor; cigars in a cigar box.

SPECIAL EFFECTS: Says Charlene Herst, stage manager for the Meadows Playhouse in Las Vegas, "I have never in my entire career worked on a show that had as many lighting and sound cues as this one." You'll also need to project a figure of Death on the back wall.

PROVIDED INSTRUMENTATION: Bass, flute, piccolo, clarinet, bass clarinet, tenor sax, alto sax, baritone sax, bassoon, horn, two trumpets, two trombones, percussion, piano-conductor.

ADVERTISING AND MARKETING: "Stop what you're doing—and make a stop at *Stop the World—I Want to Get Off.*"

SUGGESTIONS: What seemed difficult and innovative 30-plus years ago won't be a problem to today's audiences—so don't be afraid of this show's stylized approach.

RESOURCES: The original cast album on CD, cassette, and LP; the faithful 1966 movie version, and *Sammy Stops the World*, Sammy Davis's somewhat faithful 1979 version.

RIGHTS: Tams-Witmark.

ALSO WORTH A LOOK

I'm Getting My Act Together and Taking It on the Road

By Gretchen Cryer and Nancy Ford, ran off-Broadway for 1,165 performances. It's about Heather, a singer who was popular and no longer is—so she wants to try songs that are deeper, with commentary on what it's like to be a woman. This is anathema to her male manager, and, by show's end, she's singing what she likes—but he's gone. A show that's good for onstage musicians (instrumentation's provided for flute, acoustic guitar, electric guitar, percussion, bass, drums, piano-conductor), and ideal for a club setting. Rights: Samuel French.

Marry Me a Little

This is a collection of little-known songs by Stephen Sondheim, many dropped from *Company* and *Follies*, assembled by Craig Lucas and Norman René— who collaborated on the film *Longtime Companion*. It shows a single man and a single woman—seen in unassuming street clothes in one apartment, but directed so that each is alone in his or her own place—ruminate about their lives. Some of the songs are bitter (marriage is described as living "happily ever after—in hell"), some are funny (especially "Pour le Sport," about rich golfers), and some are plaintive (such as the title song, in which the woman yearns for love—but not too much of it to submerge her). Two principals. Rights: Music Theatre International.

Starting Here, Starting Now

This is a collection of songs by David Shire (who won an Oscar for his *Norma Rae* song) and Richard Maltby (who went on to write lyrics for *Miss Saigon*). Before those triumphs, though, the team was dogged by bad luck; after graduating from Yale (where Dick Cavett appeared in their musical version of *Cyrano de Bergerac*), Maltby and Shire wrote many wonderful songs for shows that closed out of town or couldn't get started in the first place. The best of them are in this 1977 off-Broadway revue. With no sets, costumes, or props to speak of, this is a fine show to do—if you have performers who can maneuver Maltby's quick-patter lyrics (a woman rails about lost love while figuring a crossword puzzle; a man lashes out at his ex-wife), this bouquet of sophisticated songs may be for you. Rights: Music Theatre International.

What About Luv?

The musicalization of Murray Schisgal's *Luv*, a smash hit during the 1964 season. Here, Jeffrey Sweet, co-editor of the annual *Best Plays* series, Howard (*Georgia Avenue*) Marren, and Susan (*Jelly's Last Jam*) Birkenhead adapted the comedy. It's still about Harry, who's just about to throw himself off a bridge when old classmate Milt comes along and convinces him that he mustn't—especially because Milt wants to foist on him wife Ellen, whom he no longer loves. A year later, however, Milt decides he does love Ellen, and Milt and Ellen, who also wants a reconciliation, try to convince Harry to throw himself off the bridge. It's a three-character show with minimal expenses, and even after all these years, still funny. "Just make sure," says librettist Sweet, "that you don't have too cheerful an actor playing Harry. He must really be someone who can express depression." Rights: Music Theatre International.

Also See: *The Act; Ain't Misbehavin'; "A" . . . My Name Is Alice; Baby; Big River; Birds of Paradise; Celebration; A Chorus Line; Company; The Cradle Will Rock; Diamond Studs; Falsettoland; Hair; In Trousers; Jesus Christ Superstar; March of the Falsettos; The Me Nobody Knows; My Old Friends; Nunsense; Oil City Symphony; Pump Boys and Dinettes; Smoke on the Mountain; Snoopy!!!; Taking My Turn; They're Playing Our Song; Three Guys Naked from the Waist Down; Two by Two; You're a Good Man, Charlie Brown.*

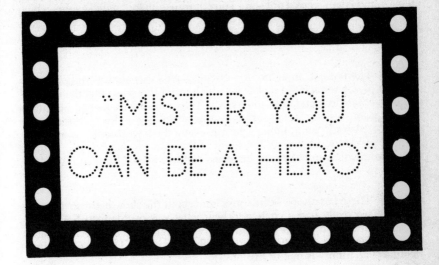

"MISTER, YOU CAN BE A HERO"

Cult Shows That Haven't Yet Found Their Audience

"The problem with doing *Dolly* or *Annie*," says director Dale Gutzman, who's directed in the Milwaukee area, "is that audiences will always compare them to previous productions they've seen. I like to try different shows where that can't happen—even shows that failed the first time around, shows that the New York critics didn't like, but have more to them than many people think."

So if you feel that you may have overdosed your audience on the warhorses, here are some musicals that might intrigue them. And given that Shakespeare's "problem comedies" get produced, "problem musicals" should, too. Who knows? Maybe you'll be the one to find a new directorial interpretation that will propel an almost-forgotten musical to new glory.

ANYONE CAN WHISTLE

CREATORS: Book by Arthur Laurents, music and lyrics by Stephen Sondheim (who had collaborated on *West Side Story*).

BACKGROUND: The 1964 production opened to three raves and three pans—but the raves were from the less important papers, and the show closed after 9 performances, literally proving that "satire is what closes on Saturday night"—and later received only one Tony nomination for choreography, which it didn't win. But record producer Goddard Lieberson believed in young Sondheim's atypical score, and recorded it, and that has kept the show alive to this day.

STORY: The present, in a "not-too-distant place." An almost-bankrupt town creates a phony miracle—a rock from which water flows—so that the religious will come there to spend time and money. When the town's mental institution inmates want to share in the fun, a visiting shrink is employed to see if they should be allowed. Soon, though, he's assessing the townspeople, saying some of them are crazy, observing that some of the inmates aren't crazy. A nurse falls in love with him before she discovers that he escaped from an institution, too.

ASSETS: There has always been a mystique about the show because it was the first time we really had a chance to hear what was on Stephen Sondheim's musical mind. And the way Sondheim's world has darkened over the years, this score, despite a "mayoress" who blithely proclaims, "There isn't a murder I couldn't commit!" is one of his most joyous.

LIABILITIES: Too many years have passed since the show was written, and the world and other writers long ago caught up with some of the wry perceptions about sanity and insanity. When one hears Sondheim in recent times talk of *Whistle,* you feel that he's proud to have written it, but has no problem admitting that time has passed it by. Sophisticated audiences may find it dated—but less discerning audiences might still be as confused as their 1964 counterparts.

RECOGNIZABLE SONGS: "Anyone Can Whistle."

WHO YOU'LL NEED: *Lead Singing Roles:* A desperate "mayoress" (Angela Lansbury); a sometimes French-accented nurse who's capable of sustaining a long monologue (Lee Remick); a most assured psychiatrist. *Supporting Singing Roles:* The town's treasurer; police chief; comptroller; a song-and-dance quartet. *Other Roles:* A sandwich sign man; a fussy doctor; a housewife and her bratty daughter; a silly married couple; a straight arrow; a black man; an old lady; a telegraph boy; a chorus. *Maximum, 44; minimum, 20.*

DESIGNATED DANCES: Ballets (conventional and un-); song-and-dance; a waltz; a parade in town.

SUGGESTED SETS: In front of a city hall in a town square; a hotel room with a workable Murphy bed that has a headboard capable of being lit from behind; a mountain; a bedroom.

COSTUMES: Colorful, costume-y street clothes; sequined song-and-dance ensemble suits; an extravagant red coat trimmed with feathers; a red wig; four pairs of very long gloves; a negligee; a pastel-colored straitjacket.

IMPORTANT PROPS: An enormous rock; a row of theater seats behind a brass rail; a massage table; a water pump; a sandwich sign; an armful of roses; a fat roll of red movie-theater tickets; a suitcase and a long oblong case; guns; a shopping bag full of vegetables.

SPECIAL EFFECTS: The rock must sprout water—and in the last scene it should spray waters of different colors.

PROVIDED INSTRUMENTATION: Five reeds, two horns, three trumpets, two trombones, two percussion, accordion, three cellos, bass, piano-conductor (and celeste).

ADVERTISING AND MARKETING: "See the Sondheim flop that just won't go away."

SUGGESTIONS: A particularly good show for a college production. Have a good, free-and-easy time with this one. If you play it with confidence and speed, you'll carry the audience.

RESOURCES: The original cast album on CD, cassette, and LP (and there was even an eight-track tape made; how's *that* for a 9-performance flop?)

RIGHTS: Music Theatre International.

BABY

CREATORS: Book by Sybille Pearson, music by David Shire *(who scored the film Norma Rae)*, lyrics by Richard *(Miss Saigon)* Maltby, Jr.

BACKGROUND: The 1983 production opened to moderate reviews, received seven Tony nominations, won none, and ran 241 performances—but has proved a popular favorite with non-professionals.

STORY: The present, in a New England college town. Middle-agers Alan and Arlene are glad their last kid has gone off to school; thirty-somethings Nick and Pam are hoping last night's lovemaking will have at last meant conception; Danny and Lizzie, who just turned twenty, are moving into a basement apartment together—though not marrying. All the women soon discover that they're pregnant (and later meet in the doctor's office). Alan's interested; Arlene is horrified. Danny now wants to get married, but Lizzie doesn't. Nick and Pam are thrilled—until they learn the nurse made a mistake. Pam insists they go to a specialist, where they discover Nick has a low sperm count. Danny, meanwhile, tours with a punk rock band that's not so good (even for a punk rock band), and Alan realizes while playing softball that he's older than he thinks. Arlene is considering abortion, but can't go through with it—which pleases Alan. Nick and Pam try some new positions and a new lifestyle that supposedly aids conception. Danny gives Lizzie a ring, saying he's marrying her; she's glad she has it when the baby starts to kick. Arlene worries that having a child will mean that she and Alan will never be able to know each other as spouses and not parents. By the end of the show, Nick and Pam know they'll never conceive, and plan to devote their lives to each other; Danny and Lizzie have their baby; and Alan and Arlene are looking forward to theirs.

ASSETS: A fine score, and an often good book. An easy show to do because the set, costume, and prop demands are minimal; it offers six almost equal in length parts.

LIABILITIES: The book sometimes meanders, and doesn't always offer satisfying resolutions. And will your audience accept Arlene's considering abortion?

WHO YOU'LL NEED: *Lead Singing Roles:* A middle-aged college administrator and his wife who has just "finished" being a mother; a thirty-ish couple, each of whom is a gym coach; a young musician and his very independent college-student girlfriend. *Other Roles:* A doctor; an intern; a nurse; a college dean; an expectant father; a chorus of townspeople. *Maximum, 20; minimum, 8.*

DESIGNATED DANCES: No difficult choreography, but some musical staging in three numbers.

SUGGESTED SETS: Three apartments, one for each couple; a doctor's waiting room; the track; on the campus; a baseball field; a bus station; the town square.

COSTUMES: Contemporary street clothes for all, though Danny does have one punk rock outfit; doctors' and nurses' uniforms; a sexy negligee; sweatpants and exercise gear.

IMPORTANT PROPS: Electronic treadmill and gym equipment; basketball; musician's equipment; bassinets; baby carriage; infant toys; a "baby."

SPECIAL EFFECTS: The Broadway production started the show with slides and cross-sections of an embryo and a fetus.

PROVIDED INSTRUMENTATION: Three reeds, French horn, three trumpets, trombone, guitar (electric and acoustic, banjo), violin, cello, bass (electric and acoustic), drums (timpani, percussion), two keyboards, piano-conductor.

ADVERTISING AND MARKETING: Use birth announcements to proclaim your newest production—er, arrival.

SUGGESTIONS: Perhaps it's best not to use the slides. They're just not musical.

RESOURCES: The original cast album on CD, cassette, and LP; videocassette–interviews with the creators.

RIGHTS: Music Theatre International.

BIRDS OF PARADISE

CREATORS: Book by Winnie Holzman and David Evans (who contributed songs to "A" . . . My Name Is Alice), music by Evans, lyrics by Holzman.

BACKGROUND: The musical was written in the New York University musical theater program, with Arthur Laurents, who wrote the book for Gypsy and West Side Story, taking an active role as godfather. When the 1987 off-Broadway production met with troubles, Laurents took over the direction; nevertheless, despite many dedicated fans, the show ran only 24 performances.

STORY: The present, on a fictional East Coast island. A community theater group will produce a musical written by one of its members; it opts for Dave's derivative A Diva by December instead of Homer's avant-garde version of Chekhov's The Sea Gull—until journeyman professional actor Lawrence Wood comes to town. Wood, having no acting prospects at the moment, is begged by the company to take on the direction and the lead role—and does. He also rewrites and reconceives Homer's work—making it clear and concise—and these changes and cuts during rehearsals both devastate and challenge Homer, but nothing prepares him for Wood's abrupt exit the night before opening when Wood is suddenly offered a part in a Broadway show. But this community of community theater actors bands together and finds a way to triumph.

ASSETS: A good score (wait till you hear a ballad called "Imagining You") and an on-the-mark book. Your actors won't have difficulty with these roles, for they'll either be playing people very much like themselves or the community theater counterparts they've come to know (and, we hope, love). This is also a very inexpensive show to mount.

LIABILITIES: Much of the time the authors spoof community theater types. Can you take a good look into this mirror and come out unscathed? And then there's that title, which can refer to flowers, birds, or even the characters. But would you have been happier with the show's original title—Amateurs? (On the other hand, the authors do remind us that the word "amateur" means someone who does something out of love.)

WHO YOU'LL NEED: Lead Singing Roles: The intense young man who wants to write something unique; his mother who gets the lead in every show; the girl he loves; the girl who loves him. Supporting Singing Roles: The early middle-aged high school music instructor whose own music proves that those who can, do, and those who can't, teach; an amiable amateur actor; the housewife who is the efficient secretary of the organization; a professional actor who's appeared on Broadway—but not lately. Maximum-minimum, 8.

DESIGNATED DANCES: One production number in which the cast portrays penguins; minimal musical staging steps.

SUGGESTED SETS: Probably none, depending on where you perform, because the show is set on the bare stage of a community theater.

COSTUMES: Primarily street clothes, though there are a few ethereal gowns for *The Sea Gull* musical and a few penguin suits.

IMPORTANT PROPS: Happily, nothing much; scripts for both *A Diva by December* and *The Sea Gull*, some newspapers—and some birds of paradise flowers.

PROVIDED INSTRUMENTATION: Reed, French horn, cello, bass, percussion, piano-conductor.

ADVERTISING AND MARKETING: Raffle birds of paradise flowers at intermission.

SUGGESTIONS: If you've just done *The Sea Gull*, this musical might be a nice follow-up, for your audience might notice the parallels between the two shows.

RESOURCES: The original cast album on CD and cassette. And do take a look at Anton Chekhov's *The Sea Gull*.

RIGHTS: Samuel French.

THE HAPPY TIME

CREATORS: Book by N. Richard (*110 in the Shade*) Nash, music by John Kander, lyrics by Fred Ebb (who had just collaborated on *Cabaret*).

BACKGROUND: Producer David Merrick put the 1968 production into Broadway's largest theater—a big mistake, for this is a small story. The result was a small 285-performance run.

STORY: "Yesterday"—in French Canada. Jacques, a photographer who left the little village of St. Pierre to see the world, returns home to take pictures of the town. His godson and nephew Bibi admires him and his lifestyle, and in turn thinks his own father is dull for living such a menial existence. Jacques encourages Bibi to embrace life as he never has, causing chaos in the family and with the boy's schoolteacher, who years ago was charmed by Jacques. Even Grandpere, who is frank about enjoying "naked pictures of girls," is angry with Jacques for the trouble he's introduced. Jacques considers staying in St. Pierre, and even thinks about marrying the schoolteacher, before they both realize it wouldn't work. When Jacques strongly suggests that Bibi come with him as his assistant for a year, Grandpere makes him tell the boy the truth, that his life is not as glamorous as it seems.

ASSETS: A fine score complements a charmingly personal book. If you do this show in a small space, it should work. If you have a good audio-visual department, here's the chance to involve them.

LIABILITIES: The costly and time-consuming concept behind the show is that we see projected on the cyclorama behind the photographer the pictures that he's taken; sometimes they represent what really happened, sometimes what he thinks happened, sometimes what he wishes had happened. Not a bad idea, but it does raise problems that you wouldn't have if you chose another show.

WHO YOU'LL NEED: *Lead Singing Roles*: A virile and worldly (baritone) photographer. *Supporting Singing Roles*: His family, all of whom still live at home: his married no-nonsense brother, levelheaded sister-in-law, and their naive young adult son; another sensible brother, his wife, and their small daughters; the family's irascible father; six nightclub chorines; the lovely local schoolteacher; *Other Roles:* Members of a boys' glee club. Maximum, 40; minimum, 20.

DESIGNATED DANCES: A few numbers involve simple musical staging, but there are two kick-line production numbers; a nightclub act involving acrobatics; spirited strut for Jacques, Bibi, and Grandpere; a balletlike sequence in which the students at Bibi's school pass around those naked pictures.

SUGGESTED SETS: Because the photographs take the place of settings, there are no realistic sets—just a few rooms and areas represented by tables and chairs; beds and end tables; folding chairs; a dressing screen; a jungle gym.

COSTUMES: Conservative provincial wear for St. Pierre residents; more flashy clothes for Jacques. In addition, a Tyrolean hat; a smoking jacket.

IMPORTANT PROPS: Many cameras, darkroom equipment; dinnerware; birthday party streamers; red paper hats; black balloons; wine bottles; hard-boiled egg; a large pocket watch.

SPECIAL EFFECTS: You'll need to take many, many slides, of the family members, the schoolteacher on a bike, the glee club boys fighting, and—toughest of all—Grandpere as a child, teenager, young man, and middle-aged man. (Cheer up, though; the photographs that come from Bibi's memory are *supposed* to be out-of-focus and double-exposed.)

ADVERTISING AND MARKETING: "Plan to enjoy yourself at our next production. It is, after all, called *The Happy Time*."

SUGGESTIONS: It's often been alleged that having the photographs on the back wall overwhelmed the production, and that theatergoers didn't watch—in fact, couldn't *see*—the actors, so you might consider having a movie screen on each side of the stage and letting the pictures project there.

RESOURCES: The original cast album on CD, cassette, and LP; the play by Samuel Taylor on which the musical was hardly based.

RIGHTS: Dramatic Publishing Co.

MACK & MABEL

CREATORS: Book by Michael Stewart, music and lyrics by Jerry Herman. (the authors of *Hello, Dolly!*).

BACKGROUND: The 1974 production may have had its flaws, but it also opened at a time when "the Jerry Herman musical" was out-of-fashion and unappreciated, and ran 66 performances. Herman's terrific score didn't even get him a Tony nomination; the show received eight, and won none.

STORY: 1911–1938, Hollywood. Mack Sennett is a workaholic who turns sandwich girl Mabel Normand into a silent-movie comedy star. She loves him and he even loves her—but work comes first, especially the work he insists she do (he won't let her out of her contract to take more challenging roles). Mabel eventually drifts to alcohol and drugs, and is even involved in a murder; an overdose kills her, leaving a guilty Mack to regret not appreciating the woman who loved him so.

ASSETS: A terrific cluster of songs. If you're the type of director who can do the pie-in-the-face routines with panache, here's your chance.

LIABILITIES: For a man who "only wants to make the world laugh," Mack is remarkably unhumorous, an arrogant slavedriver who believes he has all the answers, and whose only joy is seeing how many movies he can crank out quickly. And will your audience want to see the grisly death of the most appealing character?

WHO YOU'LL NEED: *Lead Singing Roles:* A very driven movie director; the charming young delivery girl he turns into a comic movie star. *Supporting Singing Roles:* His assistant (originally played by Lisa Kirk—though Tommy Tune later appeared in a rewritten version of the character); a soundstage worker who's Mabel's biggest fan. *Other Roles:* A studio head, a famous movie director; a drug dealer; various cameramen and grips; Keystone Kops and, if not the "hundreds of girls" stated in the song, at least a generous chorus of bathing beauties. *Maximum, 48; minimum, 20.*

DESIGNATED DANCES: Much—for you must choreograph all those silent movie sequences where those pies must be pushed into faces with perfect timing.

SUGGESTED SETS: The about-to-be-demolished Sennett Studios; Mack's first office and later his newer one; a sleeper on a train; a posh function room in a Hollywood hotel; a New York pier; a fancy home.

COSTUMES: Early twentieth-century wear—plus a bevy of Keystone Kops and bathing beauty costumes.

IMPORTANT PROPS: An ironing board; a director's chair; a flower basket; bathtub and screen; bar unit with stool; a horseshoe of roses; a steamer trunk; Keystone Kops clubs; stools; a wardrobe hamper; camera with megaphone; buzzsaw; hand movie projector; suitcases; briefcases; two pistols; film cans; red carpet for Mabel's Hollywood entrance; silver tray and champagne glasses; seventeen "custard" pies; a push broom with which to clean them from the stage.

SPECIAL EFFECTS: If you wish, a "camera crane" that can carry your Mack over the orchestra.

PROVIDED INSTRUMENTATION: Four reeds, three trumpets, horn, two trombones, two percussion, two violins, viola, cello, bass/tuba, guitar/banjo, piano-conductor.

ADVERTISING AND MARKETING: "The composer of *Hello, Dolly!* in a Hollywood mood."

SUGGESTIONS: It helps if Mack is played a little tentatively; let him *hope* (but not *know*) that he has all the answers; he can lose his head less quickly, less maniacally, and less often, with a minimum of bluster and outrage.

RESOURCES: The original cast album on CD, cassette, and LP; a London concert version (with one different song) on CD and cassette.

RIGHTS: Samuel French.

SHE LOVES ME

CREATORS: Book by Joe (*Cabaret*) Masteroff, music by Jerry Bock, lyrics by Sheldon Harnick (who next collaborated on *Fiddler on the Roof*).

BACKGROUND: The 1963 production opened quietly to mostly fine reviews, but ran only 301 performances; it later received five Tony nominations, and won one for supporting actor Jack Cassidy. However, this show has had a healthy afterlife, and many a theater has mounted this quiet and lovely show.

STORY: 1933, a middle European city. Georg and Amalia, who work together in an elegant European parfumerie (and hate each other) are each writing (and falling in love with) a "dear friend" whom neither has met. In contrast to this is a more knowing romantic couple—Ilona and Kodaly—who have their ups and downs. Kodaly is, in fact, having an affair with the proprietor's wife, but the proprietor believes it is Georg and fires him. What's worse, Georg learns just before the first date that Amalia has been writing to him, and embarrasses her without letting her in on his "true identity." The next day he comes to apologize, and she begins steadily falling in love with him. By show's end, Kodaly is found guilty and fired, Georg rehired and promoted, Ilona falls in love with someone new, and Amalia and Georg become a couple.

ASSETS: What a score! The show is really, on its own terms, a masterpiece. It also provides a nice journey back to a world when stylish elegance was expected and happily adhered to, when personal ads didn't yet insist that responses include "no femmes or fatties."

LIABILITIES: About twice as much music for your cast to learn as the average musical. There are none of the big, loud showstoppers which most theatergoers tend to enjoy, and only one song-and-dance number that approaches that level.

RECOGNIZABLE SONGS: "She Loves Me."

WHO YOU'LL NEED: *Lead Singing Roles:* Two shy lovers (here's a chance to cast your most naive members!), she with a strong soprano, he with the ability to lift her in his arms. *Supporting Singing Roles:* A slick (song-and-dance) womanizer; his worldly-wise girlfriend; a round-shouldered clerk; a perfectionist boss; a delivery boy. *Other Roles:* A chorus of store customers and cafe patrons. *Maximum, 25; minimum, 10.*

DESIGNATED DANCES: Very little; some musical staging on a song in which a cafe is established as a spot that has "a romantic atmosphere," and another (a march) in which the chorus marvels how quickly the days pass when you haven't done your Christmas shopping. Georg and his boss have an awkward extemporaneous waltz, and a song-and-dance turn for the womanizer.

SUGGESTED SETS: At most four, but especially a high-class parfumerie with two sales counters (put it on a turntable so you can quickly go from the exterior scenes to the interior ones), and a cafe that isn't as elegant as it seems at first glance. You can build (or finesse) Amalia's bedroom and a hospital's private room, with a bed (or two) for each.

COSTUMES: Old-fashioned European suits; brimmed caps; trench coats; long dresses; stylish hats; handbags; tuxedos; nurse's uniform; bathrobes; an arm-sling.

IMPORTANT PROPS: A bicycle; cafe chairs and tables; serving trays; wine bottles; champagne glasses; candles; potted plants; hatrack; Christmas decorations; wreaths; a small tree; wrapped presents; a pint of vanilla ice cream; a cash register; a telephone; perfume bottles; containers of cream; a music box; a rose; a book.

PROVIDED INSTRUMENTATION: Five reeds, two horns, three trumpets, two trombones, two percussion, accordion, three cellos, bass, piano-conductor (and celeste).

ADVERTISING AND MARKETING: "Accompany a woman to the box office when she buys her ticket, tell us *She Loves Me* and we'll give you yours free."

SUGGESTIONS: During "Tonight at Eight," after Georg has smudged his coat with cream and sings about his anxiety to Sipos (another clerk), don't just have Sipos stand there, but have him continually work to get out the stain so that Georg will look good for his "dear friend." "And make sure," says Patricia Hoag, who directed the show at Manhattan Marymount College, "that your piano starts playing the moment the music box melody opens, and stops the moment it's closed.

RESOURCES: The original cast album on CD, cassette, and LP; a British TV production; the play *Parfumerie*, on which the musical is fairly faithfully based.

RIGHTS: Tams-Witmark.

WORKING

CREATORS: Stephen (*Godspell*) Schwartz adapted the book by Studs Terkel, wrote some music and lyrics, and commissioned songs to others, such as Susan (*Jelly's Last Jam*) Birkenhead, Craig (*Is There Life After High School?*) Carnelia, Micki (*Don't Bother Me, I Can't Cope*) Grant, Mary (*Once upon a Mattress*) Rodgers, and James ("Fire and Rain") Taylor.

BACKGROUND: The 1978 production opened to moderate reviews, received five Tony nominations, won none, and played 25 performances.

STORY: The jobs that Americans do every day: white-collar occupations (vice president, executive, editor, advertising copy chief) but, more often, blue-collar workers (steelworker, parking lot attendant, gas meter reader, firefighter). There are surprising revelations from those in glamorous occupations (hockey player, flight attendant), people who use their brains (secretary, telephone and switchboard operators), and those who use their brawn (trucker, seaman). But perhaps most unexpected are the observations from those in "menial" jobs who simply decide not to see their work in an unfavorable light (the waitress, for example, is very happy).

ASSETS: A fine score and a moving book. A good show for a black-box theater— indeed, any small space. Everyone can identify with the show because, of course, everyone works, has worked, or will work. There's a good chance that some of your actors are or have been in the occupations cited (especially one very familiar to those who have an interest in show business: waitressing).

LIABILITIES: As Schwartz often says when he lectures on musical theater, "The problem with a revue is that after every song you have to get to know a whole new character and situation; as a result, you don't travel through a single journey with a character, seeing him solve a problem by the end of the show. After each blackout, you must make a completely new personal investment." Some audience members prefer not to. It's also a costume-heavy show.

WHO YOU'LL NEED: The original production used nine men and seven women playing an advertising copy chief, agency vice president, bar pianist, boxboy, bus driver, bus driver's wife, call girl (Patti LuPone), cleaning woman, copy boy, corporation executive, editor, fireman, football coach, gas meter reader, hockey player, hospital aide, hotel switchboard operator, housewife, interstate trucker (Joe Mantegna), migrant worker, millworker, parking lot attendant, receptionist, retired shipping clerk, salesman, salesman's wife, seaman, seaman's wife, secretary, steelworker, flight attendant, stonemason, supermarket checker, teacher, telephone operator, tie salesman, and waitress; one boy played a newsboy—but you can use more or fewer. *Maximum, 38; minimum, 17.*

DESIGNATED DANCES: A dance for three women; one for a husband and wife; one in which a hockey player mimes his craft; a few solo dances staged in the background while other songs are being sung.

SUGGESTED SETS: Small set pieces can represent a factory, an office, a supermarket, a parking garage, a classroom, a kitchen, house exteriors, cocktail lounge, a restaurant, a hospital, a construction site.

COSTUMES: Contemporary work clothes, plus uniforms for a bus driver; cleaning woman; firefighter; gas meter reader; hockey player; hospital aide; parking lot attendant; seaman; steelworker, flight attendant; stonemason; supermarket checker; waitress.

IMPORTANT PROPS: Supermarket carriages and bags; typewriters and office equipment; bricks; bicycle; onstage piano; mops, pails, and buckets; waitress trays and bus tables; firefighter's hose; hockey stick.

PROVIDED INSTRUMENTATION: Two keyboards, two guitars, bass, drums, percussion.

ADVERTISING AND MARKETING: The show provides an added incentive for local businesses to put ads in your program—especially if the goods and services they offer are already mentioned in the musical. Using the same typeface to refer to "The Butcher," "The Baker," "The Grocer," etc. will help the ads stand out and have greater impact than they would otherwise.

SUGGESTIONS: It might be a good idea to advertise in the local paper that you're holding auditions for the show, and you'd like to find a mason, mailman, meter reader, who can sing the song that represents his or her own life. (This would presumably mean that you'll drop the prostitute sequence.)

RESOURCES: The original cast album on cassette and LP; the 1983 TV production; Studs Terkel's book *Working*.

RIGHTS: Music Theatre International.

ALSO WORTH A LOOK

The Baker's Wife

With a book by Joseph *(Fiddler on the Roof)* Stein and music and lyrics by Stephen *(Godspell)* Schwartz, this musical has yet to play Broadway; David Merrick's 1976 tryout closed out of town. But it does have a cult following thanks to a semi-original cast recording issued long after it folded. But a more interesting story involves the London production: Trevor Nunn, the English director of *Cats* and *Les Miserables*, while auditioning actors as replacements in those megahits, often heard his applicants sing songs from *The Baker's Wife*— to the point where he had to investigate the show. He did, liked it (why not?— it *is* a glorious score), and mounted it in the West End. Would that we could report it was successful there, but it wasn't. Nevertheless, it's a tender story that could be described as *Camelot* among the working class, only with a happier ending. Aimable, a kindly middle-aged baker in a French town, has a young wife, Genevieve, who knows she should love him—but finds herself drawn to Dominique, the handsome, young, and cocksure village *Don Juan* and runs away with him. (Poor Aimable; his beloved cat runs away, too). Genevieve, though, eventually discovers that though Dominique has heat, where is the warmth? She eventually returns to Aimable, on the same day his cat reappears. It's very touching when Aimable informs the cat that he'll get one last chance as Genevieve looks on and knows he's telling her, too. A nice show for a small space. Rights: Music Theatre International.

Celebration

This is from Tom Jones and Harvey Schmidt, the authors of *The Fantasticks*, and though the 1969 Broadway production lasted only 109 performances—it's an allegory, seldom Broadway's favorite form of storytelling—the musical has its admirers. It's about an orphan who comes to the big city on New Year's Eve to see Mr. Rich, whose syndicate is about to destroy the garden he loves. When the orphan arrives at Rich's house, he sees and is smitten by Angel— really a girl dressed as such to entertain for Mr. Rich's party. Orphan meets Rich, a bored executive who challenges Orphan to move him with his pleas; Orphan tries, but when he enlists the help of Angel, Rich is moved only enough to romance the girl. Angel promises Orphan to convince Rich to give Orphan his garden. She can't. Still, Orphan's youth and idealism compensate for something: she does love him, and eventually sleeps with him, infuriating Rich, who takes away the garden. Orphan and Angel know the battle for the rest of the world will be hard to win: "The air is being poisoned," he notes; "half of the people are starving," says she. "We're destroying the other animals." Alas, *Celebration* is as timely as it was a quarter-century ago. And you may respond to the fascinating, percussionist score, the minimal set demands (one to represent the city in the first act, and another to suggest the country in the second) and the costume requirements (fanciful rags for most). "But play them as people, not as symbols," advises Steven Crowley, who directed the show's first post-Broadway production in Washington, D.C. It's also a good show to present during Christmas week, given that it takes place on New Year's Eve. Rights: Music Theatre International.

Drat! The Cat!

This does have one song your audience might recognize: "He Touched Me," thanks to a TV commercial as well as a Barbara Streisand recording made during the original production (her then-husband Elliot Gould was the star). The Milton Schaefer score is very good, but book and lyrics are even better, amazingly clever, and written by—surprise!—Ira Levin, better known for the novel *Rosemary's Baby*. True, the 1965 production lasted only 8 performances, but the musical is much better than that run suggests. It's a spoof of the type of theater found in the late nineteenth century; here, rich girl Alice is bored by her pampered life, and becomes a cat burglar who goes for the gold. The police are called in, and naive Bob Purefoy, assigned to the case, meets Alice while investigating the crime. It's love at first sight for him; she thinks he's a clod, but does find him useful, for he can tell her where the money is in town, what's being carefully guarded and what isn't. Eventually she frames him for the crimes, but they must escape together and live in the woods (not his idea of a good time; "Oh, shut up and eat your woodchuck," she tells him). Production values are admittedly elaborate, but if this is your sense of humor, the show is worth investigating. Rights: Samuel French.

Flora, The Red Menace

This was the 1965 flop that introduced Liza Minnelli to Broadway, and the Tony award to Minnelli. It's also the show that John Kander and Fred Ebb wrote immediately before *Cabaret*. But twenty-two years after its original production, the George Abbott-Robert Russell book was revised by David Thompson for an off-off-Broadway run. Should you order it, you'll get the new version, which has the WPA Theater producing a show called *Flora, the Red Menace* on a shoestring (which will be good for you, since you'll only need a few crates, wooden chairs, trunks of old clothes, and an upright piano for props). After that, the show often follows the original version. Flora, having just graduated from high school, wants a job as a fashion illustrator and, while filling out an application, meets Harry; soon they're sharing studio space; then he tells her he's a Communist and gets her to join the party. Problems arise when she gets a thirty-dollar-a-week job at a shop which, party zealot Charlotte informs her, is not union. Flora promises to work on that, unaware that Charlotte will soon be working on Harry. Eventually, Flora loses her job and the man as the curtain falls—leading many to think that the show hasn't been much improved. You, of course, may feel differently, especially if you have a talented crew of five men and four women who might be good for this material. Rights: Samuel French.

It's a Bird...It's a Plane...It's Superman!

This was written by David Newman and Robert Benton (who later collaborated on the successful *Superman* movie) with music by Charles Strouse and lyrics by Lee Adams (who collaborated on *Bye Bye Birdie*). The 1966 Broadway production opened to a rave review from the *New York Times*—usually enough to catapult a show to hit status—but the review was written by the too-good-for-the-average man critic Stanley Kauffman, who was fired around the time that the show shuttered after 129 performances. Perhaps one of the reasons the audiences didn't respond was that the authors made the mistake of adding two characters not in the comic strip—Max Mencken, a reporter jealous of Superman, and Sydney, his female assistant—while eliminating Jimmy Olsen, thus creating a too-unfamiliar *Daily Planet* staff. Still, kids love performing this show, and there's always one boy around who can be persuaded to put on the blue suit, cape, and great big red "S." Washington, D.C., audiences will get a kick out of the overture, which served as the theme music to a local newscast back in the 1970s. Rights: Tams-Witmark.

Also See: "A" . . . *My Name Is Alice; Assassins; Baker Street; Ballroom; Ben Franklin in Paris; Bring Back Birdie; Canterbury Tales; Chess; The Cradle Will Rock; Dear World; Do Black Patent Leather Shoes Really Reflect Up?; Do I Hear a Waltz?; Donnybrook; Doonesbury; The Education of Hyman Kaplan; The First; First Impressions; God Bless You, Mr. Rosewater; The Grass Harp; Grind; Happy New Year; Henry, Sweet Henry; Here's Love; How Now, Dow Jones; Is There Life After High School?; Merrily We Roll Along; Minnie's Boys; My Old Friends; The 1940's Radio Hour; Now Is the Time for All Good Men; Quilters; Rags; The Rink; Robert and Elizabeth; Runaways; 70, Girls, 70; Smile; Something's Afoot; Starmites; Starting Here, Starting Now; Tenderloin; Three Guys Naked from the Waist Down; What About Luv?; The Zulu and the Zayda.*

"STRIKE UP THE BAND!"

Musicals for Musicians Who Also Want to Act

"Let's face it," says Rob Bezubka, who's been the musical director for many shows in New England. "So many musicians are hams at heart, and love to get on stage. To be honest, I'm glad when I get the chance, too," says Bezubka, who also once played the lead in *Walking Happy*, "not just because it's fun, but also because it gives me an opportunity to see the challenges that actors face."

Whether you want your musicians to see how the other half lives, or whether you have double-threat performers, or just musicians who want to have a chance to trod the boards, here are some musicals that make the most of their musicians.

DIAMOND STUDS

CREATORS: Book by Jim (*Pump Boys and Dinettes*) Wann, music and lyrics by Bland Simpson and Wann.

BACKGROUND: The 1975 off-Broadway production charmed many critics and audiences by its transforming a theater into a Western saloon; a 232-performance run was the result.

STORY: The late 1800s in the Old West; the life of Jesse James. Because the Yankees killed their father in the Civil War, Jesse and brother Frank join the Confederates. When they find they've backed the losing side—and that Reconstruction won't allow Southerners to become doctors, lawyers, teachers, civil servants, politicians (or even voters)—they become bank robbers. They do so well, they must take on Jim, Cole, and Bob Ford as helpers. Jim and Cole get caught, serve seven years, are paroled, and join the James Gang once again. But Bob soon becomes disillusioned, and eventually betrays Jesse and kills him.

ASSETS: The book is so straightforward and simple that it has a certain charm that many audiences find fun and irresistible. The lively score mixes some Western standards with some good contemporary fare to provide toe-tapping bluegrass, ragtime, country ballads, and harmony singing.

LIABILITIES: Well, the show *is* about a bank robber, and just by its very nature (and by asking people to devote ninety minutes of their lives to seeing it) seems to glamorize a criminal. It's also not for the musical theater fan who enjoys seeing Dolly come down the staircase in a red dress.

WHO YOU'LL NEED: *Supporting Singing Roles:* The original production used twenty actors—twelve males and eight females—to play no fewer than sixty roles, ranging from Jesse James to dancehall girls to posse members to Pancho Villa. But the real challenge is to find actors who can play piano, bass, banjo, guitar, 12-string guitar, mandolin, and fiddle. *Maximum, 60; minimum, 20.*

DESIGNATED DANCES: There is a cakewalk act one finale, a hoedown act two finale, and a short tango in between, but this is a show where the musicians stand at mikes for most of the show.

SUGGESTED SETS: A Western saloon, with tables and overlong bar.

COSTUMES: Jeans, suspenders, and workshirts for all; a fancy gown for Belle Starr; otherwise, a change of hats creates the characters; thus, you'll need cowboy hats; Yankee and Confederate caps; derbies; straw boaters; sombreros; a green plastic accountant's visor; women's bonnets, Belle's feathered head-piece.

IMPORTANT PROPS: Microphones, mainly—but you'll also need a Confederate flag; 36-star American flag; a white surrender flag. For special musical needs, tambourines and maracas. While there are a number of guns written into the script, the original production had the guitarists use the necks of their guitars to simulate rifles.

PROVIDED INSTRUMENTATION: Violin, banjo, bass, percussion, piano-conductor.

ADVERTISING AND MARKETING: Says producer Robert Kalfin, "Our bar made us as much money as ticket sales"—so you might consider finding a spot with a liquor license so you, too, can reap the proceeds.

SUGGESTIONS: Try what worked so well for the original production—in which the cast members mingled with the audience before, during, and after the show.

RESOURCES: A seven-inch vinyl record was made, containing a few of the show's songs.

RIGHTS: Samuel French.

I LOVE MY WIFE

CREATORS: Book and lyrics by Michael Stewart, music by Cy Coleman (who later collaborated on *Barnum*).

BACKGROUND: After the production received bad notices in its 1977 Philadelphia tryout, little was expected; perhaps that's one of the reasons that *I Love My Wife* so charmed the critics, received six Tony nominations, won two awards, and ran for 872 performances.

STORY: Wally and Alvin, two married men of the late 1970s who live in Trenton, New Jersey, find themselves discussing wife-swapping. Alvin proposes the idea to his wife, Cleo, but Wally postpones telling his wife, Monica. When he does, she's outraged, then belligerently consents. But before very much happens, each guy comes to the conclusion that he can't go through with it, because he loves his wife.

ASSETS: Says Sean Wengroff, who directed the show at Brandeis University, "It has a truly hilarious book, a tuneful, catchy score, and a happy ending—making it a fun show to be in."

LIABILITIES: The show was written during the 1970s sexual revolution, when wife-swapping was a hot topic. Times have certainly changed, and the show has greatly dated. In a way, an audience out for a good escapist evening could leave the theater depressed for having been reminded of how unthreatening casual sex seemed once upon a time.

WHO YOU'LL NEED: *Lead Singing Roles:* Four attractive principals (two men, two women) in their late twenties (who should be good sports about stripping to their scanties for the show's long last scene). *Supporting Singing Roles:* Four other performers, one of whom is black (men were used in the original, but women could serve), who not only function as a Greek chorus (commenting as everything from tempting devils to moving men), but also are onstage musicians who play piano, guitar, bass, and drums. Should you care to get more people into the show, you could use one group as the devils, another as the movers, etc. *Maximum, 24; minimum, 8.*

DESIGNATED DANCES: A solo sexy dance for Monica, a ballroom dance, a vaudeville strut for Alvin and Wally; a jitterbug for the finale.

SUGGESTED SETS: A diner with counter and stools, Alvin and Cleo's apartment; Wally and Monica's apartment with a hide-a-bed couch. "But," suggests Wengroff, "paint a nighttime skyline of Trenton on the back wall and install small lights to represent offices in buildings—and stars, which you'll save for the final moments."

COSTUMES: Says Wengroff, "I wanted a parade on my stage of all that was *en vogue* from the famed decade: clogs, bellbottoms, ruffled tuxedo shirts, leisure suits, very thick ties, men's high-heeled dress shoes, man-tailored shirts with pointy collars, floor-length, backless halter dresses cut low in front, stiletto-heel shoes—anything in ultrasuede or one-hundred-percent polyester. And some provocative underwear for the big climactic scene. Every time your Greek chorus reenters, it's in a set of different costumes: red-devil costumes, country-western wear, togas, Santa Claus suits, moving-men coveralls, pajamas, and marching band uniforms." If need be, much of this could be accomplished merely with hats.

IMPORTANT PROPS: Onstage piano; moving men's padded cloths; two gift boxes with a knapsack and men's high-heeled shoes in each; a suitcase; a turkey; a banana-cream pie; tablecloth and tableware; a Christmas tree; a "Salvation Army" bell.

PROVIDED INSTRUMENTATION: For the onstage musicians, bass, guitar-banjo, clarinet, drums, piano-conductor; for offstage musicians, drums and piano. Says Wengroff, "My guitarist had a 'wah-wah' pedal to achieve a distinctively seventies sound in some of the numbers."

ADVERTISING AND MARKETING: "Do *you* love your wife? Why not show it by taking her to *I Love My Wife*, performed at . . ." Or: "Sex, drugs, and rock 'n' roll go Broadway—in a very adult musical of the swinging 1970s."

SUGGESTIONS: "Now it's a period piece," insists Wengroff. "The only way to do it is to do it as is. Keep the lines about 'Kojak' and living in a sexually permissive society."

RESOURCES: The original cast album on CD, cassette, and LP; the Luis Rego play, *Viens Chez Moi, J'Habite Chez une Copine*, on which the musical is somewhat based.

RIGHTS: Samuel French.

THE 1940's RADIO HOUR

CREATORS: Book by Walton Jones, who incorporated a number of 1940s hits into his libretto.

BACKGROUND: The 1979 production lasted 105 performances on Broadway and received no Tony nominations.

STORY: The pre-broadcast, broadcast, and post-broadcast of a Christmas radio show (Dec. 21, 1942) from WOV in New York City. But this is hardly a top-shelf operation; the station's comic is really a cab driver, the big band female vocalist is a secretary by day. Nevertheless, the second-rate radio show still has its charms, as do most of the colorful characters—especially Johnny Cantone, who promises would-be crooner Neal that Neal can have his featured spot once Johnny goes to Hollywood—as long as Neal lends him two dollars to play on a horse.

ASSETS: A wonderful nostalgia trip for those who remember the innocent charms of radio, its songs, comedy sketches, and giveaways; a chance to hear not only the great hits of yesteryear (one in pig Latin), but also the spoken and musical commercials for products long-gone (e.g., Nash automobiles) and those still with us (e.g. Pepsi, Chiquita Banana).

LIABILITIES: Besides being heavy on props and effects, the first half-hour of the show—the pre-broadcast in which we meet everyone—isn't as much fun as the rest of the show.

RECOGNIZABLE SONGS: "Have Yourself a Merry Little Christmas," "Love Is Here to Stay," "Chattanooga Choo-Choo," "Blues in the Night," and sixteen others of the same caliber. "But," says Kevin Chamberlin, who played a lead in the production at St. Louis's The Rep, "there are many updated editions of the show in which you can easily substitute other songs."

WHO YOU'LL NEED: *Lead Singing Roles*: A classy black female singer who can do scat and sass; a teenage bobby-soxer just starting out as a singer; a young crooner in the 1940-ish Sinatra mode. *Supporting Singing Roles*: A not-so-talented waitress who's convinced the station manager to let her sing; a squeaky-clean Yalie who wants to sing for a living; a delivery boy waiting for his big break as a singer. *Other Roles*: A bigshot stage manager; a comic; a control booth assistant; a sound effects man; a stage doorman called Pops; an orchestra leader who's also the station's general manager; a baby-faced trumpeter who's part of an orchestra that consists of anywhere from five to seventeen pieces. *Maximum, 26; minimum, 14.*

DESIGNATED DANCES: Virtually none—just some ad-lib steps whenever the mood hits the singers or those performers not involved in the number.

SUGGESTED SETS: The seedy studios of WOV, a five thousand–watt local New York City radio station: a bandstand; some chairs; a greenroom with mailboxes and call board.

COSTUMES: 1940s fashions; double-breasted suits; full skirts; sleeveless sweaters.

IMPORTANT PROPS: A grand piano; period microphones; time clock; a coffee urn; food that's delivered; mop and bucket; a board on which dancers can tap (to make the taps tappier for the radio audience); Christmas lights and a string of Christmas cards; a Coke machine; a pay phone; signs that say "Shubert Alley Exit," "On the Air," and "Applause." Most of all, you'll need a mini-door unit to create convincing slams; a working telephone; a xylophone; a plunger.

SPECIAL EFFECTS: Here's the rub: You'll have to create a number of endearing radio sound effects, including the pouring of Pepsi; sleigh bells; dog barks; carriage on cobblestones; horse hooves; window breaking; and two shoes, wood blocks, and sandpaper to create a tap routine which the sound man creates (and could very well steal the show).

PROVIDED INSTRUMENTATION: Five reeds, four trumpets, three trombones, guitar, bass, drums, percussion, piano-conductor. However, there are alternate orchestrations for thirteen, nine, seven, rhythm and horn, or even just piano—"which," says Jones, "was the way we portrayed the Zoot Doubelman Orchestra' in our first production."

ADVERTISING AND MARKETING: Given that the show relies on many aural effects, it's a show that's particularly apt for the blind; schedule a performance at a home for the visually impaired. It's also a natural for radio spots.

SUGGESTIONS: You may very well have people or groups in your community who have already adeptly performed 1940s hits; incorporate these talents into your show, and you're that much ahead of the game.

RESOURCES: No cast album, but all the songs are available on a myriad of recordings.

RIGHTS: Samuel French.

NO STRINGS

CREATORS: Book by Samuel Taylor (*who wrote the play Sabrina Fair*), music and lyrics by Richard (*Oklahoma!*) Rodgers.

BACKGROUND: After the death of Oscar Hammerstein II, Rodgers, for the first time in his Broadway career, decided to try his hand at lyrics—and did a most impressive job, writing in a style that harkened back to his days with sophisticated collaborator Lorenz Hart; the show's plot was more Hartian than Hammersteinian. It received nine Tony nominations, won three awards (Rodgers also got an honorary one "for taking the men out of the pit and putting them on stage"), and had a 580-performance run.

STORY: 1962—or now. Barbara Woodruff, a successful black American fashion model in Paris, meets David Jordan, a Pulitzer Prize–winning author who enjoys Europe so much that he no longer writes. He's made friends with such bums as Mike, who plays gigolo to a rich American woman named Comfort. Barbara has been platonically seeing the successful but aging Louis, who would like more from her; Barbara is in fact trying to oblige, but can't find it in her heart, especially when she realizes she can't get David out of her mind. She reads his book and starts pressuring him about not writing; he, in turn, pressures her about settling for someone she doesn't love. They quarrel, but reconcile; he tells her that he has access to a house at Honfleur and that she should go with him. She argues that he should instead use the time to write, but goes with him, hoping that he'll write once he gets there. And though David is soon saying they should go to Deauville "where everyone is," she persuades him to write about Maine, his home. When she finds he's writing about the people he's met in Europe, she's angry; they argue and break up. David goes to Deauville, where he finds Mike cheating on Comfort—and when she discovers it, she dismisses Mike and asks David to be her new gigolo. That makes David realize how empty his life is, and he returns to Barbara, asking for a second chance, saying he'll take a job he's been offered to write additional dialogue for an Italian film. But she convinces him he must return home if he's ever going to write another book of substance. David agrees and asks her to come with him. But Paris is her world, and they part, still in love, but with "no strings" attached.

ASSETS: A fine score; a chance for a director to use unconventional staging techniques (e.g., models positioned in a circle represent a fountain); nice, too, that Barbara's race, aside from her mentioning in song that she comes from "up north of Central Park," is a nonissue.

LIABILITIES: You've got to re-create the world of Paris fashion on the stage. Also, it's an underwritten book: Why does Barbara stay with Louis; does she need a father figure? Barbara's telling David what to write shows she doesn't understand the process. And if European jet-setters aren't worth writing about, why has bookwriter Taylor written a musical about them? Last and least, there's more than a modicum of French dialogue that may frustrate some of your audience.

RECOGNIZABLE SONGS: "The Sweetest Sounds."

WHO YOU'LL NEED: *Lead Singing Roles:* A stunning black model; her rugged alcoholic author lover. *Supporting Singing Roles:* Her fiftyish magnate would-be lover; a virile photographer and his bubbly female assistant; a *Vogue* editor; a Parisian singer; a good-humored bum; the rich young American woman who supports him. *Other Roles:* Beach boys; women to play fashion mannequins; onstage musicians who weave in and out of the action. *Maximum, 41; minimum, 19.*

DESIGNATED DANCES: Not much, one big production number, but then only three quick dances—a soft-shoe, a waltz, and a polite fan dance.

SUGGESTED SETS: The original production didn't use realistic sets, but scaffolds, lights, and blocks to represent a Paris photographer's studio; a park; an apartment; a Monte Carlo race track; a Deauville casino; the beach at Honfleur; a district of St. Tropez.

COSTUMES: A veritable fashion show of Parisian *haute couture*; gowns of chiffon, velvet, silks, and satins; party dresses; wraps; fur pieces; turbans; large pocketbooks; suits; blazers; slacks; beachwear; racing-car outfits.

IMPORTANT PROPS: Photographers' mannequins; scoop lights; reflectors; umbrellas; equipment cases; a roulette wheel; a clanging bell; a typewriter; a portable bar; champagne and cognac bottles; needlepoint; a bunch of violets; money.

PROVIDED INSTRUMENTATION: Four reeds, trumpet, trombone, percussion, kettledrum, bass, piano, piano-conductor—but literally no strings. "And what a help this is," says Bert Silverberg, Associate Professor of Theater at Community College of Rhode Island, "for I've found that stringed instruments are notoriously difficult for most nonprofessional musicians."

ADVERTISING AND MARKETING: *"No Strings* is NOT the story of Pinocchio. Come see why at . . ."

SUGGESTIONS: Using leotards in lieu of many of the high-fashion costumes could work.

RESOURCES: The original cast album on CD, cassette, and LP.

RIGHTS: Rodgers and Hammerstein.

OIL CITY SYMPHONY

CREATORS: Book and much of the music and lyrics by Mike Craver, Debra Monk (who collaborated on *Pump Boys and Dinettes*) Mark Hardwick, and Mary Murfitt.

BACKGROUND: The 1987 production opened to strong reviews, won the Outer Critics Circle Award as Best Off-Broadway Musical and the 1988 Drama Desk Award for Best Ensemble Acting, and ran 626 performances.

STORY: Tonight in a small midwestern town. A celebration of small-town life—community activities, schools, churches, families, friendships, and music lessons—as detailed by four not-very-good musicians who used to play together and are now getting back together to give a recital.

ASSETS: A lively score, and a good time to be had in seeing four people display much more of their personalities than even they are realizing. Set, costume, and production demands are minimal.

LIABILITIES: As David Barbour wrote in *TheaterWeek*, "This is the type of show many of us out-of-towners moved to New York to avoid." This is a very hokey show.

RECOGNIZABLE SONGS: "Baby, It's Cold Outside," "The Hokey Pokey," "(Don't Say No, It's) The End of the World," "Theme from *Exodus*," "Sleigh Ride."

WHO YOU'LL NEED: *Lead Singing Roles:* A geek of a guy who thinks he's up-to-date with the sounds and mores of today; a housewife who doubles as a drummer and seems to express her sexuality on the pedal; a demure young composer who seems to be untalented until we discover he does have at least one good tune in him; a virginal and unattractive female violinist. *Maximum-minimum, 4.*

DESIGNATED DANCES: None.

SUGGESTED SETS: A school's "gymnatorium" stage.

COSTUMES: Contemporary would-be fancy clothes that were just purchased from K mart.

IMPORTANT PROPS: A bouquet of flowers presented to the quartet's high school music teacher, Miss Reeves (who is chosen each night out of the audience).

PROVIDED INSTRUMENTATION: Piano/accordion, synthesizer, drums/percussion, violin/tenor, saxophone/flute.

ADVERTISING AND MARKETING: The original production found that when it advertised itself as *Oil City* and dropped the *Symphony*, more people attended; perhaps the classical music reference made audiences a bit gun-shy. Consider, then, what your community would be more likely to endorse.

SUGGESTIONS: You needn't call the "teacher" called from the audience "Miss Reeves" but can choose a real teacher you know will be attending that performance.

RESOURCES: The original cast album on CD and cassette.

RIGHTS: Music Theatre International.

PUMP BOYS AND DINETTES

CREATORS: Book, music, and lyrics by Mark Hardwick and Debra Monk (who collaborated on *Oil City Symphony*), Jim (*Diamond Studs*) Wann, John Foley, Cass Morgan, and John Schimmel.

BACKGROUND: The 1981 off-off-Broadway production was so successful that the show moved to off-Broadway for 112 performances, then onto Broadway for 573 performances.

STORY: The present—"somewhere between Frog Level and Smyrna." The thoughts of gas station attendants and waitresses on Highway 57. The guys and girls compare jobs; the women are interested in the guys, who are more interested in fishing—though they do show interest in Dolly Parton and the hot clerk at Woolworth's.

ASSETS: "It's great for small theaters in rural areas," says Melanie Larch of the Charleston (West Virginia) Light Opera Guild, "because it celebrates an evening of fun with the good ol' boys and girls. Its infectious blend of country rock gets an audience's toes tappin' and faces smiling."

LIABILITIES: It's really a glorified stand-at-mikes concert of country-and-western songs, not a musical. There's not much to it, for all the action is discussed, not dramatized.

RECOGNIZABLE SONGS: "I Need a Vacation Like Nobody's Business."

WHO YOU'LL NEED: *Lead Singing Roles:* Four guys who can effectively portray gas station workers and can play lead guitar, piano-accordion, bass, and rhythm guitar; two women who can play percussion. *Maximum-minimum,* 6.

DESIGNATED DANCES: A few modest steps at best.

SUGGESTED SETS: Billboards advertising "Jim's Gas Station" and the "Double Cupp Diner"; phone booth; diner counter with four stools.

COSTUMES: Fishing hats; baseball caps; tap shoes; fancy aprons; sunglasses for all.

IMPORTANT PROPS: Microphones for all; an upright piano and bass; an "Open/Closed" sign; pots and pans, rolling pins; a colander; coffee cups; pies; a silk rose; a coffee-can shaker; a cowbell; an air freshener tree-card for each of your performances (this very modest prize is given away at a raffle at each intermission).

PROVIDED INSTRUMENTATION: Two acoustic guitars, electric bass, piano, sticks, and tambourines.

ADVERTISING AND MARKETING: Make a deal with local gas stations and diners to display your posters. And sell all those pies.

SUGGESTIONS: "The men and women should show their affection for each other through music," says author Morgan. "And," she adds, "if the boys aren't a band when they start rehearsals, they must be by opening night."

RESOURCES: The original cast album on CD, cassette, and LP.

RIGHTS: Samuel French.

RETURN TO THE FORBIDDEN PLANET

CREATORS: Written by Bob Carlton.

BACKGROUND: In England in 1989, this small show with its skewered Shakesperean dialogue ("Woman has a mean and hungry look") and its tongue-in-cheek rock-'n'-roll songs and commentary, surprised many by beating *Miss Saigon* as Best Musical; it's still running in London as of this writing. An American version, produced off-Broadway, fared less well, and ran 207 performances.

STORY: Shakespeare's *The Tempest*, which was adapted into a 1956 sci-fi flick, *Forbidden Planet*; we're not in Ilyria, but *Deliria*, where Miranda falls in love with one crew member, then the captain. When the ship is attacked, the audience is asked to "reverse polarity" by putting their hands on their heads. The monsters turn out just to be "monsters from the id" ("Beware the ids that march"), and Miranda gets the captain.

ASSETS: Kids will have a great time performing this multiracial, imaginative show (when a guitarist plays, another character holds the hand-mike he'd been holding to his mouth). Carlton chose some of the best rock 'n' roll songs of his era.

LIABILITIES: It's much louder than the older theatergoers' favorite shows. And while the puns are well-thought-out (a funding cut in a day care program is considered "the most unkindest cut of all"), sometimes an audience has a knee-jerk reaction to groan. And you're going to have to come up with a robot costume that could run into money.

RECOGNIZABLE SONGS: "Great Balls of Fire," "Young Girl," "A Teenager in Love," "The Shoop-Shoop Song (It's in Her Kiss)," "Good Vibrations," "Only the Lonely," "All Shook Up," "Born to Be Wild," "Monster Mash," "Tell Her," "Who's Sorry Now?" "Shake, Rattle, and Roll."

WHO YOU'LL NEED: *Lead Singing Roles:* A handsome and dashing captain, his demure daughter; the crewman who's madly in love with her; the straight-arrow object of her affection. *Supporting Singing Roles:* A robot on rollerblades;

a woman scientist who's sexless when her glasses are on and can rock 'n' roll when she takes them off; three girls as a trio of backup singers (they must often play music under dialogue, too). "I could play three instruments when I joined the show," says David LaDuca, who played Ariel the robot during the off-Broadway run, "but found I had to learn seven. And it isn't easy playing the drums while in three-fingered gloves." *Maximum, 16; minimum, 12.*

DESIGNATED DANCES: Not much—just a little jitterbugging here and there, though you could augment some songs with such classic 1950s dances as the stroll. "But dancing on rollerblades is not easy," moans LaDuca.

SUGGESTED SETS: A spaceship with girder-like buttresses; wheels and wires to suggest complex equipment; wire-encased light bulbs; a glass booth to function as an air-lock elevator; a trap door that reveals a gangplank from which aliens can make their entrances. Behind it all, a star-filled cyclorama on which you'll put some cut-out stalagmites when a planet comes near. Tentacles that fall from above the proscenium arch will attack the cast (ideally, lifting the actors into the air).

COSTUMES: For the crew, identical uniforms in a *Star Trek* style; one white lab coat for a scientist; space boots; safety belts; simple 1950s bobby-soxer plaid skirt; Marilyn Monroe *Seven-Year Itch* outfit and wig. Your biggest challenge will be Ariel's robot suit, which is futuristic Tin Man; he also travels on rollerblades.

IMPORTANT PROPS: Hand microphones; telephones; beachball made to look like planet Earth; blackboard and chalk; smoke pots; test tubes; hair dryers to function as "ray guns." The original production also used a TV camera to show what the bassist was accomplishing during his dynamic solo.

SPECIAL EFFECTS: Here's a show where a lighting designer can really have some fun; the original production had red, white, and blue horizontal and vertical lights everywhere; many red lights to indicate red alert. Sound effects (especially explosions and echoes) abound. If you have the means and equipment to go audio-visual, there are many opportunities to show who and what are outside the spaceship.

PROVIDED INSTRUMENTATION: Two drumsets, keyboards, guitars, basses, trumpets, tambourines and saxes.

ADVERTISING AND MARKETING: "Once you see *Return to the Forbidden Planet*, you'll want to return to *Return to the Forbidden Planet*. To start yourself off, we're starting performances on . . ."

SUGGESTIONS: There was some audience participation in the original production, and it seemed to captivate the theatergoers in attendance. First, the flight attendants would point out where the emergency exits were, as if they were on a flight, then they primed the group on gestures and sounds that they might need later (they would) that "may save your life and the lives of ones you love." There is also a "polarity reversal drill" in which people were asked to put their hands on their heads and go "Ewwwww!"—which turned out to be important to the plot. Use them all!

RESOURCES: The original London cast album on CD, cassette, and LP; Shakespeare's *The Tempest* and the 1956 film *Forbidden Planet*, from which the musical only takes its inspiration.

RIGHTS: Not available at press time.

SMOKE ON THE MOUNTAIN

CREATORS: Book by Connie Ray (TV's Millicent Torhelson) and conceived by Alan Bailey.

BACKGROUND: Southerners Ray and Bailey met and found that they shared an affinity for blue-grass gospel music—so they got a commission from the McCarter Theater in Princeton, New Jersey to create a book around twenty-four gospel standards. The show later opened off-Broadway in 1990 and ran 490 performances.

STORY: A 1938 Saturday-night sing in a church in mythical Mount Pleasant, North Carolina. A family of gospel singers/musicians decides to return to performing after a hiatus of five years. We the congregation are waiting—but are then told that they've had an accident en route. Still, they're indomitable, and they show up to sing—and we enjoy their optimism.

ASSETS: A small-cast musical of heartwarming family fare.

LIABILITIES: Five of the seven actors must be good musicians and play a variety of instruments, including piano, guitar, mandolin, banjo and fiddle.

WHO YOU'LL NEED: *Lead Singing Roles:* A sincere father; a fervent mother; a pair of brother-and-sister twins. *Supporting Singing Roles:* A moon-faced reverend, a troublemaker. *Other Role:* One sister who does not sing (says Ray, "I wanted to appear in the show, too—but I can't sing a note. So I wrote in a part for a kid who couldn't.") *Maximum-minimum,* 7.

DESIGNATED DANCES: No dancing at all—because we're in a church.

SUGGESTED SETS: The interior of a wooden church.

COSTUMES: Simple "plain-but-clean" clothes representing lower middle-class 1930s garb, with a pair of support hose for the mother.

IMPORTANT PROPS: The instruments are all you'll need.

PROVIDED INSTRUMENTATION: Piano, guitar, mandolin, banjo, fiddle.

ADVERTISING AND MARKETING: The original production had a bake sale bazaar during intermission: brownies, pecan pie, and chess pie. You should, too.

SUGGESTIONS: "These are real people and not hillbilly caricatures," says Bailey. "The key to a successful production is playing these roles with heart and depth; the comedy will follow. If you're in the Bible Belt, emphasize the gospel-sing aspect of the show; if not, emphasize the bluegrass music and the heartwarming side."

RESOURCES: Though there is no original cast album, the songs are available on a number of records.

RIGHTS: Samuel French.

Also See: *I'm Getting My Act Together and Taking It on the Road; The Music Man.*

Musicals for Sophisticated Communities

You've seen your audiences; you've talked to them; you know who they are. If you think they're particularly enlightened, you should meet their expectations with one of the following.

ASSASSINS

CREATORS: Book by John Weidman, music and lyrics by Stephen Sondheim (who collaborated on *Pacific Overtures*).

BACKGROUND: The 1991 production debuted at Playwrights Horizons, a small, innovative, nonprofit New York theater—and though as of this writing, no Broadway or off-Broadway producer has decided to risk producing this "uncommercial" show, it has played London and many regional theaters.

STORY: An examination of those who feel the need to assassinate—from John Wilkes Booth to John Hinkley—and how they felt it gave their otherwise unsuccessful lives some meaning and made them household names.

ASSETS: Sondheim's score shows that he is still at the peak of his powers. A musical for theatergoers who complain that musicals are concerned only with love stories. A not very expensive show to do.

LIABILITIES: This is a very hard-hitting musical that will make many, many audiences squirm. Should assassins receive any more attention than they've already received? Can we really comfortably laugh at the inanities and insanities placed before us? The sequence involving Lee Harvey Oswald's deliberating on whether to kill John F. Kennedy may be the most difficult scene to sit through in any musical.

WHO YOU'LL NEED: *Supporting Singing Roles:* A shooting gallery proprietor; a balladeer; John Wilkes Booth; Charles Guiteau (a true loony who assassinated Garfield); Leon Czolgosz (a Polish immigrant who assassinated McKinley); Giuseppe Zangara (an Italian immigrant who tried to assassinate FDR); Samuel Byck (a talkative type who tried to assassinate Nixon); Squeaky Fromme (a Manson family member who tried to assassinate Ford); Sara Jane Moore (a plump housewife who tried to assassinate Ford); John Hinkley (the Jodie Foster admirer who tried to assassinate Reagan). *Other Roles:* Lee Harvey Oswald; David Herrold (Booth's frightened co-conspirator); Emma Goldman; James Garfield; James Blaine; Gerald Ford; a hangman; a warden; a bartender; bystanders. *Maximum, 31; minimum, 16.*

DESIGNATED DANCES: Just a cakewalk for Guiteau as he climbs up the stairs to the gallows.

SUGGESTED SETS: A shooting gallery; a barn; an electric chair chamber; the Pan-American Exhibition in Buffalo; at a gallows; the sixth floor of the Texas Book Depository in Dallas.

COSTUMES: Various clothes from 1865 to 1981; from waistcoats to hippie dress to K mart specials; T-shirts and jeans; a Santa Claus suit.

IMPORTANT PROPS: Pictures of every president mounted on a shooting gallery arcade; an electric chair; a flight of stairs leading to a gallows; nooses; crutches; an old-fashioned microphone; a guitar; buckets of Kentucky Fried Chicken; a pocketbook and its traditional contents; bales and boxes; a lunch pail; a radio; a long thin box that contains a rifle; guns, rifles, and more guns—which will be used to create so many gunshots that you'd better print many signs warning fainthearted patrons of the same.

SPECIAL EFFECTS: Many gunshots; the famous picture of Jack Ruby shooting Lee Harvey Oswald, enlarged to fill back wall.

PROVIDED INSTRUMENTATION: Three reeds, two trumpets, horn, trombone, violin, viola, cello, bass, guitar, two keyboards, two percussion.

ADVERTISING AND MARKETING: "The toughest musical you'll ever love."

SUGGESTIONS: Play the show without apology.

RESOURCES: The original cast album on CD and cassette; study guide and videocassette—interviews with the creators.

RIGHTS: Music Theatre International.

THE BEST LITTLE WHOREHOUSE IN TEXAS

CREATORS: Book by Larry L. King and Peter Masterston, music and lyrics by Carol Hall.

BACKGROUND: The 1978 workshop at New York's famed Actors' Studio went well enough for Tommy Tune to sign on as co-director and choreographer. Not long thereafter, the production moved to Broadway, received seven Tony nominations, won two awards for its leads, and enjoyed a 1,639-performance run.

STORY: Late 1970s in rural Texas. Miss Mona runs the Chicken Ranch, a quiet brothel in rural Texas. Sheriff Ed Earl Dodd, who loves her in his own fashion, looks the other way and allows her to stay in business. But Melvin P. Thorpe, an ambitious newscaster, begins a media campaign against the Ranch, and Dodd must reluctantly close it.

ASSETS: A riotously funny book, one of the best country-western scores for the theater, and some very endearing characters. A lesser show wouldn't have been smart enough to include the vital scene (dropped for the movie, which made it less effective) in which Miss Mona overhears her newest girl call home and talk to her young son, hiding the realities from him, but promising him many Christmas presents. After the call, Mona tells the girl she'll make sure that she is home for Christmas—and that makes Mona three-dimensional.

LIABILITIES: For many communities, the title alone will be a problem. But there is also a plethora of (admittedly funny) salty language. If you think your community will mind such lines as "I'd close you down faster than goose shit would run through a tin horn" and "I can damn sure tell when somebody's pissin' on my boots and telling me it's a rainstorm," choose another show. The show also has a what's-the-problem attitude toward illicit sex that dates it in the age of AIDS.

WHO YOU'LL NEED: *Lead Singing Roles*: A charming madam and a cantankerous sheriff, each with heart and soul. *Supporting Singing Roles*: Eight experienced prostitutes; an obvious-looking new prostitute and her totally inexperienced gawky girlfriend; a mature black maid who sings gospel; the governor of Texas; a bandleader-narrator; a bunch of strong college football players.

Other Roles: A small choir; a rural newspaper editor; the town's mayor; its main insurance man. *Maximum, 49; minimum, 30.*

DESIGNATED DANCES: Much musical staging for the girls, and much stylized movement representing sexual activity; a gospel number with tambourines for Thorpe and his followers; a production number for the brothel's maid and the girls; a strut for the football players; a sidestep soft-shoe; a drill-team tap routine for the girl chorus; and a hoedown curtain call.

SUGGESTED SETS: The original production used a two-level red-velvet brothel; the first level is its parlor, the second represented the rooms. Oversized Venetian blinds dropped whenever a sex act was taking place. Scenes in a cafe, the TV studio, a football locker room, and the sheriff's office were simply designated areas of the brothel set.

COSTUMES: 1970s street clothes with a decidedly Texan flavor, Stestons; dark suits; string ties; oversized belt buckles; ladies' Western shirts and pants; cowboy boots for men and women; lounging costumes; Fredericks of Hollywood scanties; elegant-looking ball gowns (at least one that's held together by Velcro); drill team outfits; sheriff's outfit and badge; farmers' overalls; straw hat; football uniforms (ideally red and white); choir robes; many beautifully coiffed wigs and one preposterous silver wig for Thorpe.

IMPORTANT PROPS: Ceiling fans; those oversized Venetian blinds; a jukebox; a big burlap bag in which there is a rubber chicken; an old-fashioned wheelchair; six-shooters and shotguns; a truck rearview mirror; TV sound and camera equipment, "On the Air" sign and assorted cue cards; a scarred desk with telephone; cafeteria trays, pie case, sugar containers, etc.; many flashlights; tambourines; a live microphone; corsages; Texas flags and football pennants; and life-sized dolls "worn" by drill-team members to suggest other members of the drill team.

SPECIAL EFFECTS: Black-eye makeup; a sleight-of-hand cigarette trick for one male chorus member.

PROVIDED INSTRUMENTATION: Violin, two guitars, bass, drums, piano-conductor.

ADVERTISING AND MARKETING: "The show says 'Texas has a whorehouse in it.' Well, so does [your town], starting on . . ."

SUGGESTIONS: Those life-sized dolls, with which each drill team member was buttressed on each side to give the illusion of *three* drill team members, was a wonderful *coup de theatre,* and you may actually be better off using them than real dancers.

If you can only do a one-level set, you can of course use each side of the stage to represent the girls' bedrooms.

RESOURCES: The original cast album on cassette and LP; the (somewhat faithful) 1982 movie version on videotape and laserdisc; the Larry L. King article in *Playboy* magazine (June 1976) that inspired the musical and his *Whorehouse Papers* memoirs.

RIGHTS: Samuel French.

CABARET

CREATORS: Book by Joe *(She Loves Me)* Masteroff, music by John Kander, lyrics by Fred Ebb (who later collaborated on *Zorba*).

BACKGROUND: The 1966 production of *Cabaret* was the missing link between the old-fashioned musical comedy and the newer style "concept musical." Critics responded positively to the new direction in which the show pointed, as did the Tony committee (ten nominations; eight awards—including Best Musical), and the result was a 1,165-performance run.

STORY: Cliff Bradshaw comes to 1930s Berlin to write a novel, meets the exotic Sally Bowles in the Kit Kat Klub, and is maneuvered into living with her in a rooming house run by Fraulein Schneider. While he has misgivings about her he goes along, especially when she announces she's pregnant. Schneider, meanwhile, is being courted by Jewish fruit dealer Herr Schultz, and agrees to marry him—until she realizes what's happening politically to the Jews. Cliff is distraught by the Nazi threat, and devastated when he discovers that Sally has aborted their child. He leaves Berlin for America, but with grist for his novel. Through all of this, an Emcee comments on what's happening.

ASSETS: Terrific score, and a nice opportunity to give both the younger and older members of your company some equally fat parts to play.

LIABILITIES: There are many who feel that Bob Fosse's movie, which eliminated all the "book" numbers and only included the cabaret songs (and the German anthem) is a great improvement over the stage version. "And many people are disappointed," says Linda Goss of the Victory Players of Holyoke, Massachusetts, "when they see you haven't done the movie on stage."

RECOGNIZABLE SONGS: "Wilkommen," "Cabaret."

WHO YOU'LL NEED: *Lead Singing Roles:* A dynamic cabaret emcee (which could be played by a woman; it was conceived that way, and has occasionally been played as such); a not-going-anywhere female cabaret singer; an erudite and sincere writer. *Supporting Singing Roles:* A very proper landlady; her fruit-selling suitor. *Other Roles:* A beefy boyfriend, an enterprising prostitute tenant; a covert operator; her back-up singers; the cabaret staff; German sailors; some fraus who may or may not be able to double as the hefty, unglamorous onstage band. *Maximum, 44; minimum, 26.*

DESIGNATED DANCES: Heavy, a dazzling opening; a production number involving telephones; a small dance between older lovers and then with others at a party; a short romantic dance between two men. The emcee dances with two ladies, and later with a kick-line (in which he's a female impersonator).

SUGGESTED SETS: A cabaret with stage; a train compartment; a couple of rooming house flats; a fruit shop.

COSTUMES: 1930s wear, railroad officers' outfits; both a schlocky and a fine tuxedo; Father Time and Baby New Year outfits; chorine costumes—including one representing Russia (ruble-studded), Japan (skimpy Asian suit with gong between legs), France (an Eiffel Tower headdress), and America (eagle headdress, small Revolutionary War drums on breasts); flowered dressing gown, a fur coat; Nazi uniforms with swastika armbands; waiters' outfits; a dress that could be worn to the opera; face bandages; a gorilla suit and a tutu large enough to fit around it.

IMPORTANT PROPS: Many 1930s-style telephones; a shabby bed; armoire; table and chairs; seat cushion; blanket; a suitcase, briefcase, and mountain of luggage; party decorations; a brick that breaks a window; a scythe; a cigarette holder; an old gramophone; a copy of *Mein Kampf*; a wrapped gift with crystal bowl inside; a bottle of shnapps; a nice big pineapple.

SPECIAL EFFECTS: An electronic sign that, bulb-by-bulb, spells out "Cabaret"; a tilting mirror that reflects the action in front of it.

PROVIDED INSTRUMENTATION: Four reeds, two trumpets, two trombones, horn, two violins, viola, cello, bass, percussion, accordion and celeste, guitar and banjo; piano-conductor. Also available is a reduced orchestration that eliminates the horn, violins, viola, and cello. There is also an orchestration for the stage band: tenor saxophone, trombone, piano, and drums.

ADVERTISING AND MARKETING: Take out an ad that quotes the now-famous lines from the title song: "What good is sitting alone in your room? Come to the *Cabaret!*"

SUGGESTIONS: Depending on how much your community can take, you can choose between the tamer 1966 version and the 1987 revival that openly proclaimed Cliff as a bisexual. And as Gillian Lynne's 1986 British revival proved, this is a musical that works very well—if not better—when done in a Brechtian, austere–agit prop style.

For the gorilla number, you also have the option of using one of two endings—saying that gorilla "isn't a *meeskite* [ugly one] at all," or the more severe, deleted-in-Boston (but used in the movie), "She wouldn't look Jewish at all." Your choice.

RESOURCES: The original cast album on CD, cassette, and LP; the film version on videotape and laserdisc; John Van Druten's *I Am a Camera*, the play on which the musical is based, in script and movie version on videotape;

the book *The Berlin Stories*, on which the play was based, by Christopher Isherwood.

RIGHTS: Tams-Witmark.

THE CRADLE WILL ROCK

CREATORS: Book, music, and lyrics by Mark *(Regina)* Blitzstein.

BACKGROUND: One of the most stirring stories in the history of theater. The 1937 production was funded by the WPA, but when word reached the government that the show was pro-union, the government "postponed" the premiere on the very night it was to open at a 39th Street theater. But famed director Orson Welles would not relent, and, as first-nighters waited on the sidewalk, he sent his associates scurrying to find a new theater. They did—twenty blocks away—and everyone marched there, except the musicians, whose union would not allow them to perform. In fact, Actors' Equity wouldn't consent for its members to set foot on stage, so the actors sat in the audience, and when it came time for each to perform, he or she stood, was spotlit, and spoke and sang to Blitzstein's piano accompaniment. The show opened seven months later for a commercial run, ran 107 performances, and has been revived many times.

STORY: An allegory that takes place "anytime" in Steeltown, USA. Steeltown is controlled by the mighty Mr. Mister, who owns the town newspaper, and has the doctors, professors, and, through his wife's influence, the artists and the clergy in his hip pockets. When Larry Foreman passes out leaflets to start a union in town, Mr. Mister makes certain he's involved in a factory accident, and then has the doctor who examines him say that he was drunk and brought it on himself. Afterward, Mr. Mister tries to buy Larry, but can't, and despite the obstacles, Larry vows to keep fighting to get workers their just due.

ASSETS: A musical with a haunting score that's very easy to produce.

LIABILITIES: The intended didacticism is sometimes too off-putting for audiences.

WHO YOU'LL NEED: *Lead Singing Roles:* A sincere and impassioned foreman and his girlfriend; the town tyrant; his dilettante wife. *Supporting Singing Roles:* Their preppie son and flibbertigibbet daughter; a prostitute; the man who propositions her; the detective and cop who harass them; a minister; an editor; a doctor; an artist; a violinist; a college president; two professors; a football coach; an embittered druggist and his agreeable son; a pair of Polish newlyweds. *Other Roles:* A judge; a court clerk; a thug. *Maximum, 35; minimum, 25.*

DESIGNATED DANCES: Virtually none; maybe a few steps for the Polish newlyweds.

SUGGESTED SETS: Simple furniture to represent a night court; a hotel lobby; a faculty room; a doctor's office; the lawn (with hammocks) of the Mister estate; a street corner with pay phone.

COSTUMES: 1930s suits, workers' clothes, and fashions; a few fancy but ludicrous hats for Mrs. Mister; preppie clothes for her kids; a straw hat for the editor; minister's clothes; dandies' clothes for the artists.

IMPORTANT PROPS: Soda fountain glasses; a doctor's thermometer; a police whistle.

PROVIDED INSTRUMENTATION: Piano-conductor.

ADVERTISING AND MARKETING: "See the musical that the government tried to suppress."

SUGGESTIONS: In the 1983 revival, John Houseman, who had co-produced the musical on that original opening night, gave a speech about the exhilarating evening. See if you can get that speech in John Houseman's memoirs, have one of your actors deliver it, and then do *The Cradle Will Rock* as it was performed on that improvised first night—with actors sitting in the audience, and standing when it's their moment in the spotlight.

RESOURCES: The original cast album (the first one ever made in America), the 1964 and 1983 revival cast albums on LP; the TV production of the 1983 revival.

RIGHTS: Tams-Witmark.

FALSETTOLAND

CREATORS: Book by James (*Into the Woods*) Lapine and William Finn (who earlier wrote *March of the Falsettos*), music and lyrics by Finn.

BACKGROUND: The 1990 musical, a sequel to *March of the Falsettos*, opened at Playwrights Horizons, a small, innovative nonprofit New York theater—and later moved to off-Broadway for 175 performances. It reopened on Broadway in 1992 as the second half of *Falsettos* and won two Tony awards.

STORY: It's 1981 in New York City, and Marvin is no longer Whizzer's lover—but when Whizzer is one of the first to contract AIDS, Marvin and even Marvin's ex-wife, his former psychiatrist, his son Jason, and the lesbian neighbors next door emotionally support Whizzer until his death.

ASSETS: A riveting score, and considering how difficult the subject matter is, it's all the more impressive what Finn has achieved. It's also an inexpensive musical to produce.

LIABILITIES: Will your audience be able to laugh when an actor illuminates two arbitrary people in the audience with flashlights and sings "Homosexuals"? It's a much different way than starting a musical with "There's a bright golden haze on the meadow." And that's just the beginning. *Falsettoland* is still a show that will raise the hackles of some audiences. Some may balk at having a 13-year-old boy sing material that they feel he shouldn't even be allowed to *see*. Because the musical is almost all sung, there's more music to learn than in most other musicals, though the show is only about ninety minutes long.

WHO YOU'LL NEED: *Lead Singing Roles:* A well-meaning, virile, early middle-aged man; his bright muscleboy former love. *Supporting Singing Roles:* A glib psychiatrist; a most distraught wife; a trying-to-find-himself preadolescent boy; a lesbian doctor; a lesbian caterer. *Maximum-Minimum,* 7.

DESIGNATED DANCES: Some musical staging on the title song and the opening song, but otherwise a conga line and calisthenics will swing it.

SUGGESTED SETS: A black box with a door frame and modern painting, augmented with a few pieces of modern furniture—a sofa, chairs, and Parsons tables—on rollers; a small bleachers.

COSTUMES: Contemporary casualwear; a doctor's white coat; jogging and aerobics togs; yarmulkes and prayer shawl; baseball caps; one "Jewish Center" baseball uniform.

IMPORTANT PROPS: Flashlights; a Walkman; a plate of food; baseball and bat; champagne and flutes.

PROVIDED INSTRUMENTATION: Piano, synthesizer, percussion, flute, oboe, clarinet, alto sax.

ADVERTISING AND MARKETING: Use the campaign that worked so well for the Broadway production: "Everybody's Musical!"

SUGGESTIONS: If you do this as the second act of *Falsettos,* you could cast two kids (ideally, brothers) two years apart in age, to effectively convey that Jason has aged two years.

RESOURCES: The original cast album on CD and cassette.

RIGHTS: Samuel French.

GOD BLESS YOU, MR. ROSEWATER

CREATORS: Book and lyrics by Howard Ashman, music by Alan Menken (who later collaborated on *Little Shop of Horrors*), additional lyrics by Dennis Green.

BACKGROUND: The 1979 production opened off-off-Broadway at the WPA to enthusiastic crowds and reviews, but when it later moved to a bigger off-Broadway theater, it ran only 49 performances.

STORY: The present, in an Indiana town. Eliot Rosewater, a very rich man and the son of a senator, is a sci-fi fan who believes his mentor Kilgore Trout's insistence that you "give respect to people who don't deserve it." He gives emotional and financial support to a depressed town and its people—whom his father considers "maggots in the slime at the bottom of the human garbage pail"; Eliot instead will "make them my work of art." But Norman, an unscrupulous lawyer who wants to obtain the Rosewater fortune, rustles up Fred and Caroline, distant Rosewater relatives, to take the money from Eliot—who survives the threat and continues to use his money to win rights for the average American.

ASSETS: A tuneful score and delightfully off-beat book. This show might bring in audiences who don't ordinarily go to musicals—the science-fiction fans, especially admirers of Kurt Vonnegut, on whose novel the musical was based.

LIABILITIES: This show could annoy audiences who like conventional musicals. It's about hard economic times and the death of the small American town, includes talk of suicide and divorce, and contains some salty language. Eliot, meanwhile, while wondering "What the hell are people for?" admits he might be insane, and gives his wife a nervous breakdown. For that matter, Eliot isn't even a very musical character, for, while attending the opera, he worries about the *Aida* lovers sealed in a tomb but singing, because they'll use up more oxygen that way and die quicker.

WHO YOU'LL NEED: *Lead Singing Role:* A delightfully wacky and disheveled philanthropist. *Supporting Singing Roles:* His well-bred but driven-to-insanity wife; a most smarmy lawyer; a needy and neurotic overweight middle-aged spinster; at least four firefighters. *Other Roles:* Eliot's long-suffering senator father; a semifamous science-fiction writer; a high-powered executive; a psychiatrist; a hostess; a writer; a space creature; a sergeant; a nun; various townspeople; foundation employees. *Maximum, 29; minimum, 14.*

DESIGNATED DANCES: A tango for Norman, Fred, and Caroline; soft-shoe steps for firefighters; a singular waltz for Norman; a big patriotic number for the company.

SUGGESTED SETS: Unit set used to go everywhere from Indiana to Rhode Island. (Don't make it as dully brown-colored as the original, though; that hurt the production.)

COSTUMES: Elegant lady's evening coat and gown (the latter must endure a Coke spilled on it); a maternity dress with padding; white hospital gown; red-white-and-blue coats; firefighters' outfits; old-fashioned pin-stripe suit; space creature costume; astronaut outfit; bus driver's suit; nun's habit; man's tennis outfit.

IMPORTANT PROPS: Furniture for rich, middle-class, and poor living rooms; two telephones (one red, one black); a beat-up desk; a hundred envelopes; a bicycle horn; insecticide sprayer; cassette recorder; a pizza box; Cheese Nips; a suitcase; pom-poms; batons; poster-sized photo of your lead looking a little crazy; many gum-backed signs that say "Don't Kill Yourself—Call the Rose-water Foundation."

PROVIDED INSTRUMENTATION: Guitar/banjo, bass, drums, piano, piano-conductor.

ADVERTISING AND MARKETING: Advertise the show as "Kurt Vonnegut's *God Bless You, Mr. Rosewater*"—not only because his name may sell a few tickets, but also because contractual regulations demand that he be listed before the title.

RESOURCES: No cast album; the Kurt Vonnegut novel on which the musical was faithfully based.

RIGHTS: Samuel French.

MARCH OF THE FALSETTOS

CREATORS: Book, music, and lyrics by William Finn (who later wrote *Falsettoland*).

BACKGROUND: The 1981 musical, a sequel to *In Trousers*, opened at Playwrights Horizons, a small, innovative nonprofit New York theater—and later moved to off-Broadway for 128 performances. It reopened on Broadway in 1992 as the first half of *Falsettos*, and won two Tony awards.

STORY: 1979, New York City. Marvin is married to Trina; they have a 13-year-old son, Jason. But Marvin isn't fulfilled, as he tells his psychiatrist Mendel. Soon he meets a handsome and athletic man named Whizzer and leaves his family for him; Trina goes to Mendel for psychiatric help and winds up becoming his lover. Jason, meanwhile, is angry with his father and worries that he may be homosexual as well, but at the end of the show, Marvin helps him to realize that this isn't necessarily true, and they reconcile.

ASSETS: The score is excellent, and Finn has done a good job with difficult subject matter. The musical is inexpensive to produce.

LIABILITIES: Like Falsettoland (page 273), this is still a show that will offend some audiences. Some people will be particularly upset about having a young boy in the show and singing lyrics that they feel are inappropriate. Again, this musical is almost all-sung, so there is more music to learn than with most other musicals, though the show is not long.

WHO YOU'LL NEED: *Lead Singing Roles:* A well-meaning, virile, early middle-aged man; his bright muscleboy love. *Supporting Singing Roles:* A glib psychiatrist; a most distraught wife; a trying-to-find-himself preadolescent boy. *Maximum-minimum,* 5.

DESIGNATED DANCES: An opening number for the entire company; a march for the men.

SUGGESTED SETS: Just a black box with a door frame, augmented by a few pieces of modern furniture—a sofa, chairs, and Parsons tables—on rollers.

COSTUMES: Contemporary casualwear for all, as well as a smoking jacket; kerchief; apron; T-shirt; jeans.

IMPORTANT PROPS: A vacuum cleaner; racquetball equipment; a chess set; a clipboard; a mixing bowl; a rolling pin; earthenware; a suitcase; a rose; poster-sized pictures of Freud, Jung, and Dr. Ruth; a unit that can represent a Red Sea that can part.

PROVIDED INSTRUMENTATION: Three reeds, violin, viola, bass, percussion, piano-conductor.

ADVERTISING AND MARKETING: Try the approach that worked for the Broadway producers: "Everybody's musical."

SUGGESTIONS: If you do this as the first act of *Falsettos,* you could cast two kids (ideally, brothers) two years apart in age to effectively convey that Jason is two years younger in this show.

RESOURCES: The original cast album on CD, cassette, and LP.

RIGHTS: Samuel French.

NOW IS THE TIME FOR ALL GOOD MEN

CREATORS: Book and lyrics by Gretchen Cryer, music by Nancy Ford (who later collaborated on *I'm Getting My Act Together and Taking It on the Road*).

BACKGROUND: The authors of this 1967 off-Broadway production got some encouraging reviews, and though the show only ran 112 performances, the team is still writing together today.

STORY: 1967 in Bloomdale, Indiana. Mike Butler gets a job teaching high school English in a small Indiana town—despite his five-year prison sentence resulting from his court-martial as a conscientious objector—because his father once saved the life of Albert, the school's principal. Mike is interested in expanding the kids' horizons; Tommy, the son of football coach Herbert, is especially influenced and starts considering dodging the draft. Also smitten is

Sarah, a young widow without a teaching degree to whom Albert has given a teaching job, partly because he feels sorry for her, partly because he's fallen in love with her. Sarah's worldview is expanded by Mike's free-thinking ideas and charm. When the town, celebrating its centennial, decides to choose its "Man of the Century," Tommy nominates Mike and not his father—causing Herbert to worry that Mike may be homosexually influencing the boy. Even Sarah becomes scared by all the controversies Mike's causing, and though she sees the good in Mike, she reluctantly agrees to marry Albert. When it's disclosed that Mike once was in prison, the town insists on his resignation; Mike leaves, but Sarah decides he's the man for her and goes with him.

ASSETS: A good and sincere score; a pithy book that has much strong writing in it and will be a lively discussion starter. After seeing this show, those who weren't yet born in the 1960s may better understand the attitudes and struggles of the era.

LIABILITIES: The show is dated, in that dodging the draft is no longer an issue (at least at this writing). Furthermore, Mike seems so sure of himself that we sometimes tire of his having all the answers; in the second act, when Sarah confronts him, she makes a good deal more sense than he does.

WHO YOU'LL NEED: *Lead Singing Roles:* A strong-willed schoolteacher; the not-so-educated female schoolteacher who isn't certain if she should love him. *Supporting Singing Roles:* Her feisty waitress sister; a sincere school principal; a macho-at-all-costs football coach; his rough-hewn teenage son who's unmotivated at the start of the show but grows from his teacher's influence; his admiring girlfriend; two female teachers of home economics and elementary English; two male teachers of science and agriculture; a landlady. *Maximum, 12; minimum, 10.*

DESIGNATED DANCES: Some musical staging, but only a solo rock dance for Sarah's sister and a tap number for all the men.

SUGGESTED SETS: Around Bloomdale, Indiana (pop. 973). The original production used projections—which are available from the licenser—but should you decide on realism, you'll have to re-create a schoolroom; a faculty room; a funeral home; Mike's rented room; a church.

COSTUMES: 1967 Midwestern clothes and 1867 costumes for the centennial celebration, including bride and groom outfits, a bonnet with veil, and a Confederate Civil War uniform.

IMPORTANT PROPS: Squeaky rocking chair; tables; chairs; stools; teachers' desk; settee; barber chair; suitcases; transistor tape recorder; Indian blanket; travel posters; American flag; a contemporary rifle and an antique one; antique baby buggy; rocking horse; scales; chamber pot; a snowman.

PROVIDED INSTRUMENTATION: Piano-conductor only.

ADVERTISING AND MARKETING: "Now is the time for all good men, women, and children to come see *Now Is the Time for All Good Men*," the musical we're presenting at . . ."

SUGGESTIONS: Keep it set in the '60s.

RESOURCES: The original cast album on LP.

RIGHTS: Samuel French.

SUNDAY IN THE PARK WITH GEORGE

CREATORS: Book by James Lapine, music and lyrics by Stephen Sondheim (who later collaborated on *Into the Woods*).

BACKGROUND: During previews, the 1984 production was admired, but most insiders predicted a short run because of its uncommercial nature. But this was one time that the public confounded expectations, keeping the show going for 604 performances. The voters of the New York Critics Circle chose it as Best Musical, it became one of the few musicals to win the Pulitzer Prize, and it racked up ten Tony nominations and two awards.

STORY: George Seurat is trying to find a new style of painting (pointillism), to the dismay of his girlfriend Dot, who wants him to pay much more attention to her. It's especially galling on the night he said he'd take her to the Follies, and then tells her he must finish the hat on one of his subjects. When his painting *A Sunday Afternoon on the Island of La Grande Jatte* does not get the response he wants ("I am trying to get through to something new," says George, perhaps speaking for the show's authors), he is further confounded by Dot's demands for marriage. He's upset that she can't accept him for the artist he is, and, although she's pregnant with George's child, she runs off with Louis, who's willing to raise the child. A century later, we meet a light-sculptor George and his grandmother Marie—and we find out that she is the child of George and Dot, and he is their great-grandson, and Marie is very proud of their heritage.

ASSETS: A fine score and deftly written book. The musical will appeal to anyone who's seriously tried to create—whether a painter, writer, or photographer, one who knows how difficult the process of creation is. And aren't we glad that George spent the night finishing the hat, and didn't go to the Follies?

LIABILITIES: Some audience members, though, may be bored, unable to find the message, and just plain confused when the action suddenly changes from the late nineteenth century to the late twentieth century. This is also a difficult show to do, because you must in some way replicate on stage a few of Seurat's paintings—especially *A Sunday Afternoon on the Island of La Grande Jatte*, not only in sets but also in costumes. In the second act, you'll also have to build a large machine described below.

RECOGNIZABLE SONGS: "Putting It Together"—thanks to a television commercial.

WHO YOU'LL NEED: The show has two distinct acts, with each performer playing two separate roles—though you could cast different performers in each act. *Lead Singing Roles:*: A virile and intense painter/a light-sculptor who must also affect the "voices" of two dogs (Mandy Patinkin); his marriage-minded mistress/a grandmother (Bernadette Peters). *Lesser Singing Roles:* A cantankerous old lady/an art critic; her nurse/art patron; a supercilious artist/museum director; his pretentious wife/a composer; their young daughter; their servant/ a technician; their cook/an artist; two shopgirls/waitresses. *Other Roles:* A simple baker/the critic's friend; a surly boatman/a curator; a staunch soldier/an artist; an "ugly American" couple/a publicist and patron; a woman with a baby carriage/a photographer; a man with a bicycle/a museum assistant; a little girl; a boy bathing in the river; a young man sitting on the bank; a man lying on the bank. *Maximum, 38; minimum, 19.*

DESIGNATED DANCES: Some musical staging, but no numbers as such.

SUGGESTED SETS: Here's the challenge: taking a bare white stage, and then filling it with cutouts identical to Seurat's paintings (for when Seurat paints a tree, it flies in, and when he then decides it shouldn't be there, it flies out). You'll also need cutouts of a sailboat; a tugboat; a black dog; a soldier; a horn player, and others. And that's just the first act. In the second act, you must create a series of high-rise buildings to play against the previously tranquil island.

COSTUMES: Take a look at the painting; that's exactly the type of late-nineteenth-century wear you'll need; nothing less will do. For the second act, you'll need trendy contemporary clothes apropos of the art crowd.

IMPORTANT PROPS: Act one: An easel; sketchbooks; brushes; a painter's scaffold; lanterns; a park bench; a vanity table; fishing poles; cream puffs in a pastry tray; reproductions of famous French paintings. Act two: A wheelchair; contemporary paintings; five poster cut-outs of your contemporary George; and—most significantly—a "chromolume," which is a large machine that emits laser beams *and* must convincingly catch fire. As for the film projections that accompany the lecture on Seurat, they aren't entirely necessary.

SPECIAL EFFECTS: In the first scene, Dot wears a dress that is actually more of an encasement; it opens up and she steps out of it. (You can, however, get by without this.) And there is that chromolume.

PROVIDED INSTRUMENTATION: Two reeds, two horns, two violins, viola, cello, harp, percussion, synthesizer, piano/celeste, piano-conductor.

ADVERTISING AND MARKETING: Before opening, take your cast into parks on Sundays, head for the bandshell, and do some numbers from the show—while your advance-ticket seller is there with tickets.

SUGGESTIONS: While it would be a monumental task to replicate the actual Seurat A *Sunday Afternoon on the Island of La Grande Jatte*, you might fudge it by using visual projections of the piece.

RESOURCES: In addition to the original cast album on CD, cassette, and LP, there is a videotape of the original production that features much of the original cast; study guides.

RIGHTS: Music Theatre International.

SWEENEY TODD, THE DEMON BARBER OF FLEET STREET

CREATORS: Book by Hugh Wheeler, music and lyrics by Stephen Sondheim (who collaborated on *A Little Night Music*).

BACKGROUND: The 1979 production opened to admiring notices, was nominated for eight Tonys, and, with the exception of Best Lighting, won them all—including Best Musical—thus propelling a run of 557 performances. Not long after, the musical joined City Opera's repertory, and a few years later, received a small Broadway revival.

STORY: Sweeney Todd was once Benjamin Barker, a London barber who was incarcerated on a trumped-up charge by Judge Turpin, who raped his wife and, after she disappeared, adopted their daughter Johanna. Now that Todd's escaped and been brought back to London by sailor Anthony, whose life he saved, he plans revenge on the judge. Todd is recognized by Mrs. Lovett, an unsuccessful pie seller who lusts for him; she tells him that his wife took poison after the judge raped her. Todd sets up a barber shop where he and his family once lived and becomes single-minded in his quest for revenge, pushing aside everyone from the beggar woman on the street who constantly propositions him, to Mrs. Lovett and her warped affection. Pirelli, a rival barber, happens by with his assistant Tobias, recognizes Todd, and tries to extort money from him. Todd strangles Pirelli and stuffs him in a trunk just as the judge visits his emporium for a shave. Todd is about to slit the judge's throat when Anthony rushes in to tell Todd of his new love, Johanna, the girl he saw on the judge's balcony. The judge, who plans to marry Johanna, is furious and storms out; Todd ejects Anthony unceremoniously. Mrs. Lovett, meanwhile, has come up with an idea of how to dispose of Pirelli's body: Make meat pies from it, and Todd, now totally insane, is delighted by the idea. Soon enough, most of Todd's customers get a far closer shave than they bargained for, and Mrs. Lovett's pies are such a sensation that they must hire Pirelli's Tobias to help— but the success brings no happiness to Todd, who only wishes to find a way to persuade the judge to return to his shop. When Anthony tells him that the judge has had Johanna put in a madhouse, Todd explains how Anthony can spring her, and tells him that they can hide in his shop. But when Anthony leaves, Todd writes the judge to tell him that Johanna can be found in his shop that evening. Just before the judge arrives, though, the beggar woman comes in, and Todd, not taking any chances, slits her throat. The unsuspecting judge is next, and Todd has his revenge—but then discovers that the beggar woman he killed was actually his wife gone mad. Realizing that Mrs. Lovett kept the truth from him, he pushes her into the bake oven, which causes Tobias to then slit Todd's throat and go mad himself.

ASSETS: A masterpiece score, complemented by a compelling story that's expertly told; even the minor characters are fully fleshed out.

LIABILITIES: One of the more difficult shows to pull off, for it demands strong actors with good voices, as well as a complicated set with equally complicated props. And for all that, your audience may not appreciate your efforts, for the show is too dark for many theatergoers' tastes.

RECOGNIZABLE SONGS: "Not While I'm Around," "Pretty Women."

WHO YOU'LL NEED: *Lead Singing Roles:* A crazed and vengeful barber, the unscrupulous woman who loves him (Angela Lansbury); a sincere and naive (tenor) young sailor, and the *almost* equally innocent (soprano) young woman who loves him. *Supporting Singing Roles:* A dishonest Italian barber who's really an Irishman; his simple-minded assistant; a malevolent judge and his obsequious beadle; a stark raving mad beggar woman. *Other Roles:* A chorus of Londoners, customers, madhouse inhabitants, policemen. *Maximum, 29; minimum, 14.*

DESIGNATED DANCES: Virtually none: a pantomime flashback involving a minuet; a short waltz for Todd and Mrs. Lovett.

SUGGESTED SETS: A street by a London dock; a pie shop with barbershop above; an eating garden with benches outside; the bakehouse below; outside the judge's mansion; a marketplace.

COSTUMES: Early nineteenth-century wear; for Mrs. Lovett, a plain ragged dress and apron as well as a more glamorous dress for her second act success; a flamboyant Italian suit; two wigs for Tobias; judge's robes and wig; a wigmaker's outfit.

IMPORTANT PROPS: A shabby barber's chair and a brand-new one; a case full of old-fashioned but handsome silver razors; a very large baking oven; a meat-grinding machine; trays of pies; mounds of pie dough; rolling pin; steins of ale; a Sicilian donkey cart; a steamer trunk; a tin drum; bottles of elixir; an anatomical chart of a face; a harmonium; body bags; birds in cages; pistols.

SPECIAL EFFECTS: Much stage blood to flow from the many slit throats. Some smoke effects. And you'll need a second level on the set to represent Sweeney's shop, which will have a barber's chair facing a trap door that will open, so that bodies can slide down a chute where they'll emerge on the first level.

PROVIDED INSTRUMENTATION: Five reeds, horn, two trumpets, three trombones, violin, viola, cello, bass, harp, percussion, piano-conductor.

ADVERTISING AND MARKETING: The opening line of the show can serve as your advertising slogan: "Attend the tale of *Sweeney Todd.*"

SUGGESTIONS: There's one very controversial song in which the judge whips himself with a scourge while consumed by obsession with Johanna. It was dropped during previews, but it has shown up in the New York City Opera production. Your choice.

RESOURCES: The original cast album on CD, cassette, and LP; the videotape of the touring production; the Christopher Bond adaptation of the classic play on which the musical is fairly faithfully based; a "Rehearscore" disc for Macintosh and IBM systems that eliminates the need for a rehearsal pianist.

RIGHTS: Music Theatre International.

ALSO WORTH A LOOK

In Trousers

This is the four-person William Finn revusical that began the story of Marvin and Trina, whose marriage and troubles are better detailed in *March of the Falsettos* and *Falsettoland*. The music is extraordinary—arguably better than the subsequent scores—but the lyrics sometimes make it very difficult to understand what is going on. Like its successors, it's a simple show to do—no choreography, no real sets, only contemporary street clothes, and for props, a series of Venetian blinds and a bunch of watering cans are virtually all you'll need—though it is through-sung and the music isn't particularly easy to sing. Definitely worth examining. Rights: Samuel French.

The Threepenny Opera

The Bertolt Brecht–Kurt Weill masterpiece, ran all of 12 performances in its 1933 Broadway production, but became the longest running off-Broadway show in the 1950s, mostly thanks to Marc Blitzstein's new translation. Granted, it's a masterpiece, and contains the classic "Mack the Knife," but its plot—in which militant beggars terrorize a town—may now be unsettling to contemporary audiences who have seen many homeless street people who greatly resemble the characters in the show. Still, if you do decide to do it, do hold a dress rehearsal at which you charge three pennies for admission. Rights: Rodgers and Hammerstein.

Also See: *Candide; Canterbury Tales; Celebration; A Chorus Line; Company; Dear World; Evita; Follies; Grand Hotel; Into the Woods; Les Miserables; A Little Night Music; Marry Me a Little; Merrily We Roll Along; Nine; No Strings; Three Guys Naked from the Waist Down.*

"TIME FOR
A HOLIDAY!"

Musicals with Holiday Appeal

Ever try attending a Broadway musical Thanksgiving weekend? How about the week between Christmas and New Year's Eve? If you have, you probably ordered tickets well in advance—or you sat in the upper reaches of the balcony. If you haven't been able to see a show during those times, that could be because you tried getting tickets during the two most theatrically crowded times of the year.

For that matter, theatergoing is intense during most holiday seasons—and you might tie into this by offering a musical for your audiences during these times of the year. And why not try a musical that has a holiday as its theme?

True, not every show that takes place during a holiday season is a grand and glorious celebration. (*Promises, Promises* is set at Christmas to further underline the unhappiness of the leading female character.) But here are just a few that fit the bill.

HERE'S LOVE

CREATORS: Book, music, and lyrics by Meredith *(The Music Man)* Willson.

THE BACKGROUND: The 1963 musical opened to not-so-hot reviews, received no Tony nominations, and ran 334 performances—but has had an afterlife in many theaters because it's based on the much-beloved movie *Miracle on 34th Street*.

STORY: 1963, in New York City. Doris Walker, a divorced buyer for Macy's, doesn't want her daughter, Susan, to believe in Santa Claus, so the kid won't have any romantic illusions about life. But Fred Gaily comes into their life, and wins them over by proving that there is—literally—a Santa Claus, thanks to a character named Kris Kringle who keeps insisting that he's the real thing. By the end of the show, we're believing it, too.

ASSETS: A show based on one of the most charming Christmas stories that provides a nice change of pace from doing A *Christmas Carol* yet again.

LIABILITIES: The Macy's Thanksgiving Day Parade can never, of course, be convincingly portrayed on stage. You'd forgive that if the rest of the show measured up to *Miracle on 34th Street*, but it doesn't. A couple of songs are tantalizingly good, but most would be hard to learn even after repeated hearings. It's a pretty expensive show to do, and you'll have to play it as a period piece, now that Gimbel's is gone and Macy's is in bankruptcy.

RECOGNIZABLE SONGS: "It's Beginning to Look a Lot like Christmas," which Willson wrote a dozen years before he wrote *Here's Love*, but interpolated into this show.

WHO YOU'LL NEED: *Lead Singing Roles:* An ex-Marine and current lawyer who is a sensitive man; an angry-at-life mother and businesswoman. *Supporting Singing Roles:* Her savvy (if unhappier for it) young daughter; the real Santa Claus; Mr. R. H. Macy; his store's assistant promotional director; a smarmy lawyer; a befuddled judge, a young Dutch girl who sits on Santa's lap. *Other Roles:* Mr. Gimbel; a drunk Santa Claus imitator; a governor; a mayor; a district attorney; a psychologist; a policeman; a bailiff; a mailman; a street vendor; the smarmy lawyer's young son; a nurse; a Girl Scout leader; a secretary; a kindly stepmother. For the parade, some drum majorettes; acrobats; ballerinas; clowns; a bunch of young children. *Maximum, 51; minimum, 26.*

DESIGNATED DANCES: For the entire company, the Macy's Thanksgiving Day Parade involves much musical staging; a joyous title song romp; a lengthy ballet that takes place in the land of Imagi Nation; musical staging on two other numbers.

SUGGESTED SETS: The streets of New York; two Manhattan apartments; a courtroom; an isolation ward; Macy's main store; its offices; its Santa Claus throne; a store display window that represents a suburban Connecticut home.

COSTUMES: 1960s street and work clothes; winter coats and hats; parade uniforms for a band and its marchers; pajamas for Susan; soldiers' uniforms; Native American costumes; rag doll costumes; a Girl Scout's uniform; judge's robes; two Santa Claus suits.

IMPORTANT PROPS: Both a toy Santa sleigh with reindeer, and an actual one; a bevy of band instruments, including a giant xylophone; walkie-talkies; store mannequins; balloons, both regular- and parade-sized; a seesaw; a very large birthday cake; wrapped Christmas presents; a box of Girl Scout cookies; many enormous sacks of mail; *many* plastic alligators.

PROVIDED INSTRUMENTATION: Five reeds, three trumpets, three trombones, horn, three violins, viola, two cello, bass, percussion, celeste, piano-conductor.

ADVERTISING AND MARKETING: Stan Barber of the Pax Amicus Castle Theater in Budd Lake, New Jersey, had the right idea when advertising this show to his community; he set in small black-and-white type, *"Here's Love,* the musical version of,"* and then, in much, much larger red capital letters, *"Miracle on 34th Street."* Why not?

SUGGESTIONS: *Beg* the licenser to allow you to drop "She Hadda Go Back," a great song to play for laughs late at night at a party, but one that has nothing at all to do with the show and is suspected to be a novelty song that Willson took out of his trunk. (Eliminating it would also mean no Girl Scout, no uniform, and no cookies.)

RESOURCES: The original cast album on CD, cassette, and LP; the original 1947 movie on which the musical is faithfully based is available on videotape and laserdisc, while the not-so-good 1974 TV remake is not.

RIGHTS: Music Theatre International.

ALSO WORTH A LOOK

Donnybrook

Would be a nice St. Patrick's Day production. It's a musical version of the *The Quiet Man* movie, with a good score by Johnny Burke, who co-wrote the marvelous "Swinging on a Star" for the film *Going My Way*. Robert McEnroe's book has John Enright—an Irish prizefighter who became a pacifist after killing a man in an American boxing match—returning home and falling in love with a young woman whose father thinks he's cowardly because he won't fight for what he wants. There's a terrific supporting role for a marriage broker who tries to marry off the couple and the girl's widowed father to a salty widow who's really interested in him. The musical received pretty good reviews, but debuted in 1961 right after a string of more exciting shows opened, and became lost in the crowd. Because it has many meaty parts, perhaps you'll want to revive it and give it its due—if you have actors capable of delivering convincing but not overly annoying brogues. Rights: Samuel French.

Meet Me In St. Louis

By Hugh Wheeler, with a score by Hugh Martin and Ralph Blane, is, as of this writing, only available for professional groups, though by the time this reaches you that ruling may have been changed. If it is, your audience will hear "Meet Me in St. Louis," "The Boy Next Door," "Skip to My Lou," "The

Trolley Song," and "Have Yourself a Merry Little Christmas," and will tap its collective toes for such "new" songs as "Be Anything at All but a Boy," "Banjos," and "The Luck of the Irish." It's an expensive show to do: All those turn-of-the-century costumes, and sets that must show inside and outside the upper-middle-class home at 5135 Kensington Avenue in St. Louis—the kitchen, living room, and bedroom—not to mention a ballroom *and* an ice pond, on which your dancers will be expected to skate. (It's one of seven production numbers.) And what will you do for a trolley? Come to think of it, maybe the licensers know what they're doing by not encouraging nonprofessional groups to tackle this one. Rights: Tams-Witmark.

Miss Liberty

This was a 308-performance Irving Berlin musical that celebrated France's gift of the Statue of Liberty to America. Horace Miller is a photographer for the *Herald* who is supposed to photograph the statue, yet mistakenly photographs another, and is fired. His girlfriend Maisie suggests he may do well to try to find the woman that sculptor Bartholdi used as a model for Miss Liberty, so Horace sets off for Paris. There he makes another mistake—finding the wrong girl and falling in love with her. When he brings her back to America, there's a big honoring ceremony for her, and she tells Horace he's erred; still, he and Maisie ask her to continue the ruse. They think they will get away with it, but Bartholdi shows up, causing Miller to be thrown in jail. He is sprung by *World* publisher Joseph Pulitzer, who offers him employment on his paper. *If* you can get behind a "hero" who makes not one big mistake but two; *if* you can forgive him for falling in love with another when his girlfriend gave him a good idea in the first place; *if* you can understand why a smart man like Pulitzer would offer a twice-incompetent a job; if you like the song "Give Me Your Tired, Your Poor," then you might want to do this show. Rights: Rodgers and Hammerstein.

A Wonderful Life

This is the musicalization of Frank Capra's classic film *It's a Wonderful Life* (and if you don't know the story of that movie, then you probably don't turn on your television during the month of December). The book and lyrics are by Sheldon (*Fiddler on the Roof*) Harnick; the music by Joe Raposo, who wrote many of the classic songs for "Sesame Street." The show starts with George Bailey praying for help, then moves to heaven where a deity enlists Clarence to help George. The story is augmented with perceptions of an era when a long-distance phone call was a costly event, and adds a little pop psychology ("What makes a man so power-hungry?" asks George as he tries to figure Bedford Falls bigshot Mr. Potter; "He isn't even short"). Audiences who can recite the screenplay word for word will find a nice unsentimental line ending the scene where Mary tells George she's pregnant. The music is also strong, and there's a clever song about that dance craze, the Charleston, that wonders which Charleston city in the forty-eight states was the inspiration for the dance. Definitely worth a look. Rights: Rodgers and Hammerstein.

Also See: For Christmas: *Annie; The Best Little Whorehouse in Texas; I Love My Wife; Mame; The 1940's Radio Hour; Promises, Promises; She Loves Me.*

For Easter: *Godspell*; *Jesus Christ Superstar*. For the Fourth of July: *Ben Franklin in Paris*; *George M!*; *1776*; *Take Me Along*. For Mothers' Day: *I Remember Mama*; *Minnie's Boys*. For New Year's: *Cabaret*; *Celebration*; *Happy New Year*. For Valentine's Day: *The Baker's Wife*; *Sugar*. For Sadie Hawkins Day (the first Saturday after November 11): *Li'l Abner*. For Jewish holidays, see Chapter 22.

"MELT US!"

Shows for Ethnic and Minority Casts

Here are some musicals in which you can melt black, Hispanic, Asian, and Native American talents.

DREAMGIRLS

CREATORS: Book and lyrics by Tom (*Why Hannah's Skirt Won't Stay Down*) Eyen, Henry *(The Tap Dance Kid)* Krieger.

BACKGROUND: The 1981 Michael Bennett production opened to strong reviews, received twelve Tony nominations, won six awards, and ran 1,522 performances.

STORY: Detroit—Motown—in the 1960s. The Dreamettes are a black girl group; Effie's the lead singer, Deena and Lorrell back her up. They appear in a contest at the Apollo Theatre, which they lose, but gain the attention of

Curtis, an ambitious manager, who convinces big star James Thunder Early to use the Dreamettes as his opening act. Effie's soon in love with him, but is devastated when Curtis makes a critical change that he feels will bring the group greater success: The heavy Effie and the sleek Deena are to trade places in a new group called the Dreams. Effie is devastated that she must sing backup, and loses the love of Curtis and the respect of the group for not better accepting this demotion, and is eventually replaced. By the 1970s, she's on a downward spiral, just as the Dreams are soaring. But no one's satisfied: Deena wants to leave the group to make movies, and when Effie tries a comeback with a new single, Curtis sabotages its air play. But in the end, Curtis's ruse is discovered, Effie does better, and even joins the group onstage at their final appearance before Deena begins her first film.

ASSETS: A driving Motown-flavored score and a fine book (so smart that we can tell at first glance that James Thunder Early is a star, just from the way he complains about the food that has been delivered). Richly defined characters that your performers will be thrilled to play.

LIABILITIES: The show is wall-to-wall music, and its pulsating rhythms make it imperative that your cast not lose a word to that seemingly never-stopping music. It's also a heavy costume show. And some audiences won't have much sympathy for Effie; shouldn't she just be a good soldier and accept her demotion, especially considering that it seems to be making a big difference?

RECOGNIZABLE SONGS: "And I Am Telling You I Am Not Going."

WHO YOU'LL NEED: *Lead Singing Roles:* The Dreams: One heavyweight gospel singer; her two sleek and sexy backups; her equally sleek and sexy eventual replacement; their ambitious and corrupt manager. *Supporting Singing Roles:* A hard-working dynamic James Brown prototype; the four Stepp Sisters (another girl group); two male black pop quintets; a saccharine white trio. *Other Roles:* An emcee; an ousted manager; three film executives; a nightclub owner; a press agent; various onstage performers; announcers; fans; reporters; stagehands; party guests; photographers. *Maximum, 50; minimum, 33.*

DESIGNATED DANCES: Heavy; the entire show seems to be choreographed. Much musical staging throughout—there are no fewer than twelve onstage appearances for the Dreams—and four other production numbers.

SUGGESTED SETS: A unit set that represents various stages and backstage areas of many American cities, as well as a recording studio, a dressing room, and a TV studio.

COSTUMES: 1960s bright-colored dresses, then numerous slinky nightclub gowns and fur coats and capes—ideally a different one for each city the Dreams play. Many tuxedos and nightclub costumes; 1960s street wear for the rest of the cast.

IMPORTANT PROPS: 45-rpm records; microphones; TV and electronic recording equipment; flash cameras and lighting towers for modeling sessions; makeup table.

PROVIDED INSTRUMENTATION: Two flutes, oboe, two clarinets, bass clarinet, horn, two trumpets, two trombones, tuba, percussion, four violins, viola, cello, bass, harp, guitar, piano-conductor.

ADVERTISING AND MARKETING: "What's the real story behind one of the great black girl singing groups in history? We'll tell you in our production of *Dreamgirls*, beginning on . . ."

SUGGESTIONS: Do duplicate one of the most dazzling costume effects in musical theater history: After the Dreams appear on stage in one city, they exit behind a tinseled curtain, and, as the announcer lets us know they are now in another city, they emerge, seconds later, in different dresses. No matter how many dressers and how much Velcro you might need to make this happen, *make this happen.*

RESOURCES: The (much abridged) original cast album on CD, cassette, and LP.

RIGHTS: Tams-Witmark.

FLOWER DRUM SONG

CREATORS: Book and lyrics by Oscar Hammerstein II, music by Richard Rodgers (who next collaborated on *The Sound of Music*).

BACKGROUND: The 1958 production opened to almost unanimously favorable reviews, received six Tony nominations, won only one award (for its conductor), and ran 600 performances.

STORY: 1950s, San Francisco. Tacky nightclub manager Sammy Fong was long ago promised to a "picture bride"—but he's in love with Linda, one of his singers. Linda, though, has given up on his promises of marriage and has been seeing Wang Ta, a nice young man whose family is well-bred and wealthy. Linda doesn't tell Wang Ta where she works, knowing his Old World father Chi Yang would not approve. Ironically, Sammy goes to Chi Yang with his picture bride, Mei Li, who had to slip through customs to get to America. Her expert playing and singing of a flower drum song entrances the elder, and he decides she'd be an excellent match for Wang Ta. But Wang Ta would prefer to choose his own wife—and his choice is Linda, a match neither Sammy nor Chi Yang wants to happen. Sammy arranges for the family to visit his club, where he'll unveil his lead stripper—Linda—which should put an end to the romance with Wang Ta. It does, and Wang Ta realizes the error of his ways and comes to love Mei Li. But a contract is a contract, and Mei Li must marry Sammy—until she discloses that she entered the country illegally. That voids the agreement, and allows Wang Ta to marry Mei Li and Sammy to marry Linda.

ASSETS: A show where no one singer dominates, but almost everyone has a chance to shine. A fine score, and, if that plot seems a little circuitous, it deals with a real issue: Chinese family members living in San Francisco who have different attitudes toward Americanization. The patriarch is against it, his younger son is all for it, and his "number one son" finds the dichotomy difficult. It's a story and struggle that families of every nationality have felt, and your audience will relate to its universality.

LIABILITIES: Some will find the story and situations a little too sentimental. Times have changed since the show's premiere, and "I Enjoy Being a Girl" has often been criticized for its blatant sexist values. Mei Li's father's description of his daughter—"She is strong as a cow and just as amiable"—is not what contemporary audiences like to hear—and having Mei Li say, "Thank you, Father" to this "compliment" doesn't help.

RECOGNIZABLE SONGS: "A Hundred Million Miracles," "I Enjoy Being a Girl," "Chop Suey."

WHO YOU'LL NEED: *Supporting Singing Roles:* An Asian Old World patriarch; his handsome, level-headed, and sensitive elder son; his ultra-cool all-for-Americanization younger son; his endearing and corpulent sister-in-law; a flashy Americanized Asian nightclub singer; her Americanized Asian nightclub manager and sometimes boyfriend; a lovely young Asian immigrant and her Old-World father; a (soprano) seamstress who's suffering an unrequited love. *Other Roles:* A pair of Old World parents; a nightclub emcee who also pretends to be a naval commander; a tailor; a banker; a headwaiter; a servant. *Maximum,* 42; *minimum,* 20.

DESIGNATED DANCES: Three ballets—one for the younger generation, one for Sammy and Linda; one representing Wang Ta's nightmare; three major production numbers; nightclub parade and strip numbers; soft-shoe for Mei Li and Sammy.

SUGGESTED SETS: A San Francisco Victorian house with Chinese ornamentation imposed; its garden; a bedroom; a hill near the Golden Gate Bridge; a touristy nightclub; a modest apartment.

COSTUMES: Chinese satin gowns; robes; trousers; silk pajamas; bridal gown with heavy gold veil; American street clothes; a naval commander's suit; a San Francisco Giants baseball uniform, cap, and glove; nightclub outfits for Chinese coolies, with some modifications that suggest the girls are Irish, Swedish, British, and Spanish; a man's suit in the process of being made.

IMPORTANT PROPS: Teakwood screens, tables, and straight-backed chairs; statues of Chinese gods; pagoda lamps and lanterns; water pipe; Chinese banner-streamers; an iron chest; sedan chair; card table; a bowl of soup; ice bucket with ice; goblets; decorative medals; stacks of money; a sewing machine; TV set; candelabra; gift box with handsome clock inside; suitcases bound with ropes; a corsage in a box; a flower drum and gong.

PROVIDED INSTRUMENTATION: Two flutes, oboe, two clarinets, bass clarinet, horn, two trumpets, two trombones, tuba, percussion, four violins, viola, cello, bass, harp, guitar, piano-conductor.

ADVERTISING AND MARKETING: Flower drum songs have traditionally been sung in Chinese public squares, so why not take your Mei Li to do some singing at the local mall? You may sell some tickets.

SUGGESTIONS: Play it with warmth and charm, and it will work.

RESOURCES: The original cast album on CD, cassette, and LP; the faithful 1961 film available on videotape and laserdisc; the C. Y. Lee novel on which the musical is somewhat faithfully based.

RIGHTS: Rodgers and Hammerstein.

GOLDEN BOY

CREATORS: Book by William Gibson (*who wrote the play The Miracle Worker*) and Clifford Odets (author of the original play), music by Charles Strouse, lyrics by Lee Adams (who later collaborated on *Applause*).

BACKGROUND: The 1964 Broadway production, after a tortuous tryout in which the new bookwriter had to rework the deceased author's script and a new director took the helm, opened to arguably the most mixed notices in musical theater history, then won none of its four Tony nominations. But on the strength of having Sammy Davis as its lead, it still ran 569 performances.

STORY: New York, 1964—or the present now. Joe is a young black man who's started boxing, but keeps it from the family, knowing that they won't approve. He's managed to attract the attention of Tom Moody, who doesn't have much money to promote him—or to divorce and pay alimony to his wife, no matter how much he and his longtime girlfriend Lorna want it. When Tom sees that Joe is restless and is being pursued by more glamorous and successful manager Eddie Satin, he sends Lorna to convince Joe to stay with Tom. Lorna, understanding the implication that she is even to sleep with Joe if necessary, feels debased by his command—but she goes, and does succumb to Joe, who's been attracted to her all along. And yet Lorna cannot commit herself to Joe, and when she marries Tom, Joe is devastated. He takes it out on his next opponent in the ring, and kills him. After lashing out at Lorna—"Why couldn't you love me right?"—he drives at a high speed in his new car, crashes it, and is killed.

ASSETS: A pulsating score with tart lyrics, and a black-white concept that trumps the original play's problem of Joe's being Italian and Lorna's being a WASP.

LIABILITIES: A book that became more muddled yet ironically less complex as it was successively reworked in its Philadelphia, Boston, and Detroit tryouts, when Joe had a promising piano career and was risking his hands every time he entered the ring; by the time he reached Broadway, he was just another black man searching for himself. Lorna is also a tough character to like, given that she has no self-respect (and whines about it—often). And have you the many musclebound men who can effectively portray prizefighters (both in the ring and in practice) and sing as well?

WHO YOU'LL NEED: *Lead Singing Roles:* A young black man with the body and moves of a boxer. *Supporting Singing Roles:* A very harried and miserably married two-bit fight manager; his ever-supportive but masochistic mistress; a cocksure wheeler-dealer with an appreciation for the finer expensive things; two trainers; Joe's Fat-Albert brother-in-law; a young black kid. *Other Roles:* A Hispanic boxing opponent who can maneuver the fight-dance sequence; Joe's stern and uncompromising father, militant brother, and cautious sister; a reporter; a chorus of both black and white fighters, neighbors, party guests, and hoodlums. *Maximum, 38; minimum, 17.*

DESIGNATED DANCES: An opening in which boxers train and jump rope to music; a big block party; three other production numbers; and—most important—a boxing match that is choreographed, often in slow motion.

SUGGESTED SETS: A gym; a tenement apartment; a small office; a playground with a chain-link fence; 127th Street; a train; a dressing room; a bar; a penthouse; inside and outside Madison Square Garden; its boxing ring.

COSTUMES: Many boxing trunks, boxing gloves, and terrycloth robes; clothes representative of the best and worst of Harlem; polyester suits for the whites.

IMPORTANT PROPS: Jump ropes; punching bags large and small; ironing board, iron, and laundry basket; coffee pot; first aid kit and adhesive tape; beer cans; baby carriage with black doll inside; metal milk crates; movie and flash cameras; champagne and liquor bottles; suitcases; shoeshine kit.

PROVIDED INSTRUMENTATION: Two flutes, oboe, two clarinets, bass clarinet, horn, two trumpets, two trombones, tuba, percussion, four violins, viola, cello, bass, harp, guitar, piano-conductor.

ADVERTISING AND MARKETING: The word "Golden" is a marketer's delight, and you can try everything from selling Hershey's Golden Almond Bars to sponsorship from American Express.

SUGGESTIONS: An excellent show for an intimate black-box theater; indeed, it will be enhanced in such surroundings.

RESOURCES: The original cast album on CD, cassette, and LP; the Clifford Odets play on which the musical is loosely based.

RIGHTS: Samuel French.

GRIND

CREATORS: Book by Fay (*The Gay Life*) Kanin, music by Larry (*Snoopy!!!*) Grossman, lyrics by Ellen (*Herringbone*) Fitzhugh.

BACKGROUND: Interesting that this 1985 musical about burlesque should open six years after *Sugar Babies* at the same theater, the Hellinger. That's where the similarities end; *Sugar Babies* is an escapist show, while *Grind* has racism, terrorism, blindness, and suicide on its mind—and paid the price, playing 79 performances, one-fifteenth the run of the earlier hit. It received seven Tony nominations and won two awards.

STORY: It's 1933 at Harry Earle's Burlesque Theater in Chicago, where Harry employs blacks (including comic Leroy and stripper Satin) and whites (including top banana Gus and second banana Solly), though he's careful to abide by the unwritten rules and keep them segregated when they're on- and offstage. Leroy is interested in Satin, but she's keeping her distance. Gus is going blind, and his heavy hand with his oversized hypodermic needle on his act has made other professional stooges refuse to work with him. He hires Doyle, a down-and-out bum. When Leroy sees that Satin has bought a bicycle for her young brother, he offers to help her get it to him—by asking Doyle, the only person in the company who can ride it. At Satin's mother's house, both Doyle and Leroy discover that she is disgusted with the way her daughter is making her living. But greater trouble arrives when white toughs show up and destroy the bike. It does cause the trio to become closer, and Satin agrees to have dinner with Leroy. Gus, meanwhile, is still having eye problems, and when Harry threatens to fire him, Gus takes his own life. Doyle gets drunk; Satin finds him on the way to meet Leroy and takes him back to her apartment, where she learns that he was an IRA sympathizer whose wife was accidentally killed by a bomb he made. Leroy discovers them, and is so jealous that he later humiliates Satin onstage. In the end, though, when the theater is threatened, blacks and whites join together with a better understanding of one another.

ASSETS: A good score with clever lyrics.

LIABILITIES: An unwieldy book with too many characters. And though the opening song proclaims, "This must be the place," your community may not be the place to do a show with burlesque humor, salty language, and a scene in which a woman is sexually humiliated onstage. It also requires expensive sets, costumes, and props.

WHO YOU'LL NEED: *Lead Singing Roles:* A dynamic black song-and-dance man; an elegant, young, headlining black stripper. *Supporting Singing Roles:*

An older white top banana; an equally old white second banana; a down-on-his-luck burly Irishman with a strong tenor voice. *Other Roles:* A disapproving black mother; her nine-year-old son; a wardrobe mistress; the white burlesque theater owner; his stripper wife; a stage manager, a doorman; six tough guys; six black chorus girls; six white chorus girls. *Maximum, 48; minimum, 22.*

DESIGNATED DANCES: A snazzy opening number and act one closer; a tap dance to open act two; two solo spots for Leroy; two solo strips for Satin.

SUGGESTED SETS: Much of the show takes place on a theater stage, so you're all set there. But there are the backstage areas segregated between blacks and whites, as well as a few interiors: the kitchen in Satin's mother's house; Satin's room.

COSTUMES: 1930s wear, as well as exaggerated burlesque duds; strippers' clothes—both elegant and tacky. A female cop uniform; white tuxedo; hobo outfit; bathrobes; for your chorus girls, train porter uniforms; harem costumes; a Whistler's mother costume; an outlandish array of costumes that represent exhibits (the monorail, a fountain, etc.) at the 1939–1940 World's Fair Century of Progress exhibition.

IMPORTANT PROPS: An apple-seller's stand; big balloons that can serve as women's breasts; butcher knife; breakaway chair; burlesque pig bladder; tomatoes to be thrown; liquor bottles; softball and bat; monkey wrench; cake box with a candled cake inside; oversized burlesque hypodermic needle; seltzer bottle; folding screen; trunk; gun; bicycle; wreath; juggling balls; magician's bouquet of flowers; ostrich-feather fans; ironing board and iron.

PROVIDED INSTRUMENTATION: Two flutes, oboe, two clarinets, bass clarinet, horn, two trumpets, two trombones, tuba, percussion, four violins, viola, cello, bass, harp, guitar, piano-conductor.

ADVERTISING AND MARKETING: "Burlesque wasn't all fun and games. It was also a grind, as we'll show you in our production of *Grind*, beginning on . . ."

SUGGESTIONS: In the original production, the destruction of the young black boy's bike by four white punks was accomplished by using a breakaway bicycle—but you can stage this scene with the boys in a huddle, backs to audience, and sound effects.

RESOURCES: The original cast album on CD, cassette, and LP.

RIGHTS: Broadway Play Publishing, 357 West 20th Street, New York, NY 10011; phone: 212–627–1055; fax: 212–609–6631.

ONCE ON THIS ISLAND

CREATORS: Book and lyrics by Lynn Ahrens, music by Stephen Flaherty, (who later collaborated on *My Favorite Year*).

BACKGROUND: The 1990 production moved from Playwrights Horizons to Broadway, received enthusiastic notices, eight Tony nominations, won no awards, and ran for 469 performances.

STORY: During a fierce thunderstorm in the French Antilles, some natives—who believe that "if we knew why the gods did things, we'd be gods ourselves"—calm and entertain a scared child by telling her the story of Ti Moune, a young girl adopted by a kindly middle-aged couple, who is smitten from afar by the wealthy Daniel. When Daniel is hurt in an accident, Ti Moune rescues him and feels for the first time in her life that she has a purpose. He's grateful for the attention, because he's had a tougher life than one might expect: Half-French, half-native, he's never been fully accepted by either culture, and soon falls in love with her. Her parents insist she cannot marry him, but she is sure they are wrong. They aren't; Daniel has been promised since birth to Andrea. Ti Moune commits suicide—but, the natives insist, the gods were kind in allowing her to come back to live as a tree that shelters Daniel's son, who later finds a peasant girl and loves her fully the way his father could not.

ASSETS: A fine score with solid up-tempo numbers, ballads, and gospel; a book that's very moving, and takes an unusual slant on race—light-skinned vs. dark-skinned blacks, moneyed vs. poor.

LIABILITIES: A good deal of musical staging, as the performers seldom stop dancing (but in a "story theatre" style).

WHO YOU'LL NEED: *Lead Singing Roles:* A sensitive and naive young native girl; the half-white, half-black, handsome, well-bred young man with whom she falls desperately in love. *Supporting Singing Roles:* A most concerned and advanced-in-age mother and father; a goddess of love; a goddess of earth; a god of water; a god of death; Daniel's well-bred and supercilious fiancée; his imperious father. *Other Role:* Ti Moune as a young girl. *Maximum, 20; minimum, 11.*

DESIGNATED DANCES: Heavy, many calypso-style dances for most of the company—including an opening and closing number; a ritual dance to the gods; a masquerade ball; a waltz for Daniel and Andrea; a solo dance of beauty and grace for Ti Moune; much musical staging throughout.

SUGGESTED SETS: A black box that had been brightly painted sufficed for the original production.

COSTUMES: Colorful native garb—pants, dresses, and vests in reds, vermilions, and yellows—for most of the company; costumes to represent birds, frogs, trees, moss, and rocks; brocaded masquerade-party wear; a white suit for Daniel; masks to represent the upper classes; Rastafarian wigs for the natives.

IMPORTANT PROPS: Stick of wood gathered for a fire; two trees—one simple and one very elaborate for the finale; two flashlights to represent the headlights of a car; lanterns; a peasant straw mat; a large white quilt; a machete.

SPECIAL EFFECTS: Thunder and lighting;

PROVIDED INSTRUMENTATION: Piano, two keyboards, bass, percussion, woodwinds.

ADVERTISING AND MARKETING: *"Once on This Island* is the story of Ti Moune, a young native girl. Starting on [date], Ti Moune belongs to everyone, at our theater . . ."*

SUGGESTIONS: As director-choreographer Graciela Daniele did in the original production, direct your lovers so that they fondle with an erotic and yet truly innocent sexuality.

RESOURCES: The original cast album on CD and cassette; Rosa Guy's novel *My Love, My Love,* on which the musical is fairly faithfully based; study guides.

RIGHTS: Music Theatre International.

PURLIE

CREATORS: Book by Philip Rose, Peter Udell (who respectively directed and did the lyrics for *Shenandoah*), and Ossie Davis (who wrote the play *Purlie Victorious*) music by Gary *(Shenandoah)* Geld, lyrics by Udell.

BACKGROUND: The 1970 production wasn't given much of a chance or much attention while it was rehearsing, but word spread during previews that the show was very exciting. The critics liked it well enough. Add five Tony nominations, wins for stars Cleavon Little and Melba Moore, and a resulting 688-performance run.

STORY: "Not so long ago" in South Georgia. Purlie is a Southern black preacher very much intent on wresting power from Ol' Cap'n, the tyrannical white landowner—and church owner. The Cap'n may no longer own slaves, but he certainly treats his "Negras" as such and pays them slave wages, which may be fine for Purlie's brother Gitlow, but certainly not for Purlie or the Cap'n's liberal son Charlie. Purlie also wants the five hundred dollars owed his cousin, now deceased, and enlists Lutiebelle, a young woman he's recently met, to impersonate her. Because Lutiebelle is so taken with Purlie, she agrees to do it, and fools the Cap'n—until he asks her to sign her name as a receipt and she accidentally signs her own name. The Cap'n hires her as his maid, but when he sexually harasses her, Purlie is furious enough to go kill him. En route, though, he runs into Charlie who convinces him not to, and finagles matters and betrays his father so that Purlie can become owner of the church. This so upsets the Cap'n that he dies of shock on the spot. The blacks celebrate their soon-to-be-better life at his funeral.

ASSETS: A fine score that soars when sung well; good characters, including a tell-it-like-it-is character who has right on his side and a good deal of charm as well; a young woman and too-satisfied black worker who grow a good deal by curtain's end. This also is one of the more inexpensive musicals to mount.

LIABILITIES: There's nothing endearing about the Cap'n's prejudice, no matter how folksily he expresses it. The blacks too often appear foolish, toothless, even moronic. And it takes a white man to save the day.

WHO YOU'LL NEED: *Lead Singing Roles:* A dynamic and sincere black preacher; an impressionable young black woman with a soaring voice. *Supporting Singing Roles:* A toadying worker and his cheerful wife; a black nurse; an irascible white landowner who treats the blacks no better than slaves, his gawky son who is intent on being fair-minded. *Other Roles:* A chorus of gospel singers and cotton pickers. *Maximum, 24; minimum, 7.*

DESIGNATED DANCES: A big opening gospel number; a production number for the cotton pickers.

SUGGESTED SETS: A church with a pulpit and pews; a rundown farmhouse with table and cupboard; a country store; a cotton field.

COSTUMES: A minister's claw-hammer coat and black hat; Southern black sharecropper and peasant wear (gingham clothes, aprons, a feathered hat, ragged straw hat, outsized handbag); Palm Beach linen suit; wide hat; shoestring tie; workshirt and jeans.

IMPORTANT PROPS: A coffin swathed in a Confederate flag; funeral fans and tambourines; baseball bat; bullwhip; pistol; a vest-pocket watch on a chain; department store boxes; suitcase tied with rope; kerosene lamps; cooking utensils; pie slices; parchment scroll.

PROVIDED INSTRUMENTATION: Five reeds, three trumpets, two trombones, percussion, drums, two violins, viola, cello, bass, two guitars, organ, piano, piano-conductor.

ADVERTISING AND MARKETING: The original production was fond of emphasizing the musical's source material by constantly advertising "*Purlie* is Victorious!" You might do the same.

SUGGESTIONS: Here's how to do this musical with as few as seven performers: Lutiebelle could do the song that the church soloist sings to open and close the show, with the five surviving others backing her up; as for the cotton pickers that sing the act two opener, the song could be given to the toadying brother.

RESOURCES: The original cast album on CD, cassette, and LP; a made-for-TV video; Ossie Davis's play *Purlie Victorious,* on which the musical is fairly faithfully based.

RIGHTS: Samuel French.

RAISIN

CREATORS: Book by Robert Nemiroff and Charlotte Zaltzberg, music by Judd *(King of Schnorrers)* Woldin, lyrics by Robert Brittan.

BACKGROUND: The 1973 production did so well at Washington D.C.'s Arena Stage that producers brought it to Broadway, where it won the Tony as Best Musical (albeit against rather weak opposition) and ran 847 performances.

STORY: The South side of Chicago in the 1950s. Walter lives in a rundown apartment with his wife, Ruth; son, Travis; mother, Lena; and sister, Beneatha. He works as a chauffeur but dreams of owning a liquor store with two partners, and hopes that his mother will back him with the ten thousand dollars they'll soon receive from his deceased father's insurance. But Lena decides to use the money to put Beneatha through medical school and to buy a house, until she sees how devastated Walter is by her decision. She gives him the money, only to see it lost when one of Walter's partners turns out to be a crook. In the meantime, a white resident of the neighborhood to which Lena planned to relocate the family offers to pay them a substantial sum if they choose not to move. But the family will not compromise its dignity and be bought off, and will move to their new home and somehow find a way to pay for it.

ASSETS: Fine book, music, and lyrics, meaty parts for all, and a message worth hearing, in a musical based on a neo-classic play. The original production received a good deal of acclaim for miming the use of most props, and if you go with that conception, you'll find the show far less expensive to produce.

LIABILITIES: While there are of course a number of battles yet to be fought and won in race relations, the ones depicted here, in a pre-civil rights era, do seem a little dated.

WHO YOU'LL NEED: Aside from one embarrassed white middle-class executive, the rest of the cast is black. *Lead Singing Roles:* A virile leading man; his portly gray-haired mother. *Supporting Singing Roles:* His college-student sister; his attractive wife; their ten-year-old son; a busybody housewife-neighbor; two business partners—one sincere and one smarmy; a Nigerian student; a pastor and his wife. *Other Roles:* A nightclub proprietor; a drug pusher and his victim; a chorus to represent people of Chicago's South Side, commuters, churchgoers, bar patrons and workers, moving men, African women, and warriors. *Maximum*, 43; *minimum*, 22.

DESIGNATED DANCES: An elaborate jazz ballet starts the show, which also includes some 1950s jitterbugging; musical staging representing a crowded subway ride; three African dances for Beneatha (one solo, one with Walter, one with her boyfriend); one production number for Walter and his partners; another for him, Ruth, and Beneatha; a full-chorus gospel production number.

SUGGESTED SETS: Though the action takes place in such locations as an apartment, a nightclub, and a church, the set is abstract. For example, a platform first represents a bed, and later a car.

COSTUMES: Late 1950s street clothes, as well as pajamas, housecoats, slippers, and curlers; an African head wrap, necklace, and tribal robes for Beneatha, women, and warriors; moving-men coveralls; "do-rags" for the chorus (ornate print vests, wide brimmed hats); a chauffeur's hat and jacket.

IMPORTANT PROPS: Even if you go with the convention of the mime, you'll still need one table; two chairs; a briefcase; a rocking chair; an undernourished potted plant.

SPECIAL EFFECTS: Lighting is profoundly important in this set-less show, so you must have a very well-stocked board (and, ideally, a neon effect for the bar scenes). You should also have two records: A 78 that, despite sounding old and scratchy, plays a black blues number, and a then-"new" album with African drum music.

PROVIDED INSTRUMENTATION: Four reeds, three trumpets, horn, two trombones, tuba, three percussion, two violins, viola, cello, bass, guitar, organ, drums, African drums, keyboard-conductor. There is also a smaller orchestration without strings, and a smaller one still for a single trumpet, trombone, reed, and keyboard-conductor.

ADVERTISING AND MARKETING: Stock your concession stand with raisin cookies and boxes of raisins.

SUGGESTIONS: "Budget a great deal of time to rehearsing the mime," stresses Woldin. "Though the best mime is the least noticed, you must have *exact* locations on stage for each object. Ask yourself such specific questions as 'Does the door open in or out? To right or left? How high is the doorknob?' "

RESOURCES: The original cast album on CD, cassette and LP; the script of Lorraine Hansberry's original play *A Raisin in the Sun*, and the 1961 movie *A Raisin in the Sun*, on which the musical is faithfully based, on videotape and laserdisc.

RIGHTS: Samuel French.

THE WIZ

CREATORS: Book by William F. (*The Girl in the Freudian Slip*) Brown, music and lyrics by Charlie Smalls.

BACKGROUND: "It hasn't been easy," director Gilbert Moses told the audience before the musical's first tryout performance in Baltimore in 1974. "One actor's been ill, we haven't had much time to rehearse with sets, but someday you will brag that you saw the first performance of *The Wiz*." The audience was skeptical, but the production managed to overcome its problems, receive eight Tony nominations, win seven awards—including Best Musical—and run 1,672 performances. Unfortunately, the optimistic Moses never shared in the glory, for he was fired before the show left Baltimore.

STORY: Girl has Kansas, girl loses Kansas, girl gets Kansas. If you've seen the movie of *The Wiz*, don't assume you've seen the stage version. Casting Diana Ross as a mature Dorothy was a dumb mistake, for part of Judy Garland's appeal in *The Wizard of Oz* movie and Stephanie Mills's appeal in *The Wiz* on stage was that they were little girls bravely fighting seemingly insurmoutable odds; Diana Ross was older, not wiser, and panicked and cried at what came her way. Not that any adult wouldn't—but the point is that leading the way must be a child too young to truly realize how much danger she's facing.

ASSETS: A story that everyone loves is nevertheless not too grand for a strictly-for-laughs treatment. Children of all ages will probably agree with master Broadway composer-lyricist Stephen Sondheim, who, though a writer in a far loftier style, has often gone on record as saying, "After you see *The Wiz*, you'll feel much better than you did when you entered the theater."

LIABILITIES: You'll need a wiz of a costume, set, and special effects designer—not to mention a producer with deep pockets, for this is an expensive show to mount. And there'll be times you'll wonder if it's worth it for a show with the literary merit of "a pox on both your houses" being rejoined with "Oh, no—on my summer place, too?"

RECOGNIZABLE SONGS: "Ease on Down the Road."

WHO YOU'LL NEED: *Lead Singing Role:* A charming and brave young girl. *Supporting Singing Roles:* Her kindly aunt; a soulful Scarecrow, Tin Man, and Cowardly Lion; a wild-and-crazy wizard; two good witches and one wicked one. *Other Roles:* A not-so-emotional uncle; a chorus of Munchkins, crows, witch's helpers, funky monkeys, poppies, and field mice; a gatekeeper and citizens of Emerald City; four actor-dancers who *play* and represent the yellow brick road; an adorable dog. *Maximum, 46; minimum, 20.*

SUGGESTED SETS: A Kansas farmhouse with storm cellar; Munchkinland; a cornfield; a forest with big trees; a poppy field; outside and inside Emerald City; the Wiz's throne room; the wicked witch's castle; the site of a hot-air balloon.

COSTUMES INCLUDE: Rural Kansas wear; a nice Sunday dress for Dorothy; fanciful outfits for Scarecrow, Tin Man, Cowardly Lion, crows, field mice, Munchkins, and witches; streetwalker dress for poppies; "beautiful people" outfits for Oz inhabitants; a forbidding leather outfit for the Wiz (as well as pajamas and wig with curlers); a pair of silver slippers.

DESIGNATED DANCES: Much ballet—for the tornado, a fight sequence, the lion's dream, and the funky monkeys; solo struts for Scarecrow, Tin Man, and Cowardly Lion; a rap dance for all principals as they ease on down the road; a stomp when the Wicked Witch is liquidated; a joyous romp to celebrate leaving Oz.

IMPORTANT PROPS: A clothesline with clothes; clothes basket; a magic wand that can turn into handkerchiefs; a paddy wagon; an enormous mask; a very long rope; a throne; a tent; a pair of dead witch's feet wearing detachable silver slippers; ears of corn, a box of All-Bran; a milk can; an oil can; an ax; a bucket of water; a valentine heart; oversized whiskey and seltzer bottles.

SPECIAL EFFECTS: Plenty—with the biggest challenge being having the Wicked Witch of the West disappear through a trap door. The Good Witch of the North also does a few minor magic tricks. You'll also need smoke and fire from flashpots; sounds of the jungle; police sirens.

PROVIDED INSTRUMENTATION: Four reeds, three trumpets, horn, two trombones, percussions, drums, two violins, cello, bass, guitar, piano, piano-conductor.

ADVERTISING AND MARKETING: "In the original Broadway production of *The Wiz*, playing the roles of both a Munchkin and a field mouse, was Phylicia Rashad—and look what happened to her. Who knows how many stars in the making you'll see in *our* production of the Tony-winning musical, opening..."

SUGGESTIONS: While the original Broadway production was all-black—and the musical idiom includes soul and rap music—there's no reason that you can't present *The Wiz* as an integrated show, as Christopher Catt did to great effect in an outdoor amphitheater in Albany, New York.

RESOURCES: The original cast album on cassette and LP; the barely faithful 1978 movie version on videotape and laserdisc; and, of course, the original 1939 *The Wizard of Oz* movie.

RIGHTS: Samuel French.

ALSO WORTH A LOOK

Ain't Misbehavin'

This was assembled and directed by Richard (*Miss Saigon*) Maltby, Jr., and won three 1979 Tonys of its five nominations—including Best Musical. It's really a concert of Fats Wallers's greatest hits— " 'Tain't Nobody's Biz-ness If I Do," "Honeysuckle Rose," "Mean to Me," "Keepin' Out of Mischief Now," "Black and Blue," "I'm Gonna Sit Right Down and Write Myself a Letter," "Two Sleepy People," "I Can't Give You Anything but Love," "It's a Sin to Tell a Lie," and, of course, "Ain't Misbehavin'." If you have three good female singers, two fine men singers, a down-and-dirty pianist, and a small budget, you'll have a crowd-pleaser here. Rights: Music Theatre International.

Pacific Overtures

This has a book by John Weidman, and music and lyrics by Stephen Sondheim, who later wrote *Assassins* (though Sondheim's more than occasional collaborator Hugh Wheeler helped on the book, too). The show received ten Tony nominations in 1976, but won only two for sets and costumes (it was *A Chorus Line's* year), and ran 193 performances. Many critics liked it, many audiences didn't; it's a difficult show because it employs many conventions from Japan's Kabuki theater in dealing with the peaceful and artistic land that Japan was for 250 years before Commodore Matthew Perry arrived and brought "civilization" to the island. You'll need at least twenty-two Asian or Asian-American actors—virtually all men, in the Kabuki tradition—to play nearly three times as many roles, and the set and costume demands are strong (though it can be done small, as an acclaimed off-Broadway production in 1984 proved; in fact, the provided instrumentation from the licensers offers both the Broadway and off-Broadway versions). The upshot? If you've got the horses and the inclination, this is another strong Sondheim musical that deserves to be heard and seen. Rights: Music Theatre International.

Sweet Dreams—The Inner City Musical

This was produced on Broadway in 1971 as *Inner City*, won its one Tony nomination for featured actress Linda Hopkins, and ran only 97 performances, but this rock musical is definitely worth a second look. It's based on a collection of Eve Merriam's poems, *The Inner City Mother Goose*, that parodies the classic nursery rhymes—for example, "Mary, Mary, Urban Mary, how does your garden grow? With chewing gum wads and cigarette butts, with Popsicle sticks and potato chip bags"—and sets them to a terrific Helen Miller rock score. (True, it's a through-sung musical, meaning that there's more than twice the average amount of music for your nine-member cast to learn.) It is, as bookwriter-lyricist Merriam stated, "about the perils and pleasures of being alive today and not giving up hope that we can all survive and make our cities safe for living and loving and neighborliness and regreening." Cynics will point out that things have become worse in the twenty-plus years since the show's original production; perhaps that means "Boy, do we need it now." Rights: Samuel French.

Also See: *Big River*; *Cats*; *Celebration*; *Don't Bother Me, I Can't Cope*; *The First*; *Godspell*; *Hair*; *Into the Woods*; *Jacques Brel Is Alive and Well and Living in Paris*, *Jesus Christ Superstar*; *Joseph and the Amazing Technicolor Dreamcoat*; *The King and I*; *Kismet*; *The Me Nobody Knows*; *No Strings*; *Return to the Forbidden Planet*; *The Roar of the Greasepaint—The Smell of the Crowd*; *Runaways*; *Show Boat*; *South Pacific*; *Starlight Express*; *Starmites*; *The Tap Dance Kid*; *The Wizard of Oz*; *The Zulu and the Zayda*.

"SOMETHING NEW—
SOMETHING DIFFERENT"

Rock and Folk-Rock Musicals

"Something new—something different" was actually a lyric in the Broadway musical *Harrigan 'n' Hart*, a 1985 show that celebrated what Ned Harrigan and Tony Hart brought to the stage—the "something new—something different" innovation of musical comedy.

Let's borrow "Something new—something different" and put it in a new context: the new sound that Broadway has enjoyed or endured, depending on your perspective, since *Hair* opened on Broadway in 1968. Given that many of today's high school students and young adult performers in nonprofessional theaters are more natural and familiar singing rock style than they are with "Oh, What a Beautiful Morning" or "On the Street Where You Live," you may want to investigate the following.

HAIR

CREATORS: Book and lyrics by Gerome *(Dude)* Ragni and James Rado, music by Galt *(Two Gentlemen of Verona)* MacDermot.

BACKGROUND: Legendary producer Joe Papp opened his New York Shakespeare Festival with this 1967 production, then co-produced it at a now-defunct discotheque with Michael Butler. Papp lost faith, Butler didn't, and opened it on Broadway in 1968—with the famous now-you-see-it-now-you-don't nude scene. It didn't win either of its mere two Tony nominations, but that didn't stop it from running 1,750 performances.

STORY: 1968, New York City. Claude is drafted to serve in the war in Vietnam, but his hippie values make him burn his draft card, protest loudly, swear to keep his hair, and evade the draft at all costs. In the end, he has his hair cut and goes into the army.

ASSETS: A terrific score, with some songs—especially the one about air pollution—still relevant. A show into which kids like to sink their teeth, and one that offers good opportunities for onstage musicians. And a chance to show a younger generation what the late 1960s were all about.

LIABILITIES: A virtually incomprehensible book so dated (even the Waverly Theater, alluded to in one song, is now the Waverly I and II) that contemporary theatergoers won't get all the then-trendy references. Your audience may very well contain parents who loved this musical way back when, and now are embarrassed to have their children appear in the drug-obsessed show.

RECOGNIZABLE SONGS: "Aquarius," "Frank Mills," "Good Morning, Starshine;" "Let the Sunshine In."

WHO YOU'LL NEED: *Lead Singing Roles:* Three male hippies and their three hippie girlfriends. *Supporting Singing Roles:* Two male and two female black hippies. *Other Roles:* Kids of varying races to play a myriad of roles; a middle-aged mom and pop. *Maximum, 45; minimum, 25.*

DESIGNATED DANCES: No choreography as such, but a good deal of free-form musical staging for thirteen production numbers.

SUGGESTED SETS: The authors suggest a bare, dirt-covered, and exposed-to-the-back-wall stage, with a totem pole and a modern crucifix onstage, and three American flags—two 1776 flags, one contemporary—to be hung from the rafters.

COSTUMES: Late 1960s hippie and American and Hindu Indian wear (sandals, saris, loincloths, beads, old military uniforms, leather outfits); mismatched military uniforms (including ones for George Washington, Ulysses S. Grant, Robert E. Lee, and astronauts); man's floor-length linen gown; three dresses appropriate for the Supremes which should be sewn together.

IMPORTANT PROPS: Stacks of newspapers; metal oil drums and a yellow bathtub; sleeping bags; old mattresses covered with psychedelic sheets; rolled-up rugs; tomahawks; blowguns; spears; toys; umbrellas; sticks; poles; banners; balloons; flags; leaflets and protest posters; incense burners and candles; cameras; a conservative suit on a hanger; many, many flowers.

PROVIDED INSTRUMENTATION: Guitars, trumpets, percussion, piano-conductor.

ADVERTISING AND MARKETING: "We're bringing back the Age of Aquarius so you can see what *Hair* looks like a quarter-century later."

SUGGESTIONS: No, the show doesn't lose a thing by omitting the nude act one finale.

RESOURCES: The original cast album on CD, cassette, and LP; the somewhat faithful (and better) 1979 movie on videotape and laserdisc.

RIGHTS: Tams-Witmark.

JOSEPH AND THE AMAZING TECHNICOLOR DREAMCOAT

CREATORS: Book and lyrics by Tim Rice, music by Andrew Lloyd Webber (who collaborated on *Jesus Christ Superstar*).

BACKGROUND: The authors conceived this as a musical for schoolchildren to perform and see, but it's been produced almost everywhere professionally since then. The 1982 Broadway production did not win any of its seven Tony nominations, but it ran an impressive 747 performances.

STORY: A new stylization of the biblical tale: Boy gets coat from Dad, boy's brothers become jealous, get rid of him, and tell their father he's been murdered. Happy ending, though, when he reappears and forgives everyone.

ASSETS: A driving score that kids and adults enjoy performing, for it gives them a chance to do everything from hard rock to pop rock to Elvis.

LIABILITIES: The show is wall-to-wall music, which means that much more for your cast to learn.

WHO YOU'LL NEED: *Lead Singing Roles:* A narrator (more often played by a woman, but you can use a man); a charming, young, innocent lad; his good-natured father, who considers him his favorite. *Supporting Singing Roles:* Twelve not-so-nice brothers and their intense wives; a corrupt pharaoh; his equally corrupt captain of the guard; his even more corrupt wife; a butler; a baker. *Maximum, 50; minimum, 32.*

DESIGNATED DANCES: Six production numbers in the rock style.

SUGGESTED SETS: A unit set that can represent anywhere and everywhere.

COSTUMES: Ideally, some that will give the brothers a "look," but you should also have a pair of identically designed costumes that you can stain, tear, and ruin which the brothers will wear during their hard times.

IMPORTANT PROPS: Goblets, and wine to fill them.

PROVIDED INSTRUMENTATION: Two reeds, trumpet, trombone/tuba, guitar, bass guitar, drums, percussion, piano.

ADVERTISING AND MARKETING: Have a promotion by which anyone wearing a coat of many colors gets in for half price.

SUGGESTIONS: Amita Bhalla's 1992 production at New York University was set in the Southwest; the father, Jacob, was a camera-toter constantly taking pictures of his brood in colorful T-shirts and jeans. The dreamcoat was a jacket featuring all the T-shirt colors, so what made the kids jealous was the implication that he was better than all of them. The Ishmaelites were three girls in motorcycle jackets who danced tap and calypso, as well as the Texas side-step.

RESOURCES: The original cast album on CD, cassette, and LP; the story in Genesis 30–37 on which the musical is fancifully based.

RIGHTS: Music Theatre International.

THE ROBBER BRIDEGROOM

CREATORS: Book and lyrics by Alfred Uhry (who wrote the play *Driving Miss Daisy*); music by Robert Waldman.

BACKGROUND: The 1975 musical received two Tony nominations, won neither, and ran 15 performances; the following year, it was revived for 145 performances and won a Tony for Barry Bostwick.

STORY: Around Rodney, Mississippi, "the day before yesterday." Jamie Lockhart is a country boy who proudly tells you that he "steals with style." When staying at an inn, he saves the life of rich Mr. Musgrove, knowing that the gentleman will be so grateful that he'll invite Jamie to his house—where he'll *really* make a haul. En route, while heavily disguised, he encounters Musgrove's lovely daughter Rosamund and forces her to undress and give him her clothes she's wearing—exactly the type of move that intrigues the girl who wants some excitement in her life. When she hears from her father about how wonderful Jamie Lockhart is, she's not at all interested, and she doesn't recognize him when he shows up undisguised. Meanwhile, Rosamund's jealous stepmother Salome is plotting to have her killed, but only winds up outfoxing herself and getting herself murdered. Eventually Rosamund learns the truth about Jamie and rehabilitates him into becoming a successful merchant—which is all right, he decides, because in that occupation he can *still* "steal with style."

ASSETS: A bouncy and flavorful country score that's a delight to hear and play. This is a favorite show of many people who *hate* musicals, because it eschews the more obvious conventions and has no trouble being its unpretentious self.

LIABILITIES: It's another of those stories that deeply depends on the heroine not recognizing the second identity of a man she's gotten to know. Once an audience believes that such a ruse should easily be discovered, it begins to lose respect for the heroine—and for the show for stooping to such a timeworn device.

WHO YOU'LL NEED: *Lead Singing Roles:* A charming rogue; the attractive young woman who comes to love him. *Supporting Singing Roles:* A rich merchant; his most unattractive wife; a simpleton; his equally simple mother and sister; a raven (played by an actor); a most uncharming rogue and his brother—a decapitated head who is still alive. *Other Roles:* An onstage country band; townspeople. *Maximum, 26; minimum, 10.*

DESIGNATED DANCES: A square dance to open and close the show, musical staging in a search for Rosamund, and some very stylized movement in which Rosamund is pursued by Salome's henchman, but she always turns around at the last minute (not that she sees him), and he cannot get the job done.

SUGGESTED SETS: A clearing in the woods; a country inn; and a well-to-do house.

COSTUMES: Country and rustic wear, as well as a green silk dress, a petticoat embellished with gold, a brooch, and pregnancy pad.

IMPORTANT PROPS: Knives; hatchet; oven; bowl; jug; barrel; soup ladle; silver dishes; gold candlesticks; feather duster; wine bottle; peaches; money bags; a pair of twin "babies."

SPECIAL EFFECTS: Some dark make-up for Jamie that prevents Rosamund from recognizing his secret identity. The actor playing the still-alive decapitated head must be resigned to sitting in a large box all night long with only his head showing; make it comfortable for him.

PROVIDED INSTRUMENTATION: Three violins, mandolin, two guitars, bass, banjo, piano-conductor.

ADVERTISING AND MARKETING: "Any bridegroom gets a half-price ticket when attending with his bride; any robber attending gets a visit from the police."

SUGGESTIONS: There is some nudity suggested, when Jamie demands that Rosamund give him every stitch of her clothing. In the original production, the actress's very long hair served as a cover, but you needn't have Jamie be so demanding in your production; he can just ask for her outer clothes. And Rosamund *could* wear a body stocking.

RESOURCES: The original cast album on cassette and LP; the Eudora Welty story on which the musical is loosely based.

RIGHTS: Music Theatre International.

STARMITES

CREATORS: Book by Stuart (*Forever Plaid*) Ross and Barry Keating, music and lyrics by Keating.

BACKGROUND: The 1989 production surprised quite a few when it received six Tony nominations, but it won no Tonys, and its advance sale never built to allow more than a 60-performance run.

STORY: Teenager Eleanor is a social outcast and comic book freak (she loves *Starmite Tales*) whose mother insists she get rid of the books. That's when Eleanor is suddenly transported into an intergalactic adventure: She becomes Milady to the Starmites, who are trying to save the earth and battle Shak Graa. She becomes their captain, falls in love with Space Punk, but is soon pitted against Diva, whose daughter Bizarbara (also a comic book freak—albeit one who reads *Earth Tales*) also wants Space Punk, for a prophecy says that when Bizarbara weds a groom, Shak Graa will meet his doom. When Shak Graa appears, it seems that they are doomed—but Eleanor believes that love conquers all, and her love for the Space Punk defeats Shak Graa. Eleanor is so happy that she stays in space, while Bizarbara takes her place on earth; Eleanor's unsuspecting mother is very happy with the changes in her "daughter."

ASSETS: A bouncy score, and a book that will please those who enjoy camp. (Example: When one of Diva's subjects says to her, "Excuse me, your esteemedship," she answers, "Don't call me steamship!") Nice, too, to have a girl comic book freak instead of a boy, which would have been more ordinary.

LIABILITIES: Still, having Eleanor be such a freak about comic books that she knows every volume and number may make some think that maybe her peers are right to suspect she's a little unbalanced. Worse, there are so many arcane terms and names that it's easy to lose track of who's who. On a practical level, there was no original cast album recorded, and that will hamper your cast.

WHO YOU'LL NEED: *Lead Singing Roles:* A teenage girl who becomes a superhero and can double as Bizarbara; her unassuming mother who can double as Diva. *Supporting Singing Roles:* Three Starmites and their captain; a high priest of chaos; a lizard who doubles as Shak Graa; four female banshees. *Other Roles:* Two droids to undertake scene shifts. *Maximum,* 26; *minimum,* 12.

DESIGNATED DANCES: Rock/space age choreography mixed with Motown and do-wop; six production numbers; a solo for Diva, and another for Bizarbara "which," says Keating, "combines elements of Cobra Woman, the Dance of the Seven Veils, and a Martha Graham nightmare."

SUGGESTED SETS: Eleanor's bedroom; a lab in innerspace; a forest (with vines, twines, tendrils, and flora); a great hall in a castle; a mortuary; a sorcery chamber. "Go for a rock concert feel," urges Keating. "Exposed lighting, sound equipment, and ladders."

COSTUMES: Contemporary teen wear for Eleanor; innerspace-styled clothes for almost everyone else: spandex; capes; gloves; armbands; military hats; corset costumes; chokers; tutu rag skirts; slashed jeans; purple sneakers with green laces; bicycle shorts; fingerless gloves; jumpsuits; tube hoods; a wedding dress; a lizard suit.

IMPORTANT PROPS: Boxes of comic books; a lute; a whistle; wedding garlands; bed, bedspread and pillows; hand and foot shackles.

SPECIAL EFFECTS: *Starmites* is undoubtedly the first musical to include in its script "F/X"—the Hollywood term for "special effects"—because it has an abundance of lighting effects, explosions, fog, echos, and wind chimes.

PROVIDED INSTRUMENTATION: Two synthesizers, guitar, bass, drums; a piano/vocal score is available for piano-only productions.

ADVERTISING AND MARKETING: "Comic book freaks, have we got a musical for you!" Put posters in comic shops; offer discounts to those who come dressed as super-heros.

SUGGESTIONS: While Eleanor and Bizarbara are played by the same actress (ditto Diva and Eleanor's mother), you could use four different actresses for the two parts.

RESOURCES: No original cast album.

RIGHTS: Samuel French.

TWO GENTLEMEN OF VERONA

CREATORS: Book and lyrics by John Guare *(who wrote the play Six Degrees of Separation)*, music by Galt *(Hair)* MacDermot.

BACKGROUND: "We started writing the show in March of 1971," reports Guare, "and by the summer we were performing in Central Park. Then we opened on Broadway on December 1"—which must be record time from blank page to opening. Not only that, the show received nine Tony nominations, won two awards—including Best Musical—and ran 627 performances.

STORY: Verona, "now—and then." Proteus and Valentine, best friends since childhood, say goodbye, as Valentine is leaving Verona for the high life in

Milan. Proteus won't go because he wants to win the hand of Julia, who is a bit unsure of him at first, but gives in; they trade rings. But Proteus's father wants him to go to Milan on business, and the boy must go—unaware that he's leaving a pregnant Julia. She and her maid Lucetta decide to disguise themselves as men and go to Milan, too. When they arrive, we catch up with Valentine, who has fallen for Silvia, the daughter of the stern duke. But Silvia has been promised to the foolish-but-rich Thurio—which would be problem enough for Valentine, even if it weren't exacerbated by Silvia's love for Eglamour, whom her father has banished from the kingdom. To further complicate matters, Proteus also falls in love with Silvia, and is willing to betray his best friend to get her—informing the duke of Valentine's plans to abduct Silvia. The duke then has Valentine drafted. All this is overheard by Julia and Lucetta, whom Proteus does not recognize, and he asks "the men" to be his servants, and to deliver a ring to Silvia—the ring that Julia had given him—thus breaking Julia's heart. Meanwhile, an AWOL Eglamour comes back for Silvia, and Proteus attacks them while they make love. Eglamour runs away, disappointing Silvia, who succumbs to Proteus's advances. Valentine catches them and is furious with his former friend, and is about to kill him when Eglamour returns with an enormous Chinese dragon—which turns on Eglamour and drives him off. Proteus apologizes to Valentine, who accepts, and, upon discovering that Julia is the "boy" he hired, reconciles with her. Valentine challenges Thurio to a duel, but Thurio gives up without a fight, leaving Silvia to Valentine.

ASSETS: A good score—but the whole is even more than the sum of its parts, for the musical is a joyous experience that sends most audiences home deliriously happy.

LIABILITIES: This is *not* one of Shakespeare's masterpieces, and the plot convolutions can make the head spin. There is also approximately twice the music of the average Broadway musical, which will put greater demands on your cast—and you. And some nonsense-syllable lyrics come perilously close to profanity.

WHO YOU'LL NEED: *Lead Singing Roles:* Two virile young men; a cute young woman; a sexy siren. *Supporting Singing Roles:* A silly fop (ideally with a falsetto); two manservants; one maidservant; a fascistic duke who isn't ashamed to play politics; a stern father; a tavern host; a returning soldier; a milkmaid; a chorus of citizens. *Other Roles:* A dog—the more mongrel-looking the better. *Maximum, 33; minimum, 13.*

DESIGNATED DANCES: A joyous opening number; a short dance for a manservant; a big production number for the company as Julia and Lucetta travel to Milan and yet another that includes a marching drill once they arrive; a rock romp for Silvia and Valentine, a gleeful strut for Thurio and company; a wild dance featuring Silvia and the cast; a joyous Frisbee-throwing, yo-yo-twirling frenetic finale.

SUGGESTED SETS: The original production used a three-level unit set with scaffolding, but even if you can't duplicate that, don't go for realism, but just a few pieces to represent each scene.

COSTUMES: This is one of those shows that can be costumed in a myriad of styles—whatever looks trendy—though you should have military uniforms for the Duke and Eglamour, a snow-white outfit for Thurio, and a pregnant suit for Julia.

IMPORTANT PROPS: Red tissue-paper hearts; a cupid's bow and arrow; much luggage; a tent; vellum parchments; rakes; hoes; burlap bags; military medals; a dove (ideally one that flies through the theater on a wire); a Chinese fire-breathing dragon; a large feathered quill pen; a bicycle (ideally with golden baroque trim); a very fancy Renaissance-styled telephone; a scarecrow that wears the clothes that Julia and Lucetta will use as disguises.

PROVIDED INSTRUMENTATION: Four reeds, two trumpets, two horns, trombone, two percussion, three violins, viola, cello, bass, harp, mandolin/banjo, accordion, piano-conductor.

ADVERTISING AND MARKETING: "We're doing *Two Gentlemen of Verona*, but those who fear Shakespeare needn't worry; we're doing the musical version written by the authors of *Hair* and *Six Degrees of Separation.*"

SUGGESTIONS: The original production was a multiethnic delight; Valentine and Silvia were black, Proteus Hispanic, Eglamour Chinese, Julia and Lucetta white. While you don't have to cast this way, why not give it a try?

RESOURCES: The original cast album on cassette and LP; Shakespeare's *Two Gentlemen of Verona*, on which the musical is very faithfully based.

RIGHTS: Tams-Witmark.

ALSO WORTH A LOOK

Chess

Despite its dazzling score, this Benny Anderson-Björn Ulvaeus-Tim Rice collaboration has never found success in this country—and is less likely to as time goes on. The story of a bitter chess match between an American and a Russian was written in the early 1980s, when the world was a much different place. Now that the cold war is over, the musical has become a dinosaur. By the time you read this, *Chess* could, of course, indeed once again be topical—but let's hope not. Rights: Samuel French.

The Rocky Horror Show

The 1973 Richard O'Brien hit, has become infamous as *The Rocky Horror Picture Show*, a midnight attraction around the world famous for audience members adding their own commentary to the movie. "Trouble is," says Bert Bernardi, who's directed it for the Downtown Cabaret Theater in Bridgeport, Connecticut, "they shout them to the live actors as well." On the other hand, you may have an audience that might be struck dumb at the prospect of watching a transvestite create a muscleboy that he wants to play with, while also enjoying a young married couple who just happened by his castle. None of this, however, is to disparage the show: The score is terrific, the dance numbers are electric, and it's a great deal of fun. Rights: Samuel French.

Starlight Express

The Andrew *(Cats)* Lloyd Webber 1984 London hit and 1987 Broadway failure that is, in essence, a musical version of "The Little Engine That Could." We hear via voice-over a little boy playing with his trains, commiserating with a poor little steam train that tries to win a race against some pretty impressive machinery. The irony is that the productions in both cities relied heavily on technology, all the while condemning it in the book. No matter; if you've got a bunch of roller-skaters who want to do a musical—and/or if you have access to a roller rink—there's no better show to do. Lloyd Webber's score, his heaviest rock-influenced one yet, is terrific. But one suggestion: instead of just having a little boy's voice-over, use a kid actor; it'll give the show some much-needed humanity. Rights: Music Theatre International.

Also See: "A" . . . *My Name Is Alice; Cats; Diamond Studs; Don't Bother Me, I Can't Cope; Dreamgirls; Evita; Falsettoland; God Bless You, Mr. Rosewater; Godspell; Grease; In Trousers; Jesus Christ Superstar; Little Shop of Horrors; March of the Falsettos; The Me Nobody Knows; Once on This Island; Pippin; Promises; Promises; Pump Boys and Dinettes; Purlie; Return to the Forbidden Planet; Runaways; Sweet Dreams—The Inner City Musical; Three Guys Naked from the Waist Down; The Wiz; Working.*

```
┌─────────────────────────────────────────────┐
│  ● ● ● ● ● ● ● ● ● ●                          │
│  ●                                        ●  │
│  ●    "THIS IS THE                        ●  │
│  ●                                        ●  │
│  ●    LAND OF MILK                        ●  │
│  ●                                        ●  │
│  ●    AND HONEY"                          ●  │
│  ●                                        ●  │
│  ● ● ● ● ● ● ● ● ● ●                          │
└─────────────────────────────────────────────┘
```

Musicals with Jewish Appeal

William Goldman said in his landmark 1969 book *The Season: A Candid Look at Broadway*, "Without Jews, there simply would have been no musical comedy to speak of in America." He mentions the great preponderance of Jewish writers (Arlen, Berlin, Bernstein, Bock, Ebb, the Gershwins, Hammerstein, Harburg, Harnick, Hart, Herman, Kander, Kern, Lerner, Loesser, Loewe, Rodgers, Rome, Sondheim, Styne, and Weill), and also says, "A conservative guess would be that Jews account for 50% of the attendance on Broadway."

If this figure is in tune with your community, you might consider some of the following musicals.

THE EDUCATION OF H*Y*M*A*N*K*A*P*L*A*N

CREATORS: Book by Benjamin Bernard Zavin, music and lyrics by Paul Nassau and Oscar Brand.

BACKGROUND: The 1968 production blamed its 28-performance fate on the fact that during its opening performance on April 4, word spread throughout the theater that Martin Luther King had just been assassinated, thus destroying the mood of the small and charming show. But even a smooth opening might not have made much difference, for the show did seem a little old-fashioned for 1968 Broadway, closing right around the time *Hair* opened.

STORY: Hyman Kaplan is a Jewish immigrant who's eager to learn "American" and become a citizen—but his irrepressibility causes some students to loathe him, though his harried teacher Mr. Parkhill understands his zeal. As for the industrious Rose Mitnick, she's not sure, even when Kaplan expresses his admiration for her. But Rose is promised to Yissel Fishbein, who'll be emigrating to New York in the spring. Kaplan tries to deny the arrival of spring, even wearing a heavy coat on the rather warm day that Fishbein arrives. He becomes so discouraged—Fishbein wants to take Rose out of school so she can stay home and "be a good wife"—that he absentmindedly falls in with an anarchist. He's later arrested, and is about to be deported when Rose visits him; he gives her title to his tailor shop so that she will have something in case the marriage with Fishbein doesn't work out. When Parkhill comes to visit, Kaplan tells him that he was arrested without a warrant, and Parkhill goes to work. As Rose comes to the realization that she just can't marry the man she doesn't love, Kaplan returns, having been released through Parkhill's efforts, and they begin their new life together as Americans—along with the other graduates from Mr. Parkhill's class.

ASSETS: Nice score and charming book, with much good-natured fun to be gleaned from the immigrants' many mistakes with the language. (There's a lengthy debate among them on whether there should be one or two "z's" in the word "please." A show that will give your middle-aged performers good chances to shine. Despite the quick fold on Broadway, the name recognition is there, thanks to the original novel.

LIABILITIES: No cast album was ever released, thus making it a bit more difficult for your cast to learn the songs.

WHO YOU'LL NEED: *Lead Singing Roles:* A tailor by day who's a most eager student by night; the intelligent young woman who also loves to learn—and learns to love him. *Supporting Singing Roles:* Her old-fashioned widowed mother; a very dedicated young male teacher; two female schoolteachers; an Italian immigrant; a competitive student; a more conservative student; a self-centered dandy. *Other Roles:* An Irish immigrant student; a very vocal anarchist; two other Jewish students; a pushcart vendor; an old-clothes man; a police officer; a guard; a judge. *Maximum, 31; minimum, 16.*

DESIGNATED DANCES: For most of the company, two horas (in which Kaplan is the focal point); a march; two numbers with much musical staging.

SUGGESTED SETS: A street in New York's Lower East Side; a modest night school classroom; a teacher's room; a tenement apartment; Ellis Island; Kaplan's tailor shop.

COSTUMES: Because virtually all the characters are immigrants in the 1910 decade, you need clothes that are plain, but out-of-style.

IMPORTANT PROPS: Student desks and chairs; blackboard; Palmer writing method alphabet script placards; schoolbooks; benches; sewing machines; piecework; half-mannequin; wedding dress; one cart containing glasses and false teeth and another with old clothes; bouquet of flowers; bag of fruit; suitcases; bundles; a soapbox.

PROVIDED INSTRUMENTATION: Four reeds, two trumpets, two horns, trombone, two percussion, three violins, viola, cello, bass, harp, mandolin/banjo, accordion, piano-conductor.

ADVERTISING AND MARKETING: "Go back to school—at least for one night, and get *The Education of Hyman Kaplan.*"

SUGGESTIONS: Lonny Price's 1989 production at the American Jewish Theater eliminated the scenes with the teachers and kept the action small in that vest-pocket theater. If that appeals to you, see if you can convince the licensers to allow you the same option.

RESOURCES: Leo Rosten's stories *The Education of Hyman Kaplan.*

RIGHTS: Music Theatre International.

THE GRAND TOUR

CREATORS: Book by Michael Stewart and Mark Bramble (who later collaborated on *42nd Street*), music and lyrics by Jerry (*Hello, Dolly!*) Herman.

BACKGROUND: The 1979 production starred Joel Grey, who received nicer notices than the show itself, which perished after 61 performances, and won neither of its two Tony nominations.

STORY: June, 1940, in Paris. Jacobowksy, a mild-mannered, optimistic, yet savvy Polish Jew, must escape the Nazis. So must Polish Colonel Stjerbinsky, who has important Resistance papers to deliver. With no planes available, Jacobowsky quickly buys a car; only problem is, he cannot drive—but the colonel can, and though he has no affection for Jacobowsky (they have diametrically opposed personalities), he realizes they must travel together. The colonel detours to pick up his beloved Marianne, who doesn't want to leave her homeland, but realizes she must. On their tour, Marianne comes to admire the clever and sunny qualities in Jacobowsky that the colonel cannot stand. Jacobowsky does get them in a pickle, though, when he tries to convince the Nazis that he and his friends are circus performers—which means he'll be shot from a cannon—causing Marianne to admire him even more. Eventually the colonel comes to see Jacobowksy's good qualities, and though Jacobowsky also falls in love with Marianne, she remains true to the colonel. Jacobowsky makes certain that the colonel and Marianne escape the country, while he continues to fend for himself, despite a great Nazi threat.

ASSETS: A charming score and book, with several amusing incidents that show Jacobowsky's David-like thinking in some trial-by-fire situations that the Goliath-like colonel cannot fathom. Jacobowsky also has an endearing way of looking at life—when the no-nonsense colonel complains that they won't be traveling in a first-class train compartment, Jacobowsky notes that "what makes a carriage first-class is not the number painted on the door, but the quality of passengers inside." It's also nice that the colonel is three-dimensional enough to be in love.

LIABILITIES: Jacobowsky is *so* endearing at times (and always seems to have all the answers) that he can become a bit of a pain. Theatergoers used to big Jerry Herman numbers won't find quite the same payoff here. But your biggest problems will be putting onstage a circus and all the modes of transportation that people need when taking a grand tour—car, train, horse-drawn wagon, and barge.

WHO YOU'LL NEED: *Lead Singing Roles:* A charming negotiator (Grey, a Michael Jeter type); a cocksure brute-force colonel; his lovely girlfriend. *Supporting Singing Roles:* The colonel's aide; a German officer and his soldiers; some Resistance workers; a chauffeur; a police commissioner; a hotel owner; a circus owner and her performers; a bride, groom, and her parents; two nuns; a chorus of refugees, Parisians, train travelers, and wedding guests. *Maximum, 45; minimum, 24.*

DESIGNATED DANCES: A few dance steps for Jacobowsky's opening monologue-song; a tango for him and Marianne; a hora for him and the colonel; a traditional Jewish wedding dance for much of the company.

SUGGESTED SETS: In front of a hotel, a garden wall, a circus, a parade site, a barge, a convent, and a wharf.

COSTUMES: 1940s Eastern European wear; a once-elegant but now shiny suit for Jacobowsky; Polish and German military uniforms; finery befitting a Jewish wedding; circus costumes; nuns' habits.

IMPORTANT PROPS: A Rolls-Royce (which eventually suffers a flat tire), a bicycle; restaurant table and chairs; picnic baskets; food and wine; many suitcases; chicken crates; circus banners and placards; a sharpshooting board with a figure of a man outlined in balloons; a bird cage; a hat in a hatbox; machine guns and pistols; enough small drinking glasses so that one can be broken each performance; a large French flag and small Polish flags.

SPECIAL EFFECTS: Circus performers who can do circus tricks—including a shoot-the-ballons-encircling-a-man trick *and* a dummy shot from a cannon. Some sounds of a sputtering motor; steam emerging from it.

PROVIDED INSTRUMENTATION: Four reeds, two trumpets, two horns, trombone, two percussion, three violins, viola, cello, bass, harp, mandolin/banjo, accordion, piano-conductor.

ADVERTISING AND MARKETING: Make a detailed road map of all the streets and avenues leading to your theater, replete with directions, and headline it, "Here's how to make a Grand Tour to *The Grand Tour*."

SUGGESTIONS: The musical offers a good opportunity to swell the ranks of your organization, for if you recruit people with circus skills, you may show them how much fun it is to be in a musical, and they may become long-term members.

RESOURCES: The original cast album on cassette and LP; S. N. Behrman's play that is an adaptation of Franz Werfel's novel *Jacobowsky and the Colonel*, on which the musical is loosely based.

RIGHTS: Samuel French.

I CAN GET IT FOR YOU WHOLESALE

CREATORS: Book by Jerome (*Fiorello!*) Weidman, music and lyrics by Harold (*Pins and Needles*) Rome.

BACKGROUND: The 1962 musical opened to some raves and some pans, and ran 301 performances, but is most remembered as being the launching pad for supporting player Barbra Streisand's spectacular career; she received the show's only Tony nomination.

STORY: 1930s, New York. Harry Bogen tells dress magnate Mr. Pulvermacher that his company can break the strike that is preventing dresses from being delivered. But Harry hasn't got a company, and needs five hundred dollars to start one; to get the money, he drops by his old neighborhood to see Ruthie Rivkin, who's been in love with him since grade school. She loans him the money, and Harry is on his way, soon buying expensive gifts for his mother, whom he adores, and for Martha Mills, a showgirl, whom he wants. He starts Apex Modes with two partners, the savvy Teddy and the naive Meyer, and soon hires Miss Marmelstein and everyone else from Pulvermacher's company. But Harry gives too many gifts to his mother, Martha, and even Meyer's son who's being bar-mitzvahed; Teddy soon pulls out and works against Harry. Harry eventually bilks Meyer into a tax-fraud, and Meyer is sentenced to jail. But Harry keeps him out by going to Pulvermacher, who agrees to help Harry in exchange for true devotion to him and his firm. Harry returns to Ruthie as the curtain falls.

ASSETS: A terrific score, replete with just-right Jewish harmonies; a chance for a supporting actress to steal the show just as Streisand once did with her "Miss Marmelstein" song.

LIABILITIES: Given that the musical deals with the garment industry, it's costume-heavy, and even contains a fashion show. More problematic: Harry is a very tough character with whom to spend an evening; aside from being nice to his mother, he is virtually devoid of appeal or charm.

WHO YOU'LL NEED: *Lead Singing Roles:* A ruthless would-be executive (Elliot Gould); his unpretentious housewife mother; his long-suffering plain and simple girlfriend. *Supporting Singing Roles:* A Seventh Avenue executive; his secretary (Barbra Streisand); a Broadway showgirl, a dress salesman; a dress designer; his wife. *Other Roles:* A striker; a shipping clerk; a bartender; a cigarette girl; a waiter; four office workers; four dress models; two delivery boys; a teenage boy. *Maximum, 35; minimum, 12.*

DESIGNATED DANCES: Musical staging at opening to indicate the strike; a big production with Harry, Martha, and restaurant personnel and patrons; a hora/kazatske for Harry, his mother, Ruthie, and his partners; a soft-shoe for Meyer and his wife; a sensual dance for Teddy and Martha.

SUGGESTED SETS: Seventh Avenue; Pulvermacher's office; a Bronx street; a modest kitchen; a flashy nightclub; Apex Modes offices and showroom; a penthouse.

COSTUMES: Tons of 1930s fashions, both quasi-fashionable (pinched waists, simple cuts, big peplums, shimmering gowns, one-piece culottes, play suits) and plain (office wear, street clothes, housedress). Also a fancy suit, an overcoat with a velvet collar, and a homburg hat for Harry.

IMPORTANT PROPS: Wheeled pipe racks of dresses on hangers; sewing machines; cutting machines; bolts of fabric; strike and bankruptcy signs; hatbox with fancy hat; dress box with cape; gift box with silver fox stole; jewelry box with diamond bracelet; another with a locket; a souvenir doll; dishes and dishtowels; a switchboard; swivel office chair.

PROVIDED INSTRUMENTATION: Four reeds, two trumpets, two horns, trombone, two percussion, three violins, viola, cello, bass, harp, mandolin/banjo, accordion, piano-conductor.

ADVERTISING AND MARKETING: Scour your community for all the merchants and stores that offer wholesale discounts, and strongly encourage them to take an "I Can Get It For You Wholesale" ad in your program.

SUGGESTIONS: Make certain that your Harry seems as if he's learned something at the final curtain, or we'll hate him all the more for victimizing Ruthie—and equally detest her for being so stupid. And given that Harry's mother washes a considerable amount of dishes, consider taking a page out of *Raisin*'s book, and have her mime this action; that way, the sink can be fourth wall, and we can see her while she's singing and talking to us. (Come to think of it, it wouldn't be so bad if she had her back to us washing dishes much of the night, because she is the type of mother who would do just that while talking to her son.)

RESOURCES: The original cast album on LP; the Jerome Weidman novel on which the musical is loosely based. (The 1951 movie version of the novel has no relation at all to the musical.)

RIGHTS: Tams-Witmark.

MILK AND HONEY

CREATORS: Book by Don Appell, music and lyrics by Jerry (*Hello, Dolly!*) Herman.

BACKGROUND: The 1961 production received pretty enthusiastic notices and five Tony nominations; while it won none, it was a strong enough draw during its two matinees a week to offset those empty evening performance seats early in the week, and lasted 543 performances.

STORY: 1960, Jerusalem. Phil Arkin, separated for years from his wife, meets Ruth Stein, traveling with her friend Clara and a bunch of other widows, while all are visiting Israel. Phil's interested in Ruth, but feels it would be wrong to engage her in a romance. But his daughter, Barbara, who sees the potential of the relationship, invites Ruth to the farm she shares with her husband. There, Ruth and the other widows enjoy themselves (though Clara and company are sorry to find every man's married). Phil and Ruth fall more in love, but he's yet to tell her about his wife. When he finally does, Ruth doesn't at first stop the budding relationship, but later feels guilty and goes to Tel Aviv with the other widows. Phil follows her, meets Clara, who's happily met a nice man of her own and hopes to marry (after she soliloquizes permission from her dead husband), but won't tell Phil where Ruth is. He eventually finds her, but she won't go with him until he's officially divorced. They fly from Tel Aviv—he to Paris to get a divorce, she to America to hope that he can.

ASSETS: A melodic score, and the chance for your middle-aged female performers to steal the show.

LIABILITIES: You wonder about two mature people thinking that they can fall in love so quickly, especially in an idealized situation such as a vacation. His reluctance to tell her about his separation makes him look bad.

RECOGNIZABLE SONGS: "Shalom," "Milk and Honey."

WHO YOU'LL NEED: *Lead Singing Roles:* A handsome widower; a charming widow traveling with other less attractive widows—each should have an operatic voice. *Supporting Singing Roles:* A widow who's keeping her eye out for a new husband and is the self-appointed leader of the group; a married daughter interested in her father's romantic welfare; her pro-Israeli husband; his not-so-sure-about-Israel comic friend. *Other Roles:* Seven widows; an upstanding second-husband candidate; a policeman; a Yemenite boy, a chorus of Israeli farmers, Arabs, waiters, and tradesmen. *Maximum, 34; minimum, 19.*

DESIGNATED DANCES: For the company, a hora to celebrate Independence Day and a wedding dance; a march for the widows; the title song production number for the farmers.

SUGGESTED SETS: A Jerusalem street; an Israeli farmhouse; its rocky farm; its barn; a hillside; a Tel Aviv cafe; outside a modest Israeli house; the airport.

COSTUMES: 1960s wear for both American tourists and Israeli workers; shepherd clothes; policeman and guard uniforms; Independence Day wear; rabbi's habits; a wedding dress; sunsuits.

IMPORTANT PROPS: Shepherds' staffs; pickaxes and digging equipment; banners and lights for the Independence Day ceremony; many tables and chairs; chuppa and wrapped glass for the wedding.

PROVIDED INSTRUMENTATION: Two violins, viola, cello, bass, five reeds, bassoon, two horns, three trumpets, two trombones, harp, percussion, piano-conductor.

ADVERTISING AND MARKETING: Get all the milk and honey companies in your area to advertise in the program. Try to reach the agency that handles Bit-o'-Honey candy, too.

SUGGESTIONS: The show opens with a boy tending a flock of sheep; mime them, as well as the cows and goats that made appearances in the original production.

RESOURCES: The original cast album on LP.

RIGHTS: Tams-Witmark.

RAGS

CREATORS: Book by Joseph (*Fiddler on the Roof*) Styne, music by Charles (*Annie*) Strouse, lyrics by Stephen (*Godspell*) Schwartz.

BACKGROUND: The 1986 musical opened to mixed reviews and threw in the towel after 5 performances, but was fondly remembered and received five Tony nominations.

STORY: Five Jewish immigrants come to America in 1910: Rebecca; her young son, David (who will try to find his father Nathan, who moved to America some time ago); the orthodox Avram; Bella, his young adult daughter whom he rules with an iron hand; and Ben, an enterprising young man who falls in love with Bella while on the boat. Once they arrive, Rebecca and David are crestfallen to see that Nathan has not met them; Avram and Bella take pity, and offer to put them up for a while. Rebecca tries to find her husband when she isn't working at a sweatshop; David works a pushcart with Avram, who insists that Bella stay at home and sew. Rebecca's co-worker Saul tries to unionize the shop, which scares Rebecca—though not as much as the idea of dating him (they see a Yiddish version of *Hamlet* on their first date) and beginning to fall in love with him. Ben, meanwhile, has found work in a cigar factory and brings Bella a new invention—a gramophone. While that cheers the homebound miss, she does lash out at her father because America isn't delivering what they assumed it would; he then allows her to work in the sweatshop with Rebecca. The scene shifts to a pub, where Nathan—who has Americanized his name to Nat and has been working his way in the corrupt Democratic machine—hears that Rebecca and David are in America, and he goes to find them, just as Rebecca is breaking off with Saul, whose bellicose style, she thinks, has been badly affecting David. But she doesn't like what's happened to Nathan, either. (Things are going better romantically for Avram, who's met a widow with a nice apartment, and Bella, whose Ben is doing very well selling grampophones.) But then comes the Triangle Shirtwaist fire, and Bella is killed. This convinces a devastated Rebecca that Saul was right, and though Nathan insists that she not shake the status quo, she decides to join Saul to change conditions and make America closer to the dream she had of it when she arrived.

ASSETS: A soaring score and a sincere book that serves to remind most of us of how courageous our ancestors were to come to these shores—and how much we owe them.

LIABILITIES: Too many characters to keep track of—though this will give your cast some ample opportunities to show their talents.

WHO YOU'LL NEED: *Lead Singing Role:* A charming and brave mother. *Supporting Singing Roles:* Her little boy; her wise-to-the-world husband; her would-be lover; an Old World father who is reluctant to change; his embittered young daughter; her very ardent entrepreneurial suitor; a portly widow who's tired of the single life; Sophie Tucker; three Tammany politicians. *Other Roles:* A female sweatshop worker; three fat-cat politicians; a young man and his mother; a chorus of cynical Americans, new and homesick immigrants, guards, klezmer musicians, sweatshop workers, Yiddish theater performers, shoppers, and strikers. *Maximum, 43; minimum 20.*

DESIGNATED DANCES: Much musical staging on three numbers; a hora for a Yiddish theater performance; a dance for Nathan in a pub; a dance for most of the supporting company at the politicians' ball; a ballet that shows the uptown monied people enjoying themselves.

SUGGESTED SETS: Ellis Island; a tenement apartment; a sweatshop; a Yiddish theater; a local Irish pub.

COSTUMES: Not quite rags, but old-fashioned peasant clothes (you can probably get everything you need from a thrift shop), some upper-class wear as well for the politicians, the ballet, and the political ball. And you'll need some fanciful costumes for the Yiddish *Hamlet*.

IMPORTANT PROPS: A larger-than-life Statue of Liberty; a gramophone; sewing machines and piecework; pushcarts; Ellis Island benches and gates.

PROVIDED INSTRUMENTATION: Two keyboards, four reeds, trumpet, horn, trombone, two violins, viola, guitar, bass, percussion, drums, piano-conductor, and—for onstage musicians—violin, clarinet, trumpet, trombone, tuba.

RESOURCES: Much of the original cast recorded an album after the show closed; available on CD and cassette.

RIGHTS: Rodgers and Hammerstein.

THE ZULU AND THE ZAYDA

CREATORS: Book by Howard daSilva (who portrayed Jud in *Oklahoma!* and Ben Franklin in *1776*) and Felix Leon, music and lyrics by Harold (*Pins and Needles*) Rome.

BACKGROUND: The 1965 production had to delay its November 9 premiere by one day because New York City experienced a blackout. Despite less-than-respectful reviews, the show ran 179 performances; it received no Tony nominations, but then had a national and summer stock tour.

STORY: Harry Grossman, a hardware store owner in Johannesburg, has brought his elderly father to live with him. Because "the Zayda" (grandfather) often gets lost and has a language-barrier problem, Harry hires Paulus, a Zulu, the cousin of his house servant Johannes, as the Zayda's full-time attendant. But the two become friends, and the Zayda thinks nothing of taking the Zulu into parts of town that, due to apartheid, are white-only areas, causing a bit of trouble when a policeman spots them. When the Zulu takes the Zayda to his friends' house, it leads to their all being arrested. Harry bails out the Zayda, but the old man insists on the others being released, and pays their bail. Harry decides that the two are getting too close, so he fires Paulus. The furious Zayda goes looking for him, collapses en route, and winds up in the hospital. Harry knows that only the Zulu can have a positive effect on his father, and he reunites the two friends.

ASSETS: An appealing score, and a book that details a genuine friendship and convincingly shows a man who is color-blind in the best sense of the word. If you have a small Yiddish man and a strong black man in your company, here's a good place to showcase them.

LIABILITIES: There is a good deal of time spent in the Zulu's trying to make his language and meaning known to the Zayda—and vice versa—which can become wearing. The theme of brotherhood can become a bit heavy-handed; ditto the melodramatic attacks.

WHO YOU'LL NEED: *Lead Singing Roles:* a wry and incorrigible Yiddish grandfather; a super-efficient Zulu house servant; a Zulu caregiver. *Supporting Singing Roles:* The Zulu's best friend; his brother and his wife. *Other Roles:* A harried hardware store owner; his well-meaning wife and two flip teenage sons; his business partner; a black couple; a police captain; his assistant; a policeman; a cemetery visitor. *Maximum, 22; minimum, 14.*

DESIGNATED DANCES: A spirited dance for the Zulu and the Zayda; a Zulu dance for the Zulu, Zayda, and his friends.

SUGGESTED SETS: A park; a porch; a hardware store; a dining room; a hill; a meadow; a jail; a cemetery; an alley; inside and outside a hospital.

COSTUMES: Contemporary wear for the whites; native garb for the blacks, as well as a house servant's white suit. An important plot point also involves the Zulu's wearing shoes made from automobile tires.

IMPORTANT PROPS: An African spear; a wheelchair; hedge clippers; police nightsticks; silver fruit bowls that can be worn as hats.

PROVIDED INSTRUMENTATION: Piano-conductor.

ADVERTISING AND MARKETING: "A Zulu. A Zayda. A musical."

SUGGESTIONS: The script includes a glossary of both Yiddish and Zulu terms, which isn't necessary to the enjoyment of the show but is fun to read during intermission; include it in your program.

RESOURCES: The original cast album on LP; the Dan Jacobson short story *The Zulu and the Zeide*, on which the musical is faithfully based.

RIGHTS: Dramatists Play Service.

ALSO WORTH A LOOK

Yours, Anne

This is a musical version of *The Diary of Anne Frank*. The inherent problem with musicalizing this material is that when the family members sing, they somehow appear *content* with the life they've been handed. But if you're in a community that reveres the property, or one in which it figures prominently in the school curriculum, give it a read. Rights: Rodgers and Hammerstein.

Musicals with More Than One Starring Role

Who's the best performer in your company? Can't make a decision because you've got two good leading men, or two good leading ladies? Maybe you've tried double casting before, with one star performing on Thursday night and Saturday matinee, while the other does the Friday night and Sunday matinee—and you've found it's twice the work, and you and your audiences wind up preferring one to the other, anyway.

Make it easy on yourself this time, and choose a show with two fat parts for your two stars.

THE APPLE TREE

CREATORS: Book, music, and lyrics by Jerry Bock and Sheldon Harnick (who collaborated on *Fiddler on the Roof*); additional book by Jerome *(Baker Street)* Coopersmith.

BACKGROUND: Not long before the much-anticipated 1967 Broadway production of these three one-act musicals, the songwriters decided to drop their collaborator, rewrite the first act themselves, and write two completely new acts. With a shaky start like this, the show is to be commended for its six Tony nominations, a win for Barbara Harris as Best Actress, and its 463-performance run.

STORY: Three different shows presented chronologically; the first is a whimsical look at the life of Adam and Eve, showing that their struggles regarding house, home, and children aren't much different from what today's husbands and wives experience; the second is the famed "Lady or the Tiger" story about the princess who has the choice to send her beloved either to marriage with another or to death (and lets us guess which she chooses); the third is a Cinderella spoof in which a pitiful chimneysweep asks her fairy godmother not for a handsome prince, but for a movie career. She gets it *and* a handsome prince, who later turns out to be a meek man who had the same fairy godmother.

ASSETS: A fine score, some very funny situations; the "Adam and Eve" segment with a very strong book, is especially tender and well-written. (If you don't know Adam's song "It's a Fish," you have a treat in store.) If you have versatile performers, prepare to show them now, for an audience enjoys seeing performers play three different roles in one evening.

LIABILITIES: Because the first sequence is the strongest, there seems to be a law-of-diminishing-returns feeling about this show. Some theatergoers have trouble responding to one-acters, and prefer to follow a character from overture to final curtain.

WHO YOU'LL NEED: *Lead Singing Roles:* A female who can play Eve, a sensuous barbarian princess, a charwoman, and a beautiful, glamorous, radiant, ravishing movie star (Barbara Harris); a male who can play Adam, a Dark Ages prince, a nerd, and a biker-rock star (Alan Alda). *Supporting Singing Role:* A male who can play the Devil, a balladeer, and a narrator (Larry Blyden). *Other Roles:* A chorus to play a variety of small roles in the last two acts. *Maximum,* 25, *minimum,* 6.

DESIGNATED DANCES: Not much. In the first, not a step. In the second, one big production number. In the third, a long musical scene, some musical staging for subway passengers, and a few swinging steps in another number.

SUGGESTED SETS: One for each act. The first is a Garden of Eden, but that doesn't necessarily mean that your set designer must outdo himself or herself (in fact, after designer Tony Walton had whipped up an extraordinary set for the original production, it was discarded because the actors seemed lost in it)—a climbable tree and a flowerbed will do, with a distant apple tree in the background; for the second, anything suggesting a barbaric kingdom—as long as you create an arena with bleachers and two large doors; for the third, a rooftop with a chimney, a studio apartment, a fancier apartment, a swank nightclub, and the stage of the Dorothy Chandler Pavilion.

COSTUMES: For the first act, workshirts, jeans, simple dress, a rough wool sweater, a hat crudely made from flowers, a tuxedo; for the second, medieval-styled wear (many capes and some jewelry), primitive battle wear, and a bridal outfit; for the third, some ragged clothes, then some glamorous ones—especially a gold lamé gown with enormous breasts, Brando leather jacket and pants, and a conservative man's suit.

IMPORTANT PROPS: For the first, planks of wood (both natural and red-stained), a wooden bowl, a watering can, a grass curtain, shells, plow, and rake; for the second, thrones, whips, a guitar, and a very large stuffed tiger; for the third, a chimney brush, a piggy bank, flash cameras, movie dolly, automobile mock-up, wide-screen TV, and an Oscar.

SPECIAL EFFECTS: The scene in which the chimney sweep changes to a movie star must be accomplished quickly. The original production gave Barbara Harris much more time by having *another* performer come out in an identical costume while Harris was getting into her gold lamé gown, The audience didn't notice, because by then they'd come to accept that woman in the rags was Harris. Do the same; it's easier.

PROVIDED INSTRUMENTATION: Five reeds, three trumpets, three trombones, horn, two percussion, guitar, harp, violin, viola, cello, bass, piano-conductor.

ADVERTISING AND MARKETING: Don't forget that with three acts, you have two intermissions and twice as many opportunities to sell drinks (apple cider?) and souvenirs.

SUGGESTIONS: Consider casting nine performers instead of three, giving each of them a lead—and giving you better control of the production and easier rehearsal schedules.

Incidentally, the show tried a billing rotation—the first month had Harris-Alda-Blyden over the title; the second month, Adla-Blyden-Harris; the third month Blyden-Harris-Alda, etc. You might try this for successive nights of your production.

RESOURCES: The original cast album on CD, cassette, and LP; the three stories on which the stories are fairly faithfully based: Mark Twain's "The Diary of Adam and Eve," Frank R. Stockton's "The Lady or the Tiger," and Jules Feiffer's "*Passionella.*"

RIGHTS: Music Theatre International.

CHICAGO

CREATORS: Music by John Kander, lyrics by Fred Ebb (the *Cabaret* team); book by Ebb and Bob Fosse (director-choreographer of *Sweet Charity*).

BACKGROUND: The 1975 production star Gwen Verdon fell ill soon after opening, so Fosse called Liza Minnelli, whom he'd directed in the *Cabaret* movie and the *Liza with a* Z TV special; she came in, made audience interest even greater, and propelled the show to an 898-performance run. It won none of its eleven Tony nominations (but it was the year of *A Chorus Line*).

STORY: Chicago in the late 1920's. When Roxie Hart is left by her lover, she shoots him, encouraging her weak husband to take the blame. He won't, so she goes to jail, and pretends to be pregnant to win sympathy. This doesn't sit well with Velma, a murderer who has become yesterday's news. But thanks to a smart lawyer, both get off and—only in America!—go on a vaudeville tour.

ASSETS: Murder and an ensuing trial are *not* the stuff of which a commercial musical hit is usually made—but Fosse was very smart in shaping the show as "a musical vaudeville"—using the musical styles of Eddie Cantor, Ted Lewis, Helen Morgan, and Sophie Tucker to "razzle-dazzle" us. Had it been done as a realistic musical, we would have had to deal with the realities of Roxie in a way that the surrealistic style avoids.

LIABILITIES: The show is often cold, cynical, and at times crude.

RECOGNIZABLE SONGS: "All That Jazz."

WHO YOU'LL NEED: *Lead Singing Roles:* A foxy stagestruck adulterer-murderer (Gwen Verdon; a Lesley Ann Warren type); the murderer she supplants in the headlines (Chita Rivera); their shyster lawyer (Jerry Orbach). *Supporting Singing Roles:* A meek cuckolded husband; six women murderer prisoners (one is Hungarian); a prison matron; a coluratura (ideally a male) reporter. *Other Roles:* A bailiff; a prosecutor; a sergeant; a reporter; a court clerk; a gigolo; an emcee (and/or bandleader who can handle dialogue); one actor who can use facial putty to create different faces to represent the twelve jurors. *Maximum, 47; minimum, 20.*

DESIGNATED DANCES: Heavy. Six production numbers, as well as nightclub choreogaphy; a tap dance for four men; a big solo number with chair; a solo Charleston; a brief apache dance; a fan dance around the leading man; a "hot" dance for the two female stars.

SUGGESTED SETS: The original production used an enormous center drum on which the orchestra sat, but there are many other options in defining a bedroom, cells and a visitor's area of a jail, a lawyer's office, and a courtroom with jury box.

COSTUMES: Roaring Twenties clothes, including two ladies matching raincoats and hats; a handsome man's suit; a fur stole; a ridiculously prim lace dress; a teddy; a kimono; silver shoes with rhinestone buckles; adult-sized diapers; a clown's frock coat; flap shoes; a battered top hat and oversized celluloid collar; a breakaway dress; a T-shirt and boxer shorts; a straitjacket.

IMPORTANT PROPS: Jail-bar units for the murderers to hold in front of them to represent incarceration; wheelchair; a board picturing a man and woman in bed with cutouts for actors' heads; flashbulb cameras; small megaphones; top hats and canes; card table and chairs; sword and scales of justice; guns; large burlesque-styled feather-fans; a bed; an onstage upright piano; flashlights; a newspaper that's headlined "Roxie Rocks Chicago"; jury box, old-fashioned cathedral radio.

PROVIDED INSTRUMENTATION: Five reeds, three trumpets, three trombones, horn, two percussion, guitar, harp, violin, viola, cello, bass, piano-conductor.

ADVERTISING AND MARKETING: "Take a trip to *Chicago* for [your ticket price], as we present the much-acclaimed musical, beginning on . . ."

SUGGESTIONS: Never play it straight, but always with a wink.

RESOURCES: The original cast album on CD, cassette, and LP; the play *Chicago* by Maurine Watkins, and the movie *Roxie Hart*, on which the musical is loosely based.

RIGHTS: Samuel French.

THE GRASS HARP

CREATORS: Book and lyrics by Kenward Elsmlie, music by Claibe Richardson (who later collaborated on *Lola*).

BACKGROUND: This was one of the first musicals to have a tryout at a regional theater, opening in 1966 at Trinity Square Repertory Theater, in Providence. It finally opened on Broadway in 1971, budgeted at only $160,000 in era when five times that was the norm, and, with only slightly affirmative reviews, didn't have the money to keep it running past 5 performances.

STORY: The past in the rural South. Dolly, who keeps house for her sister, Verena, has a "gypsy dropsy cure" that is developing into a modest mail-order business. When Verena's late-in-life beau Dr. Ritz finds out about it, he wants to turn it into something bigger. Dolly doesn't trust him, and when Verena humiliates her, she heads out of the house with their maid Catherine and teenage nephew Collin—but with no place to go, they wind up at a treehouse where they ensconce themselves. Soon a retired judge, Collin's girlfriend Maude, and a group of faith healers—"Babylove and Her Miracle Show"—come by and join them in the tree. When Verena discovers them, she has the sheriff come to get Dolly out of the tree and arrest the others. But Dolly won't allow it, and insists that she go to jail, too. Ritz, realizing that Dolly won't ever give him the recipe for the cure, bolts, and Verena, realizing she's been duped and how much her sister means to her, goes to the treehouse and asks forgiveness, and the two are reconciled.

ASSETS: A soaring score, one of the most unappreciated in Broadway history, and a very touching book that underlines that a sister can be a greater source of love than a man.

LIABILITIES: You'll have to build a convincing tree and an equally convincing treehouse in it—one that can withstand thirteen people on it. The character of Catherine could offend some theatergoers, for she's a black maid who denies her heritage and claims she's "an Indian"—itself no longer a politically correct term.

WHO YOU'LL NEED: *Lead Singing Role:* A demure housewife type who has a strong sense of worth; an experienced professional woman who's not very experienced in love.

SUPPORTING SINGING ROLES: Their fifteen-year-old nephew who's wondering about sex; a dazzling faith healer and her six grade-school-age children; an oversized black maid who insists she's Native American; a city-slicker conman; a retired judge who's ready to embrace life. *Other Roles:* A no-nonsense sheriff; a pretty teenage girl who's trying to behave. *Maximum, 20; minimum, 15.*

DESIGNATED DANCES: A solo turn for Dr. Ritz; a stirring march for Dolly, Catherine, and Collin; a faith-healing ceremony started by Babylove and her children, and joined by Dolly, Catherine, Collin, the judge, and Maude; some musical staging in three other songs.

SUGGESTED SETS: Inside and outside a nice Southern house; a treehouse; a jail.

COSTUMES: 1920s Southern dress; flowered dresses; traveling hats with veils; cameo lockets; underskirts; aprons; Western suits with string ties; for Verena, the best of small-town business suits; for Babylove and her children, satin cowboy shirts, suede cowhide skirts, jeans, and cowboy boots; for Catherine, a Native American outfit down to her moccasins; a sheriff's outfit.

IMPORTANT PROPS: A black tub with a funnel hooked onto it; a girlie magazine with a 1920s cover; patchwork cape and quilt; ingredients for the dropsy cure; a tea cart sporting an edible devil's food cake; a crate stating "Babylove's Miracle Show."

PROVIDED INSTRUMENTATION: Five reeds, three trumpets, three trombones, horn, two percussion, guitar, harp, violin, viola, cello, bass, piano-conductor.

ADVERTISING AND MARKETING: "Truman Capote goes musical—starting on . . ."

SUGGESTIONS: Licensers and authors stress that you're not allowed to change even one word in a script, but see if you can convince them to allow you to change one *letter*. When Verena sings "What Do I Do Now He's Gone?" she is referring to Dr. Ritz—but by the end of the song, she should sing "What do I do now *she's* gone?" referring to her sister.

RESOURCES: The original cast album on CD and LP; the Truman Capote novella on which the musical is loosely based.

RIGHTS: Samuel French.

MAME

CREATORS: Book by Jerome Lawrence and Robert E. Lee (who wrote the *Auntie Mame* play), music and lyrics by Jerry (*Hello, Dolly!*) Herman.

BACKGROUND: The 1966 production opened to strong reviews in Philadelphia, but just to be on the safe side, booked another engagement in Boston when a musical that was to star Pinky Lee suddenly closed during rehearsal. Even without the extra tune-up, the musical probably would have received its eight Tony nominations, three awards, and a 1,508-performance run.

STORY: Prohibition-era New York City. Patrick Dennis, recently orphaned in Des Moines, must come with his late father's secretary Agnes Gooch to live in New York with his Auntie Mame. The eccentric madcap Mame is happy to have him, and he's even happier, learning from her and her actress friend Vera Charles a lifestyle that he certainly never saw in Iowa. But co-trustee for Patrick is the stuffy Mr. Babcock, who is not pleased when he sees how well Patrick can make a martini. He insists on Patrick's attending a conservative school, but Mame enrolls him in a progressive one. Babcock discovers this and sends the boy to a boarding school—just as the Crash of '29 occurs, bankrupting Mame. She takes a job in one of Vera's operettas, but is fired for incompetence after the first performance. She finds employment as a manicurist, and her first customer is Beauregard Jackson Pickett Burnside. They talk quite a bit—but when Mame's boss sees what a butcher job she's done on Beau, she fires her. Beau tracks her down, though, and they are soon in love— even though Beau had been "engaged since grammar school" to Southern belle Sally Cato. He takes Mame to his plantation, where Sally maneuvers Mame into proclaiming she's a horsewoman. When it's time to prove it, Mame glues herself to the saddle, stays on, and, her ruse undetected, wins the hearts of everyone (but Sally) and marries Beau. For the next few years, with Patrick in school, Mame goes on many around-the-world trips with Beau; then on one he's killed in an accident. Mame comes home and turns her attention to Agnes, gussying her up—which eventually leads to her becoming pregnant. Patrick the collegian, meanwhile, has fallen for the *awfully* correct Gloria Upson, and he's now trying to be as respectable as she—and her parents, who offend Mame when they say that they might buy some real estate near their home so that Patrick and Gloria can live free from riffraff. Mame is disappointed in what Patrick has become, and when she has the Upsons over—after Agnes is seen in her "disgraceful" condition—Mame announces that she's buying the aforementioned property to start an unwed mothers' home. Eventually Patrick comes around, and marries a woman far more in tune with him. As the curtain falls, we see Mame ready to take their son on an adventure much like the ones his father used to have with his Auntie Mame.

ASSETS: A bouncy score and a terrific book that's as good as its source material, with meaty parts for many.

LIABILITIES: This is a very costume-heavy show. You'll also need to fly in a sturdy moon on which Mame can sit, hang, and cavort.

RECOGNIZABLE SONGS: "Mame," "We Need a Little Christmas," "If He Walked into My Life."

WHO YOU'LL NEED: *Lead Singing Role:* An eccentric aunt with the courage of her atypical convictions (a Rue McClanahan type). *Supporting Singing Roles:* Her very theatrical (if hammy) actress friend; her nephew, both as a mature ten-year-old and as a sensible man in his twenties; a frumpy comic secretary; a Southern gentleman (a Burt Reynolds type). *Other Roles:* A Japanese houseboy; a puritanical bank president and his almost as stuffy teenage son; a very progressive schoolteacher; a savvy publisher; a Greek Orthodox bishop; an art model; a dance teacher; an operetta's leading man; a stage manager; a chic Russian beauty parlor owner and her assistant; an upscale Connecticut father, mother, and daughter; a charming interior decorator; the adult Patrick's little son; a chorus to play both New York and Deep South party guests and operetta performers. *Maximum, 45; minimum, 25.*

DESIGNATED DANCES: A musical cocktail party; a big production number as Mame takes Patrick through Manhattan; an operetta parody; a spirited march; a cakewalk; a showstopper for Mame and Vera; a Charleston.

SUGGESTED SETS: A New York City street; an elegant Beekman Place penthouse (ideally with a spiral staircase); its bedroom and living room; the stage of the Shubert Theater in New Haven where an operetta (with a mountain and a moon) is playing; a Southern plantation; a prep school; an upper-class Connecticut home.

COSTUMES: Fashions from the Roaring Twenties through the postwar era. For Mame and Vera, always something flamboyant; for Agnes, always something frumpy; preppie clothes for both Patricks; riding clothes, long fancy dresses, and parasols for the Southerners; exotic wear and flapper dresses for Mame's party guests; costumes for the operetta (including a stylized lady astronomer's outfit); a houseboy's outfit; trendy 1940s barbecue wear; collegiate fashions.

IMPORTANT PROPS: A small grand piano; a bugle; a model airplane on a stick; a Picasso nude; a feminine Empress-sized bed and a mountain of pink pillows; many gift boxes; telescopes; a pair of boy's long pants.

PROVIDED INSTRUMENTATION: Two violins, viola, cello, bass, five reeds, three trumpets, three trombones, percussion, harp, guitar-banjo, piano-conductor.

ADVERTISING AND MARKETING: Print posters, placards, and bumper stickers that say "Remember the *Mame!*" followed by the information on where to see your production.

SUGGESTIONS: Be prepared to do more work than usual on this one.

RESOURCES: The original cast album on CD, cassette, and LP; the faithful 1974 movie version; the play and movie *Auntie Mame* on which the musical is faithfully based, available on videotape and laserdisc.

RIGHTS: Tams-Witmark.

OVER HERE

CREATORS: Book by Will ("Lemon Tree") Holt, music and lyrics by Richard M. Sherman and Robert B. Sherman (who wrote the score for the movie *Mary Poppins*).

BACKGROUND: The 1974 production about the 1940s starred the two surviving Andrews Sisters and was produced by the team that brought the 1950s to Broadway in *Grease*. But mediocre reviews, only one Tony out of five nominations—and the two sisters warring with each other—resulted in only 348 performances.

STORY: Paulette and Pauline, two World War II entertainers on the home front, want to be in show business, but they know it's an era in which only trios succeed. Wouldn't it be nice if they could find a voice who can blend in perfectly with theirs? They eventually do—thanks to Mitzi. What they don't know is that Mitzi is a Nazi spy who is sending signals through her electronic lipstick. Mitzi is unmasked, however, when she is discovered to know the second verse of "The Star Spangled Banner"—because "No *real* American knows the second verse of 'The Star Spangled Banner.'" Paulette and Pauline may never become big stars, but they are happy to entertain the soldiers going off to war as the show ends.

ASSETS: The songs written for the Andrews Sisters are as good as any of their hits, and the book is really deep in nostalgia, celebrating such 1940s icons as Sonja Henie, Esther Williams, and Betty Grable in that famous over-the-shoulder pin-up pose; it's also replete with many "Kilroy Is Here" lines that take an audience back.

LIABILITIES: The show seems to be a one-act musical that's been padded to make it last a full evening. As much fun as the second act "dreams from everyone's movie life" scene is, it does seem to be a time-killing device. "And," says John Pike of the Goodspeed Opera House in East Haddam, Connecticut, "this nostalgic montage involves many costume changes that are difficult to accomplish and execute."

WHO YOU'LL NEED: *Lead Singing Roles:* A realistic singer who knows she'll never make the big time; her starry-eyed sister who feels there's still a chance; a sweet young woman who's really a Nazi spy. *Supporting Singing Roles:* A bandleader; a sweet ingenue and her innocent soldier; a typical American father; an automotive executive; a young draftee; a black soldier. *Other Roles:* A railroad conductor; a typical American mother; a waitress; a city street kid. *Maximum, 42; minimum, 19.* (The script has been slightly rewritten from what played on Broadway, and eliminates two characters, Wilma and Misfit—the latter played by John Travolta—whom you'll find on the cast album.)

DESIGNATED DANCES: Four jitterbug numbers; a fox-trot; a polka; a daisy-chain dance; a solo dance for the porter; a solo for a private who'd like to be a drummer—and expresses his ambition through dance. There's also a scene that is for all intents and purposes choreographed: It involves how speedily and sneakily black market goods are bought and sold, and once it's stopped, it plays itself as if it's a movie in reverse.

SUGGESTED SETS: A train; its military coach; its civilian coach; the canteen that Paulette and Pauline establish in between; a curtained sleeper.

COSTUMES: 1940s ladies' wear (horizontal striped blouses, open skirts, knee-length skirts, seamed silk stockings held up by garters, saddle shoes) and men's wear (double-breasted suits, cardigan sweaters, zoot suits); soldiers' and general's uniforms; camouflage outfits; helmets and hats; train conductor's, waitress's and porter's uniforms; snow hat and scarf; boxing shorts; a prom gown; ladies' bathing suits and Miss America sashes; outfits that suggest Nelson Eddy, Jeannette MacDonald, Sonja Henie, Joe Louis, Esther Williams, and that Betty Grable white bathing suit.

IMPORTANT PROPS: A standing live microphone; a canoe; perfectly matched luggage; a lipstick and compact; barracks bags; rifles; a gigantic syringe; first aid bandages; small and large bouquets; a *very* long knitted scarf; period magazines; doughnuts; cigarette cartons; liquor bottles; chewing gum. On Broadway, Paulette and Pauline made their entrance in a jeep, and while it would be fun for an audience to see that, it is optional.

SPECIAL EFFECTS: Train whistle sounds.

PROVIDED INSTRUMENTATION: Five reeds, four trumpets, four trombones, horn, two percussion, guitar, harp, violin, viola, cello, bass, piano-conductor.

ADVERTISING AND MARKETING: Print street maps with detailed directions, stating "Here's how to get to *Over Here.*"

SUGGESTIONS: Cast two real sisters, and promote them.

RESOURCES: The original cast album on CD, cassette, and LP.

RIGHTS: Samuel French.

THE RINK

CREATORS: Book by Terrence McNally, music by John Kander, lyrics by Fred Ebb (who collaborated on *Kiss of the Spider Woman*).

BACKGROUND: The 1984 production linked Broadway legend Chita Rivera with two-time Tony winner Liza Minnelli, old-pro songwriters, and one of America's better playwrights—so expectations were high. When they weren't realized, the show seemed less good than it really was, and 204 performances later (not long after Minnelli left the cast), it closed—though it did receive five Tony nominations and won a Best Actress award for Rivera.

STORY: Late 1970s at a dilapidated seaside resort. Angel Antonelli, who's lived the hippie life for the past fifteen years, decides to come home to the roller rink her mother Anna owns—only to find that her mother has sold it to developers and plans to use some of the proceeds to visit Italy. Angel's upset, because for her the rink represented happiness in a time when her father lived with them. That brings up the sorest spot between mother and daughter: When Angel's father left, Anna had told her he had died, and when Angel learned the truth, she left home. Eventually, though, Angel agrees with her mother that it is time to sell the rink—the area has become depressed and Anna was recently mugged. There is a reconciliation, especially after Angel gives birth to her own young daughter, whom she names after Anna.

ASSETS: A strong score, and an opportunity for a real mother and daughter in your company to play the parts.

LIABILITIES: While every musical must have conflict, the two leads seem to have more than their share; all their arguing can become wearing. Many communities won't enjoy—at all—the scene in which Angel offers her mother some marijuana, and Anna takes it and enjoys it. And will you be able to find a chorus that can roller-skate—or will there be time for them to learn?

WHO YOU'LL NEED: *Lead Singing Roles:* A late-middle-aged traditional Italian mother (Chita Rivera) and her grown daughter who's been incorrigible and counter-cultural (Liza Minnelli). *Supporting Singing Roles:* A chorus of six wreckers (men in the original production, but they really needn't be) to play a variety of roles, from men and women, to suitors and punks, to priests and nuns. *Other Role:* A grade-school girl. *Maximum, 33; minimum, 9.*

DESIGNATED DANCES: In addition to that roller-skating sequence for your chorus, there's a number in which Anna teaches Angel how to dance, and one in which Angel's father celebrates with his friends after a night out on the town.

SUGGESTED SETS: Just one—the rink itself. But it is wrecked at the end, so you must make provisions for that.

COSTUMES: 1970s contemporary wear for both Anna (unglamorous dresses) and Angel (inexpensively trendy wear); wreckers' uniforms for the chorus.

IMPORTANT PROPS: A suitcase and knapsack; blue crystal goblets; a mirror ball.

PROVIDED INSTRUMENTATION: Five reeds, three trumpets, three trombones, horn, two percussion, guitar, harp, violin, viola, cello, bass, piano-conductor.

ADVERTISING AND MARKETING: Not only should you seek program ads from your local ice-skating and roller-skating rinks, but you should arrange for your chorus to perform the title number on roller skates (or ice skates, if they can) at the rink.

SUGGESTIONS: If the marijuana sequence is too much for your community the same effect can be accomplished with liquor, if it's established in advance that Anna is a teetotaler.

RESOURCES: The original cast album on CD, cassette, and LP.

RIGHTS: Music Theatre International.

WONDERFUL TOWN

CREATORS: Book by Joseph Fields and Jerome Chodorov (who wrote the play *My Sister Eileen*, on which this musical is based), music by Leonard Bernstein, lyrics by Betty Comden and Adolph Green (who wrote *On the Town*).

BACKGROUND: The 1953 production was about to go into rehearsal with music by Leroy Anderson and lyrics by Arnold Horwitt, but too many people didn't like the score, and Bernstein, Comden, and Green were quickly dispatched to provide a new score in four weeks. They apparently rose to the occasion, given that the musical opened to unanimous raves, won five Tony awards—including Best Musical—and ran 559 performances.

STORY: 1930s, New York. Ruth and Eileen move to Greenwich Village from Columbus, Ohio. Ruth, common sense and plain, plans to be a writer, while Eileen, fetching and charming, wants to be an actress. They rent a horrid basement apartment for thirty days and meet such colorful characters as Wreck, who's married to Helen—but with her mother coming to town, could he room with them for the duration? Worse, they're getting nowhere in their careers, though Eileen has her share of admirers. But so does Ruth—including Bob, an editor, whom Eileen invites to dinner. It's a disaster, as the girls are mistaken for the streetwalker who used to inhabit the space, causing Helen's mother to boil with umbrage. But Ruth is more disturbed to hear that Bob doesn't like her work—though she feels better when she gets a newspaper assignment to interview Brazilian naval cadets. They like her so much that they follow her home, and when Helen's mother sees all these men being entertained by Ruth and Eileen, she calls the cops and the girls are arrested. But the police officers like Eileen and let both girls go. Ruth is now relegated to wearing an electronic sandwich sign advertising the Vortex nightclub, but Bob soon shows up—with Eileen's help—to offer his support, encouragement, and love, as Eileen happily looks on.

ASSETS: It's nice to see Eileen, the beauty, think highly of her sister and take a sincere interest in her sister's welfare. The score is top-notch, too.

LIABILITIES: Musical theater has changed a good deal since this show was written, and it's evident in the book—and not just because Ruth chides herself for showing men she's bright ("We might have written it a little differently today," says Comden, "our consciousnesses having risen"). Also, there's no real second act, just one scene after another that doesn't particularly further the plot. The scene change from the basement to other locales won't be easy to accomplish.

RECOGNIZABLE SONGS: "Ohio."

WHO YOU'LL NEED: *Lead Singing Roles:* A no-nonsense and not-afraid-to-be-herself aspiring writer (a Candice Bergen type); her demure and very attractive younger sister. *Supporting Singing Roles:* A Greenwich Village tour guide; a disillusioned editor; a dumb football player; his adoring wife; her stern mother; an Italian chef; a waiter; a nightclub owner; a dining counter manager; a crude newspaperman. *Other Roles:* A blustery landlord who also paints; an endearing streetwalker; a zoot-suited character; a young thief; a chorus of gaping tourists, editors, party guests, and policemen, a dog. *Maximum, 47; minimum, 22.*

DESIGNATED DANCES: Much musical staging in the opening number; a dance pantomime that shows Ruth and Eileen looking for work; a solo pantomime for Ruth; a football dance for Wreck and his admirers; a conga for Ruth and the naval cadets; an Irish jig for Eileen and the policemen; a jazz dance for Ruth and some Villagers; a nightclub number for Ruth and Eileen.

SUGGESTED SETS: Christopher Street in Greenwich Village; a basement studio apartment with a barred window at its top; its outside not-at-all- glamorous garden with a moldy tree; the Brooklyn Navy Yard; the local jail; inside and outside a Village nightclub.

COSTUMES: 1930s fashions; colorful Greenwich Village wear for its denizens, more subdued wear for the tourists, editors, and white-collar workers; uniforms for Brazilian naval cadets, and policemen, and a guide, outfits for the girls' nightclub appearance; a zoot suit.

IMPORTANT PROPS: Two day beds; suitcases; empty milk bottles and sample cereal boxes; an ironing board; electronic sandwich signs; riotously painted canvases on easels.

SPECIAL EFFECTS: The sound of a subterranean explosion.

PROVIDED INSTRUMENTATION: Five reeds, three trumpets, three trombones, horn, two percussion, guitar, harp, violin, viola, cello, bass, piano-conductor.

ADVERTISING AND MARKETING: "A musical about a *Wonderful Town* is coming to our Wonderful Town, beginning on . . ."

SUGGESTIONS: Resist the temptation to update.

RESOURCES: The original cast album on CD, cassette, and LP; the play and movie *My Sister Eileen*, on which the musical is loosely based.

RIGHTS: Tams-Witmark.

Also See: *Anyone Can Whistle; Applause; The Boy Friend; Brigadoon; Cabaret; Chess; City of Angels; Dames at Sea; First Impressions; Follies; Gentlemen Prefer Blondes; Grand Hotel; How Now, Dow Jones; Is There Life After High School?; Jacques Brel Is Alive and Well and Living in Paris; Merrily We Roll Along; No, No, Nanette; Nunsense; She Loves Me; Sugar; Two Gentlemen of Verona.*

Musicals Simply Out for Fun

Here we go, again quoting from that Broadway musical called A *Broadway Musical*, which had an I-hate-musicals young playwright sing, "It doesn't have one redeeming feature—a Broadway musical."

But theatergoers who *do* like musicals can have a good time at shows that aren't heavy on redeeming features, that aren't masterpieces, but do have some tuneful numbers and funny characters, and offer up a good time.

HAPPY HUNTING

CREATORS: Book by Howard Lindsay and Russel Crouse (who later collaborated on *The Sound of Music*), music by Harold Karr, lyrics by Matt Dubey.

BACKGROUND: Ethel Merman gave a chance to two songwriting newcomers (the composer was a dentist), and starred in the 1956 production that turned out to be her least acclaimed show. Nevertheless, it did receive four Tony nominations, and the star's drawing power kept it playing for 408 performances.

STORY: Liz Livingstone is a diamond-in-the-rough rich widow who goes to Monaco in 1956 in hopes of being invited to Grace Kelly and Prince Rainier's wedding—but finds she isn't. Wanting an entree into society for her and daughter Beth, she tries to arrange a marriage between Beth and an impoverished duke who believes he has claim to the Spanish throne—and can use her money. Just as the story reaches reporters that he'll marry the daughter— who has already fallen in love with a lawyer—the duke indicates he loves Liz. She becomes convinced that he isn't just marrying her for her money once he gives up his claim to the Spanish throne for her.

ASSETS: The show whisks us back to a simpler, more innocent, pre–rock-'n'-roll era for those audiences who enjoy such fare. (Merman's character is even said to be shooting dice with Aristotle Onassis.) The score, albeit undistinguished, is fun.

LIABILITIES: There's a blinding predictability that the two mismatched couples will of course wind up with the right people, and the script offers no suspense to suggest they won't. And as Walter Kerr said in his review, "What kind of Merman show is a show that never gives Merman the chance to stop it—not once?"

RECOGNIZABLE SONGS: "(We Belong to a) Mutual Admiration Society."

WHO YOU'LL NEED: *Lead Singing Roles*: A nouveau riche would-be socialite (Merman); the duke of Granada. *Supporting Singing Roles*: an attractive twenty-ish daughter; an equally attractive lawyer. *Other Roles*: An old friend; a Philadelphia grande dame; a lord chamberlain; Main Line ladies; a French police sergeant and beat cop; a hotel manager; a horse groom; a chorus of tourists, reporters, photographers, celebrities, schoolchildren, barmen, and waiters. An onstage ship combo is optional. *Maximum, 45; minimum, 23.*

DESIGNATED DANCES: Musical staging for the opening; an on-ship number; a new-fangled tango for the entire company; the title song production number; a short dance between the two young lovers.

SUGGESTED SETS: Outside Monaco's palace; a posh hotel suite; its terrace and veranda; a quay (with ocean liner backdrop); a ship's deck (with railing) and its bar; a Philadelphia estate; its boudoir, stables, and garden; a hunt club; another part of the forest.

COSTUMES: 1950s street clothes, formalwear, and shipwear; handsome lady's suit and face-obscuring hat; a woman's silk pajamas, jacket, negligee, and bikini; a prince's formal uniform with gold trim, and an auto racing outfit; hunt club finery; Spanish ball costumes; jewel-studded necklaces, brooches, and bracelets.

IMPORTANT PROPS: Cafe table, chair, tablecloth skirt, and china; chaise longue; cameras; a beach ball; an attache case; riding crops that "become" umbrellas; saddles. If you care to include a live poodle and a horse (one who's been trained to answer yes and no questions), so much the better.

SPECIAL EFFECTS: A tape recording of your star's "inner thoughts" played over your sound system; sounds of hounds barking as well as horses galloping and neighing. Liz must appear to have been thrown from a horse.

PROVIDED INSTRUMENTATION: Five reeds, three trumpets, two trombones, horn, four violins, viola, cello, bass, guitar, percussion, piano-conductor.

ADVERTISING AND MARKETING: "Remember when Grace Kelly married Prince Rainier? We will, too—in *Happy Hunting*, on . . ."

SUGGESTIONS: You could dress your chorus as then-famous people (Groucho Marx, Marlene Dietrich, et al.) who came to Grace Kelly's wedding.

RESOURCES: The original cast album on LP.

RIGHTS: Music Theatre International.

HAPPY NEW YEAR

CREATORS: Book by Bert (*A Funny Thing Happened on the Way to the Forum*) Shevelove, music and lyrics by Cole Porter (using songs from other shows).

BACKGROUND: The 1980 production was much maligned by Broadway critics who (among other things) were bored that old Porter hits had been recycled into the show, causing it to close after 17 performances. Only a Best Costume Tony nomination followed.

STORY: 1930s, New York. A narrator tells us the story of Wall Street banker Edward Seton's family—Ned, his wastrel son; Linda, his irrepressible daughter; and Julia, the proper daughter—who on a trip met and quickly fell in love with Johnny Case. Johnny's worked his way up from poverty to become a corporation lawyer, but, he finally tells the family, he's really interested in retiring and just having fun for a while after he makes his pile. While Linda admires the man's lust for life and his irreverence for riches, Julia is terribly concerned that everyone will assume he's marrying her for her money. Still, Julia will marry him—but two weeks before the wedding, Johnny announces that he's closed a deal that will allow the early retirement. When he sees that Julia still won't come around, he offers a compromise: He'll work for three more years, and then try his experiment. It strikes Linda as reasonable, and Julia as horrid, and she breaks the engagement. Johnny starts on a world cruise—joined by Linda, with whom he should have been involved in the first place.

ASSETS: A score that will please much of your audience, who probably won't be bothered that the songs originally weren't from this piece. A strong book, thanks to the original play on which it is based—Philip Barry's *Holiday*.

LIABILITIES: You'll have to create a convincingly posh mansion and elegant costumes for your characters. And can your performers convincingly turn out upper-class elocution?

RECOGNIZABLE SONGS: "At Long Last Love," "Easy to Love," "You Do Something to Me," "Night and Day."

WHO YOU'LL NEED: *Lead Singing Roles:* A down-to-earth rich woman (Katharine Hepburn in the movie *Holiday*); an equally down-to-earth young man (Cary Grant in the movie). *Supporting Singing Roles:* A not at all down-to-earth rich young woman, her habitually drunk brother. *Other Roles:* Their stuffy father; four male and female friends of Linda's; a chorus to represent Stork Club patrons, the staff, and wedding guests. *Maximum, 25; minimum, 16.*

DESIGNATED DANCES: Not much: a soft-shoe and fox-trot for Johnny and Linda; a waltz for Johnny and Julia; a Charleston for Linda and her friends.

SUGGESTED SETS: A Fifth Avenue mansion's great hall with a Rembrandt displayed, though you could indicate this fourth-wall; a chandeliered dining room; a playroom.

COSTUMES: Pretty demanding 1930s high fashion (evening gowns, tuxes, even skating outfits and a bridal gown that are in good taste); maids' and butlers' uniforms; a crimson Harvard sweater.

IMPORTANT PROPS: Hip flask; many trays of drinks and/or bottles; big boxes of presents; feather dusters; fanciful toys, dolls, games, and musical instruments for the playroom.

PROVIDED INSTRUMENTATION: Two reeds, two trumpets, trombone, percussion, piano, piano-conductor.

ADVERTISING AND MARKETING: "We're celebrating New Year's a little early this year—on [dates]—when we produce *Happy New Year.*"

SUGGESTIONS: Sophistication is the key.

RESOURCES: No original cast album, but all the recycled songs in the score are available on various CDs, cassettes, and LPs; Philip Barry's play *Holiday*, from which the musical was faithfully adapted, on videotape and laserdisc.

RIGHTS: Samuel French.

MINNIE'S BOYS

CREATORS: Book by Arthur Marx (Groucho's son) and Robert Fisher (who collaborated on *The Impossible Years*), music by Larry Grossman, lyrics by Hal Hackady (who collaborated on *Snoopy!!!*).

BACKGROUND: Shelley Winters was cast as Minnie in the 1970 Broadway production, wasn't good, and, during previews, came an eyelash away from being replaced by Totie Fields. There's a good chance that if *your* eventual leading lady had played the part on Broadway, it would have run longer than its 76 performances. No Tony nominations.

STORY: The show follows the Marx Brothers from their Lower East Side boyhood (after the turn of the century) to the point where they're just about to make it big in show business (the early 1920s). Minnie Marx is having trouble with her five adolescent sons—Julius, Leonard, Adolph, Herbie, and Milton—who are always getting into mischief and seem to be going nowhere. But the success of Minnie's brother (he's Al Shean, half of the hit vaudevillian team Gallagher and Shean) convinces her that if he can make it in show business, so can her boys. The four interested brothers do, both because of her insistence and despite her meddling.

ASSETS: Almost everyone enjoys the Marx Brothers—and will relish seeing four actors who can impersonate then in scenes reminscent of their movies (Julius does a number with a Margaret Dumont prototype) and from their real life (such as the time they broke into producer Irving Thalberg's office and roasted hot dogs in his fireplace). The most amusing sequence, however, is an original, occurring when the boys—billed as the Four Nightingales—are just about to go onstage and perform, when Leonard (Chico) is lured into a card game. Julius (Groucho) then must run from one end of the line to the other to represent two Nightingales, all the while hoping that no one will notice.

LIABILITIES: Very little happens in the second act. It contains only five songs, which is often a clue that much of what's going to happen in the show has already occurred.

WHO YOU'LL NEED: *Lead Singing Roles:* Four boys who not only can successfully impersonate the Marx Brothers, but also can show us a youthful dimension we haven't seen from Julius, Leonard, Adolph, and Herbie; their middle-aged mother. *Supporting Singing Roles:* Their tailor father; a successful vaudevillian; a female impersonator; a boardinghouse owner (Margaret Dumont type). *Other Roles:* Their not-involved-in-show-biz brother Milton; an unsympathetic landlord; three acrobats; a small-time Louisiana vaudeville house owner; the premier New York vaudeville impresario; showgirls to represent the Taj Mahal, White House, and Eiffel Tower; a telegraph boy, a policeman; neighbors. *Maximum, 46; minimum, 25.*

DESIGNATED DANCES: There are four production numbers that could employ the simplest of choreography. Minnie is a character who purposely looks awkward when she dances, so a lead-footed leading lady wouldn't be a particular problem.

SUGGESTED SETS: A Lower East Side street; a tenement apartment; backstage and onstage at a theater; a hotel room; a boardinghouse; a posh office; a Long Island home.

COSTUMES: Early twentieth-century Lower East Side wear; a snazzy outfit and boater for Shean; identical vaudeville costumes for the boys; three acrobat costumes; an elaborate gown for the female impersonator; Taj Mahal, White House, and Eiffel Tower headdresses; a bunny suit for Minnie.

IMPORTANT PROPS: An ironing board; a vaudeville "hook"; a six-shooter; a school blackboard and dunce cap; a large harp.

PROVIDED INSTRUMENTATION: Two reeds, two trumpets, trombone, percussion, piano, piano-conductor.

ADVERTISING AND MARKETING: You might schedule your production for early May, as one enterprising company in Portland, Oregon, did—opening on May 1, trumpeting this as "a big day in Marxist history," and closing on May 11, which was Mother's Day—significant, they argued, in a show that celebrated a mother.

SUGGESTIONS: As a late-night "midnight show" or "nightcap," use your Marx Brothers in the one-act *A Night in the Ukraine*, a musical written in the late 1970s as "the Marx Brothers movie that never was made" and was very loosely based on Chekhov's *The Bear*. In this, Groucho plays Samovar the lawyer who tries to romance Mrs. Pavlenko (a Margaret Dumont type), all the while encountering obstacles from Carlo the footman (Chico) and his brother Gino (Harpo).

RESOURCES: The original cast album on CD, cassette, and LP; the book *The Marx Brothers at the Movies* by Paul D. Zimmerman and Burt Goldblatt gives a feel for the boys and the era.

RIGHTS: Tams-Witmark.

PETER PAN

CREATORS: Music by Moose *(Whoop-up)* Charlap and Jule *(Gypsy)* Styne, lyrics by Carolyn *(Little Me)* Leigh, Betty *(Do Re Mi)* Comden and Adolph *(Two on the Aisle)* Green (book never credited, but presumably adapted by Charlap and Leigh).

BACKGROUND: The 1954 production was greatly reworked out of town, and the effort paid off: the show won Tonys for stars Mary Martin and Cyril Ritchard (and for its stage technician), and ran 152 performances before being telecast and becoming a national phenomenon. The 1979 revival received two Tony nominations (for star Sandy Duncan and as Best Revival) and ran 578 performances. The 1991 revival also received two Tony nominations (for star Cathy Rigby and as Best Revival) and played a limited Christmas engagement.

STORY: Turn-of-the-century London. Peter Pan, returning to the London house where he inadvertently left his shadow, awakens young Wendy, Michael, and John—and takes them to Neverland, where they meet and defeat Captain Hook before returning home to grow up.

ASSETS: A fine score, a good book, and one of the best first acts in musical theater history. Great audience appeal for the entire family; many, many kids have become musical theater aficionados for life after seeing a production of this show.

LIABILITIES: How will you make your Peter Pan, Wendy, Michael, and John fly? "And," moans Kenneth Kantor, who played Captain Hook at the Alabama Shakespeare Festival, "it's very frustrating in the swordfight to stab at Peter and find that he isn't anywhere near where he's supposed to be. Don't get angry with Peter, but the person flying him."

RECOGNIZABLE SONGS: "I'm Flying," "I've Got to Crow," "Never-Land," "Wendy."

WHO YOU'LL NEED: *Lead Singing Roles:* A young man (usually played by a woman, because the flying harnesses better suit the female anatomy; a Janine Turner type) with a mischievous side and a vulnerable one as well; an outrageous pirate captain who doubles as an upper-class father. *Supporting Singing Roles:* An adolescent girl, her two younger brothers (all of whom have a good sense of wonder); an upper-class mother; a young Native American woman. *Other Roles:* A pirate first mate, a bosun; other pirates; other Native Americans; a bunch of young boys; Wendy as an adult; her young daughter; actors to play a lion, a bird, a kangaroo, an ostrich, a crocodile, and a sheep dog. *Maximum, 52; minimum, 20.*

DESIGNATED DANCES: A march, tango and a tarantella for Hook and the pirates; a solo waltz for Hook; a strut for Peter and the boys; a beguine for Peter and Hook; much musical staging throughout.

SUGGESTED SETS: The nursery of a Victorian house; a fanciful world called Neverland—its tree-laden woods, a trap door leading to a subterranean home; a pirate ship.

COSTUMES: Victoriana for the scenes in London; nightdress and Doctor Dentons for the kids; ragged clothes for Peter and the boys; Indian costumes; lion, bird, kangaroo, ostrich, crocodile, and sheep dog suits; an outrageously elaborate and foppish outfit for Hook that includes a hook that replaces one hand. Says Kantor, "Don't have your actor play in rehearsal clothes for too long; he's got to get used to that hook and that big costume—not to mention that wig."

IMPORTANT PROPS: Peter's "shadow" (made from sheer nylon); fairy dust; a harness that sports an arrow that shot Wendy; swords; tepee; makeshift house built on the spot; a large alarm clock; a peacepipe.

SPECIAL EFFECTS: Flying for Peter, Wendy, Michael, and John; a beam of light that represents Tinkerbell; tick-tocking for the crocodile; a vial of medicine that smokes.

PROVIDED INSTRUMENTATION: Flute, piccolo, oboe, bassoon, two clarinets, three trumpets, horn, trombone, drums, four violins, viola, cello, bass, harp, piano-conductor.

ADVERTISING AND MARKETING: "We're doing *Peter Pan;* don't run, don't walk to our box office—*fly.*"

SUGGESTIONS: There's no real reason why the actor playing Hook must double as Mr. Darling; after all, none of the kids ever says to Hook, "Gee, you look like Daddy." So if you want to give an extra actor something to do, you could cast him as the father and have a separate Hook.

RESOURCES: The original cast album on CD, cassette, and LP; the videotape of the 1960 TV production with Mary Martin; the original James M. Barrie play and novel on which the musical is fairly faithfully based.

RIGHTS: Samuel French.

SILK STOCKINGS

CREATORS: Book by George S. Kaufman *(who wrote the play* The Man Who Came to Dinner) and his wife, Leueen MacGrath (and Abe *[Guys and Dolls]* Burrows, who, according to legend, wrote most of it), music and lyrics by Cole *(Anything Goes)* Porter.

BACKGROUND: The 1955 production had a rough time out of town and added many cities to its tryout tour rather than risk the wrath of New York critics. When the show finally did come in, enough work had been done to make it respectable and, despite no Tony nominations, it ran for 478 performances.

STORY: 1950s Paris. Show business agent Steve Canfield is in Paris to get Soviet composer Peter Ilyitch Boroff to defect and write the music for his client Janice Dayton's next picture. Russia attempts to get Boroff back, first sending to Paris three Soviet agents, and then Ninotchka, a no-nonsense Communist who winds up falling in love with Canfield, Paris, capitalism, and freedom.

ASSETS: A good score and a fine role for an actress, as we watch her turn from an ice queen to a happier person.

LIABILITIES: The book goes to great lengths to mock the Soviet way of life in order to glorify our own, and now, after the fall of that empire, it might strike audiences that you're kicking a country when it's down and out. As for those who argue that it's sexist to watch a woman so easily fall to capitalism through a man, point out that the three male Russian agents come to the same conclusion.

RECOGNIZABLE SONGS: "All of You."

WHO YOU'LL NEED: *Lead Singing Roles:* A steely Russian woman capable of eventual warmth; a charming diplomat type. *Supporting Singing Roles:* A not-very-bright movie temptress; three Russian comrades. *Other Roles:* A very serious classical composer; a hotel doorman and manager; a flower girl; three commissars; a foreign prime minister and president; two guards; three reporters; a saleslady; a bookseller; a movie director and his assistant; a choreographer; three musicians; two Russian women; two Frenchmen. *Maximum, 55; minimum, 17.*

DESIGNATED DANCES: Three Russian-style dances; a solo dance for the movie temptress; three production numbers and one ballet for the entire company; a romantic ballroom turn by your lovers.

SUGGESTED SETS: A Parisian hotel lobby and two of its handsomely appointed suites; a dressmaker's salon; outside and inside a French movie studio; bookstalls representative of the Left Bank; the commissar's Soviet office; a Russian apartment.

COSTUMES: Your biggest obstacle will be the many French *haute couture* gowns, hats, and lingerie—but there are also some Louis XIV-styled costumes for a movie production number. Then there are utilitarian men's suits and a woman's dress, tuxedos, and trenchcoats.

IMPORTANT PROPS: A noisy typewriter; fresh flowers; a pair of silk stockings.

PROVIDED INSTRUMENTATION: Violins, viola, cello, bass, guitar, clarinet, bass clarinet, tenor sax, alto sax, bass sax, flute, piccolo, horn, trumpets, trombones, harp, percussion, piano-conductor.

ADVERTISING AND MARKETING: "Once it was difficult to get silk stockings. We've made it easier, for starting on . . ."

SUGGESTIONS: Keep it in its period, or it'll never work.

RESOURCES: The original cast album on CD, cassette, and LP; the faithful 1957 movie version on videotape and laserdisc, and *Ninotchka*, the movie on which the musical is fairly faithfully based.

RIGHTS: Tams-Witmark.

SUGAR

CREATORS: Book by Peter (*The Will Rogers Follies*) Stone, music by Jule Styne, lyrics by Bob Merrill (who collaborated on *Funny Girl*).

BACKGROUND: The 1972 production was roundly criticized for not being up to its source—the movie *Some Like It Hot*—and received only four Tony nominations, winning none. But audiences liked it enough to keep it running 505 performances.

STORY: Joe and Jerry, two musicians working Chicago in the 1920s, inadvertently witness the St. Valentine's Day Massacre and must get out of town. The only way is to take jobs as two female musicians in an all-girl band. Once they're dressed and have joined as Josephine and Daphne, both take a shine to Sugar Kane, the featured singer. When she tells them she wants to marry for money, Joe/Josephine takes on yet another new identity as a (male) millionaire. Speaking of millionaires—Jerry/Daphne's attracted one, named Osgood, and Jerry doesn't tell Osgood he's really a man until the final curtain, when he finds Osgood doesn't care. Joe eventually tells Sugar the truth, too, and she doesn't care, either.

ASSETS: A show that gives audiences the chance to enjoy the sight of men struggling to be convincing females. An especially good musical for high school groups.

LIABILITIES: While the score and book have their moments, no, the musical isn't as good as *Some Like It Hot*.

WHO YOU'LL NEED: *Lead Singing Roles:* Two funny and scared guys—one a comic, one a romantic lead—who can later adopt a high class accent—who dress as women. *Supporting Singing Roles:* A charming and gullible girl who, if not a Marilyn Monroe, is at least a very pretty blond (a Donna Dixon type); an elegant but dirty old man; the leader of an all-girl orchestra; a tap-dancing head gangster. *Other Roles:* Female orchestra members on piano, drums, bass, trumpets, trombones, and saxophones; the band's male manager; twelve gang members; sunbathers; a cab driver; a train conductor; an employment agency clerk; a bellboy. *Maximum, 47; Minimum, 20.*

DESIGNATED DANCES: Three production numbers for Joe and Jerry and most of the company; a strut for Joe and Jerry; a dance for Sugar and the male chorus. When the show opened on Broadway, the character of Spats, the gangster, tap-danced throughout, but if you don't have a tap dancer, you can easily eliminate this. (Indeed, this was an element that was added during the tryout.)

SUGGESTED SETS: An employment agency; a garage; a train; a Miami beach; onstage at some theaters.

COSTUMES: Roaring Twenties fashions; dark gangster suits; teddies and negligees; orchestra uniforms; Palm Beach-style fashions for Osgood.

IMPORTANT PROPS: A saxophone, a bass fiddle, and their cases; automobile shells; a moveable wicker chair.

PROVIDED INSTRUMENTATION: Four reeds, three trumpets, two trombones, horn, two violins, cello, bass, harp, guitar-banjo, two percussion, piano-conductor. But all the stage band music is cued into the pit orchestra parts.

ADVERTISING AND MARKETING: When the musical was produced in London in 1992, the title was changed to *Some Like It Hot*; if you think that that title might better sell your show, ask the licensers if you can change it, too.

SUGGESTIONS: Too often the drama club and the school orchestra are at odds, but here's a way to have some of them join forces—by having the girls in the orchestra play Sweet Sue and Her Society Syncopators' All-Girl Band.

RESOURCES: The original cast album on cassette and LP; *Some Like It Hot*, the movie on which the musical is based, on videotape.

RIGHTS: Tams-Witmark.

TOP BANANA

CREATORS: Book by Hy (*Cafe Crown*) Kraft, music and lyrics by Johnny (*St. Louis Woman*) Mercer.

BACKGROUND: The 1950 production received many raves, all accenting its Tony-winning star, Phil Silvers; when he left after 317 performances, business plummeted so much that the show closed after 33 more.

STORY: A 1950s New York television studio. Jerry Biffle is a burlesque veteran who's now starring in that brand new medium, television. His variety show, featuring Tommy, a crackerjack tap-dancer, but mostly old burlesque skits, is doing well, but the vice president of Blendo Soap, his sponsor, decides that the show needs a love interest—so Sally is hired. Though Jerry covets her for himself, she quickly falls in love with Cliff, the show's vocalist. A scheduling conflict causes a fight between them, which Sally's roommate Betty tries to ameliorate. Jerry again stakes his claim to Sally—after doing a "duet" with a "singing" dog on the show—but when he sees she's really in love with Cliff, he makes sure they wind up together. They're such a lovely couple that the sponsor suggests that they have their own TV show—which will replace Jerry's. But that doesn't come to pass, and Jerry remains top banana.

ASSETS: Time has endearingly metamorphosed the book and much of the score from satire to nostalgia, as it comments on the craziness of early live television. Audiences who saw those Milton Berle and Sid Caesar shows will be charmed, and lyrics about "Lana Turner turns green" will evoke the same feeling.

LIABILITIES: The ballads are quintessentially Old World, pre-Presley 1950s, aimed at what was then "The Hit Parade," and now look and sound rather silly. Can you also find a dog who will bay and bark at the right times to interrupt Jerry's spiel?

WHO YOU'LL NEED: *Lead Singing Role:* A loud, brash old vaudevillian with a bit of the devil and a truckload of energy in him. *Supporting Singing Roles:* A young man with hit parade ambitions; the lovely young model he comes to love; her wise-in-the-ways-of-the-world girlfriend; the show's premier tap dancer; a gag writer; a stage manager; a barber; a waiter. *Other Roles:* A soap company vice president; a script girl; a TV technician; an elevator operator; a doctor; a stagehand; a juggler; a widow; a magician; his assistant; "Miss Pillsbury"; a chorus that also can portray models, sales girls, photographers, and dance teams; a "singing" dog. *Maximum, 54; minimum 26.*

DESIGNATED DANCES: Four production numbers that should look like those extravaganzas that were done on weekly variety shows; some musical staging on two others; a tap solo for Tommy; a ballet in which Jerry remembers his burlesque days.

SUGGESTED SETS: A 1950s TV studio and its dressing room; a department store's elevator bank and its gown shop.

COSTUMES: 1950s fashions and street clothes; French costumes for a Gallic production number; showgirl costumes; a "Miss Blendo" beauty contest winner outfit; baggy-pants burlesque outfits for the title song.

IMPORTANT PROPS: Old-fashioned television cameras, equipment, and microphones; flash cameras; mock-ups of Blendo Soap detergent boxes.

PROVIDED INSTRUMENTATION: Two violins, viola, cello, bass, flute-piccolo, oboe-English horn, two clarinets, bass clarinet-bassoon, two horns, two trumpets, two trombones, percussion, harp, guitar-banjo, piano-celeste, piano-conductor.

ADVERTISING AND MARKETING: Aside from the obvious—selling banana-flavored food and drink during intermission—you could give a "Top Banana" award at each performance to a deserving townsperson you know will be in attendance.

SUGGESTIONS: Play early '50s music in the lobby so that your theatregoers can be in the mood right from the start.

RESOURCES: The original cast album on CD, cassette, and LP; the 1954 (3-D!) rather faithful movie of the musical; a 1982 HBO special merely used the title and a few numbers, but bears no resemblance to the musical.

RIGHTS: Tams-Witmark.

TWO BY TWO

CREATORS: Book by Peter (*1776*) Stone, music by Richard (*Oklahoma!*) Rodgers, lyrics by Martin (*Annie*) Charnin.

BACKGROUND: The 1970 musical about Noah and the flood opened to decent enough reviews, but a few months after opening, star Danny Kaye broke his leg. Director Joe Layton, noting that Noah was supposed to be an old man, suggested that Kaye could play the role in a wheelchair, and while Kaye did, he also took it as license to improvise "funny" lines into a most sincere script, even mentioning the then-current *No, No, Nanette* production in a show set in Biblical times. Bad word-of-mouth and even poorer press resulted, and the show closed after 351 performances.

STORY: Noah is told by God to build an ark and collect two of each species, for He's about to destroy the rest of the world. This does not go over well with Noah's family—wife Esther, eldest son Shem and his wife Leah, middle son Ham (a gambler) and his wife Rachel, and especially youngest son Japheth, who may be "at that age" when he protests everything, but also makes sense when he criticizes God for wanting to destroy almost everything in the world. Japheth is also bothered by the fact that Ham has been insensitive to Rachel—whom Japheth loves from afar. When Noah announces that God said everyone on the ark must be in pairs, and Japheth doesn't have anyone, he goes to a nearby town to tell the people what God has planned, and meets Goldie, who likes him. Noah is pleased that here is a wife for Japheth—even though Japheth doesn't love her. Noah actually knocks Japheth unconscious to get him on the ark as the flood begins. After the forty days and forty nights (we hear rain all through the intermission), Ham is lusting after Goldie, and Noah is displeased to find that Shem and Leah are stockpiling manure that will be needed once they're off the boat. Noah is further displeased when Japheth and Rachel, as well as Ham and Goldie, ask to be married, but a dying Esther begs Noah to sanction the new unions. He does—but also asks God for a sign that He will never again destroy the world. God answers by placing a beautiful rainbow in the sky.

ASSETS: This show—with a fine score, good book, and a very nice effect at the end when Noah sees the rainbow—is one of the few musicals that plays as a big musical but isn't too expensive to produce; it has only two sets, a cast of eight, and no chorus.

LIABILITIES: Things do become a bit boring in the middle of the second act, so a director must compensate with some vigorous pacing.

RECOGNIZABLE SONGS: "I Do Not Know a Day I Did Not Love You."

WHO YOU'LL NEED: *Lead Singing Role:* A six-hundred-year-old man who, through God's miracle, is transformed to a "young" ninety-year-old man. *Supporting Singing Roles:* His tender and loving wife; their eldest enterprising son and his equally enterprising wife; their middle son who's a swinger, and the long-suffering-in-silence wife who's tried to stay in love with him; their youngest sincere but argumentative son; a well-built woman with a coloratura voice. *Maximum,* 20 (if you'd like to augment the early scenes with a chorus of townspeople); *minimum,* 8.

DESIGNATED DANCES: Only one real production number—a joyous stomp after the ark lands—as well as some musical staging for three other songs.

SUGGESTED SETS: One set representing where Noah and his family live; the ark they build on stage.

COSTUMES: Primitive-looking costumes in earth tones of brown and gray.

IMPORTANT PROPS: Many pieces of wood and a rudder that will eventually make up the ark; a bird cage.

SPECIAL EFFECTS: Much thunder and lightning representing the voice of God; fifteen minutes' worth of pouring rain sounds; sounds of the various animals as they're taken onto the ark; a projection of a rainbow at play's end.

PROVIDED INSTRUMENTATION: Three reeds, two trumpets, trombone, two percussion, two violins, viola, cello, bass, piano, piano-conductor.

ADVERTISING AND MARKETING: Try to have a promotion with a local store that sells stuffed animals so that you can raffle off a few during inter-mission. Or at least get them to advertise in your program. In addition, perhaps try to do a performance, or a few numbers, at your local zoo.

SUGGESTIONS: "Instead of just miming the animals," says Carol Lucha-Burns, Chairman of the Theater Department at the University of New Hampshire, "use puppets. This is especially effective when the gitka bird—which we created as an adorable loony bird—dies; the audience really shared the sorrow, because they had actually seen the bird."

RESOURCES: The original cast album on CD, cassette, and LP; Clifford Odets's *The Flowering Peach*, the play on which the musical is based.

RIGHTS: Rodgers and Hammerstein.

ALSO WORTH A LOOK

Finian's Rainbow

This still has that wonderful E. Y. Harburg–Burton Lane score ("How Are Things in Glocca Morra?," "Old Devil Moon," "If This Isn't Love?") that seemed daringly ahead of its time in 1947, but has been embarrassingly dated ever since the civil rights movement. Its observations on "left-wing" socialism, taxes, anti-black legislation, sharecropping, and even the Tennessee Valley Authority are no longer relevant, but the worst problem is that Finian, who has three wishes, uses one to change a Southern senator into a black evangelist—but treats the fate as one worse than death. To undercut the embarrassing racial issues, you might provide black and white masks for much of your cast, but that won't solve everything. Rights: Tams-Witmark.

Golden Rainbow

This starred Steve Lawrence and Eydie Gorme and featured the hit song "I've Gotta Be Me," but was one of the great disappointments of the 1967–1968 season. This is the Ernest Kinoy-Walter Marks musical version of A *Hole in the Head*, in which a Miami wheeler-dealer has an upstanding retired brother and sister-in-law who believe he's a bad influence on his son, and want to take the boy away. Here, the locale has been switched to Las Vegas, and the part of the brother was replaced by Gorme, who plays a working sister-in-law who wants to take away the boy. If you think that Vegas is tacky to begin with, do imagine what your production will look like without the ability to throw money at the problem. Rights: Samuel French.

Goldilocks

This was co-written by Walter Kerr, the esteemed *New York Herald Tribune* and *New York Times* critic, with his wife Jean *(Mary, Mary)* Kerr; Leroy ("The Syncopated Clock") Anderson and lyricist Joan Ford. Kerr nicely acquitted himself, though the show didn't run that long in 1958. It's a more lighthearted version of *Mack & Mabel*, dealing with the infancy of the movie industry when it was still located in Astoria, New York—and snow would fall while a movie was being made about Egypt. It's got a terrific score, but don't make the mistake that director Kerr made with the original production: Featured as the ambitious young silent-movie maker who'd do anything to get his film made was Don Ameche, and as the new vamp star, Elaine Stritch; both, even in 1958, were too old to play the leads. Had the roles been given to young performers, the musical would have been much better—so cast with an eye toward youthful energy. Rights: Samuel French.

Take Me Along

This is the Joseph Stein-Robert Russell musical version of Eugene O'Neill's one comedy, *Ah, Wilderness*, but with O'Neill's supporting character, Sid, reconfigured as the lead—it was a vehicle for Jackie Gleason. It will be a reasonably costly musical to produce, because of its early twentieth-century small-town sets and costumes, but it may be worth it, because it has a glorious score by Bob *(Carnival)* Merrill. It also includes one song your audience might recognize: "Take Me Along"—if only because it was much heard as "Nixon's the One!" during Richard M. Nixon's 1972 campaign. If you have a corpulent performer who's talented and can sing and dance (at least as well as Gleason, who won a Tony), here is a musical to show him off. And if you're trying to develop new audiences, this show naturally lends itself to a two-tickets-for-the-price-of-one promotion: "Buy a ticket to *Take Me Along* and take along a friend." Rights: Tams-Witmark.

LICENSERS

Dramatists Play Service, Inc.
440 Park Avenue South
New York, NY 10016
Phone: 212–683–8960
Fax: 212–213–1539

Music Theatre International
545 Eighth Avenue
New York, NY 10018
Phone: 212–868–6668
Fax: 212–643–8465

Rodgers and Hammerstein
1633 Broadway
New York, NY 10019
Phone: 212–541–6900
Fax: 212–586–6155

Samuel French, Inc.
45 West 25th Street
New York, NY 10010-2751
Phone: 212-206-8990
Fax: 212-206-1429

Tams-Witmark Music Library, Inc.
560 Lexington Avenue
New York, NY 10022
Phone: NY (800) 522-2181
         US (800) 221-7196
Fax: 212-688-3232

INDEX